# KINGS, HEROES AND LOVERS

*Pictorial Rugs from the
Tribes and Villages of Iran*

## PARVIZ TANAVOLI

Scorpion Publishing
London

*To Manijeh*

© Parviz Tanavoli

Translation by John Wertime

All rights reserved. No part of this publication may be reproduced, stored in a retrieval system, or transmitted in any form or by any means, electronic, mechanical, photocopying, recording or otherwise, without the prior permission of the copyright owner.

First published in 1994 by
Scorpion Publishing Ltd
Victoria House
Victoria Road
Buckhurst Hill
Essex
England

ISBN 0 905906 86 1

Typeset by MasterType, Newport, Essex, England

Printed and bound in Singapore by Craft Print

# CONTENTS

| | |
|---|---|
| Acknowledgements | 4 |
| Introduction | 7 |
| Chapter One  Kings | 13 |
|    Hushang Shah | |
|    Darius I and Xerxes I | |
|    Shapur I | |
|    Shah 'Abbas I | |
|    Nadir Shah | |
|    Fath 'Ali Shah | |
|    Nasir al-Din Shah | |
|    Muhammad 'Ali Shah | |
|    Ahmad Shah | |
|    Reza Shah | |
| Chapter Two  Stories from Classical Persian Literature | 30 |
|    The *Shahnamah* of Firdawsi, Rustam | |
|       Rustam and Suhrab | |
|       Rustam and Akvan the Demon | |
|    The *Khamsah* of Nizami | |
|       Khusraw, Shirin, Farhad | |
|       Layla and Majnun | |
| Chapter Three  Stories From the Qur'an | 39 |
|    Abraham's Sacrifice of Ishmael | |
|    Gabriel | |
|    Mary and Jesus | |
| Chapter Four  Sufism and Pictorial Rugs | 42 |
|    Dervishes | |
|    Shaykh San'an | |
| Chapter Five  Armenians and Pictorial Rugs | 47 |
|    David of Sassoun | |
| Chapter Six  Rugs Depicting Tribal People | 50 |
|    Persian-speaking tribes | |
|    Turkish-speaking tribes | |
|    Arab tribes | |
| Chapter Seven  Beautiful Women | 56 |
| Chapter Eight  Animals | 58 |
| Chapter Nine  An Explanation of the Analysis of the Structural and Other Physical Characteristics of the Rugs | 61 |
| Figures | 68 |
| Illustrations | 98 |
| The Plates | 103 |
| Notes | 294 |
| Bibliography | 297 |
| Index | 299 |

# ACKNOWLEDGEMENTS

This book was written during the 1970s, but the completion and publication of the manuscript were delayed by complications due to the Iranian revolution of 1979. Now that it is to be published, with the aim of familiarizing the general public with the rich heritage of Iranian history and culture, through the medium of the pictorial carpets woven in the tribes and villages of Iran, I would like to acknowledge the many and varied contributions of friends and colleagues, without which this book could not have been written.

My deepest appreciation goes to Sarah B Sherrill, who from the beginning of this project to the very end has generously devoted herself to the numerous revisions of this work, and particularly to the chapter on structural analysis, with an enthusiasm, patience, and dedication that reflects her great love of the art and culture of Iran, and especially of the weavings and life of the tribes and villages, which she studied during field-trips to many parts of the country.

I owe a very special debt of gratitude also to Yahya Zoka and Ahmad Tafazzoli for their extremely valuable assistance and guidance on the historical and cultural background.

Other friends who have been especially helpful in a number of ways are: Abby W Grey, Trudy S Kawami, John T Wertime, Anne R Gossett, Houshang Adorbehi, Martha Deese, Parviz Varjavand, and Manijeh Tanavoli.

And we owe the most important debt of all to those skilful rug weavers, most of them women, who have imaginatively created such engaging works of art, which reflect their deeply rooted cultural heritage.

The drawings in the chapter on structural analysis (see p. 98 infra) are by Houshang Adorbehi.

The following people and institutions are responsible for the photographs. The colour and black and white photographs of the rugs are by Peter John Gates, except for Nos. 16, 24, 27, 35, 44, 78, 81, 82 and 90, which are by Bahman Jalali, and Nos. 11 and 65, which are by courtesy of the Smithsonian Institution.

The black and white photographs supplementing the text were contributed as follows:
Ministry of Culture, Tehran: 6, 7, 10, 17, 63
H Haraji: 8, 9
Victoria and Albert Museum, London: 23, 52
Metropolitan Museum of Art, New York City: 37
Fogg Museum of Art, Harvard University, Cambridge, Massachusetts: 44
Royal Asiatic Society, London: 32
India Office Library, London: 5
New York Public Library: 24
Siawosch Azadi: 60
John Taylor Bigelow: 58
Yahya Deghanpour: 2, 19, 42, 62
Peter John Gates: 1, 22, 31, 46, 50
Bahman Jalali: 27, 34, 35, 43, 51, 55, 61, 65
Jean Lefevre: 16
Sarah B Sherrill: 13, 39, 49, 59
Parviz Tanavoli: 3, 4, 11, 12, 14, 15, 18, 20, 21, 30, 33, 38, 40, 41, 45, 47, 48, 53, 56, 57, 64
Photographers unknown: 25, 26, 28, 29, 54

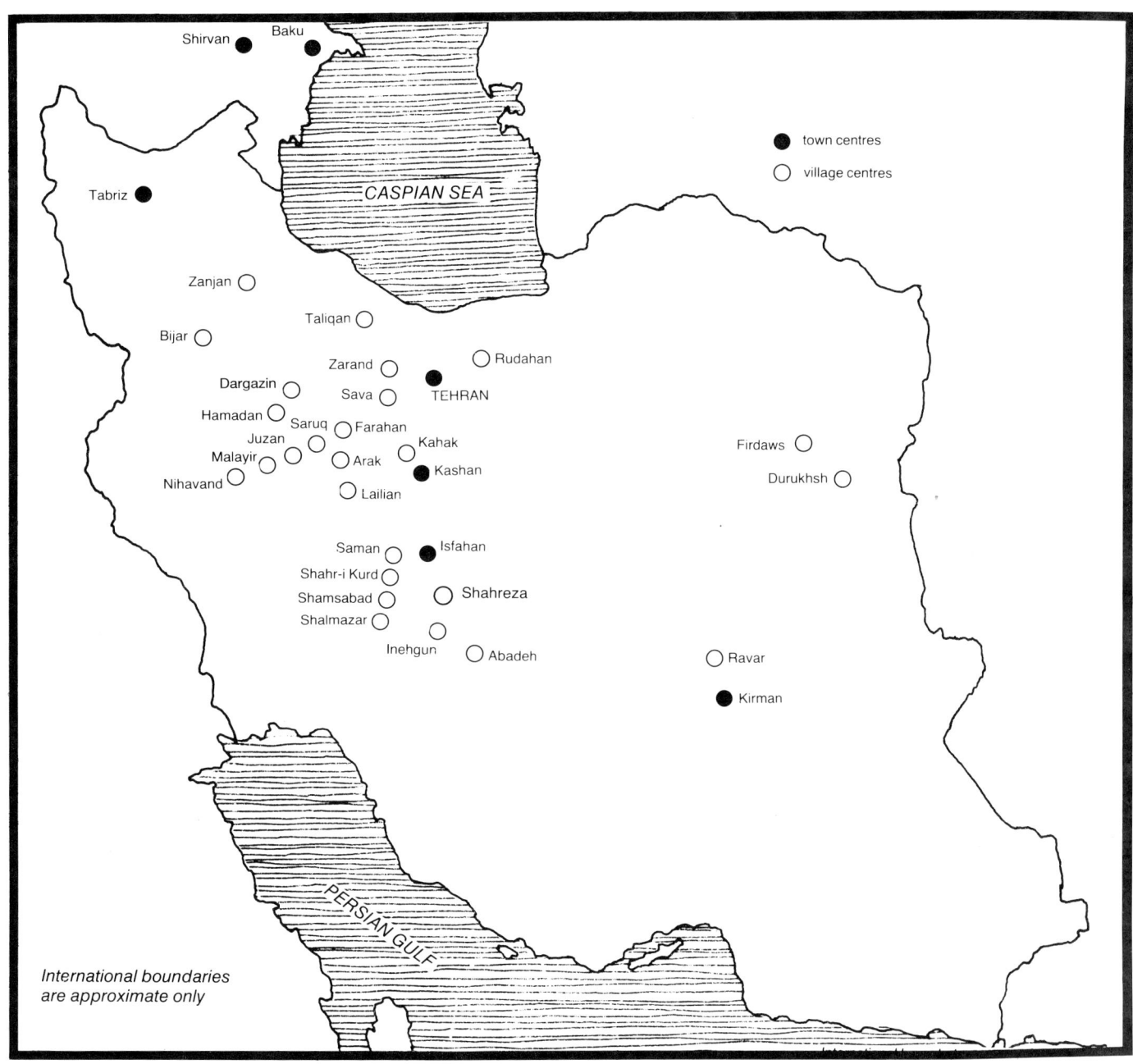

**The villages and cities of Iran involved in the production of pictorial rugs**

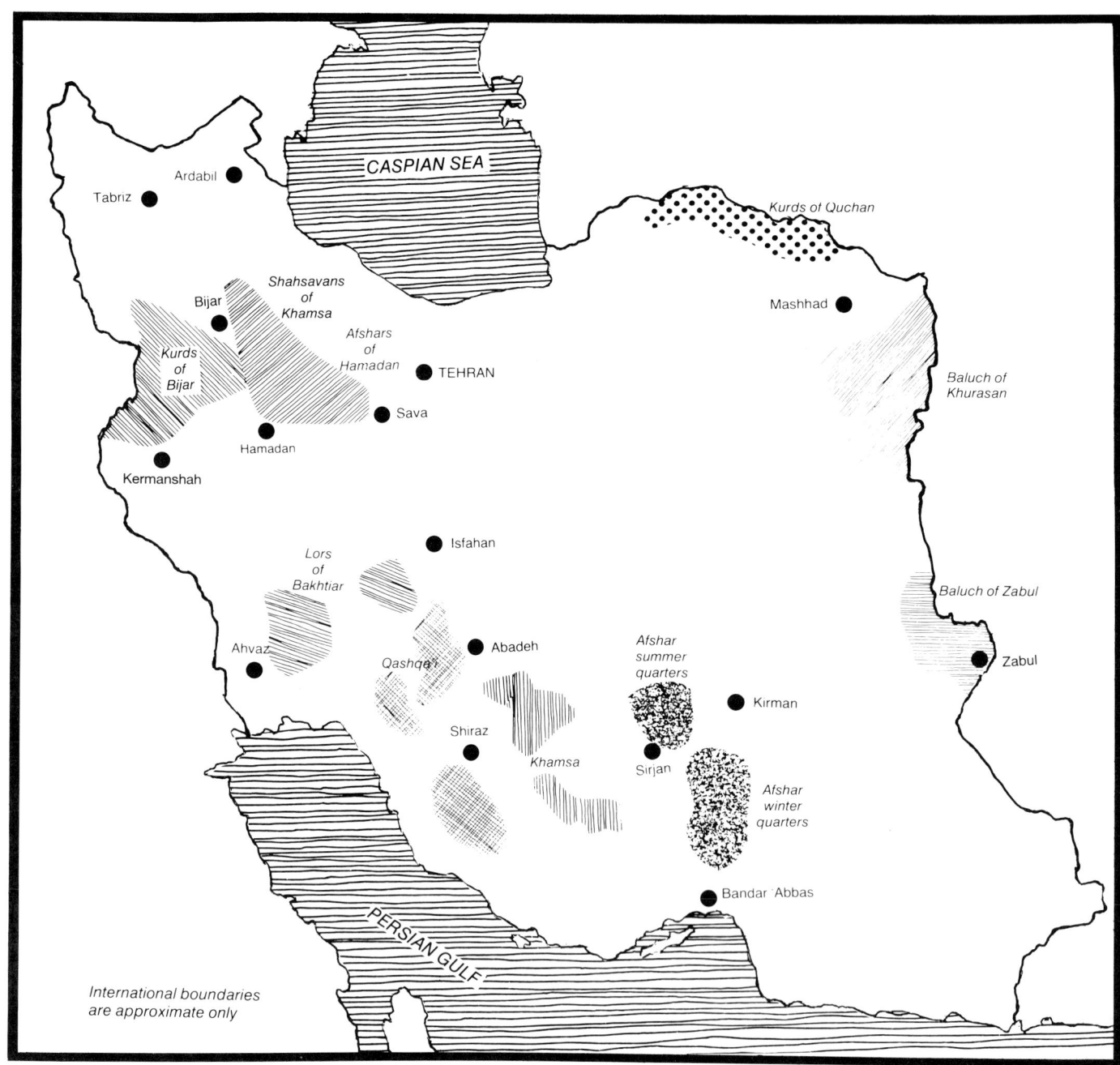

**Tribal map of Iran with regard to pictorial rugs**

# INTRODUCTION

IN THE numerous articles and books about Persian carpets there are few references to pictorial rugs with large-scale human and animal figures, and the infrequent examples that have been published often appear as little more than curiosities, especially when not accompanied by adequate explanations and background material. One of the reasons for this situation is the relative scarcity of pictorial rugs in comparison to more traditional types with abstract designs. Pictorial rugs made by villagers and tribeswomen were usually woven to suit the personal taste of the weaver or the weaver's patron, and not for the general market; consequently the more spontaneous and vigorous type of pictorial carpet, with images created on the loom from the weaver's imagination, never gained the wide circulation and recognition that the more commercial pictorial rugs, woven in city workshops from cartoons painted by commercial artists and based on miniature paintings, enjoyed both in Iran and abroad.

Pictorial rugs with large-scale figures may have come into existence at the end of the eighteenth century during the Qajar period, when large-scale oil paintings were becoming increasingly popular in Iran and printed pictures and, somewhat later, photographs were becoming readily available as models for new subjects in Iranian arts and crafts. These new sources of inspiration created an entirely new genre in traditional rug-weaving in Iran. This new type of rug came to be called *qalichaha-yi surati*, literally 'rugs with faces', i.e., rugs with representations of human figures. Although I have undertaken to introduce in this book only those rugs that were woven in villages and tribal nomadic areas, I will at times refer to city-woven rugs, which in many cases influenced village and nomadic pictorial rugs, especially since both groups have common roots.

The rugs illustrated in this book were woven during the past two centuries. The subjects represented include historical and mythical figures of Iran, as well as favourite characters in well-loved stories from Iran's literary classics, which were handed down by story tellers through the oral tradition. In order to appreciate the role of pictorial rugs in the art of Iran in general, and in its rug-weaving tradition in particular, it is necessary to consider the factors that have affected the evolution of pictorial rugs up to the present.

Following the Islamic conquest of Iran in the mid-seventh century AD, Iranian art eventually conformed to the orthodox Islamic prohibition against pictorial representation. This stricture was aimed at the practice of idolatry, which was widespread among the tribes of Arabia at the time of Muhammad. This prohibition was enforced in all Islamic territories, including Iran in spite of its ancient culture and highly developed traditions of figural representation.

The first Iranian converts to the Islamic faith, in accepting its teachings, gradually brought their culture and art into conformity with the precepts of the new faith. But a century had not elapsed after the Islamic conquest of Iran before movements for independence from Arab rule began to appear in Iran. Some of these movements led to the achievement of local autonomy and the disregard of the commands of the caliphs. In the revival of the Persian language and the ancient culture of Iran, poets and writers were encouraged to record ancient Iranian history and legends, and in medieval times artists illustrated historical manuscripts commissioned by royal patrons. Despite the fact that many later dynasties in Iran were Turkic or Mongol and not native Iranian, the Persian language and Iranian culture were adapted for secular expression.

The emergence of Iran as an Islamic nation was politically enforced in the early sixteenth century when the Safavid rulers proclaimed Shi'ism, the minority sect of Islam, as the official religion of Iran. This manoeuvre effected a distinct break from the traditional Iranian adherence to Sunnism (the majority sect of Islam), yet it distinguished the Iranian state within the greater Islamic community and especially from its greatest political adversary, Ottoman Turkey. Since

Iranians have adhered to Shi'ism ever since, this shift has profoundly affected Iranian history and culture for the past five and a half centuries.[1]

Besides ancient Iranian traditions, the general acceptance of figural representation is in part to be explained by Iranians' veneration of the Shi'ite imams in their religious worship. The common practice of representing religious figures publicly occurred regularly throughout Safavid Iran where the *ta'ziya* (mourning) ceremonies included members of the faithful enacting the lives of the Shi'ite imams, particularly the death of Imam Husayn who was martyred on the plains of Kerbala during the first ten days of Muharram in 680 AD. It was also in the Safavid period that paintings of figures, which had been confined largely to private quarters of the court, appeared life-size on palace walls and even in such public places as bazaar gates. In this sense, the Qajar pictorial rug genre is a late development of the greater laxity exercised toward Islamic strictures, which had begun during the Safavid period.[2]

Some early historians and other writers mention paintings with large-scale figural representations, thus indicating the existence of such paintings in the Islamic era. Among these is the eleventh-century Persian historian al-Tha'labi (d. 1037/8 AD) who says, 'In books as well as in palaces and on sculptural monuments Iranians have painted the picture of Tahmuras riding Ahriman [the Devil].'[3] And Sa'di, the great thirteenth-century Persian poet (d. between 1292 and 1296 AD), mentions in one of his poems an imaginary depiction of Iblis (Satan) in one of the royal palaces.[4]

Pictorial representation in rug weaving lagged behind its appearance in other art forms, perhaps because a rug was something upon which people lived and prayed. The first signs of pictorial subjects in carpets are seen in some of the surviving pile and flat-woven examples produced in court and urban workshops in the sixteenth- and seventeenth centuries. Tribal and village rugs of that period in Iran do not survive today. The figures in these sixteenth- and seventeenth-century carpets, however, are usually very small in scale and do not normally constitute the main emphasis of the over-all carpet design, unlike the rugs in this book. The subjects of the surviving sixteenth and seventeenth-century rugs with figural elements are generally birds, animals, or vignettes of kings and princes hunting and feasting. These are comparable to similar figures in many silk brocade textiles of that period, which were drawn by court artists who also executed miniature paintings.

The progress of the arts was interrupted for some time at the end of the Safavid period in the early eighteenth century with the Afghan invasions and the rise of Nadir Shah (r. 1736-1747) and his continual military campaigns both inside and outside of Iran. During the first half of the eighteenth century, artistic production in Iran declined from its peak during the Safavid dynasty. This decline, however, did not last long and with the Zand dynasty (1750-1794), peace was once again restored in Iran. Shiraz became the artistic centre and pictorial art again flourished, fashioned in stone, tiles, and plaster. Artists also executed paintings of princes, dancers, and musicians. No longer confined to palaces, pictorial art now entered the homes of the upper classes.

The short reign of the Zand rulers was supplanted by the Qajars, who made Tehran their capital. In the reign of the second Qajar, Fath 'Ali Shah (r. 1797-1834), artistic activity increased and royal studios were established as they had been under the Safavids. In addition to the traditional subjects, portraiture became a genre of its own. In spite of the fact that the painting techniques and idealization and stylization of motifs taken from nature that characterized art in the Safavid period continued, a new trend toward naturalism was seen in features such as beards and clothing.

With the growth of commercial relations with the West during the nineteenth century, the Persian carpet, which until that time had been considered a relatively rare commodity in Europe and was usually found in the possession only of rulers, churches, and nobles of the highest rank, began to be more available to a larger number of appreciative customers in a rapidly expanding market.[5] Although this increase in exports was taking place at the same time as the growing popularity of pictorial carpets in Iran, the latter type appealed only to Iranians and found very few foreign customers.

The high degree of naturalism in the European prints and postcards that reached Iran in the nineteenth and twentieth centuries was new for many Iranians, and greatly admired. Commonly found on European imports, including chocolate boxes and toilet articles, such paintings gained prestige in Iran and were used to decorate homes and shops and were also carefully kept in albums. Some of them were reproduced in Iran and found their way to the most remote parts of the country where they influenced tribal and village weavers.

The nineteenth and twentieth centuries represent a major period of the growth of pictorial art in Iran. In all the art forms in these two centuries there has been movement toward figural representation. The acceptance of figural representation among the lower classes of society was unprecedented, whether through the work of those who painted story-telling pictures to be hung in teahouses (such artists have been particularly active in the last two hundred years), painters of religious pictures, or craftsmen.

These developments also influenced rug weaving, for figural subjects inspired weavers as well. City weavers, for example, drew on classical stories such as those of Khusraw and Shirin or Layla and Majnun for their material. Patterns for their work have been provided by commercial artists as well as by the makers of blockprinted curtains (*qalamkar*, literally, pen work). These curtains are based on the general style of miniature paintings but with figures of a much larger scale, simplified lines, and a more limited colour range. Some of the blockprinted curtains, because their dimensions are similar to those of carpets, are employed as patterns for rug weavers in rug weaving centres such as Kerman, Kashan, Isfahan, and Tabriz. Such rugs are known as *pardeh* (curtain).

With the coming of photography to Iran in the second half of the nineteenth century the production of pictorial rugs greatly increased. Weavers who had heretofore contented themselves with scenes from traditional Persian stories and ancient national epics turned to portraits of kings and dignitaries of the mid-nineteenth century and later. The patrons and buyers of these various types of pictorial rugs have been Iranians, who received the new form with enthusiasm.

This new attitude has caused pictorial rugs to be taken up from the floor and hung on the wall like paintings. The rug is thus transformed from a utilitarian to a non-utilitarian object. But this does not mean to say that before there were pictorial rugs Iranians did not recognize the decorative value of their carpets and that they wove them only for utilitarian purposes. On the contrary, the rug in Iran has always been one of the most necessary, valued, and intimate objects in an Iranian house, and beauty, as much as utility, has always been an important consideration, reflecting the weaver's as well as the owner's taste. However, a rug was woven to be used for its function as a floor or ground cover. Of course exceptions occurred, but these were temporary, as, for example, at weddings and religious celebrations, and on the occasion of the birthdays of the imams, when rugs were used to decorate doors and walls of houses, stores, and bazaars, a custom that still exists today.

For these celebrations the finest and most expensive rugs, even figural ones, were used in places where participants and honoured guests were seated. Production of pictorial rugs was limited since they never became an object of mass consumption and remained mostly in the hands of the upper classes, especially wealthy city dwellers and village and tribal leaders. The best market for these rugs has been inside Iran and to an extent in the neighbouring Arab countries. Another reason for limited production of pictorial rugs is the lack of Western interest in them. This disinterest is partly due to the very different tradition of pictorial representation in the West, particularly the emphasis on three-dimensionality and naturalism after the medieval period. The two-dimensional and idealized rather than naturalistic qualities of Iranian pictorial art were uncongenial to Westerners. Pictorial rugs were therefore shunned in favour of the more traditional Persian rug which seemed an exotic art form to Westerners with its abstract and harmonious patterns of geometric and arabesque designs full of stylized flowers and leaves.

This European attitude toward Iranian representational art in general is illustrated in the mid-nineteenth century by Comte Julien de Rochechouart, who wrote: 'The paintings which Iranians produce themselves are enough to make one gnash one's teeth; not only do they ignore the principles of perspective and of design, not only are their colours bad, and their brushwork detestable, but one cannot explain how a people, who have such delicate taste in certain cases and who possess such a high degree of knowledge of colour, can consent to look at such horrors.'[6] An envoy of Napoleon Bonaparte, P. Amédée Jaubert, who in 1806 visited the painters' workshop of the Persian court, said: 'It seems to me that they cultivate their art with more zeal than success.'[7] Because the Iranian painter was still seeking to portray idealized forms of beauty, and therefore did not use natural proportions in depicting humans and animals, shading, three-dimensionality, or life-like portraiture, the Western viewer was unable to appreciate and admire Iranian art.

The ways in which Iranian painters conceived and depicted representational subjects were shared by weavers of pictorial rugs in Iran, although their materials and techniques resulted in differences in the final products. Thus these peculiarly Iranian artistic concepts of idealization rather than naturalism, in addition to other influences such as inexpensive lithographed book illustrations, photographs, posters, and blockprinted curtains, also affected the formation of the pictorial rug.

Since various factors have played an important role in the development of pictorial rugs, each is reviewed below.

**Illustrated books**

Book illustration has a long history in Iran. While

this art is best known in examples of the Islamic period, there are indications that it existed at least as early as the Sasanian period. In fact, at the beginning of the present century a number of illustrated fragments of Manichaean literature were discovered in Turfan,[8] in Central Asia. One of these fragments, all of which date between the third and ninth centuries AD, refers to a mission sent to Khurasan (in the northeastern part of present-day Iran) to promote Manichaeism. This mission included a linguist, a translator, a writer, and a book illustrator. Another reference to this expedition reads:

> Then when the Apostle of Light [Manes, 216-276 AD] was in the city of Holvan, he called Marammo the teacher who knew the Parthian language [the language of Khurasan] . . . he sent him to Abashahr together with Prince Ardavan and brethren who were scribes [and a] miniature painter.[9]

Production of a book illustrated by miniature paintings entailed months or years of work. As a result, only rulers and a few wealthy courtiers could afford to commission or to buy such books. With the introduction of printing by lithography in the 1840s,[10] the works of painters and illustrators became accessible to all levels of society and inspired many craftsmen in different fields. Craftsmen, particularly those employed in workshops that produced painted or printed curtains and ceramic tiles, needed a variety of new designs and found illustrated books a fruitful source. Also, illustrated printed books of beloved tales from the national epics appeared to be a primary source of inspiration for many craftsmen, including rug weavers.

Another virtue of the pictures in printed books, usually illustrated with lithographed line drawings, was their simplicity. Because of technical limitations the illustrations were often only in black and white. Even book illustrations coloured by hand after being printed lacked the fine brushwork of the miniatures produced earlier exclusively for court patrons. The simplicity of lithographed illustrations made the printed books a particularly congenial design source for Iranian artists and craftsmen in other fields, including village rug weaving.

This was brought to Iran in the reign of Fath 'Ali Shah by his son and crown prince, 'Abbas Mirza, who governed Tabriz. In the first printing house in Iran, which was established in Tabriz about 1816, movable type was used. Since this method was expensive, the effort was soon abandoned. Lithography proved to be an easier and less costly method, and great numbers of illustrated books printed by that method were published in Tehran and Tabriz, as well as in Bombay, Calcutta, and elsewhere, from about 1845 until well into the twentieth century. A wide variety of books, historical works and stories in particular, were printed throughout Iran.

## Painted and wood-block-printed curtains (qalamkar)

*Qalamkar*[11] in its strictest sense refers to painting directly on cloth by means of a pen, using colours made from natural rather than synthetic materials. In the Safavid period this art was associated with Isfahan, a city that still remains the centre of *qalamkar* production. A number of Safavid *qalamkar* textiles, and shirts made from them, have survived. (Some of these are in the Iran Bastan Museum in Tehran.) This art became even more popular in the Qajar period. At that time the great demand for *qalamkar*, especially curtains, so increased production that only the central part of the textile was drawn by pen, while the borders, which usually consisted of repetitive patterns, were printed with wooden blocks. Only in recent times has the entire surface of the curtain, whether pictorial or purely ornamental, been covered by block printing.

Because *qalamkar* curtains were close in size to rugs and, like rugs, had borders, they were of particular interest to rug weavers and served as models for their work.

The main source of inspiration for the makers of figural *qalamkar* textiles was illustrations in lithographed books. This was in part because the illustrated stories were widely known and also because the simplified forms of the line drawings were easily copied. In these line drawings, as in the pictorial designs on the *qalamkar* curtains, colour was of secondary importance. So similar are the drawing and composition of the illustrations in such books and curtains that the same artists may, in some cases, have designed for both mediums.

The most important influence that lithographed books had on Iranian *qalamkar* textiles was not style, however, but content. The subjects of *qalamkar* textiles before the Qajar period consisted mostly of abstract designs and stylized flower and *boteh* (the so-called Paisley motif) patterns. The use of figural representations on these textiles, as on rugs, was very limited before the Qajar period, and in fact coincided with the appearance of lithographed books.

## Photography

Photography also had a significant effect on

## Introduction

pictorial rugs. It appeared in Iran during Nasir al-Din Shah's reign (1848-1896) at the Dar al-Funun, the first European-style school in Tehran. A European French teacher—known locally as Richard Khan, *khan* being an Iranian title of respect—occasionally photographed the shah and his courtiers, thus exciting much interest at court in this newest of Western imports.[12] Nasir al-Din's interest in photography led to the appointment of one of his adjutants, Reza Khan, Iqbal al-Saltanah, to the post of chief photographer in 1863. In this capacity he accompanied the shah on his journeys to Europe in 1873 and 1878.[13]

The collection of European postcards, photographs, and prints became a pastime of the Iranian upper classes, who kept such precious souvenirs in albums at home. A more public viewing of such European exotica was the peep show called *shahr-i farang* (city of Europe), which consisted of a series of pictures of European women, buildings, and street scenes shown one after the other. Its operator carried the 'show' in a box on his shoulders, and walked about town in search of customers.

The results of these various influences on rug weaving in the Qajar period were so dissimilar in the cities or towns and in the villages and nomadic tribes that the pictorial rugs of Iran must be divided into two separate groups: city rugs, on the one hand, and village and nomadic rugs, on the other.

The most important urban centres of pictorial rug production have been Kerman, Tabriz, Kashan, and Isfahan. The city rug weaver begins his or her work with a cartoon painted on squared paper by a commercial artist (see Fig. 36). Designers of pictorial rugs usually select their subjects from paintings or photographs and transfer them to squared paper on the same scale as the actual rugs. This painted cartoon is then given to the weaver. From this cartoon are normally woven a number of rugs more or less similar to each other.

The subjects of city rugs are abundant and diverse. Besides Iranian themes and stories, unusual subjects, such as the map of the United States or the discovery of America by Columbus, or Napoleon mounted on a horse, are also seen. Most, however, consist of scenes from classical literature or portraits of shahs or various other Iranian figures. A. Cecil Edwards, in publishing a design for a rug drawn around the year 1900 by a Kermani designer named Hasan Khan, said, 'It is not an uncommon practice in Persia to weave the portrait of a gentleman into a rug.'[14]

Only a few exceptional examples of city rugs are included in this book, which is primarily devoted to pictorial rugs woven by nomadic tribes and villagers.

The imagery of tribal and village rugs, which are not woven from cartoons, is varied. Some of these rugs were copied directly from photographs or block-printed curtains. Others were inspired by lithographs. A few depict subjects that may have been invented by the weaver. In a number of regions of Iran details of the principal elements of a rug, such as the border, centre medallion, and corner pieces, have been first woven close together in haphazard order in a *vagirah* (a woven sampler) to show to potential consumers. Either the *dastur* (a rug borrowed to serve as a model) or the *vagirah* was placed in front of the weaver as a general model. By glancing at it periodically she would get sufficient guidance for her own rug. She did not follow her model exactly, but improvised her own version of the colours, motifs, and general composition. This improvisation is one of the most important differences between the city rugs and the tribal and village rugs. The city weaver in fact is only a copyist, for everything is arranged and planned by a professional designer in advance. But the tribal and village weavers are free to vary aspects of the design as they see fit. While the subject of their pictorial rugs may in some cases be derivative, the execution of the design reflects the personal expression of the weaver.

In some of the rugs illustrated in this book a particular subject has been treated by various weavers in different ways. I have classified the rugs in this book by subject matter. Some subjects may have been specific to a particular region, but eventually most subjects came to be treated in rugs from almost all parts of Iran. The circumstances underlying this distribution are interesting. In a number of cases a photograph seems to have served as a model. In some instances the origins of a particular pictorial subject must be sought in a more distant past.

The dimensions of pictorial rugs in each district of Iran are usually related to the architectural setting in which they are to be placed, and in particular to the height of ceilings, niches in walls, etc. Except for a few rugs which are larger in size and clearly meant for use on the floor, the majority have dimensions suitable for hanging on walls of private houses and tea houses. Smaller rugs were intended to be hung in the *taqcheh* (a recess in the thick walls of traditional Iranian houses). Some figural rugs, such as those with lions, were used on the ground by tribal people. However, other tribal figural rugs were usually commissioned by *khans* (tribal leaders), who hung them in their houses. Unfortunately such respectful treatment of the pictorial rug by villagers and tribal people has not continued, and with the coming of the large colour photograph, poster, and so forth, this type of rug has gradually lost its honoured place on the wall of homes and shops and has been relegated to the floor, causing some of these rugs to have become woefully worn and torn. But, very happily, many of them have survived up to the recent past in their place or origin, protected there by the remoteness of those tribes and villages from the influences of modern ways of life. It is interesting that these rugs were never valued by city rug dealers until relatively recently because of their unnatural proportions and angularity of their over-sized figures. The city rug dealers called such rugs *naqsh-i ghalat* (mistaken designs) because the figures were much less naturalistic than those in city-made examples. Characteristic features of these so-called 'mistaken designs' include straight, broken, and only very slightly curved lines; areas of solid colours without shading that would indicate dimensionality; and figures with exaggerated or otherwise unnatural proportions. However, the pictorial element in tribal and village rugs is very harmoniously integrated intuitively by the weaver into the over-all composition. All aspects of the design, including the border and subsidiary motifs in the field surrounding the dominant figure portrayed, work successfully together. The harmony and compatibility of the pictorial element with the more traditional non-figural aspects of the rug design are usually lacking in pictorial city rugs.

That is to say, it often seems as if the pictorial subject of some city-made rugs is merely glued or fastened to a ready-made, previously existing rug design conceived quite independently of the subject portrayed. In contrast, the intuitive skill of tribal nomadic and village weavers, whose manner of conceiving rug designs whether pictorial or traditional, as well as in selecting the colours, is infinitely freer and less rigid. Their work is therefore more appealing and lively to many people than that of the city weaver. One senses that the tribal or village weaver, by means of her eyes and fingers, puts something of herself into the rug in a way that escapes the city weaver, who mechanically and very precisely follows a formal pattern painted on squared paper by another artisan.

The large-scale pictorial element in a tribal or village rug is incorporated as the central design unit, thus replacing the large *turanj* (central medallion) of traditional rug designs. As in the classical central-medallion format, corner elements (called *lachak* after the triangular shape of women's head scarves) inside the border frame the large central pictorial element that replaces the central medallions of traditional rugs (for example, see rugs Nos. 14, 15, 44, 56). Also, the tribal or village weaver, with a spontaneity unknown in city-made rugs, embellishes the central pictorial element with small traditional motifs and traditional colours, but does not necessarily attempt to use colours naturalistically for people's faces and hands or for animals.

CHAPTER ONE
# KINGS

WEAVERS OF pictorial rugs seem to have favoured the images of Iranian rulers above most other subjects. Besides being very numerous, rugs bearing royal figures also show a great deal of variation in composition. Sometimes these figures are shown seated on a throne or horse, but often only the face is represented.

Rugs that depict royal personages portray rulers from the earliest period of Iranian history as well as legendary kings. The earliest figure represented is a mythical figure, Hushang Shah (see p. 15 infra). Monarchs from the pre-Islamic period of Iranian history represented in rugs include rulers of the Achaemenid and Sasanian periods. The majority, however, are kings who governed Iran during the last few centuries. Some of the ten of these more recent kings who play a role in this book were among the most active and significant in Iran's history.

The image of the ruler was also important in the art of pre-Islamic Iran. Found on large rocky cliffs and palace walls as well as on smaller items such as bowls, textiles, and coins, the features (idealized) of many earlier kings have been preserved down to our own day. Although figural representation declined in Iran for a time after the coming of Islam in the mid-seventh century AD, there is evidence that interest in the lives of kings and their likenesses continued. In 915 AD the Arab historian, 'Ali ibn Husayn Mas'udi in the city of Istakhr, saw an illustrated book about Sasanian monarchs that had been written in Arabic in 730 AD for Hisham ibn 'Abd al-Malik, an Umayyad caliph.[15]

In the late Sasanian period (224-642 AD), biographies of the kings were written in books known as *Khuda'i-namah*, ('Book of Lords', a precursor of the *Shahnamah*, 'Book of Kings'). In the second Islamic century (8th century AD) the *Khuda'i-namah* was translated into Arabic from Middle Persian, an Iranian language used in the Sasanian period (in which it had already been written), under the name of *Siyar al-Muluk* or *Siyar al-Muluk al-Fars*.

The *Shahnamah* by Firdawsi (940-ca. 1020 AD) is one of the greatest masterpieces of Persian literature. During a period of about thirty years (981-1010 AD) Firdawsi laboured to put his stories into verse, which eventually ran to about 60,000 couplets, most of which did not contain words borrowed from Arabic, which had crept into the Iranian language. In time the *Shahnamah* of Firdawsi became the book most familiar to Iranians of all ages (after the Qur'an), and inspired many people, including painters. The stories in the *Shahnamah* (often passed down through oral tradition), have had a very considerable influence on the art of Iran. Many subjects of pictorial rugs, especially kings, come from stories and miniatures related to this work.

Kings have a special place in the miniature paintings that illustrate manuscripts of the *Shahnamah*. Their regal presence in scenes of hunting, feasting, and war is emphasized in various ways, in their placement within the composition and by the depiction of thrones, crowns, and costume, but not by means of an individualized portrayal of their faces, which remained stylized and uniform. This similarity and idealization of facial features is a trait seen in Iranian painting until the end of the nineteenth century. But apparently there was some attempt on the part of a few Iranian artists at least as early as the tenth century to make portrait faces recognizable as those of specific individuals. We learn from certain writings that some Iranian painters at that time knew about naturalistic portraiture and, if required, could practise it. In the *Chahar Maqalah* ('Four Discourses') of 'Aruzi Samarqandi, the author writes that Abu Nasr 'Iraqi, a painter contemporary with Mahmud Ghaznavi (997-1030 AD), 'drew the face of Abu 'Ali Sina on paper in such a way that anyone using it could find him in the far corners of the kingdom.'[16] Apart from this early instance of a naturalistic likeness, the beginning of naturalistic portraiture came in the Safavid period. From that time on, the attempts of painters to show diversity in the drawing of faces increased and individual portraiture became more common than before.

*Kings, Heroes and Lovers*

One of the reasons for the spread of this more naturalistic approach in portraiture in Iran was the increasing presence during the Safavid period of European travellers and traders, who introduced the style of European painting into Iran. Until that time, Iranians had a very different concept of portraiture (consciously preferring idealization to naturalism) and before the Safavid period they had not seen a completely naturalistic painting of a person's face or a scene from nature with naturalistic perspective and observation of detail. The sight of European paintings of this kind proved exciting, especially to kings and their courtiers, who wanted their own faces and forms preserved in paintings for posterity, with individual features carefully portrayed. So it was that the first two rulers of the Safavid dynasty, Isma'il and his son, Tahmasp, permitted European painters to make portraits of them, works that are now preserved in Florence in the Uffizi.[17] Shah 'Abbas I (r. 1588-1629) was also much taken by European painting. During his reign several European artists, mainly Dutch, enjoyed his patronage.

Shah 'Abbas' successor, Shah Safi, was so eager to have European-style paintings that in 1635 he sent an order to Holland for special paint brushes and oil colours said to be sufficient for one thousand painters. The representative of the Dutch East India Company in Isfahan even assigned two painters to teach the king to paint in the European manner.[18]

European-style painting and naturalistic portraiture gradually made an impression on Iranian painters. The fact that this painting was done in oil colours and in a large-scale format emboldened Iranian artists in other fields both to draw figures on a larger scale and to present them in isolation instead of confining them to the small scale and company of other diminutive figures characteristic of miniature paintings. From that time on, royal personages, heretofore seen mostly in battle, hunting, and feasting scenes, were often depicted as single figures, in independent portraits. Such paintings include likenesses of nearly all of the kings of the last five centuries; and in the past two centuries, during the Qajar dynasty, such an approach to the royal figure also appeared in rug weaving and other art forms, such as printed textiles.

As has been discussed in the introductory chapter, one of the original sources of inspiration for pictorial representations employed by these artists and craftspeople from the 1840s onward was illustrated lithographed books. Of these books, the *Namah-yi Khusravan* ('Book of Kings') and the *Athar-i 'Ajam* ('Works of the Iranians') were the most used. In rugs portraying kings, some of the illustrations from these two books are copied very directly. In other rugs based on these sources sections from different illustrations are juxtaposed in one rug.

The *Namah-yi Khusravan* by Jalal al-Din Mirza (a son of Fath 'Ali Shah) was first published in Tehran in 1868 and then in Vienna in 1880. This book is a summary of the lineage of the rulers of Iran (following the sequence in Firdawsi's *Shahnamah*) with black and white pictures of each. These illustrations were done with great mastery and good taste by Mirza Mutallib. His efforts to achieve variety in portraying the successive kings, especially their faces and clothes, were successful. Undoubtedly sources such as coins of the pre-Islamic kings, Achaemenid and Sasanian bas-reliefs, and other artifacts were influential in the drawing of some of these pictures. Mirza Mutallib used his imagination in those cases in which he did not have access to early sources. Fig. 20 is an example of an illustration by Mirza Mutallib that is related to one of the rugs in this book (rug No. 16).

The other book, *Athar-i 'Ajam*, by Fursat al-Dawlah-yi Shirazi, was first published in 1892 AD in Bombay. It is an account of Fursat al-Dawlah's trips to the southern regions of Iran and the ancient monuments there. While alluding in the introduction of this book to his audience with Nasir al-Din Shah (1848-1896), the author also mentions how the king encouraged him in this undertaking. Fursat al-Dawlah both wrote the text and drew the illustrations. Although his drawings are not totally naturalistic, they give a true enough picture of the object in question. One of the most important sections of the *Athar-i 'Ajam* is the description of the monuments of Persepolis and accompanying drawings (see Figs. 15, 65). Likewise, Fursat al-Dawlah's visit to the statue of Shapur is one of the more exciting parts of his trip. Elsewhere in this book is an account of his trip and an engraving of a drawing he made of the statue (see p. 27 and Fig. 18).

To give variety to their work, painters of *qalamkar* curtains depicting many kings tried to differentiate their portrayals of each king by using individual traits and different poses (Fig. 3). The rulers are distinguished from each other by means of their crowns; their hair, beard, and moustache styles; and by the colour of these physical traits, which gives some idea of the rulers' respective ages.

Such multiple portrayals are found in pictorial rugs as well, and these are woven primarily by city rug weavers in general and those of Kerman in particular. Some of these rugs measure more than ten square metres (ninety square feet) and depict kings from the beginning of history (from the

*Shahnamah*) up to the end of the Qajar period. Others even go beyond group portraits of Iranian monarchs and include world-famous figures such as Pythagoras, Galileo, and Queen Victoria in groups of Iranian rulers.

Only a small number of kings have been the subjects of rugs woven by tribal and village weavers. These rugs will be dealt with in chronological order according to the reigns of the rulers portrayed. A consideration of the distribution of such weavings shows that the kings of ancient times are found only in products of certain areas, whereas rulers of more recent centuries are seen in rugs from all parts of Iran. For example, a great many of the rugs depicting the legendary Iranian king Hushang Shah are from Hamadan and surrounding towns, and rugs portraying Shapur I (241-272 AD) are usually from Saruq and nearby villages, while many of the rugs showing kings of the Qajar dynasty have been woven everywhere, but for different reasons. At times the appearance of a photograph, painting, or printed textile in a village seems to have inspired the weaving of a rug based on the likeness in these other mediums. Such a rug might later attract the attention of weavers in the same village and then of weavers in neighbouring villages as a model for their own rugs, and thereby caused the spread of that particular type. In some cases the proximity of a village or tribe to the ancient monuments of a district has provided an inspiration for royal figures in pictorial rugs.

## Hushang Shah

In spite of the fact that most rugs depicting Hushang Shah include the same design elements, and thus at first glance appear to be somewhat alike, each has a personality all its own. Before discussing how these rugs came into being, it will be helpful to know something of the story of this mythical king.

The legend of Hushang Shah is one of the first accounts of Firdawsi's *Shahnamah*.[19] Transmitted by story tellers over the centuries, the tale gained wide circulation among the people of Iran and eventually came to be woven into rugs.

According to legend, the mythical king Hushang Shah was the founder of the first imperial dynasty in Iran. His name in the *Avesta* (the sacred book of early Iran, which was used by the Zoroastrians, but pre-dated them) is Haushangeh and his title is *Paradhata* (later Pishdad), which means 'a first appointed' (to rule over the world) or 'first created'. In the *Shahnamah* he is mentioned as the founder of the Pishdadi dynasty, the first imperial dynasty of Iran.[20] After the death of his great-grandfather Kiyumars he ruled for forty years. He avenged his father, Siyamak, who had been killed by demons. Hushang Shah is also credited with the discovery of fire. The Sadeh festival (during which bonfires are lit) of the tenth day of Bahman (fifty days before the Iranian New Year, or Naw Ruz, which falls on March 21) is said to have been instituted by him. The origin of this festival, as related in the *Shahnamah*, is as follows: one day Hushang Shah saw a black snake with black smoke pouring out of its mouth, enveloping the world in gloom, and he threw a stone at it. The stone landed on another stone and caused a spark to fly up. This God-given spark fell on some dry plants and a fire started. Taking this to be a good omen, he established the Sadeh festival. Many dictionary writers in the past (by popular etymology; no scholarly etymology is known) considered his name to be made up of *hush* (intelligence) and *farhang* (culture). The origin of this popular etymology was doubtless a couplet from the *Shahnamah*, 'His noble name was Hushang. You might say he was all intelligence (*hush*) and culture (*farhang*).[21] The Danish Iranologist Arthur Christensen[22] considers Hushang to be Targitaos, the primordial man according to the Scythians (an Iranian-speaking nomadic tribe who probably originated in Siberia and who were newcomers to the Eurasian steppes north of the Black Sea in the first millenium BC) and that pre-Zoroastrian Iranians borrowed the story from some of the Scythian people. He also believed that Hushang was the father of the Paralatos family, which he considered the same as the Pishdadi dynasty.

The story of Hushang is also related to the origins and lineage of the Iranians and their migrations. In the books in Middle Persian (the official language of the Sasanians) the migration of the Iranians from the Aral-Caspian region in the Eurasian steppes took place in the time of Hushang. Orientalists hold different opinions about the dates of this migration. Some believe that the migration of the Aryans (Indo-Iranians) to Iran and India took place about the third millennium BC.[23] Others give a later date, in the second millennium BC,[24] while still others put the date between the second and first millennia BC.[25] After the separation of other Aryan groups, the Iranians settled in north-eastern Iran (northern Khurasan) and named the region Iran Vij (Aeryana Vaeja).[26] After becoming rooted in this region the Iranians began to expand and came into conflict with their neighbours. The accounts of their wars often took on a legendary aspect.

The story of most of these events centres on the war between the kings and demons. The kings are created by God, while the demons are representatives of Ahriman, the Devil. How they came into being is told in the *Bundahishn* (an encyclopedic book about religious lore, written in Middle Persian, but the main source of it was the book of *Avesta*; this part contains mythological stories about the creation of the world). Ormazd (God), who was omniscient, was aware of the existence of Ahriman and the fact that there would be a war between him and Ahriman. For this reason, he created the world, which for three thousand years was the dwelling place of spirits. When Ahriman saw that there was light (the symbol of truth, introduced by Ormazd) he attacked it, but was defeated. He then prepared himself for a new battle with Ormazd and for this created the demons (*divs*). Ormazd created water, earth, trees, animals, and man. The mythical first man was called Gayomard (later Kiyumars), meaning 'mortal life'.

Forty years after being purified by light and entrusted to the earth, the seed of Kiyumars produced Mashig and Mashiyanag (variously spelled also Mashi and Mashiyaneh, or Mehri and Mehriyaneh—these are the Iranian equivalents of Adam and Eve) who grew up out of the ground in the form of the rhubarb plant. At the beginning they were joined together and indistinguishable from each other sexually. Thereafter they were infused with souls and Ormazd told them that they were human and the ancestors of mankind and that they should do good deeds, think good thoughts, speak good words, and not worship the demons.[27]

Hushang fought the demons who had killed his father, Siyamak, who was the son of Mashig and Mashiyang and grandson of Kiyumars. He killed many of them and took the rest prisoners. This war is illustrated in many manuscripts of the *Shahnamah*. While these miniature paintings do not closely resemble the scenes depicted in any of the rugs in this book, they must be considered the general source of inspiration for the Hushang Shah group (even though the original model—perhaps a lithographed line drawing based on miniature paintings—used by the rug weavers has yet to be discovered).

The general composition of the rugs depicting Hushang is not unlike the composition of a number of the scenes found in the relief carvings at Persepolis. In my opinion, the original designer of this type of rug was aware of the scenes carved in relief at that site. Also, I believe that this person was very familiar with miniature paintings illustrating manuscripts of the *Shahnamah*. Thus he was able to effect a successful union of the style of the monumental scale of the figures in the stone reliefs at Persepolis with the small-scale *Shahnamah* miniatures.

The impression of the Persepolis reliefs given by these rugs must be attributed to the weavers' beliefs about that ancient site, which, according to books, legends, and popular lore, was the abode of the legendary, mythical king Jamshid. According to the *Bundahishn*, Jamshid was the brother of Tahmuras and son of Hushang, whereas in the *Shahnamah* he appears as the son of Tahmuras and grandson of Hushang. Jamshid is said to have reigned for seven hundred years.

Many inventions and discoveries are attributed to Jamshid in the *Shahnamah*, among them the smelting of iron, spinning and weaving, as well as house and ship building. He built a throne which the demons carried from the earth into the heavens. The coming of the new year (Naw Ruz, or, literally, new day, the first of the new year, which corresponds to March 21) is said to have been first celebrated by Jamshid. In Iranian legends he is credited with the expansion and population of the cities of Istakhr and Persepolis (which was never a city, but a palace that seems to have been used only for the celebration of the new year), the building of the first bath, and the invention of wine, gold leaf, and gilding. He also owned the legendary Bowl of Jam (an abbreviated form of the name Jamshid), which is now believed to have been an astrolabe. At the end of his life Jamshid became overly proud, claimed divinity for himself, and lost favour among the Iranians. Eventually he was killed by Zahhak, an evil king of a neighbouring territory, who had been proclaimed the new king of Iran.

A confusion between Jamshid and Darius I the Great (522-486 BC) and his eldest son, Xerxes I (486-465 BC), has persisted in the popular lore of Iranians. This confusion is seen in Figs. 1, 2. Above the seated figure of Darius I (repeated in mirror image for symmetry) the name of Jamshid is written. Actually, it was natural for Iranians to assume that the king depicted was Jamshid, since the history of Darius I was not known to them before the inscriptions were deciphered in the nineteenth century. Before that Darius I was known only through the Greek historians, whose works were little known in Iran until the twentieth century.

In lithographed illustrations and *qalamkar* curtains as well as in paintings Jamshid is usually shown in profile and wearing the Achaemenid crown, of Darius the Great (see Fig. 3, upper right corner, and Fig. 4).

Some Iranians, according to popular lore, have thought Jamshid to be the same person as Solomon. In the *Bustan al-Siyahah* ('Garden of Travelling', the account of the travels of a dervish) it is written 'Jamshid [is the] son of Tahmuras, and some say that he is his grandson. The Zoroastrians believe that he ruled over the world, that the races of men, djinns, demons, and fairies were under his control, and that Solomon was the same person as he.'[28] The confusion between the stories of these heroic figures arises from the common elements they all share. Hushang, Jamshid, Solomon, and Darius I (or Xerxes I) are linked together in many scenes and stories in such a way that it appears they are all one and the same person. This is true of Jamshid and Solomon because they were both great and powerful kings and had golden thrones encrusted with jewels. Both built large edifices and sanctuaries, Jamshid at Istakhr and Solomon at Jerusalem. And, finally, both had the demons, djinns, and animals in their power. The demons carried the throne of Jamshid into the air on their shoulders as they did that of Solomon (in some stories it was a rug instead of a throne). The story of the animals' submission to Solomon, which is seen in various rugs, influenced some of the weavers of Hushang Shah rugs as well. As a result, Hushang Shah is shown with a few animals in rugs Nos. 5 and 7. This confusion between Jamshid and Solomon is seen in Islamic times in many Iranian stories as well as Jewish ones from the Old Testament. One reason for the confusion is the preservation of pre-Islamic buildings in Iran because of their attribution to Jewish prophets who are cited in the Qur'an. Furthermore, Hushang Shah shares certain traits in common with Jamshid. Both tamed the demons. Some say Hushang Shah was the builder of Persepolis[29] (Jamshid has been credited with this also).

The rugs depicting Hushang Shah follow a characteristic general scheme. The front view of the king seated in the throne, the details of the throne including its stairs, and the viziers seen on either side of the king remind one of some of the paintings of the court of Fath 'Ali Shah (see Fig. 5).

The throne upon which Hushang Shah is depicted in the rugs was inspired by the famous royal thrones of Iran. A few words about the influence three such thrones in particular had on pictorial rugs may provide a better understanding of the scene depicted in Hushang Shah rugs, and the source of signs and symbols that are found in and around Hushang Shah's throne.[30]

## The Peacock Throne (*Takht-i Tavus*)

This large, jewel-studded throne, which at present sits in the Gulistan Palace in Tehran, is often mistaken for the Peacock Throne brought as plunder from India to Iran in the second quarter of the eighteenth century by Nadir Shah. In fact, that Peacock Throne was destroyed soon after Nadir Shah's death. The present throne was made in Iran some fifty years after his death. As part of a superficial movement to return to the splendour of ancient Iranian courts, sometime between 1799 and 1800 Fath 'Ali Shah ordered the construction of the throne now in the Gulistan Palace by craftsmen in Isfahan (Fig. 6). This throne appears in a Qajar painting of Fath 'Ali Shah (Fig. 5).

At first this throne was known as the 'Throne of the Sun' (*Takht-i Khurshidi*) because at the top of it was a rotating sun made of diamonds. Its name was changed several years later, however, when Fath 'Ali Shah married a beautiful girl from Isfahan. The king was so taken with this girl, whose name was Tavus (Peacock), that those in charge of the wedding celebration decided that this throne should be used as a bed on their wedding night in order to ensure the king's happiness and the splendour of the occasion. For this reason, Fath 'Ali Shah named this the *Takht-i Tavus* or Peacock Throne after his wife, Tavus. Later this new name became so well known that the former name was forgotten.

A reflection of some of the parts of this throne, especially its 'sun', can be seen in Hushang Shah rugs, such as Nos. 1-3.

## The Nadir Throne (*Takht-i Nadiri*)

This throne was at one time in the Gulistan Palace, and was transferred to the Crown Jewels Museum in the Bank Melli in Tehran some years ago (Fig. 7).[31] It too was made in the period of Fath 'Ali Shah.

Apparently Fath 'Ali Shah used this throne only when he was at Sultaniyah, a small town west of Tehran, where he had one of his summer residences. He had the throne carried back and forth for each visit. On the riser of the first step of the throne is the jewel-studded figure of a lion executed in relief and spotted like a leopard. This lion is undoubtedly the source of inspiration for the leopard that appears in many Hushang Shah rugs at the feet of the king (rugs Nos. 4, 6, 7). Sometimes the sun of the Peacock Throne is seen behind this lion (rug No. 5). The lion is both a symbol of power and a means of emphasizing, through the lion and sun emblem of the flag of Iran, that the court scene is an Iranian one. In rug No. 5 there is a complete example of this lion and sun emblem (sometimes the lion is shown without the sun). In most rugs there are two viziers, one standing on either side of Hushang Shah (in some rugs only one vizier is seen because there is not enough room to show both). In rug No. 3 the vizier is seen on both sides of the king, to provide symmetry. The columns beside the throne and the curtains above it (usually simplified to a canopy shape but also seen in other forms) are taken from paintings of the Qajar period and from *qalamkar* curtains that reflect such curtains (see Fig. 31).

## The Marble Throne (*Takht-i Marmar*), also known as the Throne of Solomon (*Takht-i Sulaymani*)

The Marble Throne (Fig. 8), unlike the Peacock and Nadir thrones, which were portable, is fixed in place in a portico (*ivan*) in the Gulistan Palace in Tehran. The Marble Throne was built about 1804 by the order of Fath 'Ali Shah, who commissioned craftsmen from Isfahan to create a splendid throne that would evoke the legendary magnificence of the ancient court of King Solomon, whose large gilded-ivory throne embellished with carved lions is described in the Bible.[32] It was said that Solomon's throne could be carried into the sky by demons and angels. To emphasize the splendour of his new marble throne, Fath 'Ali Shah called it the Throne of Solomon. In accordance with the legend of the imaginary creatures who sometimes carried Solomon's throne into the heavens, Fath 'Ali Shah's marble throne was built with figures of angels and demons supporting it.

This Marble Throne and the related legend of Solomon's throne were the source of inspiration for weavers of some of the rugs that depict Hushang Shah. The demons are seen in rugs Nos. 1-7, 9-12. The spiral-fluted columns at the back of the Marble Throne are also seen in most of the Hushang Shah rugs (Nos. 1-8, 11, 12, and Fig. 8). Weavers occasionally used attributes of more than one of these thrones in a single Hushang Shah rug.

Other aspects of the elements in many of the Hushang Shah rugs relate to reliefs at Persepolis, such as the soldiers of the lower row and the way they stand in line, which seem to be inspired by the Persian soldiers in relief illustrated in Fig. 10. This impression is reinforced by the soldiers' hats, spears, long garments, and faces shown in profile (the front view of the soldier in the middle is the axis of symmetry and serves to maintain balance).

Furthermore, the larger size of the king in comparison to the figures surrounding him is characteristic of pre-Islamic art in Iran. In nearly every rug that shows Hushang the royal throne rests on the shoulders of demons which are always depicted as ugly monsters. Such creatures are described in Iranian literature as having ugly faces and as non-Aryan. Firdawsi, in a description of a demon in his *Shahnamah*, says:

> His head is like an elephant's and his hair is long;
> His mouth is full of teeth like those of a wild boar;
> His two eyes are white and his lips are black;
> His body should not be looked at.[33]

Horns and tails also indicate the demons' wildness and the fact that they are of an inferior race which, ignorant of the arts of weaving and sewing, is obliged to wear animal skins for clothing and cattle horns for head decorations. The most dangerous demons were said to come from Mazandaran (a heavily forested area near the Caspian Sea). They are of strange build and large proportions and live in caves.[34]

In most Hushang Shah rugs the classic form of Hushang Shah (as in rugs such as Nos. 1 and 2) has been used, but in some, Hushang Shah shows a greater resemblance to Qajar rulers in general and to the reigning monarch of the time the rug was woven in particular. Thus, along with the characteristic design elements of most Hushang Shah rugs, instead of Hushang Shah with his white beard (see Fig. 11, and rug No. 11) and hair, we may see a young king without a beard. Such an anachronism is frequently seen in the case of other figures surrounding the king as well. In rugs Nos. 9 and 10 the faces of two young male slaves (who were characteristic features of the Qajar court) replace the faces of the two demons under the king's throne. Finally, in rug No. 2 both the legendary era of Hushang Shah and the historic period in which the rug was woven are brought together in one scene in which European diplomats of the Qajar period are shown lined up for an audience with Hushang Shah.

Hushang Shah rugs have been produced in western Iran in general and in Hamadan in particular. While examples of Hushang Shah rugs have been woven in other areas of Iran, the majority are the work of people in the villages of the Hamadan province and surrounding towns in neighbouring provinces. The oldest dated Hushang rug that I have seen so far (No. 2), woven in 1230 AH (1815 AD), is from this region.

Besides having the most influential role in the creation of Hushang Shah rugs, Hamadan has played a significant role in the production of other pictorial rugs. While most of these were not woven in the town of Hamadan itself, but rather in surrounding villages and tribal areas within the province of Hamadan, the importance of Hamadan as a market place for them was such that they became known as Hamadan rugs.

Hamadan is one of Iran's ancient towns. It lies at the foot of Mt. Alvand (elevation 11,717 feet). In the course of history it has attracted considerable attention from shahs and other people. At one time it was the capital (under the name Ecbatana) of the Medes, who formed a loose confederacy in the seventh and early sixth centuries. It also served as the summer residence of the Achaemenid monarchs (550-330 BC). The cool summers of Hamadan and its environs attracted not only the Achaemenids but also many others, especially tribal people. Some of the latter settled down in villages in this region in past centuries. Most important among these are the Afshar and Shahsavan tribes, who speak a Turkic dialect.

Most of the rugs of interest to me as a collector were woven by the two above-mentioned tribal groups or by other villagers in the Hamadan area who speak a Turkic dialect. One of the most important of these villages is Dargazin. In addition to the fact that the most outstanding pictorial rugs of Hamadan province were woven in and near Dargazin, that village enjoys a general reputation for having the best rug weaving in general in the Hamadan area. Its tradition of rug weaving goes back at least four or five centuries. In the town's cemetery, which is located next to the Azhar Imamzadeh (a shrine built in the Seljuk period [c. 1000-1157 AD]), there are many gravestones with pictures carved in low relief showing rug weaving implements, such as scissors and beaters (see Fig. 12, which is dated 1223 [1808 AD]). These carved images on the gravestones confirm the importance of the rug-weaving industry in that village. Some of the stones there are two hundred years old.

The influence of the pictorial rugs of Hamadan on neighbouring areas extends to a considerable degree to the districts around Hamadan. The most important of them include: Khamsah, Saveh, Zarand, Zanjan, Kahak, Nahavand and Malayer. Examples of pictorial rugs from all of these areas are found in this book.

## Darius I and Xerxes I: Persepolis

The repeated use of scenes from the carved reliefs at Persepolis in the art and handicrafts of Iran in recent centuries has caused these scenes to enter the repertoire of motifs depicted in rugs. Rug weavers have utilized these scenes extensively, most especially in products of the last hundred years. The main reason for this is that during that period numerous pictures and photographs of Persepolis became widely available throughout Iran. A second reason is related to the discovery in the last hundred years of the historical realities of Persepolis, a place which was virtually unknown to Iranians until the eighteenth century. Before that time knowledge of it was limited to a few legends, and few accurate representations of Persepolis are known before the mid-nineteenth century. For the most part, the correct name (Pars) of the region was omitted from Iranian chronicles before the eighteenth century and if, on occasion, reference was made to it, these references had a mythical or folkloric aspect that is reflected in the names the Mulk-i Jam (Estate of Jam, that is, Jamshid), Takht-i Sulayman (the Throne of Solomon), Chihil Menar (the Forty Minarets), or Hazar Sutun (Thousand Columns). The name used by all Persians even today is a folkloric one: Takht-i Jamshid (Throne of Jamshid).

In the early nineteenth century some of the first attempts to unlock the secrets of the accurate history of Persepolis were made by Georg Friedrich Grotefend (1775-1853), whose early work deciphering cuneiform inscriptions at Persepolis laid the foundation of knowledge that was confirmed and developed further by H. C. Rawlinson's famous translation of the Bisotun inscription of Darius I.[35] Sir John Malcolm, in writing about the ancient period,[36] was still obliged to draw on Iranian legends and epics which could only be partially reconciled with the information given by Herodotus and Xenophon. However, the later efforts of archaeologists and the translation of different inscriptions at Persepolis finally brought the story of this splendid complex out of oblivion and into the light of history.

Persepolis was begun by Darius I between 518 and 516 BC at the foot of Mt Rahmat overlooking the vast Marvdasht plain. It is believed to have been a ceremonial palace of the Achaemenid monarchs, who may have celebrated Farvardegan (Naw Ruz, the first day of the new year in the Persian calendar) there at the beginning of spring (March 21) as well as Mehregan (the first day of autumn).[37] The expansion of Persepolis continued until the invasion of Alexander the Great in 330 BC, when Persepolis, not yet completed, was burned. It was partially repaired after Alexander destroyed it, and the site was occupied until at least the second century BC.

While most pictorial rugs with scenes of Persepolis are products of the past hundred years and show the influence of photography, the existence of rug No. 13, ordered by Jan(-i) Khan Qashqa'i at the beginning of the nineteenth century, makes it imperative that we look deeply into the origins of the pictorial rug that depicts reliefs at Persepolis (see Fig. 13). This is especially true since rug No. 13 was woven years before the appearance of the camera in Iran and most probably in the time of Jan(-i) Khan Qashqa'i himself.

We lack precise information concerning the length of Jan-i Khan's life and the exact date when he ordered this rug, but we do know that in 1234 AH. (1819 AD) he was officially made Il Khan (over-all chief of all of the Qashqa'i sub-tribes) by Fath 'Ali Shah and was the first person to hold such a position officially in Fars province. Perhaps it was this important post, which was influential in the expansion of the Qashqa'i Confederation, that caused Jan-i Khan to be known as the real founder of that confederation. After being Il Khan for no more than five years, he died in 1239 AH. (1824 AD).[38]

Naturalistic aspects such as true-to-life proportions, attempts at shading, and the realistic depiction of a break in a column base make it certain that rug No. 13 (with the inscription Jan Khan Qashqa'i) was woven from the painting by a non-Iranian (probably European) artist. Qashqa'i weavers have a special talent for copying from models (such as pictures, photographs, other rugs). Several years ago I gave a Qashqa'i weaver one of my own paintings in order to have it woven into a rug. The weaver recreated the proportions and colours of the painting astonishingly exactly. The rug was woven by the weaver with the painting in front of her. For many years the Qashqa'i have drawn inspiration from Persepolis for their rugs in many ways. In some of their rugs aspects of Persepolis such as columns, capitals, and certain individual motifs, such as the lotus, as well as pictorial scenes with one or more human or animal figures are seen. The Qashqa'i are familiar with Persepolis at first hand, for they pass it twice each year during their seasonal migrations. In spite of this, the weaver did not base the design of the rug inscribed to Jan(-i) Khan on her own personal experience of the site but on a painting by a skilful non-Iranian (probably European) painter who depicted the site with great naturalism. At the bottom of the rug the words *roi sur son trône* ('king on his throne') are seen, which must have been taken from the foreign painting that served as a model for the weaver (the whereabouts of the painting is unknown today).

As pointed out earlier, European painters have been in contact with Iran from the sixteenth century on and, according to their writings, some visited Persepolis and made drawings of it. Among these drawings are some done by a Dutch painter named Jan Janszoon Struys (1630-1694) about 1671.[39] Many other travellers made similar drawings as well. In 1667 three famous travellers, Jean Chardin, Jean-Baptiste Tavernier, and André Daulier des Landes met each other at Persepolis. Some of these travellers personally made drawings at Persepolis (see Fig. 14).[40] This site later drew the attention of other travellers, Iranian (see Fig. 15) as well as Europeans such as Eugene Flandin and Pascal Coste.[41] André Daulier des Landes writes that his drawings in his book (which include Persepolis) were the first of Persepolis ever published in Europe and he also claims that he made these drawings on the spot.[42] Finally, the agents of the Dutch, French and English East India companies in Shiraz and the foreigners who encountered nomadic tribes during their travels in Iran may well have had a degree of influence on the original model (now lost) on which this rug was based.

Several other carpets with the same subject and composition as this rug were woven. In all of them the name of the person who commissioned the rug or the date of weaving, or both, are inscribed. One such rug (Fig. 16), now in a private collection, is dated 1222 (1807 AD). In the largely illegible inscription at the top of this particular rug are the words: Hazrat-i Sulayman (His Holiness Solomon). As stated above, before the middle of the nineteenth century diverse beliefs about Persepolis were found among the people of Iran, and the name Takht-i Jamshid (Throne of Jamshid) was only one of several names used to designate Persepolis, and had not yet become the most common or established name used by Persians for that site.

The words Takht-i Sulayman (literally, the Throne of Solomon), appear in inscriptions on the walls of the ruins at Persepolis as graffiti left by travellers in past centuries. Among these is one by Sultan Ibrahim b. Shah Rukh Shah, the grandson of Timur (Tamerlane), done in the year 826 AH. (1343 AD).

Because when this rug was woven the present-day name Takht-i Jamshid was not yet the name most often used by Persians for Persepolis, it seems safe to assume that the date woven into this rug inscribed Hazrat-i Sulayman accurately indicates when it was woven, a time when that was one of the several names used by Persians for Persepolis. But once Takht-i Jamshid became the generally accepted name among Persians for the site in the mid-nineteenth century, it was used in carpets depicting Persepolis, including one with the same subject published by Siawosch Azadi.[43] That rug was commissioned by 'Abdullah Qashqa'i and woven in 1318 AH. (1900 AD). The words *Arayish-i Jamshid* (Throne of Jamshid, using an older term for throne than the currently used *takht*) appear in its inscription. The use of Jamshid rather than Sulayman, as stated above, is compatible with the late date of this rug. A garbled rendition of the words *roi sur son trône* appear under the depiction of the king.

Bearing in mind that the earliest date seen on a rug with Persepolis motifs is 1222 (1807 AD) (the rug inscribed Takht-i Sulayman discussed above, Fig. 16), the undated rug ordered by Jan-i Khan

(No. 13) may well be at least several years older than that dated rug and might have been the model on which some of the later rugs with Persepolis scenes were based. The reverse seems unlikely. That is to say, the dated rug cannot be the model for the rug of Jan-i Khan, since the weaver of the dated rug changed many parts of the design and wove a rug that contains elements of both reality and imagination. It is also possible that the rug of Jan-i Khan was not the first rug to depict Persepolis and that it too was based on even older ones, especially since its reversed, mirror-image inscription suggests that this rug was woven from the back of another (the individual knots of inscriptions on pile rugs are usually clearer on the back of the rug for the weaver—usually illiterate—to copy). Rugs depicting scenes drawn from the ruins at Persepolis show the king seated on the throne. When the unknown European artist prepared his drawing of Persepolis on which the rug inscribed to Jan-i Khan seems to have been based, he probably was not aware which king was actually portrayed at Persepolis (or he might have named him instead of just indicating *roi sur son trône*). The weavers of this group of rugs[44] based on Persepolis themes were also mistaken in their understanding of the identity of the exact king they were portraying, and simply copied this French inscription (which they were unable to read) from rugs based on the drawing. Generally speaking, the names of Darius I and Xerxes I were omitted in historical writings in Iran before the eighteenth century. For example, no mention of them is made in the *Shahnamah* of Firdawsi. In general the Achaemenid dynasty and most of its representatives, including Cyrus the Great and Xerxes I were completely forgotten in Iranian histories before the eighteenth century.

The source of the subject of this group of rugs based on Persepolis motifs is a scene carved in relief (Fig. 13) on the southern gateway of the Palace of One Hundred Columns (the largest reception hall of Xerxes). In this, Xerxes I is portrayed sitting on his throne with a servant behind him. Above the king's head are shown two rows of lions and bison and then the image of Farvahar (the winged symbol of Ahura Mazda). Under the king's throne are fourteen people in three rows (in the rugs only two rows appear), the representatives of different countries ruled by the Achaemenid king. From top to bottom these representatives are from Elam, Armenia, Syria, Cilicia, Egypt, coastal Greece, Kandahar, Sagarati, Sakae, Sind, Arabia and Lebanon.[45]

Xerxes I was the son of Darius I by his wife Atossa,[46] the daughter of Cyrus I, 'the Great'. Xerxes I succeeded to the throne in the year 486 BC at the age of thirty-five. After quelling revolts in Egypt and Babylonia (which were subject to Iran at that time), Xerxes I went with his famous army to Greece. Herodotus claims that Xerxes I's army numbered 2,310,000 men, an overstatement to put the Greek defence in a good light. Despite the fact that Xerxes I reached the heart of Greece and occupied Athens, he was unable to conquer Greece and returned, unsuccessful, to Iran. According to Greek sources he was handsome and generous. At the time of the burning of Persepolis, legend has it that Alexander the Great saw a statue of Xerxes I on the ground and said: 'Shall I leave you fallen on the ground so that you are punished for having invaded Greece, or shall I raise you up out of respect for the great spirit and good qualities that you possessed?'[47]

After reigning for nearly twenty years, Xerxes I was killed in the year 465 BC

## Shapur I

Despite the fact that not all of the rugs that bear the symbolic likeness of the Sasanian ruler Shapur I (see p. 24) were woven in the village of Saruq itself (many were produced in the surrounding villages as well), Saruq can still be considered the most important village in the weaving of Shapur rugs because more of them have been woven there than elsewhere, and over a longer period of time. Furthermore, the geographical location of Saruq made that village a centre for the villages around it. The influence of the Saruq rugs depicting Shapur on the rugs of these surrounding villages is very evident.

The village of Saruq lies twenty-five kilometres to the north of Arak in western Iran. Its population consists of about one thousand households. Nearly every home has a rug-weaving loom set up in it. Most of the rugs woven there at the present time have either variants of the design Westerners call *herati* (Iranian weavers call it *morgh u mahi*, bird and fish, after two elements that are nearly always included in that pattern) or else central medallion patterns (called by Iranian weavers *lachak turanj*, corner and centre medallion). During a trip to Saruq in 1977, we found neither examples of Shapur or pictorial rugs nor information about the circumstances of their creation. From this it was apparent that for the previous fifty or so years (within living memory) there had been no weaving of Shapur rugs in that area. Only one of the older weavers, who was over fifty, recalled that during her youth her mother had woven a rug with a picture of one of the shahs. Although there was not sufficient information in Saruq and surrounding villages to answer all our questions, we found many answers to queries concerning the kind of weave, the use of colours, and the designs still in use there, all of which were helpful in distinguishing the groups and relative ages of the Shapur rugs.

As was pointed out above, a considerable number of Shapur rugs were woven in the villages around Saruq. Most came from the Ferahan district, which covers a wide area to the east of Saruq and includes a group of villages circumscribed by the towns of Arak, Tafresh, Saruq and Ashtiyan. Despite the fact that the large number of villages in that area include different types of weaves, all of the rugs of that region are known as Ferahans. We, too, are compelled to call the Shapur rugs woven in the various villages of Ferahan 'Ferahani'.

Likewise, in spite of the fact that the villages of Jozan and Manizan fall into the administrative district of Malayer, their rug weaving has been greatly influenced by that of Saruq, and continues to be today.

In delicacy and fineness the rugs of Jozan sometimes overshadow Saruq rugs. An example of this is the Shapur rug No.14, which from the point of view of weave and colour comes close to perfection.

Apart from a small number of Shapur rugs from Jozan, Shapur rugs can be divided into two groups: those of Saruq and those of Ferahan. The Saruq Shapurs are both the oldest and most numerous that depict this figure. These rugs are woven with two different patterns. The first (Nos.14, 21 22) consists of Shapur figures in a roughly oval-shape frame. These Shapur figures wear modern (European-style) trousers and shoes. Approximately the same curve is given to the shoulders and the hips. In general the Shapur rugs woven this way are simpler in terms of design and number of colours than those with the second type of pattern.

In the Shapur rugs of the second group (Nos. 17, 18, 19), the upper part of the body, with broad shoulders, is similar to that part of the figure in the rugs of the first group. But in the second group, trousers are straight, rather than curved out at the hips and narrow at the ankles, and the shoes are sandals, as seen in two nineteenth-century drawings of the third-century AD statue of Shapur I near Bishapur (see Figs 17, 18 and 19), discussed below. The style of the trousers in this second group of Shapur rugs is not European but similar to the costume of the large statue at Bishapur (see Fig. 17). In the rugs the entire surface of the trousers is covered with irregular lines meant to depict folds.

Only a few small examples of Shapur rugs from Ferahan district are known and these are probably inspired by Saruq rugs of the first type, with modern, European-style trousers. The attribution of rugs Nos. 21 and 22 to Ferahan is based largely on their more mellow, muted colours and fairly angular lines, as well as their structure.

Dated examples of Shapur rugs are helpful in judging the age of the undated examples. Two Shapur rugs (Nos. 17, 19) dated 1331 (1913 AD) and 1333 (1915 AD) also bear the name of the designer, a Muhammad 'Ali. It is quite probable that rug No. 17, which was woven in 1913, two years before No. 19, was the original model for several other rugs, including No. 18 (which is undated). Rug No. 17 was apparently woven from a cartoon, as implied by the inscription 'designed (by) Muhammad 'Ali the carpet designer . . .' (although the inscription could have been copied from an earlier model). But that inscription in any case indicates that a rug of this design was first woven from a cartoon. Although rug No. 19 bears the same carpet designer's inscription as does rug No. 17, it is nearly illegible in No. 19, which would seem to indicate that the inscription in rug No. 19 was based on a rug such as No. 17 rather than a cartoon. Rug No. 18, also, was apparently not woven from a cartoon but used an earlier Shapur rug as a model, because if rugs No. 17 and 19 had been woven from the same cartoon as No. 17, they could be expected to resemble No. 17 in all details more closely than they do, meaning that the weaver of Nos. 18 and 19 felt freer to change certain details than she would have if she had been following a cartoon.

Cecil Edwards, who observed rug weaving in Saruq in 1912 considered the only shortcoming in the otherwise excellent quality of weaving there to be mistakes made due to a lack of the use of cartoons still were not customarily employed in Saruq and neighbouring villages at the time and that starting in 1913, through the efforts of George Stevens (probably the representative of a large carpet company in Arak), they were first introduced in Sultanabad (which is the old name for the city of Arak) and then in other villages in that region.[48] However, it is possible that cartoons were sometimes used earlier than 1913 in the Saruq area because the curvilinear aspect to the design of rug No. 16, which is dated 1296 (1879 AD), seems to indicate that a cartoon may have been used. Rug No. 16, which is over a hundred years old, indicated that the origins of the Shapur rugs (at least those that are now known) must be attributed to at least the end of the nineteenth century, with their apogees coming at the beginning of the twentieth century.

The answer to the question of where the idea and design for the Shapur rugs first arose must be sought in some of the events of the time these rugs were woven. While keeping in mind the fact that the shape and composition of the principal figure in the known Shapur rugs very closely resembles the statue of Shapur I of the Sasanian era in the cave of Shapur (Fig. 17) roughly a hundred kilometres from Shiraz, it remains to be seen how that statue could be the source of inspiration for the rug weavers of Arak.

In the general introduction it is explained how the publication of some scenes of ancient Iranian monuments in nineteenth-century European and Iranian books inspired many artists, and how Fursat al-Dawlah Shirazi went to Fars and other parts of the country to record ancient monuments (see Fig. 18). Under the heading 'Concerning the Cave and Mausoleum of Shahpur', Fursat al-Dawlah Shirazi writes of how he sketched the statue of Shapur:

> This mausoleum is one of the strangest remains in the world. Its story is as follows: Half a parasong from the afore-mentioned pass [Tang-i Chogan] as you go toward Nowdan, one of the dependencies of Kazerun, there is a mausoleum on top of the mountain. The mouth of the mausoleum faces south. Being a frightening place, it is impossible to enter this cave without help. Likewise, one cannot go forward without a light and even with one, reaching the end is an impossible task. In short, through the promise of a reward I got six of the local inhabitants to accompany me, and together with the three persons who were already with me we climbed up the mountain for half a parasong, a distance equivalent to two normal parasongs. What a difficult road it was, all full of stones and bounded by cliffs! When we got close to the cave another difficulty appeared in the form of a sheer wall in the mountain about three metres high. The only way we could go up was by gripping the cracks and crannies in the mountain. I was thinking of fore-going this excursion and returning, but in the end at the urging of the others I got myself up somehow. When I first entered the cave I went forward for fifteen paces and saw a statue which was the representation of a shah. It had an elaborate crown on its head, a short, curly beard, and very thick tresses falling in curls over its two shoulders. It also had a necklace, a weapon like a short sword hanging at his side, and the clothes it was wearing had a fringe hanging from them as intervals. Each fringe resembled the tail of a mouse (that is, the top was thicker than the bottom). A cloth passed behind the neck of the statue and fell down its back. This was a hair band. It was also wearing shoes. The height of the statue from the top of its crown to the bottom of its feet was seven metres. That image was placed on a very large square stone slab in the middle of the cave. However, over the years its two legs were broken above the shins by blows from axes, which caused the statue to fall. This is most lamentable. From the resemblance it bears to the figure carved in stone at the beginning of the pass; this statue is said to be of Shapur.

Following his account of these events Fursat al-Dawlah drew a sketch of the statue (see Fig. 18) and wrote this explanation:

> Although, as I have written, the legs of the above-mentioned statue are broken and its body has fallen on the ground, for the sake of the viewer I have sketched it to look as it originally appeared. This sketch is number 42.

This sketch, published in his book *Athar-i 'Ajam*, is one of the first sources of inspiration for the Shapur rugs. It is possible that before Fursat al-Dawlah other travellers sketched the statue of Shapur and that these sketches were seen by Fursat al-Dawlah and by the weavers of the Shapur rugs.

A mid-nineteenth century French traveller named Charles Felix Marie Texier also published a sketch of the statue of Shapur I. This appeared in an account of his travels published in Paris in two volumes in 1842 and 1852[50] (see Fig. 19). Although this sketch is in some respects similar to Fursat al-Dawlah's, a close inspection of various details shows that the sketch of Fursat al-Dawlah was more often utilized by rug weavers.

Another nineteenth century lithographed book that may have served as a source of inspiration for pictorial rugs Jalal al-Din Mirza's *Namah-yi Khusravan* published in Vienna in 1880, which includes a drawing of a seated figure of Shapur I (Fig. 20) that seems to be related to rug No. 16.

The statue of Shapur I stands in the entrance of a cave situated in the mountains near the Chowgan pass of Bishapur. It is carved from a single piece of stone extending from the floor of the cave to the roof. For unknown reasons this statue was broken in the middle and as a consequence fell to the ground. In recent years it was lifted back to its original position. Carved during the reign of Shapur I, the statue was originally seven or eight metres high (some twenty-one to twenty-four feet).[51]

Shapur I, son of Ardeshir Babakan, the founder of the Sasanian dynasty, came to the throne in 241 AD.[52] He is one of the rulers who have been well remembered by Iranians. Firdawsi considered him a benevolent and culture-promoting king, and recorded his wars with the Romans in the *Shahnamah*, written between about 975 AD and about 1010 AD. These historical encounters led to the capture of the Roman Emperor Valerian along with seventy thousand of his troops, an event that shook the Roman Empire.

There are many monuments from Shapur I's reign of nearly thirty-two years.[53] Some of these still retain a particular glory and magnificence, such as Shapur I's imperial city of Bishapur[54] in Fars, which has been called the 'Sasanian Versailles'. All the imposing reliefs carved on rocky cliffs and the cities, bridges and dams that he left behind should be mentioned as well.

## Shah 'Abbas I

Without a doubt the Safavid ruler Shah 'Abbas I 'the Great' (r. 1588-1629), is one of the best-known figures in Iranian history. Not only his name, but also his wide, masculine face, extraordinarily long moustache, and jewel-incrusted aigrette (*boteh jegheh*) attached to a plain turban are familiar to all Iranians. Artists and craftsmen such as tile makers, engravers, steel forgers, painters, pen-box makers, painted- and printed-curtain makers, and rug weavers have found varying ways to incorporate his visage into their work.

A great many rugs depict Shah 'Abbas I's face. Most city-made examples were designed by artists in Isfahan, Kerman and Tabriz. On occasion, however, his image is seen in village rugs as well, but these are far fewer in number than the city-made ones. Of the village weavers, those of the Bakhtiyari province have shown the most interest in this subject (see rug No. 23). This may be due to the proximity of the Bakhtiyari villages to Isfahan, Shah 'Abbas I's capital, and the good relations that he had with the Bakhtiyaris.

The origins of the design found in rugs bearing Shah 'Abbas I's image are very probably a portrait attributed to Muhammad Zaman (Fig. 21). This painting was among the gifts that Fath 'Ali Shah presented to the British envoy Sir John Malcolm at the end of his trip to Iran.[55] The publication of the above-mentioned portrait (which was probably painted in the mid-seventeenth century) in the Persian translation of Sir John Malcolm's *History of Persia*, published in 1815 in London and in 1886 in Bombay (in Persian) gave Iranians an idea of what Shah 'Abbas I looked like.[56] Rug designers and weavers were directly inspired by his likeness.

In most Shah 'Abbas rugs the ruler is portrayed from the waist up as in this painting.

Shah 'Abbas I came to power at the age of seventeen in 1588 when the entire country was in turmoil.[57] The eastern part of Iran was in the hands of the Uzbeks and the western part was under the control of the Ottoman Turks. Internal conditions in Iran were also chaotic because of disputes between rival leaders seeking power. The young Shah 'Abbas solved these problems in a way no one thought possible. He first expelled the Uzbeks from the country. For his confrontation with the Ottoman Turks, who were the premier power in the Asian world at that time, he brought about changes in the army and other areas. One such innovation was aimed at reducing the influence of the Turkic-speaking Qizilbash leaders of northern Iran who, because of the role their tribes had played in the establishment of the Safavid dynasty in the early sixteenth century, considered that they had the right to interfere in all aspects of the country's affairs. Shah 'Abbas I successfully invited members from all these tribes to enrol in a national army called the Shah-savan ('Shahsavan' in Turkish means 'those who love the Shah'). The Shahsavan gradually became a large and powerful tribal group, the remnants of which are still found today in various parts of Iran.

It took fifteen years for Shah 'Abbas to prepare for his campaigns against the Ottoman Turks. In the end he succeeded in regaining the lost lands and in re-establishing security.

Shah 'Abbas I must be considered the person responsible for the expansion of Iran's relations with European countries. Many Europeans visited Iran during his reign and were encouraged to make that country known to Europe.

In the Islamic period of Iranian history, beginning in the seventh century AD, no other monarch played a more constructive role in architecture or in improving the country. Hundreds of roads, water cisterns and caravan-serais from Shah 'Abbas I's time still remain standing. The city of Isfahan (famed in an alliterative pun in Persian as *Isfahan nesf-i Jahan*, or 'Isfahan is half the world') is his most enduring monument, with many splendid mosques, palaces, other buildings and gardens.

In 1629, at the age of sixty, Shah 'Abbas I died in his palace at Farahabad in Mazandaran and was buried secretly in the Habib b. Musa Imamzadeh in Kashan.

## Nadir Shah

With the exception of portrayals of Nadir Shah

woven into rugs in the last few years, the coronation in 1736 of Nadir Shah, who ruled until his death in 1747, is one of the best-known scenes left to us in pictorial rugs. This scene was woven mostly by Kermani, Isfahani and Bakhtiyari weavers. Their depictions were based on illustrated lithographed books or block-printed curtains showing the coronation of Nadir Shah in the Moghan plain in north-western Iran (Fig. 22).

Nadir Shah's coronation is one of the important events in Iranian history.[58] To understand how this came about we are obliged to trace the career of this great commander from his days as a shepherd to his acquisition of power.

The unworthy successors of Shah 'Abbas I had allowed Iran to fall into such weakness and corruption in the early eighteenth century that every section of the country sought independence and the stage was set for the Afghans to seize Isfahan, the capital of the country, and remove the Safavid dynasty from power. The Ottoman Turks seized Azarbayjan, Kurdistan, Kermanshah and Hamadan, and hundreds of thousands of Iranian women were taken captive and sold into slavery.[59] However, this situation did not last for long, for the hand of fate brought a young man named Nadir Quli, who was a member of the Afshar tribe of Khurasan, onto the stage of these troubled times. After participating in several local wars, Nadir Quli displayed such bravery that his fame soon caused all patriots who were distressed at the plight of Iran to join him. During the difficult wars that he fought against the Turkish, and Afghan invaders, Nadir Quli expelled all of them from the country and regained lost lands. He placed Shah Tahmasp II, the former Safavid shah, who had been in hiding, on the throne in 1722. But when the Safavid shah made several mistakes, including fighting the Turks on several occasions, Nadir Quli seized the opportunity and put into effect a masterful plan to seize the throne for himself.

This plan was to invite the principal commanders of Iran to a Naw Ruz (New Year) celebration on the Moghan Plain (to the west of the Caspian Sea). When Nadir Quli met with all of the dignitaries of the realm gathered there, he said it was time to choose from among the members of the imperial family someone worthy of leadership. All of those assembled were unanimous in wanting Nadir Quli himself to ascend the throne. He refrained from accepting this request for a month, but after being persuaded by the people he accepted with certain conditions and officially became shah of Iran in 1736.

Thereafter Nadir Shah gave full rein to his bellicose nature and embarked on numerous military campaigns, which led to the spread of his control over many territories. His invasion of India and the fabulous plunder brought back to Iran resembles a fairy tale more than it does history. The number of jewels taken was so great that it required a large caravan to transport them. The famous jewelled Peacock Throne was among this loot. (Figs. 5, 6, as is explained on p. 17, illustrate a second throne of this name, made in Iran for Fath 'Ali Shah, rather than the Peacock Throne Nadir Shah brought back from India).

Nadir Shah's invasions and conquests initially met with the approval of the Iranian people and his own lieutenants, but toward the end of his reign the Shi'ite religious leaders tried to find a successor to Nadir Shah, because he was a Sunni. Such ingratitude caused this great commander to become progressively more suspicious and finally, at the end of his life, to kill and blind opponents as a matter of course until, hated by all, he was finally killed in 1747 by one of the members of his own tribe.

## Fath 'Ali Shah

One of the most prolific periods of Iranian art coincided with the reign of Fath 'Ali Shah (1797-1834).[60] During his time the pictorial arts, especially oil painting, became very widespread. The figure of the shah himself constituted one of the principal subjects for artists in various mediums, especially in painting. Although figural representation in that period was common in many artistic mediums, it was only in its initial stages in rug weaving. Only a few pictorial rugs that depict Fath 'Ali Shah are known today (I have seen two examples of them to date, both of which were woven in Kashan and show a full length figure of the king).

In these rugs, as in the portraits executed by painters, Fath 'Ali Shah has a well-proportioned physique, an attractive face, a very long black beard, and sumptuous clothes (see Fig. 23, 24). These characteristic features of the king were constantly repeated in paintings and are also reflected in the writings of many Europeans who saw him close up. The verbal portrait of this king in one of these accounts, published in 1821 by Sir Robert Ker Porter, is remarkably similar to the portrait of Fath 'Ali Shah seen in rug No. 25. His description is also reflected in his sensitive drawing of the king, which appears as the frontispiece in Porter's book (see Fig. 24). Sir Robert wrote:

> I never before beheld any thing like such perfect majesty; and he seated himself on his throne with the same undescribable unaffected dignity. Had there been any

assumption in his manner, I could not have been so impressed. I should have then seen a man, though a king, theatrically acting his state; here, I beheld a great sovereign feeling himself a such, and he looked the majesty he felt. He was one blaze of jewels, which literally dazzled the sight on first looking at him; . . . His face seemed exceedingly pale, of polished marble hue; with the finest contour of features; and eyes dark, brilliant, and piercing; a beard black as jet, and of length which fell below his chest, over a large portion of the effulgent belt which held his diamond dagger. This extraordinary amplitude of beard, appears to have been a badge of Persian royalty, from the earliest times; for we find it attached to the heads of sovereigns, in all the ancient sculptured remains throughout the empire.[61]

Fath 'Ali Shah must be considered one of the last powerful traditional eastern rulers. He had nearly one thousand wives and at his death he was survived by approximately five thousand close relatives and descendants. Some considered his court the most splendid in the world and the ceremonies surrounding his audiences the most striking. On such occasions, as Porter indicated, the king was covered with incredible jewels.

Many have considered Fath 'Ali Shah to be a stingy and cowardly ruler. At crucial times, such as when the crown prince was fighting to regain lost territory from the Russians, he was parsimonious in paying the salaries of his troops and giving them rations.

Following the death of his uncle, Agha Muhammad Khan, the founder of the Qajar dynasty, Fath 'Ali Shah succeeded to the throne 1797, and from that time the kingdom was involved in wars with the Russians. These wars, which continued nearly to the end of his reign (1834), had most unfortunate results for Iran, and ended in the loss of much Iranian territory. The treaties of Golestan in 1813 and Torkmanchay in 1828 gave some of the cities and provinces of northwestern Iran, including Georgia, Shirvan, Karabagh, Baku, Erivan, Daghestan and part of Talesh, to the Russians. These treaties were a prelude to an encroachment on other parts of Iran that came about in subsequent years and separated some of the eastern provinces from the rest of the country. Furthermore, the interference of Russia in the internal affairs of Iran grew continually due to other clauses of these treaties and brought many misfortunes to Iran.

With the weakening of the country and the concessions that the Russians were able to extract from Fath 'Ali Shah, England became aroused and competed with Russia in the division of the country.

While Fath 'Ali Shah lacked experience in diplomacy and administering the country, he had a considerable interest in poetry and art, and was himself a poet. During his reign the new style of large-scale oil painting grew in popularity.

## Muhammad Shah

After the death of Fath 'Ali Shah in 1834, his sons in Tehran, Isfahan, and Fars each claimed the throne as his successor. Zil as-Sultan, who was governor of Tehran, took the names 'Adil Shah and 'Ali Shah and struck coins celebrating his rulership, and proclaimed himself shah. At the same time Muhammad Mirza, a grandson of Fath 'Ali Shah and the son of 'Abbas Mirza (Fath 'Ali Shah's favourite son and his crown prince, who died unexpectedly in 1833, at the age of forty-four, with the help of Abulqasem-i Qa'im Maqam (later Muhammad Shah's prime minister) and the sponsorship of the Russian and British ambassadors, was crowned in Tabriz. A week later he moved to Tehran and took possession of the throne. Zil al-Sultan accepted his claim with no resistance. Muhammad Shah (Fig. 25) ruled until 1848, when he was succeeded by his son Nasir al-Din Shah.

## Nasir al-Din Shah

The reign of Nasir al-Din Shah (1848-1896)[62] coincided with the largest production of pictorial rugs. Expansion in contacts between Iran and Europe, the continued interest in European paintings and lithographs in Iran, Iranians' new familiarity with photography, and the excitement that this new phenomenon created, all had a profound influence on the arts of the time (for more information concerning the history of photography in Iran, see the general introduction, pp. 16-17). The efforts made by Iranian artists of this period toward the realistic portrayal of objects and people is itself very noteworthy. Even the shah himself was not unaffected by the excitement.

Nasir al-Din Shah's trips to Europe had many beneficial results. European painting, in addition to photographs and photography, so fascinated the shah that he sent Kemal al-Mulk, the court painter, to Italy and France to learn portraiture and copy from European paintings.

The shah's interest in European painting was such that he spent many hours of his time with painters in their studios giving them encouragement. Some of Nasir al-Din's own paintings are of interest and show his personal efforts at portraiture.

The photographs and painting as one of the cultural gifts of European culture were not of interest solely to the shah and his retainers; with great rapidity they gained the attention of the common people as well and influenced their arts and crafts. Despite the widespread appearance of pictures of Nasir al-Din Shah on objects ranging from lamps and candlesticks to bowls and plates; and despite the fact that his reign lasted nearly half a century, not many rugs depicting that monarch are known. Fortunately those rugs that do exist are good examples of the taste of rug weavers in that day and age. Of them, rug No. 28, woven in Dorokhsh, is outstanding. The widespread public display of photographs of the king (Fig. 26) seems to have influenced the weavers of some of the rugs that portray Nasir al-Din Shah, especially rug No. 30. Rug No. 31, which shows a king on a horse, is probably of Nasir al-Din Shah. This was inspired by a photograph or painting of the shah on horseback.

Nasir al-Din Shah came to the throne in 1264 (1848 AD) at the age of sixteen. His nearly fifty-year reign was contemporaneous with many major events, the most important of which was the influence of western culture and the beginning of liberal movements in Iran.

During his trips to Europe Nasir al-Din Shah was greatly impressed by the progress of European countries and it was thought that his fascination with western culture would bring about changes in Iran. Although he established several ministries and ministerial councils, his fear that the Europeanization of Iran would reduce his own power and influence caused him to deprive his ministers of freedom of action and innovation and to prevent anyone from interfering in the affairs of the country. He also appointed sycophants and unworthy people to various positions. The embassies of Russia and England were not without influence in the worsening of this disturbed situation. All changes took place under their supervision, and most Iranians involved in running the country openly took orders and received pensions from them.

The Russians, who in the time of Fath 'Ali Shah were able to seize the Iranian provinces to the west of the Caspian Sea only with difficulty, now easily annexed the cities east of that sea, including Khiva, Samarkand and Bokhara, actions that were formalised in a treaty in 1881. The British, rivals of the Russians at all stages and not wanting to be outdone, separated some parts of eastern Iran, including a section of Afghanistan and Baluchistan, from the rest of the country and added them to their own colonies.

These unpleasant events increased the anger of the Iranian people until one of the freedom seekers assassinated Nasir al-Din Shah. This was done during a pilgrimage in 1896.

## Muhammad 'Ali Shah

Muhammad 'Ali (r. 1907-1909)[63] is one of the shahs who are rejected and despised by Iranians. The common people in Iran are aware of his unworthy actions and consider him a tyrant and an enemy of freedom. It is difficult to believe that Iranians would have woven the portrait of this unpopular shah into their rugs. Yet there are indications that seem to indicate that the figure in one of the rugs (No. 32) is of him. Therefore a discussion of this is included here.

As is apparent in the photograph of this ruler (Fig. 27), Muhammad 'Ali Shah was fat and had a thick moustache. Many medals and emblems as well as gold braid trim covered his chest. All of these distinctive features are seen in the figure in rug No. 32. This rug may have been ordered by one of the *khans* or courtiers who supported him. It is also possible that a weaver based her portrayal on a photograph without knowing the true identity of its subject. In any case I do not insist that this rug depicts Muhammad Shah.

Muhammad 'Ali Shah ascended the throne in 1907, replacing his father, Muzaffar al-Din Shah, who was a feckless, cowardly and sickly ruler. From the very beginning of his reign Muhammad 'Ali Shah was determined to suppress the freedoms that the Iranian people had obtained through the constitutional revolution. Ignoring the legitimate parliament and the representatives of the nation, he acted in a perverse and dictatorial manner, which led him to attack the people and parliament with cannon, aided by the Russian embassy. But the unity and alertness of the people forced him to surrender. After each defeat, Muhammad 'Ali Shah expressed regret for his actions. Through false oaths he soothed the anger of the nation for a time and prepared for further subversion. Finally, in 1909, the parliament removed him from the throne, exiled him to the Russian port of Odessa, and installed his twelve-year-old son, Ahmad, as shah.

## Ahmad Shah

Ahmad Shah (r. 1909-1924) was one of the most popular subjects for pictorial rugs depicting royal personages. The figure of this shah (see Fig. 28) was woven by rug weavers in several different parts of the country. The following couplet, seen at the top of one of the Ahmad Shah rugs (No. 33), is expressive of the viewpoint of rug weavers, who were usually among the lowest classes of society:

> People, make way so our dear one can pass, so the Shah of Iran, the moon of Caanan [i.e. Joseph] can pass.

The bitter memories that the deposed Qajar ruler Muhammad 'Ali Shah left the people of Iran caused trouble for his son, Ahmad Shah. However, the truth is that during his sixteen-year reign Ahmad Shah in practice had little to do with the affairs of state and was nothing more than a figurehead. If he was not able to do anything productive for the troubled state of the country, he at least took no hostile action against the people. Perhaps this harmlessness is what made him popular among the people, or at least among rug weavers.

I have seen about a dozen Ahmad Shah rugs from different places in Iran, some of them from the most remote regions. Of them, Fig. 28, a Baluchi piece, from eastern Iran, and Fig. 51, woven in Karabagh, in the southern Caucasus, must be mentioned in particular. However, I have included in this book only some of those examples, all of which were produced by tribal or village weavers.

The source of inspiration for all of these rugs were official photographs showing both bust (Fig. 29) and full-length views of Ahmad Shah. What the weavers achieved on the basis of this inspiration is so masterful that it reminds one of the work of avant-gardes and modern artists. It should be remembered that these photographs were usually black and white, or, only occasionally, tinted, but the weavers of the Ahmad Shah rugs employed colour very effectively. The villagers of western Iran and the tribes of Fars province played the largest role in the weaving of Ahmad Shah rugs.

The Ahmad Shah rugs woven by village weavers in western Iran in the Hamadan and Malayer districts mostly show the figure from the waist up (Nos. 33, 34), whereas in the Ahmad Shah rugs of the tribes of Fars (Boyer Ahmad, Qashqa'i, and sometimes Afshar) the shah is portrayed standing (No. 35).

When Ahmad Shah acceded to the throne in 1909 he was no more than twelve years old.[64] Because of his youth a regent (Azod al-Mulk) was appointed to administer the affairs of state. Once Ahmad Shah reached the legal age and was crowned, in 1914, Iran faced such problems that only an unusual person could solve them. The unsettled internal conditions of Iran reached a critical stage with the outbreak of World War I. In spite of the fact that Iran declared itself neutral, some of the countries engaged in the war turned parts of the country into a battlefield. The weakness of the central government caused local powers in the outlying provinces to rebel and claim independence. It was under such circumstances that Russia and Great Britain formally divided Iran between themselves. The north was to be under Russian control and the south under British control. At that time all patriotic movements were doomed to failure. Following the Bolshevik Revolution in 1917 the Russians evacuated the northern regions of Iran and the entire country came under British influence. The last years of Ahmad Shah's reign were contemporaneous with the rise to power of Reza Khan, the commander of the armed forces. Ahmad Shah, who had in effect been divested of most of his powers, spent his time in Europe and died there in 1930.

## Reza Shah

The end of Ahmad Shah's reign and the overthrow of the Qajar dynasty (1924) conclude, for purposes of this book, the period of production of rugs depicting shahs of Iran. This is not to say that the likenesses of shahs were no longer woven into rugs. In fact, in recent decades a great many rugs were woven portraying the last and earlier shahs. However, these rugs lack all the authenticity, imagination and sincerity of the folk art of nomads and villagers. They are products of city workshops and are made with the help of advanced photographic techniques, cartoons and synthetic dyes, and they have no goal other than the unimaginative copying of a photograph. Such rugs fall outside the scope of this book.

The weaving of pictorial rugs depicting the shahs very quickly declined with the rise of Reza Shah and, except for a small number of attractive rugs, almost disappeared. Among the reasons for this situation were the expansion of printing and the spread of colour posters as well as the modernisation of the country.

The few pictorial rugs that portray Reza Shah cannot compare in artistry with other pictorial rugs. There is only one known rug from the last sixty or so years that can be considered a masterpiece of pictorial rug weaving (rug No. 36). This example was woven during the last years of the reign of Ahmad Shah when Reza Khan was still head of the armed forces (1921-1925) and on the verge of becoming king. This rug is strongly reminiscent of the formal photographs of Reza Khan at the time (Fig. 30). Such photographs also influenced makers of *qalamkar* curtains that portray Reza Shah (Fig. 31). Fig. 32 shows another pictorial rug that reflects similar conventions of that period for formal photographs. During the last years of Ahmad Shah the country was in turmoil. Poverty, disease, unemployment and insecurity cast a dark shadow over Iran. Reza

Shah rose through the ranks of the army and capitalising on the unsettled conditions of the day, he surrounded and took Tehran on February 21, 1921.[65] From that date until 1924, when the constituent assembly voted to overthrow the Qajar dynasty, Reza Khan had progressed to the position of prime minister and temporary head of state. The people, however, continued to call him *sardar-i sepah* (commander of the armed forces). In 1925 he was chosen by the constituent assembly to become shah of Iran, with the name Reza Shah Pahlavi.

From the time he was commander of the armed forces Reza Shah instituted fundamental reforms. He endeavoured to strengthen the army in the manner of his predecessors. Having suppressed insurgency, he was able to establish security in the country. Then he set about developing the country. He discarded corrupt methods of the past and replaced them with new systems in the newly formed ministries and institutions. He also set about building roads, a railroad, factories, banks, schools, a university and in general improving the towns and cities. Reza Shah was a hardworking and strong-willed man. His tall stature, masculine face and stern disposition had great influence on the success of his programs. When he was angry no one had the strength to stand up to him. Any excuse-making or weakness in executing his programs were severely punished. With the outbreak of World War II and the occupation of Iran by the Allies (despite the proclamation of neutrality) Reza Shah was obliged in 1941 to leave the country, abdicate in favour of his son and spend the rest of his life on the island of Mauritius. He died in Johannesburg, South Africa, in 1944.

CHAPTER TWO
# STORIES FROM CLASSICAL PERSIAN LITERATURE

AMONG THE pictorial rugs of Iran, those that tell stories have a special place. They are among the most numerous of all pictorial rugs and are largely the products of city weavers. The proportion woven by tribal and village weavers is very limited. For that reason storytelling rugs are represented in smaller numbers in this book than those with other subject matter. Storytelling rugs were woven more often in the cities than in villages or among the tribes because city dwellers were more familiar with the different stories, partly because there is generally greater literacy in cities than in the villages and among tribal groups. Thus city dwellers would have more access than rural people to illustrated books, which could serve as inspiration for pictorial rugs. Other factors that facilitated the city production of such rugs include the professional story-tellers in tea houses and the paintings and other depictions of various stories in tea houses and other public places such as butcher shops, *zurk hanahs* (traditional Iranian-style gymnasiums), and public baths.

One aspect of storytelling pictorial rugs woven in the cities, in contrast to village and tribal examples, is the great repertory of stories city weavers, who had many different sources on which to base their scenes, often wove into their rugs. The classical literature of Iran is extremely rich in engaging stories, thus there is a great range of famous and well-loved scenes (particularly those from the *Shahnamah* or 'Book of Kings', by the tenth-century poet Firdawsi, or the *Khamsah*, or 'Quintet', by the twelfth- to thirteenth-century poet Nizami) from which city rug weavers could draw, working from detailed cartoons prepared by professional artists.

In contrast, the number of stories depicted in village and tribal rugs is more limited. The scenes that have inspired these weavers are from the best-known and most popular tales in Iranian classical literature that have been handed down in the oral tradition. Since the rural weavers did not work from cartoons but from their own imagination, their pictorial rugs have a spontaneity and vitality not seen in the storytelling rugs woven in cities. And occasionally village and tribal weavers have combined scenes from two different stories, as in rug No.42, which shows Khusraw and Shirin out hunting as well as Majnun in the wilderness with birds and a gazelle, and rug No. 48, in which the meeting of Shirin with Farhad and that of Layla with Majnun have been depicted as one scene.

## Rustam (from the *Shahnamah* of Firdawsi)

Many of the Iranian epic tales celebrate great national heroes, some of them partly or entirely legendary. The narratives recount their exploits of fighting evil-doers, defending truth and justice, or gaining honour for the nation in other ways. With the smallest of differences they are all characterised as enjoying powerful physiques, masculine faces, and exceptional physical strength. Of all the heroes of the stories of Iran, however, none can be found who possesses all of the characteristics of Rustam.[66] Rustam, a hero among heroes, is invincible. His life from birth to death is full of amazing events and superhuman deeds. He belonged to a family of heroes and dignitaries of Sistan, in eastern Iran. His father, Zal, and all of his ancestors were among the famous heroes of Sistan, but Rustam surpassed his forebears. Firdawsi (in his *Shahnamah*, written between about 975 and 1010 AD) developed the character of the legendary figure Rustam very fully and differentiated Rustam's fate, beginning with his birth, from that of other heroes. According to Firdawsi Rustam's body at birth was so big that he had to be delivered by Caesarian section. Before that no one had been born in such a manner. He was no more than eight years old when he subdued a large elephant, and as a youth he did battle with Afrasiyab, the famous king and hero of Turan. Until that time no one had the strength to resist Afrasiyab, but Rustam lifted him over his head and dashed him on the ground. Rustam also killed one hundred and sixteen of Afrasiyab's soldiers by himself, and spent most of his six-hundred-year lifetime fighting the enemies of Iran—demons and other evil-doers was always victorious in the end. The description of these brave deeds constitutes a considerable portion of the *Shahnamah* of Firdawsi, and Rustam's exploits, more than those of any other hero, are widely admired by the Iranian people. When these tales of Rustam are told by professional reciters in Iran, they arouse great excitement.

As a king himself, the Safavid ruler Shah 'Abbas I had a special interest in the *Shahnamah* of Firdawsi. Shah 'Abbas I had in his employ two reciters of this book.[67] Furthermore, in order to maintain the bellicose spirit of their Qizilbash troops, the Safavids encouraged their soldiers to listen to reciters of the *Shahnamah* in the tea houses.[68]

The busiest night for the teahouses and story-tellers is the night when the story of Suhrab's death at the hands of his father, Rustam, is recited. On this night the teahouses are packed. In the past the walls of teahouses were hung with paintings of different scenes from the *Shahnamah* (a few still are today), some of them showing the various deeds of Rustam. Whenever necessary, the story-tellers point out these scenes to their audience and utilize the paintings to bring the scenes and heroes to life. Occasionally a story-telling rug is hung on the wall of a teahouse and used in the same way. Rug No. 45 was in fact obtained from a teahouse.

In this book there are three rugs depicting Rustam. They are rare pieces. One (No. 38 shows Rustam standing, and includes many of the characteristics attributed to him in the *Shahnamah*. Further aspects of the story of Rustam are depicted in two other rugs in this book (rugs No. 39 and 40). The episodes involved are recounted in the following pages.

## Rustam and Suhrab (from the *Shahnamah* of Firdawsi)

Out on a hunt one day Rustam, Iran's greatest warrior and defender, headed into the Samangan Plain where he killed a wild ass, roasted and ate it, and then fell asleep.[69] Several Turkish horsemen in the area noticed the footprints of Rustam's famous horse, Rakhsh, and went after him. They captured him and took him off with them. When Rustam awoke he looked for Rakhsh, but all he could find was a trail of hoofprints. Following this he went into Samangan and asked the king of that place for his horse. The king recognised the renowned warrior and invited him to his castle. There the king's daughter Tahminah caught sight of Rustam and fell in love with him. One night she went to him and urged him to ask her father for her hand in marriage. This was granted and Rustam then married the princess, who was soon with child. Rakhsh was finally found and Rustam set out for Zabulistan. But before leaving he gave his pregnant wife a special bead and told her to attach it to their child's hair if it should be a girl, and to a band for the child's arm if it turned out to be a boy.

From this union a son, Suhrab, was born. One day while he was growing up Suhrab asked his mother why he always felt compelled to seek superiority over others of his age when playing games. He also wanted to know the name of his father, who had never come back to his wife and had never seen his son. Tahminah told him he was the son of Rustam, the champion of Iran, but that this had to remain a secret lest Afrasiyab, the enemy of Rustam and Iran, learn of it. Suhrab answered that he had heard of Rustam, and that it was time to engage in battle an army of Turks (the traditional enemies of Iran) in order to rid Iran of its various enemies, depose the king, Kavus, and place his father, Rustam, and his mother Tahminah, on the throne of that country.

Suhrab selected for himself a valiant and strong horse and went to his grandfather, the king of Samangan, saying that he wanted to lead an army into Iran. The king was happy to hear this and equipped him for war. Afrasiyab, the king of Turan, the arch enemy of Iran, learned of this plan and sent a force of twelve thousand men with orders not to let the father and son recognise each other so that Rustam would either be killed by his son or die of a broken heart if Suhrab were to be killed by him before he recognised his son.

Suhrab thus set out for Iran. He conquered the White Fortress and captured its warden, Hajir. When news of Suhrab's invasion reached Kavus, he sent for Rustam who was in Zabulistan. Rustam came to the royal court and then with a large army headed toward Suhrab's camp. At night Rustam came close to Suhrab's tent in order to catch a glimpse of his adversary. It was on this occasion that the champion of Suhrab's army, Zhandah Razm, was killed in the dark by Rustam.

The next day both armies drew up in battle formation. Suhrab, who wanted to know which man was his father, summoned Hajir, the captured Iranian general, and told him to identify the leaders of Iran. Hajir named them one by one until he reached Rustam. Then fearing Suhrab might attack and kill Rustam and thereby leave the army of Iran defenceless, Hajir lied about Rustam's identity and said he did not know him but had heard that he was from China. This report of Rustam's supposed absence saddened the young warrior hopeful of meeting his father for the first time.

When the time for battle arrived, Rustam put on his armour, mounted Rakhsh, and came out to fight. Suhrab did the same. Rustam then addressed Suhrab and expressed feelings of compassion toward his opponent and wonder at his strength unequalled among the Turks and Iranians. Suhrab in turn spoke to the champion of Iran, suspecting instinctively that he might be his father, Rustam, and asked him to confirm that he was in fact Rustam and gladden him with this news. Still unaware of the identity of Suhrab, Rustam denied that he was of the lineage of Sam and Nariman, the father and grandfather of Rustam.

On the first day of battle the two champions used every weapon they had on each other, but neither gained the advantage. That night both returned to their camps tired, thirsty and bleeding. The following morning they fought each other, but this time without horses, in hand to hand combat on the ground. Suhrab seized Rustam's belt, lifted him up and threw him to the ground. Sitting on his chest Suhrab drew a dagger with which to sever his head. Then Rustam cried out that it was customary in Iran for one warrior to spare the life of his rival on the first fall. Suhrab acted accordingly and Rustam crawled back to his army and implored God to give him greater strength.

The next time Rustam came out to do battle, he felled Suhrab but gave him no quarter and ripped open his side with a dagger. The fatally wounded Suhrab moaned and lamented that he would die without ever seeing his father. Then he told his opponent that wherever he went he would never be able to escape the revenge that Rustam, his father, would take when he heard about the death of his son. Horrified on hearing this, Rustam looked at the arm of the man he had fatally wounded, saw that he wore the arm band with the bead he had given his wife long ago and thus recognised, too late, that it was his own son with whom he had been fighting. Suhrab then closed his eyes and breathed his last while a heartbroken Rustam was left to revile himself.

Rug No. 39 shows Rustam seated next to his son Suhrab. This is perhaps the scene before their final battle.

**Rustam and Akvan the Demon (from the *Shahnamah* of Firdawsi)**

One day Kay Khusraw, the king of Iran, was feasting in a meadow with his entourage.[70] Toward sunset a shepherd came in from the plain and reported to the royal assembly that a wild ass, yellow in colour with a black streak from its mane to its tail, had appeared and attacked a herd of horses. Remembering that they were in Turan, the land of their enemy, the king at once realised that what the shepherd had seen was no wild ass, but rather Akvan the Demon in disguise.

Kay Khusraw turned to the dignitaries to see which one of them was capable of killing the demon, but found no one equal to the task. He then ordered that a letter be written to Rustam summoning him from Zabulistan to deal with Akvan. Rustam responded at once and upon arriving at court kissed the foot of the royal throne and declared himself ready for action. After showering him with honours the king told Iran's greatest champion what had occurred. Thereupon Rustam mounted his famous horse, Rakhsh, and set out to capture the wild ass.

He waited for three days and on the fourth day this strange animal appeared looking just as the shepherd had described him. Rustam thought it best to capture him with a lasso and take him to his monarch. But as Rustam threw his rope the wild ass suddenly disappeared. Rustam then realised that this was in fact Akvan the Demon.

For three days Rustam chased the animal about and each time he tried to use a weapon on it, it disappeared. Finally the great warrior became tired and hungry. With his weapons still close about his body, he lay down beside a spring, put his head on Rakhsh's saddle, drew the saddle felt under himself, and went to sleep.

When the demon found his pursuer asleep, he lifted Rustam together with the patch of earth on which Iran's hero was sleeping high over his head, and flew up into the air. (This is the scene depicted in rug No. 40 and Figs. 33 and 34). Rustam then awoke to find himself a prisoner in Akvan's arms. Noticing that his captive was awake, the demon asked him where he would like to be thrown. Since Rustam knew that the demon would do the exact opposite of what he said, he told him that he wanted to be thrown into the mountains. It was thus that the hero was thrown into the sea, where Rustam swam with one hand, using the other to fend off whales.

Following this temporary setback Rustam returned to the spring where he had previously fallen asleep. However, Rakhsh was not to be seen there. Rustam became angry at this, picked up his horse's saddle and bridle, and set out to retrieve him. He finally found him in a meadow among some horses owned by Afrasiyab, Iran's arch enemy. Mounted on Rakhsh once again, Rustam gathered up some of Afrasiyab's horses and took them with him. When Afrasiyab learned what had happened, he and his soldiers set out after the horses. This led to an encounter with the great Rustam, who routed them and then returned once more to the same spring where he had fallen asleep.

Once again Akvan the Demon appeared. He told Rustam that he would not escape a second time, but, as fate would have it, one blow from Rustam's club crushed the demon's skull and finished him off. Then with a stroke of his dagger the hero of Iran severed the demon's head from his body.

## The *Khamsah* of Nizami

Without a doubt the five stories of the *Khamsah* (literally, 'five', in Arabic) of Nizami (c. 1140-c. 1217 AD) is one of the chief sources of inspiration of representational art in Iran.[71] After the *Shahnamah* of Firdawsi, no other literary work has had a greater influence on all the pictorial arts of Iran, and not only on miniature painting. The subjects of these stories, especially during the last two centuries, have appeared in all the handicrafts of Iran, especially in block-printed curtains. Scenes from the stories of the *Khamsah* are also widely found in pictorial rugs. Various subjects of the *Khamsah* constitute a considerable proportion of the rugs in this book.

Nizami was born and also died in the Caucasian town of Ganjeh. His most outstanding work is his *Khamsah*, which consists of five stories: 'The Treasury of Mysteries', 'Khusraw and Shirin', 'Layla and Majnun', 'Bahrum Gur and the Seven Princesses', and 'Iskandar'. With the exception of the first, which has a moral and mystical bent to it, the tales have very engaging story lines. In this book only the stories of Khusraw and Shirin and Layla and Majnun are summarised, since it is on scenes from these that some of the pictorial rugs have been based. Of these three stories, that of Khusraw and Shirin has been the most popular among rug weavers. Originating at the end of the Sasanian period, this story tells about the love of Khusraw Parviz for Shirin, an Armenian princess. In the Islamic period (after the mid-seventh century AD in Iran) this story was further elaborated and many poets and writers, including Firdawsi, told it in different versions. By strengthening its romantic aspects Nizami gave the story a new life.

The historical figure Khusraw Parviz was the last impressive ruler in Iran before the end of the pre-Islamic period. In wealth and the number of wives he had no peers. A description of his treasures would itself require many pages. In his crown alone there were sixty man (about one hundred and eighty kilos) of pure gold.[72] Each of the pearls in the crown were the size of a sparrow's egg and each of its rubies shone like a light. A gold chain about seventy cubits (slightly more than seventy metres) long hung from the ceiling of the *ivan* (entrance arch) and suspended the crown above his head. Khusraw Parviz's most precious possession was the throne known as Taqdis. According to the descriptions written by Tha'labi, the Arab historian (d. 1038 AD),[73] this throne was made of ivory and teak and had a silver and gold balustrade and ebony stairs inlaid with gold. The length of this throne was one hundred and eight cubits (slightly more than one hundred and eighty metres) and its width one hundred and fifty cubits (slightly more than one hundred and fifty metres).

The ceiling above this throne was of gold and lapis lazuli, and engraved on it were celestial figures, stars, signs of the zodiac, the seven climes, faces of the shahs, and representations of them at feasts, war, and on hunts. It also contained a mechanism for telling the time of day.[74]

In Nizami's rendition of the story, which he gives great psychological depth, Shirin was an exceptional woman. Not only was she unrivalled in beauty and perfection but also she was exemplary in faithfulness to love and devotion to morality. In the face of Khusraw's infidelities she did not step outside the bounds of fidelity and even a fervent lover such as Farhad, who dug through a mountain for her sake, only received a respectful look from her.

Of the numerous episodes from the story of Khusraw and Shirin and of Shirin and Farhad only several well-known scenes have inspired village and tribal rug weavers. Among these scenes that of Khusraw and Shirin hunting enjoyed the widest popularity. Several woven examples of this scene from several regions of Iran are included in this book. We see different versions of this scene in rugs Nos. 41 and 42. Except for rug No. 43, which shows both Khusraw and Shirin out hunting, the rest depict Khusraw hunting and Shirin usually seated or standing in the midst of her companions. In some rugs depicting scenes from this story, only a few of the characters are depicted. Such rugs include Figs. 35 and 36. Another famous scene shows Shirin taking a bath in a spring, while Khusraw, who comes upon her unexpectedly, watches her from a distance. This particular bathing scene seems to have been woven most often in Lilihan, near Arak (see No.46; and, as compared to rugs depicting Khusraw and Shirin hunting, the bathing scene is very infrequently found. The scene appears with two others from the story in a cartoon drawn in

*Kings, Heroes and Lovers*

the mid-nineteenth century for a city weaver, probably in Kashan, see Figs. 37, 37a, 37b and 37c). The number of rugs depicting Khusraw and Shirin hunting that come from other areas (such as No. 43 from Nahavand, near Hamadan; No. 44 from Zabul in southeastern Iran; and No. 45 from Rudehen, northeast of Tehran) included in this book is very insignificant when compared with those of this scene woven in the Ferdows area of the province of Khurasan in eastern Iran. I have seen more than fifty rugs from the Ferdows area depicting Khusraw and Shirin hunting. While most of these have been made in recent years, some are nearly a hundred years old. Examples of the latter are Nos. 41 and 42.

In all the Khusraw and Shirin rugs, Khusraw is mounted on his favourite horse, Shabdiz (which means 'the colour of night'), whom he had acquired from Shirin. Khusraw Parviz was said to have so loved this horse that he swore to put to death the person who brought the news of its death.[75] The day Shabdiz died the master of the stables fled in fear to Barbad, the shah's bard. In a song Barbad hinted at the horse's death and the shah cried out 'Oh ill-fated one, has Shabdiz died?' The singer answered, 'The shah himself has said so.' Khusraw then said, 'Very well, you have saved both yourself and the other person.'

Ferdows was one of the major centres of pictorial rug production, and rugs with pictorial subjects other than Khusraw and Shirin were also produced there. Ferdows, one of the older towns of Khurasan, is located at the edge of the Salt Desert. Its former name was Tun, which was linked to the name Tabas, as in Tun-u-Tabas. In recent years this town was severely damaged in violent earthquakes, but in the past it was a thriving place and had a long tradition of rug weaving. Nasir Khusraw Qubadiyani, who in the eleventh century AD passed through Ferdows, mentions four hundred zilu (a type of pileless, flat-woven carpeting) weaving factories in Ferdows.[76]

Many of the older rugs of Ferdows were woven by tribes said to be Arab and to have been in residence in villages around the town for many centuries. I have included in this book one of the oldest of these rugs that were woven by the Arab tribes of Ferdows (rug No. 60). Although today these people are intermingled with Persian-speaking groups and it is difficult to differentiate their rugs from those of others, the role that they played in the spread of pictorial rug weaving must not be overlooked.

The influence of the Khusraw and Shirin rugs of Ferdows, especially in Baluchi rugs, is considerable. Rug No. 44 is an example from this region. In recent years this design has also attracted the attention of weavers in Afghanistan. I saw a number of fairly recent examples of such rugs in the bazaars of that country in 1978.

In this book there is only one rug (No. 48) related to the tale of Shirin and Farhad, which is part of the over-all story of Khusraw and Shirin. (The top part of this rug pertains to the meeting of Shirin and Farhad; the lower part to the meeting of Layla and Majnun, which is a completely separate story). Despite the fact that the story of Shirin and Farhad is as well known as the story of Khusraw and Shirin, the scenes of Farhad's digging into the mountain and his meeting with Shirin are much less frequently encountered. Some of the rugs depicting episodes from the story of Khusraw and Shirin involving Shirin and Farhad are reminiscent of lithographed drawings of these scenes. For example, rug No. 48 may be compared with Fig. 41 and rug No. 50, with Fig. 42.

The tale of Layla and Majnun is another of the stories that have had a great influence on painting and other kinds of pictorial representation. The story is of Arab origin and came to Iran after the Islamic conquest of that country in the mid-seventh century. Nizami's version of the story differs considerably from the earlier Arab version. Nizami gave the old story a new colour and lustre. His changes, which are chiefly due to his sensitivity and mastery in expressing romantic subjects, reach their most affecting in the story of Layla and Majnun. The number of rugs woven depicting episodes in the Layla and Majnun story is limited. Of these only a very small number woven by village and tribal weavers has come to light (Nos. 48, 49, 54).

More than any other scene, that of Majnun and his animal companions has been a favourite with painters and designers of other forms of pictorial art. This scene shows Majnun (who has become nothing but skin and bones, and lives in the wilderness) in the midst of desert animals which he has tamed and which have become his friends. In rug No. 48 this scene is shown in the bottom section, which includes Layla who has come to see Majnun (the top of the rug depicts the meeting of Shirin and Farhad from the story of Khusraw and Shirin). The figure of Majnun in the lower right corner of this rug is reminiscent of the emaciated figure of Majnun in Fig. 43. In some depictions of this Majnun scene Layla's camel is shown as a combination of several different animals, as seen in Fig. 44, and in rug No. 49, where the animals composing the camel are so stylized that only suggestions of species and of animal heads are to be distinguished. A similar mythical beast is seen in rug No. 52 (see also Fig. 49). This composite camel is related to other similar animals from Indian mythology (such as camels, elephants and horses) whose bodies are composed of demons' heads, symbolising the power of magic possessed by demons. That Layla should be riding such a creature is the result of the oral transmission of the stories and the embellishments that the people create around the main elements of the narrative. The basis for this elaboration is this: the desert animals, which for a long time had comforted and accompanied Majnun and were aware of Majnun's need to see Layla, were all lumped together by the weaver and from them a camel was created to carry Layla to see Majnun. This particular representation of Layla's camel based on Indian mythology has become common in the art of Iran in the last few centuries. Iranian artists have long depicted such creatures (see Figs. 45, 46).

## Khusraw, Shirin, and Farhad (from the *Khamsah* of Nizami

One evening Prince Khusraw[77] and his retinue alighted at a peasant's house, seeking food and lodging. There they prepared for a night of pleasure. While Khusraw was making merry, one of his slaves went into a nobleman's vineyard and stole some grapes. One of the prince's horses also did some damage to the peasant's planted fields. When Hormuzd, king of Iran and father of Khusraw, was informed of this he became angry and ordered that the slave be given to the peasant. The roaming horse was captured, and his hooves savagely slashed. In addition, Khusraw's princely throne was given to the peasant. As a further punishment the fingernails of Khusraw's musicians were clipped, as were the musical instruments themselves.

Following this incident, Khusraw went to sleep one night greatly disturbed. He saw his grandfather Anushirvan in a dream. Anushirvan told him that as a reward for his patience in the face of his father's anger God would bestow upon him a beautiful woman named Shirin. In place of the horse given away by his father he would receive an exceptional horse named Shabdiz. To replace the musicians whose fingernails were clipped he would have the famous musician Barbad, and in place of his former throne there would be a far more glorious one known as Taqdis. Khusraw was gladdened by his dream and waited for it to become a reality.

One day Khusraw's companion Shapur the painter came and informed him that on the other side of the mountain there was a woman named Mahin Banu, the queen of Armenia, who had a beautiful niece named Shirin, who was her heiress and who owned a horse named Shabdiz. Khusraw then sent his companion to find Shirin.

When he reached the Armenian mountains (in what is today northeastern Turkey and the southern Caucasus) he inquired about Shirin and was sent to a pleasant meadow where Shirin and her companions were seated. In a place out of sight of the group of girls Shapur found a tree and hung in it a portrait that he had drawn of Khusraw. When Shirin's eyes fell upon that image she immediately fell in love with it. Wondering how to find the person portrayed, she consulted Shapur, who gave her Khusraw's ring and told her to leave her companions on the pretext of going out to hunt. Once at the hunting ground she was to flee on Mahin Banu's swiftest horse, Shabdiz, and take herself to the royal palace Moshku, in the capital city Mada'in. Shirin followed these instructions and headed for Mada'in. When she reached a spring she was tired and covered with dust, and sat down to rest. She then decided to bathe herself in the spring.

It so happened that Khusraw had already set out toward Armenia, out of fear of his father's wrath over a false accusation of Khusraw's alleged plotting to seize his father's throne, concocted by jealous enemies of Khusraw. But before he left he instructed the women of the harem to treat Shirin well if she appeared during his absence, even to build a new dwelling for her if she so wished. Arriving at a meadow on the way Khusraw rode off by himself and came upon a woman bathing in a spring. The sight of this beauty lit a flame in him. When Shirin saw a horseman watching her from a distance she jumped out of the water, clothed herself, mounted her swift horse, and fled. Once Khusraw regained his composure he saw no trace of Shirin, and searched the entire area for her, but without success.

Khusraw then went on into Armenia, and Shirin arrived at the capital city, where she was admitted to the royal palace Moshku after showing the prince's ring.

Sometime later Shirin, homesick for the mountains of her native Armenia, requested an abode in the mountains, for the weather in the city did not agree with her. However, she was placed by jealous women of the harem in a stone castle ten farasangs from Kermanshah, a place noted for its bad climate.

Meanwhile Khusraw reached Armenia and went to see Mahin Banu. One night when he was seated at a banquet Shapur entered and informed the prince that he had tricked Shirin into going to Mada'in. When he described her, Khusraw realised that the woman he had seen bathing in the spring was none other than Shirin. Once again Shapur was sent after Shirin while Khusraw waited. Mahin Banu provided her second fastest

35

horse, Golgun, for Shirin to ride, in case she no longer had Shabdiz. Shapur seated the princess on the bright bay horse and set out for Armenia. But when the news of Khusraw's father's death reached the prince, he was obliged to return to the capital city Mada'in before her arrival. For a second time the lovers missed seeing each other.

Khusraw succeeded his father on the throne only to find a rival in Bahram Chubin, a scheming general who attacked him and forced him to flee on Shabdiz to Armenia. There he found Shirin in a hunting field where the two lovers finally met each other face to face. The next day they played polo together, and each day thereafter feasted together. One day a lion attacked their camp. Khusraw, somewhat intoxicated, came out and with a blow of his fist killed the lion.

One spring night Khusraw came to Shirin and asked her to grant him that which his heart desired. Shirin refused his advances saying that he should first rid himself of his rivals and secure the throne of Iran, and only then think of pleasure and love making. Khusraw, thus inspired to regain his throne, left Shirin and went to Constantinople to enlist the aid of the Byzantine emperor.

With Byzantine help Khusraw defeated Bahram Chubin and won back his father's throne. But before he would lend his aid, the shrewd Byzantine emperor required Khusraw to marry the emperor's daughter, Princess Maryam Banu, to seal their alliance, but Khusraw's heart still belonged to Shirin. In the meantime Mahin Banu, queen of Armenia, died and Shirin succeeded her on the throne. However, it was not long before she learned of Khusraw's marriage. Heartbroken, she gave her throne into the hands of a regent and left with the faithful Shapur for Mada'in, stopping en route at the unhealthful stone castle she had previously occupied near Kermanshah. Khusraw heard of her return, but out of fear of Maryam Banu did nothing more than send a message to her through Shapur.

As the Kermanshah region of her castle was so unhealthy Shirin craved some fresh, pure milk, which was unobtainable near the palace because the surrounding fields were full of weeds that poisoned the cows. She requested Shapur's help in solving this problem, and in turn Shapur consulted his sculptor friend Farhad, who was both clever and very strong. Shirin summoned Farhad, and the sound of her voice so captivated Farhad that all he could do was stand speechless and signal without words his acceptance of the task assigned him.

For one month Farhad worked to cut a channel in the mountainside and to fashion a pool at the end of the channel. This he did so masterfully that the shepherds in the distant pasture could milk the animals and the milk would flow down the channel into the pool. Meanwhile, Farhad's love for Shirin had become such that it caused him to wander aimlessly in the mountains and desert, calling out Shirin's name.

Khusraw heard of this, became jealous, and consulted his advisers about courses of action. They told him to summon Farhad and buy him off with gold and silver. Farhad, however, could not be diverted from his love for Shirin. Finally Khusraw told him that there was an enormous mountain called Bisotun blocking a road he wanted to use. He commanded Farhad to remove the mountain. Farhad agreed to remove the mountain on the condition that Khusraw have nothing more to do with Shirin. This angered Khusraw, but he thought that Farhad would fail in this task and therefore have to give up his attempt to win Shirin for himself.

Farhad worked day and night without cease and carved the images of Shirin, the king, and Shabdiz on the side of the mountain. One day Shirin went to see Farhad at Bisotun. She gave him a cup of milk and asked about his health. On that occasion Shirin's horse died and Farhad at once picked up the dead horse and its rider and carried them to the door of the castle.

Khusraw learned that after Shirin's visit to Farhad, the sculptor's strength and speed had increased to such an extent that it became apparent that he would open a road through the mountain in one month's time. In consultation with his advisers Khusraw decided that someone should be sent to Farhad to tell him that Shirin had died so that he would lose hope and cease his efforts. This plan was carried out and when Farhad heard the lie about Shirin, he threw himself off the mountain and was killed.

It came to pass that Maryam Banu, the daughter of the Byzantine emperor, died not long after this. Khusraw sent for Shirin, intending to marry her at last. But in the meantime he met a deceitful beauty of Isfahan named Shekar and took her for his wife. Shirin in loneliness and isolation tried to hide her distress, but soon fell prey to deep despair. She spent her time supplicating God until her prayers were answered and Khusraw lost interest in Shekar. One snowy day Khusraw, riding Shabdiz, went to see Shirin after a hunt. Upon hearing the news of his arrival she locked the doors of the castle and went up to the roof, from which she spoke with him. A lovers' quarrel resulted. She reproached him for her sufferings and said if he desired her, she would only come to him as his wife. She did not give Khusraw permission to enter the palace because she did not want to be accused of being unchaste.

Khusraw was unhappy at this and left. Regretful of her treatment of him, Shirin mounted Golgun and went to Khusraw's camp. It was a moonlit night. Khusraw was asleep but Shapur was awake. Shirin told Shapur what had happened. By chance, that night Khusraw dreamed that he was in a beautiful garden with a lovely maiden. The next day Shapur told Khusraw this surely foretold his reconciliation with Shirin, and Shapur persuaded Khusraw to hold a banquet so they could celebrate this sweet dream with wine and music by Barbad and Nikisa. At that banquet Barbad sang a love song on behalf of Khusraw, while Nikisa sang one on behalf of Shirin, each musician voicing the feelings of the royal pair. In time Shirin was unable to contain herself and let out a cry that was heard by Khusraw. Shapur urged him to promise to wed Shirin. Khusraw agreed and Shirin appeared from behind a curtain and the two lovers embraced each other.

Many years later Shiruyeh, a son of Khusraw and Maryam Banu, fell in love with Shirin and plotted to seize his father's throne. He imprisoned his father. Shirin volunteered to share his dungeon and stay awake to guard him from danger. One night she fell asleep and an assassin crept into the cell, plunged a dagger into Khusraw's side and killed him. Shiruyeh then asked Shirin to be his wife. Shirin made pretence of consenting. When Khusraw's body had been placed in the tomb chamber, Shirin obtained permission to be alone with the body. She then stabbed herself with a dagger, drew Khusraw to herself, and died embracing him.

## Layla and Majnun (from the *Khamsah* of Nizami)

The chief of the Bani Amir tribe in Arabia had no son and heir.[78] His goodness of heart was as great as his boundless wealth, and he made many pious vows and gave alms to the poor until one day God bestowed a son on him. The boy was named Qays, and his father selected wet nurses for him. At the age of ten Qays, who was already famous for his beauty, was sent to school by his father. Qays excelled in all his lessons, and among the girls who were in his class was the beautiful and tender Layla. Qays and Layla fell in love with each other and in time this love became the talk of the tribesmen. As a consequence, Layla's father withdrew her from school, in order to separate the two young lovers. This separation increased the intensity of their feelings to such a degree that Qays, in a fit of madness, ran off into the desert and from that time on became known as Majnun ('the mad one').

This situation caused much grief to his father, whose efforts to advise his crazed son were of no avail. In the end he and several of the elders of the tribe were compelled to call on Layla's father to ask him to grant Layla's hand to Majnun in marriage. Layla's father, who was much disturbed by Majnun's unnatural behaviour, replied that he would not grant such a request because he did not want to lose all honour among the Arab tribes. The head of the Bani Amir tribes thus returned brokenhearted.

Majnun subsequently became more disturbed than ever. When the father saw that neither counsel nor reproach had any effect, he took Majnun on a pilgrimage to the Ka'ba at Mecca to grasp the ring of that sacred edifice and beseech God for help in finding a remedy for his love. The weeping Majnun grasped the ring of the Ka'ba and prayed to God that his devotion to Layla increase daily and that whatever remained of his lifetime be taken and given to his beloved. Upon hearing this prayer Majnun's father realised that his son's situation was even worse than he had imagined.

The story of the love of Majnun and Layla brought the ridicule of the Arab rabble upon both their families. The members of Layla's tribe met and decided to avenge this loss of honour by sending someone to seek Majnun out in the mountains or desert and kill him. However, one of the Bani Amir tribesmen revealed this plot to Majnun's father, who with some of his own friends searched high and low for Majnun, but without success.

Meanwhile Layla was burning with love for Majnun, but there was nothing she could do except cry in solitude and compose poetry. This she wrote on pieces of paper, which she threw from the roof into the street so that someone would find them and take them to Majnun and bring back his replies.

One day in spring Layla went to visit a garden. There she overheard a passer-by reciting poetry by Majnun. This caused her to weep and lose control of her senses. Someone informed Layla's mother, who forbade her to compose and send poetry anymore.

The same day that Layla went to the garden a youth named Ibn Salam from the Assad tribe saw her and fell in love with her. He went to her father to ask for her hand. Layla's parents agreed to this request but since Layla was very weak they wanted to wait a few months until their daughter regained her strength.

In the meantime a Bedouin prince named Nowfal, while travelling through the desert, came across Majnun. Majnun, though friendly with the animals of the desert, was greatly afflicted, weak, and distressed. When Nowfal heard Majnun's story he promised that he would bring him and Layla together. When Nowfal failed to achieve this goal through negotiation with Layla's father, he resorted to the sword and led his own tribe into battle against Layla's tribe. However, he was defeated in this attempt and was persuaded by Layla's father to abandon his efforts on behalf on Majnun. Majnun was bitter at this defection and went off alone into the desert again. He came upon a hunter who had trapped two gazelles. Majnun wanted to free these gazelles because their eyes resembled those of Layla. The hunter said that Majnun should buy them and free them himself. Majnun gave the hunter his horse and set the gazelles free. The next day he gave away the remainder of his possessions to a hunter in order to free a stag that had been caught in a trap.

In the end Layla was married to Ibn Salam and taken to his house. However, she refused to consummate the marriage and the bridegroom contented himself with merely looking at her and enjoying her beauty. The news of Layla's marriage made Majnun even more distressed than before and he began to reproach her despite the fact that he had been told that she had remained chaste. Meanwhile Majnun's father, who had become feeble from despairing over his son, made one final visit to his son and again failed to bring him to his senses. Soon after that he died, leaving Majnun alone in the world except for the wild animals of the desert over whom he ruled as king. Majnun's way with these animals was such that they lost their predatory instincts and lived with him and each other in peace and harmony. An old man carried a letter from Layla to Majnun, and a reply back to her, and even arranged for Majnun to see Layla one night in a grove.

After a time Ibn Salam died from a fever. Layla mourned unrestrainedly, but for Majnun rather than her husband. At length she became so weak she developed a fever, called for her mother, and asked to be dressed in bridal robes after her death. Her mother carried out her daughter's last wishes. On hearing of Layla's death Majnun came to her grave and remained there. The animals of the desert came with him as well. Majnun laid his head on her grave and surrendered his soul out of love for her. He was buried next to his beloved and their graves became a place of pilgrimage for the distressed and homeless.

# CHAPTER THREE
# STORIES FROM THE QUR'AN

A CERTAIN number of pictorial rugs show religious subjects drawn from the Qur'an. These include Abraham and Ishmael (rug No. 51, Gabriel (rug No. 52) and Mary and Jesus (rug No. 53), all of whom are mentioned in various parts of the Qur'an; their stories are based on narratives in the Bible.

In principle, the weaving of the likeness of the Prophet and Imams into rugs which might one day be used underfoot is a sin, and as a consequence such rugs were not produced in the past. During the last decade or two the weaving of the images of the Prophet Muhammad and the First Imam, 'Ali, has become common, but rugs of this sort are framed like pictures. Such rugs now being woven usually lack colour and artistry. Most are copied from photographs or black and white drawings based on photographs. These rugs fall outside the scope of this book.

A few rugs depicting religious subjects such as Imams, however, are of interest, because they were not copied from photographs but were imaginative interpretations by the weaver of a relatively unsophisticated pictorial source such as folk paintings on glass. A small rug woven in Qom is an example of this type (Fig. 47). The Imam 'Ali is shown seated in the middle of the rug, flanked by his sons, the Imams Hasan and Husayn. On the right-hand side, wearing the clothes of a dervish, stands Qanbar, one of 'Ali's companions; and on the left stands Abazar Ghaffari, another of 'Ali's supporters. This mid-twentieth century rug was undoubtedly inspired by a reverse painting on glass (*shamayel*). In order to support themselves, dervishes called *shamayel-khan* used to suspend such paintings from their necks and walk through the streets and bazaars reciting poetry about Imam 'Ali.

## Abraham's Sacrifice of Ishmael

Rug No. 51 depicts an episode in an elaboration of the narrative of Abraham and Ishmael in the Qur'an, which is based on the story that is given somewhat differently in the book of Genesis (Chapter 22) in the Bible, where Isaac, the son of Abraham's wife Sarah, is the son whom God asks Abraham to sacrifice. While the Judeo-Christian heritage is based on the lineage descending from Abraham's son Isaac, Muslims identify with the descendants of Ishmael, the son of Sarah's handmaiden Hagar. Thus Muslims give Ishmael, rather than Isaac, prominence as the son offered as a sacrifice (see the Qur'an, Sura 37, verses 101-111).

Books of commentary on figures in the Qur'an (many of whom are shared by the Judeo-Christian heritage), such as Mawlana Muhammad Jazayiri's *Stories of the Prophets*, further elaborate on the story. One such version goes as follows: Abraham made a vow that if he were given a son he would sacrifice him to God, and the Lord gave him Ishmael. When Ishmael grew to be a youth, an angel in a dream reminded Abraham of his vow, and Abraham resolved to sacrifice his son.

Abraham told the boy's mother to send her son with him to do some work. He instructed Ishmael to fetch a rope and come with him to the mountain to cut firewood. The boy took up the rope and Abraham picked up a knife and set out with all of the creatures of the heavens and the angels looking on.

When they came to Mount Shubayr (near Mecca) all of the angels wept and told God what a good servant He had in Abraham who had been cast into a fire for His sake and had not been afraid and who was now ready to sacrifice his own son without fear. As the father and son made their way up the mountain, the mountain trembled and exclaimed how difficult it was for it to bear the weight of a prophet bringing his son up to be sacrificed. Ishmael asked his father why the mountain shook and was told that it was God's will that it did so.

The devil (Iblis) was distressed by Abraham's faith and did not know what to do. He approached Ishmael's mother in the disguise of an old man and asked where Abraham had taken her son. She replied that he had gone out to cut

39

wood. The devil told her she had been deceived, for Abraham had taken a knife along in order to kill their son. The woman said she thought him to be the devil because he said a prophet of God was going to kill his own son. The devil replied that God had given Abraham such a command. 'If it be the command of God, I too will obey' was her answer.

Giving up all hope of influencing the mother, the devil approached the son and repeated all he had previously said, but only to hear the same answer. Despairing again, he went to Abraham and told him that the one who had instructed him in his dream to kill his son was not an angel but rather Iblis, the devil. Abraham addressed him saying, 'Oh enemy of God, you are Iblis. I will not disobey God's command.' The devil once again was disappointed and accompanied Abraham and Ishmael up the mountain.

Tired out, Abraham sat down, seated his son in front of him and withdrew the knife from his sleeve. Drawing his son's head to him, he began to cry. Ishmael asked his father why he was crying and what the knife was for, and then was told about the dream in which his father had been instructed to sacrifice him. Upon hearing this, Ishamael said, 'Do that which has been commanded. I shall not resist.' Then he cried and said, 'Oh father, if only you had told me at home so I could have bid mother and the others farewell.' Abraham was still hugging his son and crying, as was Ishmael. The sky, earth and mountains, and the angels wept with them.

When Ishmael realised what was happening, he told his father to rise and carry out God's command so that they would not be disobedient to the Lord. Abraham asked how he should proceed and Ishmael told his father to bind his hands and feet so that he could not move when the knife touched his flesh and thereby cause his father's robe to be spattered with blood and his mother to know what had taken place.

Abraham arose, tied his son's hands and feet, and turned him on his right side. He wanted to place the knife on Ishmael's throat but his hand trembled and he started to cry. When his father did not cut his throat, Ishmael opened his eyes and saw his father weeping. Ishmael addressed him thus: 'Oh father, if you look at my face, your hand and knife will not move. I am afraid that you and I will be disobedient to God. Turn my face away from yourself and put the knife against the nape of my neck and cut my throat.' The angels in the sky watched and were astounded by the father's courage and the son's submission.

Abraham attempted to act accordingly, but each time he tried, the knife would not cut. Both became amazed at this. Ishmael told his father he was not doing it correctly, and that he should first place the sharp part on the nape of his neck and then plunge it into his neck without hesitating. Abraham agreed to do so. Just at that time the Lord sent Gabriel with a sheep from heaven. Gabriel came holding the sheep by the ears and stood on the mountain near Abraham. The next time Abraham wielded the knife, it bent and he exclaimed to his son that something was going on that they were not aware of. Ishmael again expressed his fear of disobeying God's command and told his father to straighten the knife. Abraham did this, then placed it against the nape of his son's neck and prepared to plunge it in when suddenly God called to him and said, 'Oh Abraham, the dream that you had has been reality and you have been faithful to my command'.

Abraham was awed by the words of God and trembled. The knife fell from his hand and he sat down on a stone. Gabriel cried out 'God is great'. Abraham raised his head and saw Gabriel with a sheep. He too cried 'God is great', and said to Ishmael, 'Oh son, rise up and see how God has given comfort.' Ishmael also looked up and said 'God is great.' Abraham unbound Ishmael's hands and feet. God instructed Abraham to tell Ishmael to make a wish. When Abraham informed Ishmael of God's command, Ishmael looked up and said, 'Oh Lord, whoever of the faithful comes to you with many sins, forgive his sins for my sake.' Abraham then sacrificed the sheep in place of his son.

## Gabriel

Another rug with religious subject matter is rug No. 52. This shows Gabriel mounted on a camel. The design may have been inspired by a drawing such as Fig. 49. The camel here is also reminiscent of the camel composed of many animals that is associated with the Layla and Majnun story (see p. 107; see also rug No. 49) and other sources for such composite camels (see Figs. 44, 45 and 46).

## Mary and Jesus

Another rug that appears to have a religious subject is No. 53, a Baluchi product. The source of inspiration for this rug, also, was perhaps a folk art reverse painting on glass depicting Mary and Jesus, such as Fig. 50. It should be remembered that the figure of Mary, which in the past was a favourite subject for rug weavers, not only for the religious significance (she is mentioned in the Qur'an), but rug weavers were attracted to portrayals of Mary (such as in paintings on glass or in prints) which showed her as pure and beautiful. As discussed in the section on Beautiful Women (see p. 56 infra), in the late nineteenth and early twentieth centuries the picture of any beautiful woman that rug weavers (and painters and pen box makers as well) came in contact with could serve as a source of inspiration to a weaver or artist. For this reason the picture of the Madonna and Child are frequently seen in handicrafts from the end of the last century and beginning of this one.

# CHAPTER FOUR
# SUFISM AND PICTORIAL RUGS

## Dervishes

BEFORE DISCUSSING rugs that depict dervishes, and iconographic objects related to dervishes, we would like to provide a little background information about dervishes, their doctrines, and way of life. This is particularly important because dervish rugs, in addition to sharing the characteristics of other pictorial rugs, to an extent also have a symbolic and ceremonial function.

In the *Encyclopedia of Islam* the definition of the word *darvish* includes the following: 'Broadly through Islam it is used in the sense of a member of a religious fraternity, but in Persian and Turkish more narrowly for a mendicant religious called in Arabic a *fakir*'.[79]

The word dervish in fact is a general term applied to all members of the ascetic Sufi mystical movement of Islam, chiefly because of the importance they attach to poverty.

Of the different opinions concerning the original meaning of the word 'Sufi', the view that this word is derived from the Arabic word *suf* (wool) has the largest number of adherents. The reason for this appellation is that the Sufis wore woollen clothes, an ancient practice among ascetics.[80]

Although the term Sufi gained currency at the beginning of the eighth century AD, some people think that followers of this movement already existed at the time of the Prophet's death (632 AD) and that they were not satisfied with the mere performance of their religious duties but sought a greater closeness to God by means of asceticism and special devotions. This group gradually took root all over the Islamic world and gave a special depth and lustre to Islamic mysticism. The Sufis' wearing of woollen clothing was a sign of their asceticism and their rejection of the lifestyle of the wealthy and the worldly.

This asceticism was not limited to their dress but included a continual struggle against carnal desires and pleasure because the Sufis believed that all love of wealth, rank, wife and children were nothing but pride. Although it is not necessary for man to renounce all of them he must avoid attachment to them so they do not become an obstacle to his quest for union with divine Reality and Truth, which is the goal of man's existence (and the allegorical meaning of the book of which the story of Shaykh San'an is a part, see pp. 45-46). To succeed in this quest, one must practice asceticism so that all of the obstacles that are in the way will be removed and union with Reality will be realised. The achievement of this goal entails successive stages through which the seeker must pass.[81]

The first step is repentance, so that the heart and soul of the disciple become pure and are worthy of union with divine Reality. After that the main task is struggle with the self, which beckons man to the world and pleasure and carnal desire.[82]

A condition of the struggle is that the traveller along the path to union with Reality be assisted by a spiritual guide (*shaykh*) in whose hands he must be, like a dead man, without power or will. In accordance with the disciple's capacities the *shaykh* leads him to asceticism, struggle, seclusion, fasting, prolonged silence, meditation, calling oneself to account, and so forth.[83]

The number and order of the stages differ in the opinion of the *shaykhs*. The path begins with the stage of repentance and after passing through the stages of abstinence, renunciation, poverty and patience, reaches the final stage, which is fulfilment.[84]

Passage through the stages depends on the capacity and purity of the disciple's heart. As a result of this purity it is possible for the mystic to achieve ecstasy without going through all the stages or even a single stage. Other mystical states are not acquired through striving. Rather, they are the gift of God and come to the disciple from the unknown. Like lightning, they light up the passages of his heart and sooner or later are extinguished.[85]

The repetition of a mystical state might carry the disciple to a higher stage. Meditation, affection, fear, hope, fervour, familiarity and tranquillity are among the mystical states that are not describable. It is possible that for different disciples the order of the various mystic states might be different. The goal of all is the union with divine Reality.[86] In addition to majesty and grandeur, Reality encompasses Perfection and Beauty. If there is a path to the attainment of Beauty (in the divine, ideal and absolute sense), it is the path of love and not of the intellect. It is for this reason that Sufi poetry is full of poetic complaints of love.

This poetry is expressed mostly in the metaphorical language of love. The ecstasy that comes with union with divine Reality is called 'drunkenness' by the Sufi poets and anything that is the source of drunkenness is called 'wine'. These metaphorical terms have engendered much misunderstanding and suspicion of Sufism among orthodox Shi'ites and caused accusations of impiety to be levelled against the Sufis. The use of these terms has also brought death to many Sufis.

The state of ecstasy or seizure is usually attained in sessions of music, singing and dancing. During these sessions the Sufis sit silently on the ground and hold their breath in order not to break the silence. Suddenly a Sufi rises to dance while repeating sacred words or verses. With the repetition of these words or verses (which are usually about love for God, His Prophet, and the Prophet's companions) the others too experience joy and join that Sufi in recitation and chanting. These words and movements are repeated over and over until the Sufis are overcome by ecstasy.

Some Sufis do not even refrain from singing and dancing in the streets and bazaars. While in a mystical state Sufis sometimes tear their clothes or utter blasphemies, which can cause trouble for them.

Most of these rites take place in a special type of meeting place called *khanaqah*. The *khanaqah* is also the place where many spiritual exercises such as prescribed group prayer, fasting, individual prayer, lamentation, remaining awake at night, and seclusion and mortification for forty days are performed under the guidance of the *shaykh*. Service with respect to the physical maintenance of the *khanaqah* is also one of the duties the disciple must perform. The spiritual guide, who is a fully developed and mature teacher and manifestation of Perfection, supervises his followers through these stages. The disciple might pass through some of these stages while in the desert or at cemeteries or famous tombs.

After achieving sufficient progress along the mystical path, the disciple receives permission from his *shaykh* to supervise others and to establish a new *khanaqah* which is in fact a branch of the main *khanaqah*. The existence of these Sufi convents and their connections with the *shaykhs* create a kind of brotherhood among Sufis that transcends national borders and regional boundaries and gives the Sufis a home wherever they go in the Islamic world.

The portraying of dervishes and their symbolic equipment in large and small rugs must be considered a phenomenon of the last two centuries and a part of the movement of pictorial expression in rugs. These rugs can be divided into two groups. The first group consists of rugs decorated with the images of dervishes (see rugs Nos. 54, 55), and the second group depicts objects that are ceremonial aids to the dervishes (see rugs Nos. 56, 57).

Of the pictures of dervishes, none has been more popular among rug weavers than that of Nur 'Ali Shah (d. 1797). He was a member of the Ni'matullahi Sufi order and was one of the last dervishes to lead the exciting and tumultuous kind of life experienced by the dervishes of earlier centuries. The Ni'matullahi order is one of the largest Shi'ite Sufi orders. The founder of this order, Shah Ni'matullah Vali, was one of the famous Sufis of the fifteenth century AD. He was a contemporary of Timur (Tamerlane) and his son Shahrukh. The Timurid sultans, especially Shahrukh, had great faith in him. Shah Ni'matullah Vali spent the last twenty-five years of his life near Kerman engaged in agricultural and developmental projects. He constructed gardens and buildings in Yazd and near his own *khanaqah* in Mahan. (His tomb in Mahan is one of the most pleasant holy places of all of Iran, and still serves as a place of pilgrimage for many people). He contributed a special quality to the world of Sufism.

The eighteenth-century member of the Ni'matullahi Sufi order, Nur 'Ali Shah, who is portrayed in many pictorial rugs, was originally named Muhammad 'Ali. The name Nur 'Ali Shah was given him by his order. Most of the names given to members of the Ni'matullahi order are preceded by 'Ali Shah'. The use of this name comes from the devotion of the order to Imam 'Ali, who is called the 'King of men'. Seen in most of the reverse paintings on glass carried by dervishes is the portrait of a Sufi named Qambar, a companion of Imam 'Ali. A rug that was possibly inspired by such a painting on glass is Fig. 47.

Nur 'Ali Shah was the son of Fayz 'Ali Shah Khurasani, who was also one of the important Ni'matullahi Sufis of the nineteenth century. When Nur 'Ali Shah was young he and his father went to Shiraz to see Ma'sum 'Ali Shah Dakani, who served as spiritual guide to both of them and gave them the names Fayz 'Ali Shah and Nur 'Ali Shah. Following the killing of Ma'sum 'Ali Shah

*Kings, Heroes and Lovers*

by anti-Sufi Muslims, Nur 'Ali Shah succeeded his former spiritual master.

Nur 'Ali Shah went to Isfahan for a time and then, with Mushtaq 'Ali Shah and a group, went to Kerman. After the episode in which Mushtaq 'Ali Shah was killed by anti-Sufi Muslims, Nur 'Ali Shah went back to Shiraz, where he encountered the hostility of Lutf 'Ali Khan Zand. Therefore he left Shiraz for the shrines of Iraq where he took up residence.

Due to some of the claims he made while in a state of ecstasy, Nur 'Ali Shah angered Muslims unsympathetic to the Sufi order. This led some to accuse him of seeking secular power and others to claim that he did not observe the sacred law of Islam. These charges led to an uproar wherever he went and to the barring of his entry to many places. His opponents as well as his followers were greatly influenced by him. After enduring many hardships and travels Nur 'Ali Shah finally died in Mosul in 1797.[87]

In the borders of most rugs that depict Nur 'Ali Shah there are quotations from poetry composed by or about him (rugs Nos. 54 and 55).

Translation of Sufi poetry in Persian into English can never be totally satisfactory for several reasons. Mystical poetry by its very nature is not accessible to the uninitiated. Also, for the Persian reader Persian poetry is full of verbal images on more than one level of interpretation that are recognizable, and therefore evocative and meaningful, only to those who have an extensive familiarity with Iranian culture in general, and its language and literature in particular, as well as with Sufism and its veiled and multilayered metaphorical symbolism for ecstatic experience that cannot be adequately rendered in rational, 'down-to-earth', everyday language.

> Serve in the tavern, be a sultan on the battlefield, obey the cup bearer, be the commander of the time.
> One must not be inactive among the wine drinkers; either act like a commander or a follower.
> If you are eager to hear a tale of Joseph, either be the mirror of his face or be the holder of the mirror.
> If you don't drink wine, feel ashamed of yourself before the cup bearer.
> If you have not made love, regret it.
> Lessen your animal instincts toward others, leave the animal world behind and be human.
> If you happen to go his way one day, don't seek paradise or be inclined toward heaven.
> Far from the waves of his hair, bow to his face; seek faith in the world of the dervish.
> If you are a disciple or Nur 'Ali Shah, seek the life to come.
> If you seek earthly treasures, you will be destroyed instantly.

In rugs depicting Nur 'Ali Shah, the weaver's efforts to show the beauty of this dervish's face are apparent. In one of the rugs (No. 54) he is seen with his seated companion Mushtaq 'Ali Shah. Concerning the meeting of these two dervishes it is said that when Mushtaq 'Ali Shah came to Nur 'Ali Shah he was awestruck by the degree of spirituality that Nur 'Ali Shah had attained and decided to become his companion.

These two Sufis spent time at the tomb of Shah Ni'matullah Vali in Mahan. During one of the riots incited by the orthodox preachers of Kerman against these dervishes, Mushtaq 'Ali Shah was stoned and beaten to death (1791).[88]

Another rug that is possibly related to dervishes is No. 61. One of its two figures is Ahmad Shah, while the other resembles both a dervish and a tribal *khan*. In any case, as is explained in the introduction of the section on tribes, tribal weavers gave their subjects a tribal character, even if the figure depicted was not a tribal person.

Rugs that portray dervishes constitute one group. A second group of rugs bearing a dervish imprint is made up of a type of rug design known in Persian as *pust-i palang* (leopard skin). These are more or less similar to each other in subject matter and composition. In all of them we see the usual ceremonial paraphernalia of the dervishes (see Figs. 55-58 and rugs Nos. 56 and 57). Some of this paraphernalia appears in a tile wall revetment in the Mu'avin al-Mulk mosque in Kermanshah (Figs. 56, 56a).[89]

This paraphernalia consists of a hat (*taqieh*), axe (*tabarzin*, see Fig. 57, beggar's bowl (*kashkul*, see Fig. 58, leopard skin (*pust-i palang*), pouch (*chantah*), and cudgel (*mantasha*). The hat (which usually has twelve vertical folds) is a symbol of the twelve Shi'ite dervishes. (Some dervish caps have only seven sides, which symbolise their condemnation of the seven sins). Around the hat are usually written couplets of poetry about the owner's Sufi order.

Laleh Bakhtiar explains that 'the bowl (*kashkul*) symbolises the individual's passive, receptive nature, and the double axe (*tabar*) symbolises the individual's active nature as agent. The animal skin (*pustin*) serves the purpose of orientation in two ways: first, it is upon this space that one sits and meditates; second, it is to this space that one relates one's possessions. To own more than would fit upon this skin, or more than would fit in one's *chantah* or rug bag, is to have reached the state of forgetfulness.'[90]

The dervish's beggar's bowl is usually made

from half of an exotic type of double-lobed coconut (Fig. 59) known as coco de mer, or is an imitation of that form made of steel or brass (Fig. 58). The original coconut is an unusual double-lobed fruit about ten to fourteen inches long. This variety of coconut, among the largest known, ripens only after ten years. After the seed has germinated, the empty coconuts are found floating in the Indian Ocean (whence its name coco de mer) and were discovered long before the palm that bears them was discovered. In India yogi sadhus (wandering Hindu mystics) use the whole double-lobed coconut, hollowed out and with the top of the fruit cut off and re-attached with hinges at the back. When cut in two at the point of juncture, each half of the coco de mer can be used as a dervishes' beggar's bowl. The dervish uses the beggar's bowl in a variety of ways, including as a container for his food and drink.

The dervish's bag (*chantah*) is a pouch (which is often woven with a pile like a rug) that hangs from the shoulder and contains whatever the dervish needs. In most of these nothing is usually found due to his renunciation of worldly possessions.

The dervish's axe (*tabarzin*) normally has two steel blades either decorated with designs and poetry or completely plain. The cudgel (*mantasha*) that some dervishes carry instead of the axe is usually of a knotty wood, but sometimes it is made from the long saw-like bone that projects from the upper jaw of a fish (*arrah-mahi*, saw-fish) found in the Persian Gulf. The axe and/or cudgel are used by the dervish to defend himself against animals. The axe is symbolically held in the right hand and the beggar's bowl in the left, in accordance with Tantric symbolism of Hindu yogis, whose mystic beliefs are similar in some respects to those of the Muslim Sufis.

The animal skin has many uses. The dervishes sit and sleep on it and use it for protection was well as for meditation and prayer. It can represent the skin of a sheep, gazelle and sometimes of a lion, tiger or leopard. The dervish who styles himself the 'shah of the kingdom of poverty and abstinence' considers his hat a crown and this skin a throne and in fact calls the latter his 'throne'. Among the songs and poems dervishes commonly sing and recite is this verse:

> We are the shahs of the kingdom of poverty and abstinence is our clothing our hat is our crown and our animal skin our throne.

This paraphernalia, which is used in the daily life of the dervish, assumes a ceremonial character in the *khanaqah* during various rites.

There are different opinions about this animal skin, which is shown in most pictorial rugs as that of a leopard or tiger. Of these opinions, Marilyn Ereshefsky's are the noteworthy.[91] She believes that the depiction of a leopard or tiger skin in dervish rugs is not unrelated to earlier traditions.

After pointing out a number of Persian miniatures in which a leopard skin covers shahs and legendary heroes such as Kiyumars and Rustam, she broaches the subject of rugs depicting animal skins, and also of the wearing of leopard skins by shahs and dervishes.

While examples of rugs that feature leopard skins and dervishes are known from the last two centuries only, there are indications that rugs woven with leopard-skin designs have a longer history. One of these indications is a rug from the eighteenth century.[92] Greatly simplified in that rug, the animal skin is treated as a kind of large rectangular medallion which occupies almost all of the field. Another reflection of the leopard skin can be found in certain Indian (Kashmir) and South Persian rugs with an arch design.[93] (These rugs are known as 'Haji Khanomi' in the Tehran bazaar and as 'Nazem' in the Shiraz bazaar and among the Qashqa'i.) The arch-shape form that nearly fills the field of this rug design is reminiscent of the shape of the leopard skin in rugs such as Nos. 56 and 57 in this book. That this resemblance is more than coincidental is strongly suggested by the two 'legs' at the lower corners of the field in some examples of the Indian and South Persian rug designs.[94]

## Shaykh San'an (from *Mantiq al-Tayar* ('The Conference of the Birds') of Farid al-Din 'Attar written in the second half of the twelfth century AD)

This story comes from the *Mantiq al-Tayar* (variously translated as 'the Conference, Language, Parliament, Speech, or Discourse of the Birds'), an allegorical, philosophical, and religious poem in prose written by Farid al-Din 'Attar, born in Nishapur in Khurasan and generally believed to have died in 1220 AD 'Attar is one of the great writers of Sufi didactic poetry. Shaykh San'an was the leading Sufi mystic of his age (see rug No. 58). With four hundred disciples he lived in rigourous asceticism day and night. During a fifty-year residence in Mecca he performed the rites of pilgrimage every year without fail and healed the sick. His miraculous powers and spiritual attainments were such that his followers stood in a awe of him.

For several nights in a row this mystic saw a dream in which he left Mecca and went to lands that were once part of the Byzantine empire, where he prostrated himself before an idol.

Informing his disciples of this dream, he and four hundred of them set out for that territory. Once there they travelled from town to town in search of the secret contained in the dream. Finally Shaykh San'an's eyes fell upon a beautiful Christian girl. The Shaykh was completely smitten by her beauty and instantly fell in love with her. His disciples were astounded by their master's behaviour and tried to reason with him, but to no avail. For nearly a month Shaykh San'an sat on the ground in her quarter of the town with his eyes fixed in her direction. The girl became aware of his infatuation and one day came to see him.

Pretending not to know of his feelings she asked him why he remained in the Christian quarter. Then she told him if he were to fall in love with her, it would lead to madness. This did not dissuade the Shaykh, and after hearing his entreaties she stipulated that he would have to renounce Islam in order to be acceptable to her. This he agreed to do. She then proceeded to lay down four tasks he would have to perform: prostration in front of an idol, burning the Qur'an, drinking wine (forbidden to strict Muslims), and renunciation of his faith.

From the hand of the girl he took a goblet of wine and drank it. This caused his love to grow even stronger. He began to cry and called for another goblet of wine. The Shaykh, who is said to have written almost one hundred books and memorised the Qur'an by heart, had all of this washed away by the wine.

The girl then made him accept her religion, and when the news of this reached the Christians they took Shaykh San'an to a monastery and bound around him the girdle which Christians in Muslim lands were required to wear.

Once more the girl tried to put the Shaykh off by telling him that her marriage portion was very high and that since he was poor, he should leave her alone and return to his own country. To this the Shaykh responded: 'Oh beautiful mistress, you too all that I have. Are you now discarding me?' Upon hearing this the girl took pity on the Shaykh and waived her right to the marriage portion on the condition that the Shaykh look after her herd of swine for a year (a particularly demeaning and repugnant task because pigs were considered unclean, impure from a religious point of view by Muslims).

With the shaykh's acceptance of this ignominious task (with its insulting implications toward their religion and that of their master) there remained little his disciples could do. Some of them left him and others declared their willingness to become Christians and stay with him. The Shaykh rejected this offer and sent them back to Mecca.

Meanwhile one of the shaykh's chief disciples, who had been away on a trip when his master had left Mecca to discover the significance of his dream, returned to Mecca. When he heard the news about Shaykh San'an, he berated the other disciples for not having remained with their master. He then led them back to the lands once ruled by Byzantium. There they beseeched God for forty days and nights until their prayers were answered. In a dream the leader of the disciples was told that Shaykh San'an had been delivered from his tribulations and that they should go and find him. Upon their arrival they discovered that their Shaykh had regained his senses. He renounced Christianity and purified himself. Then he set off for Mecca with his followers.

When the Christian girl woke up in the morning she was inspired to arise and follow the Shaykh she had deceived. The Shaykh in turn was inspired to return and look for the girl. This caused an uproar among the disciples, but Shaykh San'an informed them of his inspiration and they all went back after her. When they found her she had fallen on the ground and was covered with dust. The sight of the Shaykh caused tears to fall from her eyes and she asked for his forgiveness. She also asked that the Shaykh make her a Muslim. This he did and the disciples celebrated loudly. Then she called the Shaykh to her side, bid him adieu, and died.

# CHAPTER FIVE
# ARMENIANS AND PICTORIAL RUGS

ARMENIANS HAVE played a significant role in the weaving of pictorial rugs, as have weavers in some of the towns in the Caucasus, which was part of the Iranian sphere of influence until the first decades of the present century but is now part of the former Soviet Union.

Although these towns were formally separated from Iran during the last two centuries by various treaties (these treaties and the way in which this separation came about are discussed in the chapter on kings, pp. 76-77), it must not be forgotten that a change in borders did not influence the characters, customs and culture of the people of the territories, or if it did, at least it took some time. Also, people of similar ethnic origin and culture were divided by the arbitrary border separating Soviet Azarbayjan from the Iranian province of Azarbayjan. It was during the past two centuries, when all of these changes were taking place, that the pictorial rugs in this book were woven. Moreover, we learn from travellers' accounts written during these two centuries of change that, spite of the new borders, extensive contacts between the people on both sides existed until the Bolshevik Revolution of 1917. This included the border crossings of tribal groups such as the Shahsavan and Turkoman.

Most of the pictorial rugs in this book woven outside the present borders of Iran were produced in the Caucasian towns closest to the Iranian border and mostly in two districts: Shirvan and Karabagh.

Haj Zayn al-'Abidin Shirvani, an Iranian Sufi who visited Shirvan and Karabagh about 1831 AD, wrote the following about these two regions in his book entitled Bustan al-Siyahah:

> Shirvan is the name of two places, one of which is a town in Khurasan and the other a country to the west of Mughan... with agreeable springs, pleasant pastures, and attractive places... On the north it is bounded by the Alborz Mountains and Daghestan, on the south by the Kor River and Mughan, on the east by the Caspian sea, and on the west by Georgia. It contains seven cities, ten towns, eight fortresses, and three ports. There are more mountains than deserts there. The mountains are rugged and the forests thick... Since Anushirvan made great efforts to build the place up, it took its name from that just ruler. With the first three letters of his name being dropped for the sake of ease, this place came to be called 'Shirvan'... In Shirvan there are various tribes, principally of Turkish speech... Most of them are Hanafi Muslims, and the rest Imami Shi'ites. There are many Christians too. The small number of Jews there are very despised. The Arab, Qizilbash, and Khanchapanlu tribes have about 100,000 houses.[95]

Concerning Karabagh he writes:

> Karabagh is one of the districts of Azarbayjan. It is a heavenly place. Everything there is abundant. Its people are Turkish speakers. The climate is excellent. It is a very secure place and cannot be taken by force.[96]

Although there is nothing about rug weaving and weavers in the above account, the mention of the inhabitants of these cities and other religions to an extent gives insight into the background of the weavers of some of the rugs under discussion in this book. It is especially important that Zayn al-Abedin Shirvani travelled in the area at about the same time that the rugs of interest to us were being woven. As pointed out in the general introduction of this book, the weaving of pictorial rugs started and spread in Iran during the last two centuries. In all places—cities, villages, and tribal areas—this kind of rug weaving flourished among Iranian Shi'ites. Armenian weavers too looked favourably upon this innovation.

The fact that there is a considerable Shi'ite population in the Karabagh and Shirvan regions of the southern Caucasus, including a number of Qizilbash nomads in Shirvan (who were adherents of Shi'ism) and Shahsavan and Afshars who descended from the Qizilbash, suggests that the few pictorial rugs woven in the Caucasus were probably woven by Shi'ite nomads and villagers and Armenians.

I base my attribution of certain pictorial rugs to Armenian weavers in part on inscriptions in Armenian writing (such as on rug No. 59 and Fig.51) and on Armenian subject matter (as in rug No. 59, which depicts an episode in the Armenian national epic; and Fig. 52, which includes dogs, a subject that would be very exceptional for a Muslim to treat). But in some of the pictorial rugs woven by Armenians in the Karabagh district of the Caucasus the weaver preferred to use Iranian subjects and even copied Persian inscriptions and poetry from the source being copied (rug No. 39 and Fig. 51).

To appreciate the role of the Armenians in pictorial rug weaving it is necessary to study the nature of their relations with Iranians in the past. Armenia has played an important part in the history of Iran. With the expansion of the Roman Empire, Armenia was bordered on two sides by two great empires. the Iranian and the Roman and as a consequence was caught up in their struggles. These conflicts began in the middle of the Parthian period (100 BC) and continued more or less until the end of the Sasanian period (mid-seventh century AD). At times Armenia was under Iranian rule and at times under that of Rome, or else was divided between the two.

In the eighth century AD, during the Islamic conquest, Armenia came under Muslim domination and at the end of the eleventh century was once again occupied by the Byzantine Empire. Thereafter it was invaded by the Seljuks, Mongols and Tartars. In the sixteenth century the Safavid-Ottoman conflict brought more troubles to Armenia and in 1639 AD that territory was formally divided by the Safavid and Ottoman governments. During these years Shah 'Abbas I brought thousands of Armenian families (the number of these Armenians is variously estimated at between 10,000 and 250,000 people) to the town of Julfa next to Isfahan.[97]

By the treaty of Turkomanchay (in 1828 AD) eastern Armenia, which had been a part of Iran, became Russia and Turkey.

Despite the oppression suffered by the Armenians throughout history, this hardworking and artistic people have had a considerable effect on all cultural and artistic manifestations of this region. The Armenian role in the weaving of pictorial and traditional rugs has been considerable. There was a great deal of cultural cross-fertilization between the Armenians and other peoples in the Karabagh and Shirvan regions of the Azerbayjan Soviet Socialist Republic and the Iranian provinces of Azerbayjan, Arak and Bijar. This is also evident in the rugs woven in these areas. One such rug which evokes some of the history of Armenia is Fig. 51. The general composition of this rug was based on the layout of an Iranian block-printed cotton cloth of the type (called a *sufrah*) spread on the floor and on which dishes of food are placed, and around which people in that part of the world sit to eat. Although Iranian block-printed table-cloths usually have no design in the centre, which is intended for dishes of food, the centre of this rug is divided into three parts and contains the portraits of kings of Iran, Turkey and Russia. A well-known verse from Sa'di's *Bustan*, which is often written in the borders of block-printed cotton cloths used for meals, is written in Persian:

> The hide of earth, His open banquet-cloth: At such a free-for-all, enemies and friends are one.[98]

From the point of view of pictorial rug weaving, the most important groups of Armenians are those who live in villages around the town of Arak, in western Iran. What in the past were completely Armenian villages in that area have now mixed Armenian and Muslim populations due to the migration of most Armenians to the cities. One of these villages is Lilihan, located to the south of the town of Arak. In the past this village enjoyed a great reputation for its rug weaving. Rug No. 46 is probably the work of an Armenian rug weaver of Lilihan. Rug No.51, which was woven somewhat later than No. 46, could be the work of either an Armenian or a Muslim weaver of Lilihan. The Armenian rugs of both Iran and the part of the Caucasus near the Iranian border display a special attachment to Iranian themes. Occasional carpets, such as rug No. 59, draw on Armenian nationalism.

## David of Sassoun

The Armenian national folk epic of the legendary hero David of Sassoun is evoked in rug No.59, woven in the Karabagh region of the southern Caucasus, where many Armenians live. Sassoun is the symbolic name used both to designate the nation of Armenia in general as well as occasionally (in the traditional epic) to represent a village in a mountainous part of what was once the western part of Armenia, in present-day Turkey (mountain men were known for their bravery). The epic was handed down orally until part of it was first published in written form in 1875 by Karekin Vartabed Servantziants, Bishop of Van, in the eastern part of present-day Turkey. There are now over fifty written versions of the tale, transcribed from the oral traditions of different villages, which vary slightly in minor details. The story as it relates to this rug is briefly as follows. The Armenian inscription above the three central figures reads David M Arka, which means 'David and the King of Egypt'. ('M' is the abbreviation for the Armenian word *Mesra* [or *Musra*] for Egypt. *Arka* is the Armenian word for King). David himself is not pictured here. The episode referred to by the three men and four horses shown in this rug is one of battles in the mid-ninth century during the heroic struggle of the Armenian people against the Arabs during the seventh to tenth centuries AD when Armenia was dominated by the Islamic Caliphate, in this case represented by the King of Egypt (the central figure in this rug), one of the Fatimid caliphs. David, a legendary super-hero who embodied all the strengths and virtues of the Armenian people was the son of the legendary Armenian King Mher, or Great Mher, or Lion Mher, who ruled Armenia before the Arab conquest, and who was the son of Sanassar, the founder of Sassoun. David had been raised by his maternal and paternal uncles (who are shown in this rug on either side of the Egyptian king) as a shepherd (like the Biblical hero David who fought Goliath) in a small village in his father's conquered territory, but he was expected one day to reclaim his patrimony and save his country from the invaders. The zig-zag-patterned costumes worn by the two uncles in this rug represent the animal skins (symbolically those of tigers, emblematic of strength, courage and protection) they wore as symbols of their legendary heroic characteristics: the paternal uncle, Tzenov Ohan (John of the big voice, which could be heard for hundreds of miles); the maternal uncle, Keri Toros (Keri is the Armenian word specifically designating the uncle that is the mother's brother). On one occasion when the Egyptian king invaded Armenia, so the legend goes, he set up his tents and threatened to increase his domination of the entire region. In his own tent he dug a deep pit with pointed stakes at the bottom and covered it with skins (or, in some versions, carpets over screens). This was designed as a trap for David, whom the wily Egyptian king invited to talk with him. David, unsuspecting of such treachery, fell into the pit, but his cries for help were heard miles away by his uncle of the big voice who, alarmed by a dream that David was in danger, called out to ask where David could be found. The uncle then ran to his stable and asked three horses in turn (white, red and black) how quickly they could carry him to rescue David. (The fourth horse depicted here, probably the black horse in the upper left, with three symbols over him that seem to single him out as a famous animal, is Kourkik Jelalin—horse born of fire—the heroic legendary horse David inherited from his father). The uncle chose the third horse, who said he could get the uncle to David between the time it would take him to put his feet first in one stirrup and then in the other. David, hearing his uncle's voice from a great distance, gathered strength to jump out of the pit and escape. He then challenged the Egyptian king to a series of three personal combats to determine the fate of his people, in order to avoid the bloodshed of full-scale war. The king's mother and sister persuaded David to relinquish the right to the first two contests (begging him to strike them instead of the king); but before the third, the cowardly king of Egypt hid in the pit in his tent and covered it with forty ox hides and forty mill stones. It is thus that he is portrayed in the centre of this rug, with the pit and its snakes shown below him, and clutching skins around himself. However, David managed to strike through all of the king's defences with his lightning sword and kill him nonetheless. The heart-shape motif above the king, on the right, may represent David's shield; the object to the left of it may be the king's battle mace or, more likely, David's sword wrought from lightning (Toor Gaitzagin), which he inherited from his father and grandfather.

The other Armenian inscriptions on the rug are, counter-clockwise from the upper left: the Armenian letter for N, possibly an abbreviation of Nakhshetz, designer (of the rug). Behind the feet of the black horse is the Armenian letter equivalent to M, for either the month of Mard (March) or Mais (May). Below that is 10 for the day of the month. Between the two horses on the left side of the rug are two names, shown in different colours: Verti Osepiantz and Arisaq Osep. It is impossible to know if these are the names of a weaver or owner. The suffix *-iantz* is used with names in the eastern part of Armenia (which are in parts of 'Russia' and Iran today). Behind the horse at the lower left is the date 1916 and below that the first letter of the Armenian word for year (Teev, which is the short form for Tvagan or Toovagan, in different dialects). Below the right-hand male figure is the word '*aziz* (dear), which can also be a man's name. The three letters on the lower part of that figure's costume have been satisfactorily interpreted.[99]

# CHAPTER SIX
# RUGS DEPICTING TRIBAL PEOPLE

SOME OF the rugs woven by tribal nomads included in this book depict the tribal people themselves, in contrast to other tribal rugs portraying non-tribal subjects such as Hushang Shah or Ahmad Shah or animals, for example. The rugs showing tribal subjects constitute two groups. In the first, the composition of the over-all field design is very simple. It consists of the rhythmic repetition of similar figures in one or more vertical rows. In some of these rugs the weaver is successful in creating within this simple layout a certain amount of variety by alternating colours or small details. The rugs in this first group draw on tribal sources for both their subject and the rhythmic and geometric simplicity of their over-all composition, such as rugs Nos. 60 through 69.

The second group of pictorial rugs woven by tribal nomads (Nos. 70 through 73) consists of examples in which the subject has its origins in non-tribal sources such as pictorial rugs woven in cities (which in most cases were based on miniature paintings), textiles (other than rugs) that include pictorial motifs, and prints of Qajar paintings. In this second group, however, the figures have been transformed by the tribal weaver into representations of tribespeople. This is due to the fact that the nomadic weaver has interpreted her model in an imaginative way and has not followed a cartoon. Also, most of the rugs in this group do not have the rhythmic, repetitive arrangement of the figures that is seen in the first group, a concept that is more characteristic of tribal rugs in general. However, with the passing of time, and through repeated weavings, these figural subjects assumed a tribal character and were, so to speak, absorbed into the tribal culture, as is true of rug No. 73, the original model of which was a Qajar painting of a cupbearer (see Fig. 53), which a weaver could have seen in a *khan's* house. The original subject in this tribal rug from a Qajar painting has been transformed into a portrayal of a tribeswoman. Another subject that undergoes this transformation is seen in rugs Nos. 61, 62.

To shed additional light on these tribal rugs it is helpful to know something about the geographical and historical background of the people who wove them. This of course applies to all tribal rugs, not only those depicting tribal people.

The geography of Iran, with its high mountains, fertile valleys, and low-lying plains, provides ideal regions for nomadic tribal life, which is based on herding and animal husbandry. The procuring of fodder for the animals is the most important objective of the tribes. Because of this need they live in tents and migrate seasonally in search of favourable climates and pastures for their flocks of sheep and goats. Their longest move of the year is the migration from their winter quarters to their summer quarters. This is because, although the same route is taken for the return trip back to winter quarters, the tribes travel more slowly in the spring, when the weather is pleasant and pauses are made along the way as the animals give birth and the young animals are cared for. Also, the new grass along the migration route is abundant in the spring, and the tribes take advantage of this by staying for several days at a time in one place to feed the flocks along the migration route. On the way back to winter quarters the weather becomes progressively cooler and the grass is much less plentiful in that season, so the tribes travel much more rapidly. For instance, some Qashqa'i tribes travel about four hundred kilometres between these two seasonal camping grounds and are in motion a total of almost six months a year. On the other hand, for example, some Boyer Ahmadi Lor tribes move only very short distances and can accomplish each twice-yearly migration in a matter of several days.

Precise statistics for the population of the nomadic tribes of Iran are lacking. From the writings of scholars and travellers it can be inferred that until the nineteenth century half of the population of Iran was nomadic. In a report on the nomadic population of Iran issued in 1967 by the Iranian Bureau of Statistics their number was put at 640,000. It would seem that this figure is less than what it should be since the population of the Qashqa'i tribes alone, as given by their own leaders in the late 1970s, was 400,000. If that estimate is correct, the population of all of the tribes of Iran must be more than the previous figure cited above, especially when the other tribes, such as the Lors, Bakhtiyari, Baluchi and Shahsavan, all of which still have a large number who are nomadic, are taken into consideration. It should be stressed that these figures include people who live in tents throughout the year. When the number of tribes living one part of the year in tents and the other part in villages is calculated, in addition the figure for nomadic plus semi nomadic peoples reaches about three to four million people.[100]

In addition to responsibilities such as running the family, cooking meals, milking the animals and making yogurt, butter, bread, and so forth, the women of the tribes spin wool between chores as well as during migrations. In their leisure time they weave pile and flat-woven rugs, and also other utilitarian items such as saddle-bags and decorative trappings for the family's horses and camels. The hard work and dedication of these women cannot be adequately described in words.

The men, whose most important qualities are courage and strength in battle, have for a long time been the objects of attention of various governments in Iran. Most of the dynasties that ruled in Iran after the Islamic conquest in the mid-seventh century AD came to power with tribal assistance and when opposed by the tribes, these dynasties declined. Among these are the Safavid, Afshar, Zand and Qajar dynasties. The founders of most of these dynasties were tribesmen themselves (Nadir Shah of the Afshar tribe, Karim Khan of the Lor tribes and Agha Muhammad Khan of the Ashaqibash Turkoman tribe).

This tribal bravery and bellicosity caused shahs to move tribes from one region to another to use them to help protect the frontiers and preserve the balance of power in a given region. These compulsory displacements naturally had a large impact on tribal customs, as well as on the traditional designs and colours of their weavings. A little background on these transplantings is in order.

From the point of view of origins and lineage, the tribes now living in Iran can be divided into three groups: Iranian (Persian-speaking), Turkish-speaking, and Arab.

# 1 Persian-speaking tribes

According to Professor Sa'id Nafisy, 'In different parts of Iran in the time of Tahir b. Husayn (of the Tahirid dynasty, 820-872 AD, who ruled northeastern Iran) there are many ethnic Iranian nomadic tribes to whom Iranians applied the general name "Kurd". It is clear that "Kurd", as used in the past by the people of Iran, was a term for all shepherds and nomads of Iranian ethnic origin as opposed to Turkic and Arab nomads. In Persian, "Kurd" also means "shepherd".[101] An example of this general use of the term "Kurd" in Iran is the long-used name of a town west of Isfahan, Shahr-i Kurd. This town is the capital of the Chahar Mahal-i Bakhtiyari province, a region of Bakhtiyari villages which is also the summer pasture land of the nomadic Bakhtiyari. The use of "Kurd" in the name of this town has never referred to the Kurdish tribes, who are further west of this region, but rather indicates that this town is the centre for a Persian-speaking tribal group, the Bakhtiyari. The most important Persian-speaking tribes (all of which play an important role in the pictorial rugs in this book) are the Lors and Bakhtiyari, Kurds, and Baluchi. (It must be remembered here that the provinces of Iran named Kurdistan, Loristan and Baluchistan are not the only parts of the country in which Kurds, Lors and Baluchi respectively, live; and these provinces are not exclusively inhabited by those tribal groups).

*a Lors and Bakhtiyari*
Western Iran is one of the oldest centres of settled life and civilisation. The many Lorestan bronze objects dating from the second millennium BC are indicative of the creativity of the people in that region.

The Lors are among the most important people of this region. They are divided into two groups: (1) Lor-i Kuchik (literally, the Lesser Lors), which includes the tribes of Lorestan in western Iran, bordering on Iraq (these groups are not under discussion in connection with the rugs in this book), and (2) Lor-i Buzurg (the Greater Lors), which includes the tribes in a vast area (not as far west as Lorestan) contained within the provinces of Isfahan, Fars and Khuzistan. Among them are the Bakhtiyari Lors and the Boyer Ahmadi Lors, who wove some of the pictorial rugs in this book. One of the groups of Bakhtiyari Lors is still nomadic.[102] These nomads are called in Iran 'Lor-i Bakhtiyari' in contradistinction to the people who have settled down in the villages of the Chahar Mahal-i Bakhtiyari province and who are known in Iran simply as 'Bakhtiyari'.

According to Lisan al-Saltanah Sipihr, the Bakhtiyari were among the first Iranians to become Shi'ite. He says further, 'The origin of the name "Bakhtiyari" is not precisely known because until the beginning of the Safavid period (early sixteenth century AD) that tribal group was known as Lor-i Bozorg (literally the Greater Lors) and after that was named Bakhtiyari.'[103] It is said that one of the Safavid rulers, apparently Shah Isma'il, was greatly in need of help in a battle. He was near defeat when suddenly a group of Lor horsemen forcefully attacked the enemy and routed it. The shah was greatly pleased by this action and said, 'Today good fortune [*bakht*] was my companion [*yar*].' From that day the tribe was named 'Bakhtiyari' (according to popular, not scholarly, etymology).

There are many examples of the bravery of the Bakhtiyari men. The difficult conquest of Kandahar (in present-day Afghanistan) in the mid-eighteenth century by the Bakhtiyari soldiers who accompanied Nadir Shah, the conquest of Tehran in the early twentieth century, and the role they played in the establishment of the Constitution at that time, are among the better-known instances that can be cited in this regard. Tangible witnesses commemorating Bakhtiyari heroism are the many stone lions that mark the graves of youths and men who died bravely in battle (see Fig. 54 and p.59).

In most of the Bakhtiyari villages of the Chahar Mahal-i Bakhtiyari province the weaving of pile rugs is common, while various kinds of flat-woven pieces are made by nomadic Lors. The capital of the Chahar Mahal-i Bakhtiyari province is Shahr-i Kurd (115 kilometres west of Isfahan). Some of the most important Bakhtiyari villages of the Chahar Mahal-i Bakhtiyari province where pictorial rugs have been woven are indicated on the maps on pp. 5, 6.

*b Boyer Ahmadi Lors*
Living in the Koh kiluyeh region (about two hundred kilometres northwest of Shiraz) is another branch of the Lor-i Buzurg, the Boyer Ahmadi, who are also Shi'ite. Koh Kiluyeh is one of the most pleasant and heavily wooded regions of any inhabited by Lors. The summer quarters of the Boyer Ahmadi are located on the slopes of Mount Dena (the highest peak of the Zagros, 4276 metres), where the summer is very cool and agreeable. On the way to their winter quarters the Lors cover a short distance which ends in the low-lying plains above the Persian Gulf.

The Boyer Ahmadi have enjoyed considerable fame for their bravery and skill in battle. History books mention that the people of Koh kiluyeh were the only ones who were able to pose a serious obstacle to the passage of Alexander the Great's troops on their way to Persepolis.[104] The capital of Koh kiluyeh is Yasuj (see map p. 6). It is difficult to distinguish many Boyer Ahmadi rugs from Qashqa'i rugs. The similarity of the rugs of these two groups is largely due to their geographical proximity.

*c The Kurds of Khurasan*
As was pointed out earlier, the Kurds must be considered among the oldest nomads of Iran. The section of present day Iran that was the traditional region of these people was the west and north of Iran (Kurdistan and Azarbayjan). Most of the Kurds of this region are Sunni. This group does not seem to have woven pictorial rugs. The group of Kurds who have woven pictorial rugs, however, lives in the general area of the town of Quchan in northern Khurasan in eastern Iran. These people are known as the Kurds of Quchan. An example of their weaving is rug No. 69. Following the defeat in the late sixteenth century of the Uzbeks in northeastern Iran by Shah 'Abbas the Great, who expelled them from Khurasan in 1597, that ruler transferred some of the Kurds from Azarbayjan to that area with their families and animals in order to fend off probable counter-attacks of the Uzbeks. After the settlement of these Kurds in the area around Quchan, Shirvan and Bojnurd (see map p. 6) they began to be known as the Kurds of Quchan. Their weavings are very different from those of the Kurds of western Iran. The Kurds of Khurasan now live on either side of the upper Atrak River, one of the most fertile regions of Khurasan. They still speak Kurdish (which is related to Persian), mixed with Turkish words, but most of them have been converted to the Shi'ite form of Islam, unlike the Sunni Kurds of western Iran. While many of the Kurds of Khurasan have become sedentary, a large number still maintain a nomadic way of life. In Kurdish rugs from Quchan the influences of their neighbours, especially the Baluchi, can be seen.

*d The Baluchi*
Baluchi rugs have been associated by some people with the province of Baluchistan (which is located in south-eastern Iran and borders on Pakistani Baluchistan), whereas most Iranian Baluchi rugs are the products of the Baluchi of Khurasan province and to an extent of the Baluchi of Sistan province (see map p. 6). Although most Baluchi rugs in this book were made by Baluchi who live around Zabul (in Sistan) and only one example by the Baluchi of Khurasan, the importance of the Baluchi of Khurasan in weaving and the influences they have had on their neighbours necessitate a short description of them here.

The origin of the Baluchi people is not known, but it is believed that they entered the region once known as Makran, in south eastern Iran, from Karman and Sistan about the period of the Seljuk invasion of Iran in the eleventh century and soon spread as far as the Indian frontier. From that time that region became known as Baluchistan (the land of the Baluch).[105]

Some of the weavings of the Afshars of the Kerman area greatly resemble Baluchi weavings and give added strength to this view. The Baluchi were transferred to Khurasan by Nadir Shah (r. 1736-1747). These Baluchi then spread throughout the eastern part of Iran. A considerable number of Baluchi who live around Zabul and in the delta of the Hirmand river are responsible for the largest share of the Baluchi pictorial rugs in this book. Most of the Baluchi of Khurasan province and some of those in Sistan province during the last two centuries have inclined toward the Shi'ite sect of Islam.

## 2 Turkish-speaking tribes

The study of the origins of the Turkish-speaking tribes of Iran needs more careful research because at least a thousand years have passed since the migration of Turks from their Central Asian homeland to Iran. During these thousand years many groups from different Turkic clans have come to Iran at different times and taken up residence there. Among the earliest and the most prominent of Turkic peoples that came from Central Asia to Iran were the Seljuks, in the eleventh century AD. The Seljuk Turks ruled for nearly three hundred years in Iran (1037-1300) and influenced that country in many ways. After the Seljuks, all of the dynasties that held power in Iran were in some way indebted to the power and influence of Turkic peoples.

Given the passage of much time, various population shifts and the intermingling of peoples, the task of uncovering the original roots of the Turks, especially the tribes in Iran that speak Turkic dialects, is not an easy one. Nevertheless, I have attempted a summary of the antecedents and situation of the Turkic tribes that share in the creation of the pictorial rugs in this book. The Turkoman tribes do not seem to have woven pictorial rugs, although several tent bands and camel trappings are known that include a few small figures related to caravan scenes. Thus the Turkoman in Iran do not come into the scope of this book.

*a The Qashqa'i*
Although many difficulties and pressures have affected the lives of the tribes of Iran during the last half century because of rapidly changing social conditions—and this is especially true for the Qashqa'i tribal groups in relation to the central government and the efforts the government has made to settle this large tribe over the last fifty years—the Qashqa'i tribe still enjoys a special importance and status.[106] This tribe is still the best organised in Iran. The tribe is very large and covers a vast territory from Galleh-Dar and Farrashband near the Persian Gulf and extends to Mehrgerd near Borujen, by road 150 kilometres southwest of Isfahan. The Qashqa'i winter quarters are near the Persian Gulf and their summer quarters are on the slopes of the Zagros mountains to the north, west of the road between Shahreza and Abadeh. The vastness of the Qashqa'i territory brings them into contact with many other tribes, including the Bakhtiyari, Lors, Afshar and Khamsah Confederation, and thus causes great diversity in their weavings.

There are different opinions concerning the origins of the Qashaq'i. Most consider them to be descendants of the Seljuk Turks and Khalaj Turks. It is certain, however, that the Qashqa'i do not all originate from a single Turkic clan. Rather, they are composed of different groups of Turkic peoples who banded together at different times. These differences are revealed in the variety of their facial structures and skin and hair colours.

The organisation and unity of the Qashqa'i as a powerful confederation increased during the past two centuries. The first official Qashqa'i chief was Jan-i Khan (see pp. 19-20), who commissioned rug No. 13.

*b The Afshar*
A brief look at the history of the Afshar tribes in Iran shows that this group is among the oldest of the Turkic-speaking tribes of Iran and also among the most widely scattered.

Kasravi, in the article on the Afshar,[107] maintains that the Afshar tribes in Iran go back to Seljuk times in the eleventh to thirteenth centuries AD and he says in the time of the Seljuks the Turkic people from the region of the Qapchakh Plain in Central Asia began to migrate toward regions in the west, including Iran, Asia Minor and Syria; and a few even reached north Africa. Among these Turkic people who remained in Iran the Afshar, who settled at first in Khuzistan, were the most important. In the same article Kasravi mentions that there were other groups of Afshar that lived in Azarbayjan, Mazandaran, Khurasan, Kerman, Fars, Koh Kiluyeh, Hamadan and other parts of Iran. One of the best-organised Afshar groups in Iran is that in the province of Kerman.

This group is also well known for its rug weaving, which is represented in this book by such rugs as Nos. 68 and 72. This Afshar group spends the summers in the mountainous districts around Sirjan, Rafsanjan and Baft, and they winter in the area around Bandar 'Abbas.

Cecil Edwards[108] believed that the Afshar of Kerman are a section of the Afshar of Azarbayjan; the Afshars of Azarbayjan were one of the seven powerful Turkic tribes that formed the large Qizilbash Confederation at the time of the Safavid ruler Shah Tahmasp I (1524-1576). To punish the leaders of this tribe for being rebellious, Shah Tahmasp I transported a large section of them to Kerman.

*c Shahsavan*
The Shahsavan are a confederation made up of tribes that are mainly Turkic.[109] While their origins are not easily traced, the name is first heard of during the reign of the first Safavid shah, Isma'il (1499-1524). Shah 'Abbas I, the Great (r. 1588-1629) very likely used them to help put down an earlier Turkic confederation, the Qizilbash. The Shahsavan, however, were apparently not formed into a real confederation until the eighteenth century. The Turkic term means 'those who love the shah'.

The best-organised Shahsavan group today lives to the west of the Caspian Sea. Their summer quarters are the well-watered, grassy slopes of Mount Sabalon, between Ardabil and Tabriz. For even greater access to grass and water some of them go to heights close to the 15,784-foot peak that is covered with snow most of the year to pitch their tents. The Shahsavan tent is hemispherical and is covered with felt, a thick, non-woven wool material that is very effective in helping to prevent the penetration of cold into the tent (the black goat-hair tent of the tribes of Fars province and Bakhtiyari province, on the other hand permits breezes to enter the tent, which is desirable in the warmer climates of the southern regions of the country). With the coming of colder weather at the beginning of autumn the Shahsavan return to the Moghan Plain where the weather is milder. Many Shahsavan spend the winter in houses they have built in towns, such as Germi and Parsabad, on the Moghan Plain. others pass the winter months in felt tents that are no less warm than houses.

In addition to the Shahsavan of the Moghan Plain there are many Shahsavan groups in different areas between Tabriz and Tehran. The most important ones are those who live around Hashtrud, Bijar, Zanjan, Hamadan, Qazvin, Saveh, Qum and Varamin (see map p. 6). Some of these Shahsavan have become intermingled with other Turkic-speaking tribes such as the Afshar, a situation that makes it hard to differentiate the weavings of one group from another. Rugs Nos. 2 and 58, which have been included as representing the Shahsavan and Afshar, are the work of these elements of the Shahsavan and Afshar tribes that have become intermingled.

## 3 Arab tribes

The migrations of Arab tribes to Iran were simultaneous with the Islamic conquest in the mid-seventh century AD. In the first Islamic century such cities as Hamadan, Isfahan and Kashan particularly attracted the Arab invaders. Qum, especially, was an important centre for the Arabs, who achieved great power and wealth there. More than any other region Khurasan was favoured by the Arab tribes who settled there, because it offered a way of living similar to what they had been used to. The desert-crossing Arab was able to traverse the deserts of Khurasan with the help of the camel. In the year 672 alone 200,000 Arabs are estimated to have entered the province of Khurasan. In 684 another group of Arab tribes also came to Khurasan.[110]

During the course of the centuries that followed, the Arab tribes that had settled in Iran intermingled with their Iranian neighbours to such an extent that they even forgot their original language. Among these are tribes of Arab descent in western Iran around Qum and Saveh, and in eastern Iran around Ferdows. Rug No. 60 was woven by the latter group (see also p. 34).

The most cohesive of the Arab tribes in Iran today who weave rugs live in the province of Fars, and the most important of these are known as the Arab and Baseri tribes, which constitutes sections of the Khamsah Confederation.

*a Arab tribes of the Khamsah Confederation*
This confederation was formed not along common ethnic lines but for political reasons mutually advantageous to the five different tribes that compose it, known as Arab, Baseri,[111] Inanlu, Baharlu and Nafar. Qavam al-Mulk Shirazi, one of the leaders of the powerful families of Shiraz, founded the Khamsah Confederation in 1826 by gathering these five tribal groups together to counter balance the powerful Qashqa'i tribes. Of the five tribes mentioned above, the Arab and Baseri are of ethnic Arab stock. The Inanlu and Baharlu are Turkish-speaking, and the Nafar tribe is a mixture of Persian-speaking Lori and Turkish-speaking elements. The two tribes of

ethnic Arab origin constitute the majority of the Khamsah Confederation. The language spoken by these two tribes is a mixture of Arabic, Lori, Persian and Turkish, which is difficult for anyone else to understand. The two ethnic Arab tribes in the Khamsah Confederation are considered to be among the best rug weavers of Fars, though many influences from other tribes of Fars, especially the Qashqa'i, can be seen in their rug weaving. Rug No. 77 is an example woven by the Khamsah Confederation, and bears an illegible inscription in Arabic and Persian.

In the summer the tribes of the Khamsah Confederation are in the area of Neyriz and Dih Bid; in the winter they go to the districts of Bandar 'Abbas and Lar, near the Persian Gulf.

## CHAPTER SEVEN
# BEAUTIFUL WOMEN

UNTIL VERY recently a colour picture based on a European painting of the face of an idealised beautiful woman (see Fig. 69) was often seen in Iranian homes, shops and tea houses. In addition to this example, there were other pictures of beautiful women's faces. These pictures were sometimes woven into rugs in accordance with the wishes either of the weavers or of those who placed special orders for the rugs.

Rugs depicting the face of a beautiful woman, in large-scale, dominating the entire field of the rug, constitute one of the small groups of pictorial rugs. These rugs were woven during a sixty-year period (the last two decades of the nineteenth century and first four decades of the twentieth), which was concurrent with certain social events in Iran. Among the more important of these events (as far as rugs are concerned) were the reports and gifts relating to European women that Iranian travellers brought back to Iran with them from Europe in the late nineteenth and early twentieth centuries. The ways in which European women lived and appeared in public with their faces and hair unveiled were noteworthy items of gossip in Iran in those days. Iranians were particularly struck by such innovations when such reports were accompanied by naturalistic pictures and postcards of beautiful European women with uncovered heads, ornate clothes, jewellery and make-up (very different from stylized pictures that Iranian artists made of women). This was because at that time all Iranian women were concealing their faces and bodies with various kinds of veils and coverings when they left the privacy of private homes. Concerning this, Ruhollah Khaleqi wrote: 'In those days [late nineteenth and early twentieth centuries] all women wore the black chador. The most modern-minded wore a large veil, called *pichah*, over their faces, while the old fashioned ones employed the *ru-bandi*. The former was short and the latter was long and white. Those who wore the *ru-bandi* also wore ankle-length baggy trousers bound tightly at the ankles and known as *chaqchur*. When people went out for a walk one side of the street was for men and the other side for women. Even husbands had to go on one side while their wives walked on the other. If there were public performances, women were not permitted to participate.[112]

The veiling of women was so important that anyone who spoke of doing away with it was called a heretic. From that time until 1936, when Reza Shah's queen and daughters participated unveiled in ceremonies at a boy's college and the removal of the veil became officially sanctioned, all efforts to end the institution of purdah met with violent opposition in Iran.

The period during which rugs featuring beautiful women were woven in Iran was concurrent with the modernisations discussed in this chapter. Although in recent years pictures of beautiful women, like many other subjects, have been woven into carpets, the reasons for the production of these later rugs are very different from those that lay behind the weaving of the earlier ones.

Of the pictorial sources of faces of beautiful women, the one most favoured by rug weavers was named Fatima (Fig. 60). In the absence of concrete knowledge the origins of the chromolithograph portrait of this woman, which inspired a number of pictorial rugs made in various part of Iran from the late nineteenth to the mid-twentieth century (rugs Nos. 75, 76, 77, 78), several imaginative stories have circulated in different parts of the Middle East. In Iran rug weavers and others have thought she might be Egyptian. It has also been suggested that she is perhaps a Turk painted by a European during the late nineteenth century. Still others have believed this woman represents Belkis, the Queen of Sheba, whose beauty and connection with King Solomon are famous.

In 1955 I saw in Iran prints of this female portrait in large dimensions (about 50 x 70 cm.) displayed in barbershops and teahouses. (An example of one of these is seen in Fig. 60). These dimensions correspond to those of the oldest rug known that depicts this woman (rug No.75); the rug was woven in Kerman. That rug, or one like it, apparently fell into the hands of weavers in neighbouring regions, such as the Baluchi (rug No.76) and the Khamsah Confederation (rug No. 77).

Chromolithographs of this kind were printed in Germany (as this one was) for various foreign markets. One line of research[113] which may yield more solid information about this particular print of an idealised female beauty, with Western features and complexion and pseudo-Turkish costume, is suggested by the fact that chromolithographed portraits of exotic beautiful women were featured on packages of cigarettes from the late nineteenth century to the 1930s,[114] as an overt lure to the male consumer. One of the many exotically named American brands that capitalised on the popularity of Turkish and Egyptian cigarettes was in fact called Fatima. The brand was first registered with the United States Patent and Trademark Office in February 1898, by Cameron and Cameron, later succeeded by Liggett and Myers, who kept the brand in use until at least the late 1940s.[115] Late packages of Fatima cigarettes do not show this some what dated late nineteenth-century female portrait, and early packages of that brand have not so far been found; but a British brand of a Turkish or Egyptian type of cigarette of about 1900—called Crayol—features a chromolithograph of a similar lush female portrait[116] which, like this one titled at the edge of the lithograph depicting Fatima (Fig. 60), suggests the turn of the century.

Copies of this particular chromolithograph can still be found in bazaars in Iran as well as in suqs in Cairo and Tunisia, where this woman's portrait has also been seen pasted to colourful painted wooden gun racks.[117] It would thus seem that chromolithographs of this woman's portrait, possible originally intended to lure the Western male consumer to buy a certain brand of Turkish or Egyptian type cigarettes, evidently had strong and wide-spread appeal in certain parts of the Middle East and North Africa from the late nineteenth century to the present day. Whatever its specific origins, it has inspired a group of pictorial carpets, made by villagers and tribal weavers in the provinces of Kerman as well as by Baluchi tribal weavers in the province of Khurasan, each individually conceived but clearly evoking the same chromolithograph. In the woven depictions of this woman's portrait, however, the three-dimensionality of the image in the European print in translated into the time-honoured two-dimensionality of Iranian pictorial art.

The identity of another beautiful woman whose full length portrait has been woven into rugs is unknown (rugs Nos. 79-81). She seems to have been of interest to only one Bakhtiyari *khan*, Yusuf Khan Amir Mujahid, who ordered rugs showing her in different poses. In rug No. 79 a standing woman is portrayed holding a bag in her hand, with a dog standing in front of her, and a basket of flowers. In rug No. 80 this woman is shown with her hands in her hair, and in rug No. 81 she has the same pose but stands between two women whose clothes are of the Qajar period. The latter rug is very large and is one of a very limited number of pictorial rugs woven to be used as a floor covering.

Yusuf Khan Amir Mujahid (the youngest son of Husayn Quli Khan, a great Bakhtiyari chief) died in 1938 at more than seventy years of age. According to his son, Rustam Bakhtiyar, it is believed that the three above-mentioned rugs were ordered by his father for a particular family residence known as the Shamsabad villa, in the village of Shamsabad, eighteen kilometres south of Shahr-i Kurd. Rustam Bakhtiyar remembers that during his youth he saw these very weavings. Despite all of the destruction it has seen, this building still has a special quality to it. It contains two large rooms and several small ones. The large rug was spread out in the middle of one of the large rooms and the small rugs were hung on the wall. Rustam Bakhtiyar felt that the source of inspiration for rugs Nos. 79-81 might possibly have been a European postcard, because in his father's day it was the fashion in Iran to collect European postcards in albums, and his father had such albums.

The Bakhtiyari *khans* built splendid residences in the villages of the Bakhtiyari district during the last century or two. The walls of such houses were decorated with rugs as well as paintings and mirrors.

Another example of a woven portrait of a beautiful woman is a Kerman saddle cover in the collection of Siawosch Azadi (Fig. 61). This portrait was probably taken from a woman's powder box; such boxes were brought from Paris for Iranian women in the late nineteenth and early twentieth century. These boxes were often decorated with the portrait of a woman. In those days many people were interested in European boxes containing candy, powder and so forth, decorated with the pictures of beautiful women. Not only rug weavers, but also many painters and pen-box makers were inspired by the pictures on such imported boxes.

# CHAPTER EIGHT
# ANIMALS

ANIMALS AND and birds, like flowers and plants, play a leading role in the repertory of motifs used in the traditional rugs of Iran, especially tribal and village examples. Their appearance in rug designs among flowers and *boteh* ('paisley') motifs gives such rugs great animation. We are not concerned in this book with rugs that feature small-scale representations of animals or birds, but only with rugs in which large-scale animal forms are featured as the main subject of the rug. The origins of most rugs with large-scale animal designs differ from those of other pictorial rugs. A small number of the former type, such as the two rugs each depicting a horse and groom (Nos. 91 and 92), however, have design sources similar to those of certain other pictorial rugs and were probably based on photographs or pictures. A sizable group of rugs with large-scale figures, such as the rugs featuring lions (Nos. 78-85), continued ancient traditions that have been preserved in Iran over the centuries.[118] Furthermore, most specimens of this group of animal rugs have had a function different from that of the rest of the pictorial rugs: These were not woven to be hung on walls but rather to be used on the ground inside nomads' tents. They also have had a special significance, such as guarding of the tent or symbolising a man's bravery. Another group of these rugs depicting large-scale animals such as the deer in Fig. 62 were probably taken from velvet wall hangings decorated with large-scale subjects. Rugs with large-scale animal motifs are a natural result of the importance of animals in the lives of village and tribal peoples. Animals have always had a special place in Iranian art and culture. Special beliefs concerning different creatures have given artifacts decorated with representations of animals a profound significance in Iran. Some animals symbolise good fortune, happiness and success, while others are symbols of bad luck. Auspicious creatures such as the lion, horse, bird[119] and fish were used more often than others in the ornamentation of objects.

Inauspicious animals such as the owl and black cat were usually avoided in the decorative arts.

Certain animals and birds derived from pre-Islamic traditions and religions maintained their importance in the Islamic era, but they were assimilated by the new culture with changes in their meanings and functions. One such animal is the lion, which had a special place in pre-Islamic and Islamic religions and traditions. In some of the art and religion of the pre-historic peoples of Iran as well as the Achaemenids the lion was the symbol of Mithra.[120] In the rites of Mithraism the sun had a special place, and the lion symbolised the astrological figure Leo.[121] The month governed by the sign of Leo is in the house of the sun.[122] This month (the month of Murdad in the Persian calendar) falls in the middle of summer, when the sun is extremely hot and brilliant. This astrological sign has been familiar in Iran since ancient times and for the last six hundred years was the national emblem of the flag and coins of Iran. Among Iranian Shi'ites the lion is also the symbol of His Holiness, 'Ali, who had the nickname Shir-i Khuda ('Lion of God').[123]

In some lion rugs the combined lion-and-sun motif, an ancient form, has been used, with the sun shown rising above the lion's back (see Figs. 63a, 63b). An example of this is seen in rug No.86. In the Achaemenid and Sasanian periods the image of the lion was used in many rites and ceremonies, especially to show the power and strength of the king who was usually depicted fighting or hunting the lion. One of these scenes is found in the rug illustrated in Fig. 66. The original of this scene is related to a design executed in a bas-relief at Persepolis (see Figs. 64, 65).

During the Islamic era in Iran the lion became a major symbolic image, and it appears on many artifacts and paintings. The lion retains the same symbolic representation in the Islamic period as in the previous era, such as in scenes of a king hunting the lion, which is seen in numerous ceramic and metal works as well as in carpets and other textiles.[124]

From the Safavid period on, the importance of

the lion reached such a point that despite the prohibition against making statues, three-dimensional representations of this animal were placed in local shrines and over the graves of heroic warriors. Valuable stone lions dating from the Safavid period and later are still seen in some of the shrines of Isfahan, among them the Ahmad and Harun-i Velayat shrines.

Until very recently this tradition of using stone lions over special graves was common in the villages and nomadic areas of the Bakhtiyari, Fars and Azarbayjan provinces. Stone lions are still to be seen in many graveyards in and near villages in those regions (Fig. 54). (In the villages of Azarbayjan stone rams as well as stone lions are seen marking graves).

The large-scale lion motif in rugs is not unrelated to the stone lions and the ancient traditions and rites mentioned above. Most lion rugs I know of come from districts in which stone lions are found. The considerable similarity that exists between some lion rugs and the chunky, angular style of lion depictions in the stone lions, as well as the necklace on both the stone lions and some of the lion rugs, is the best proof of this connection. An example of this is a comparison between rug No. 85 and Fig. 54.[125]

The category of animal rugs also includes rugs in which numerous animals are seen (rugs Nos. 94 and 95). The subjects of these rugs are related to certain stories, ancient myths and paintings called by artists of teahouse paintings *jangal-i mawla* (the term refers to a scene of many animals in a haphazard arrangement, as in rug No. 94, and comes from the colloquial phrase, which literally means 'forest of the master' and is the equivalent of the American colloquialism 'a zoo' for a frenetic gathering of people).

Among the few rugs in this book that were woven outside the present-day borders of Iran is rug No. 96. Despite all my efforts to identify the subject of this rug, I have still not succeeded. I have, however, obtained interesting information concerning its provenance. At first it was thought that this rug was woven in one of the towns of the Caucasus, probably by an Armenian. The rug was brought to Iran right after the First World War by an Armenian family that had owned it for as long as surviving family members could remember. The inwoven date (which appears to be 1210—which is 1795 AD) in numerals like those used by Europeans and the subject of one of the four panels of the field seemed to support this attribution. One panel depicts the figure of a man wearing a soft red cap, a green jacket and red trousers tucked into brown boots. This costume seems to suggest an army officer, either Armenian or Russian, from the Caucasus. Other factors, however, lessen the probability that the rug was the work of Caucasian or Armenian weavers.

The most important of the factors that help pinpoint a probable provenance are the weaving technique, the colours, and the softness of the rug. Considering these aspects, it is more like the so-called Samarkand rugs (actually from Khotan). I base my final attribution of the provenance of this rug on information in Hans Bidder's book *Carpets from Eastern Turkestan*, the most comprehensive work to date on rugs from this region. Many of the characteristics of this rug (with the exception of materials and subject matter about which I will speak more later) correspond to the information that Bidder gives about Khotan rugs. These correspondences are as follows:[126]

Khotan rugs Observed by Hans Bidder
    Knot: asymmetrical open to the left
    Weft: three shoots between each row of knots
    End finishes: 1. Lower end A. 9-18 rows of single-wefted balanced plain weave in cotton
      B. 2-4 rows of double-wefted balanced plain weave in cotton
      C. Warp ends—uncut, twisted loops

2. Upper end
    A. 9-18 rows of single-wefted balanced plain weave in cotton
    B. 2-4 row of double-wefted balanced plain weave in cotton
    C. Warp ends knotted in groups of 8-10 warps

Rug 96
Knot: asymmetrical open to the left
Weft: three shoots between each row of knots, occasionally two shoots
End finishes: 1. Lower end
    A. 9 rows of single-wefted balanced plain weave in silk
    B. 4 rows of double-wefted balanced plain weave in silk
    C. Warp ends—uncut, twisted loops

2. Upper end
    A. 9 rows of single-wefted balanced plain weave in silk
    B. 2 rows of double-wefted balanced plain weave in silk
    C. Remnants of warp ends knotted in groups of 6-8 warps

There are certain differences, however, between rug No. 96 and Bidder's observations of the structure in Khotan rugs, such as the number of threads plied together on the warp, weft and pile,[127] and the density fo the knots. I consider

*Kings, Heroes and Lovers*

these differences to be due mainly to the material of rug No. 96, which is entirely made of silk: warp, weft and pile.[127] Not much attention is given in Bidder's book to the silk rugs of eastern Turkestan. Perhaps this is due to the small number of silk rugs woven in this region as compared with examples with wool pile. However, silk rugs from eastern Turkestan of the seventeenth century and later do exist. Another factor that is different in rug No. 96 from the rugs in Bidder's book is the subject matter; to my knowledge there is no other rug that depicts the same figures as rug No. 96. Even the border, which depicts snakes, seems unusual. But elements in rug No. 96 that are similar to certain elements in Khotan and Yarkand rugs observed by Bidder are the over-all composition of the design with its placement of images in four horizontal compartments (when the rug is turned sideways, to follow the direction of the design), the fret motif in the inner border that surrounds each panel, and the pomegranate branches in the upper corners of each panel. The division into three or four sections is seen particularly in Khotan and Yarkand rugs with multiple medallions observed by Bidder. The pomegranate branch is a very characteristic motif of eastern Turkestan rugs. It is also one of the motifs used in Iran since ancient times. Because of its many seeds, this fruit is a symbol of blessing and abundance. In Bidder's discussion of the appearance of the pomegranate branch in rugs from Khotan and Yarkand, he talks about the relationship between the appearance of this motif in rugs of Turkestan and those of Turkic tribes in Iran and he suggests that these tribes brought the pattern with them from Central Asia.[128]

Another aspect that unites rug No. 96 and the rugs of eastern Turkestan observed by Bidder is the colour scheme that includes red, brown and yellow (though none of these may be the dominant colour of the rug), all colours that are characteristic of rugs of that region. The proportions of the rug and its considerable length relative to its width are also similar to those features of Yarkand and Khotan rugs. The biggest problem in determining the provenance of this rug is its date in European numerals, 1210, which probably indicates when it was woven if it is considered according to the Islamic calendar (which would be 1795 AD), which seems a reasonable age for this rug. These numerals in a script foreign to Iran and to eastern Turkestan are not unrelated to the European appearance of the man depicted in the rug. Possibly the date in these numeral was given to the weaver by the person who ordered the rug. Possibly there is some relationship between the male figure depicted in the rug and the person who may have commissioned it. Also, perhaps the reason why the rug is all silk is that it was a special order.

Although this rug is so unlike any of the other rugs in this book, it has been included because of the lion in this rug which, in my opinion, is not totally unrelated to the lion rugs of Iran.[129] The lion motif was used all over Iran as well as in Turkestan in the past. The lion motif may be seen in works from the Seljuk and Timurid periods. The Spanish diplomat Clavijo commented, in his account of his trip from 1403 to 1406 to the court of Timur in Samarkand, on the lion-and-sun motif that he saw on the wall of one of the palace buildings of Samarkand during his visit.

This gateway is throughout beautifully adorned with very fine work in gold and blue tiles, and over the entrance are seen the figures of the Lion and the Sun, these same figures being repeated over the summit of each of the arches round the courtyard, and this emblem of the Lion and the Sun was, they told us, the armorial bearing of the former lord of Samarkand [whom Timur dispossessed]. We were assured that it had been Timur himself who was the builder of this great palace, but I imagine in truth that some part of it must have been built by that lord of Samarkand who lived before the time of Timur's sovereignty; for the Lion and the Sun which we saw here set up are the emblems of this former sovereign.

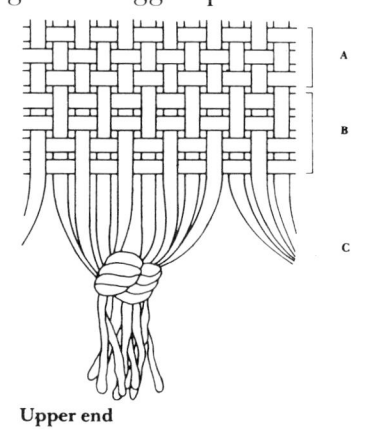

**Upper end**

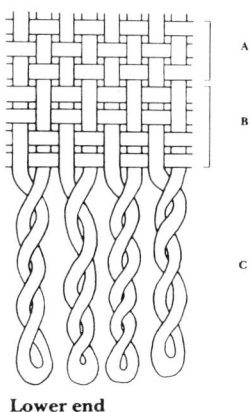

**Lower end**

# CHAPTER NINE
# AN EXPLANATION OF THE ANALYSIS OF THE STRUCTURAL AND OTHER PHYSICAL CHARACTERISTICS OF THE RUGS

OPPOSITE THE plate of each pictorial rug is a discussion of it, divided into two sections. In the first section, at the top of the page, is a general interpretation of the scene depicted, and some of the particular characteristics and aesthetic qualities of the rug are examined. In those cases in which the historical background and subject depicted required greater elaboration, I have dealt with these aspects in the appropriate chapters elsewhere in the book.

At the bottom of the page, I have concentrated on the structural aspects of each rug, since this information is essential in the quest for knowledge about where a rug may have been woven.

Contemporary Persian is sadly lacking in technical weaving terminology. Only a few general terms are used in Iran for a number of what are often quite dissimilar techniques. In recent years more precise terms have been developed in English. Before going into the specific explanations of the terminology used in this book, it is important to distinguish between the words structure and technique. Structure, strictly speaking, is the term used to refer to the objective observation and description of the way the elements such as warp, weft and pile relate to each other in the finished textile. Technique, by contrast, refers to the various ways in which that structure can be created. Structure, thus, describes what exists, while technique describes how the structure is made. It is important to remember that more than one technique can be used to create the same structure, and when observing a finished textile it is not always possible to determine from studying the structure alone exactly which technique was used to produce it.

With due respect for certain rug specialists who spent many years of their lives doing research on Persian rugs, I would like to point out some of the mistakes in structural analysis that have been made in the past by writers generalising about the products of different rug-weaving regions because certain exceptions were not taken into consideration. Even A. Cecil Edwards, author of *The Persian Carpet* (first published in 1953), made mistakes due to his generalising about what he saw on his trips in rug-weaving regions of Iran. For example, among other erroneous generalisations he mentions with certainty that the only knot used in Saruq is asymmetrical (Persian) and that Baluchi rugs are single-wefted, whereas in this book there are rugs from Saruq with symmetrical (so-called Turkish) knots (Nos. 17, 38) and numerous Baluchi rugs with two wefts (Nos. 63, 64, 65, 78). The multiplicity of knot types in the rugs of a single village, tribe or region, and even occasionally within a single rug, is due to several factors related to the individual weavers. For example, in addition to the principal weaver of a given village or tribal rug, friends and neighbours may also occasionally participate in its production. At times even the number of wefts varies in different sections of a single rug, as well as in rugs from the same village or tribe. Furthermore, the movement of weavers from one village to another or from one tribe to another that takes place through marriage, for example, makes for exceptions from the 'norm'. I have encountered some tribal rugs that are woven with two different types of knot: one part of the rug in the symmetrical knot and the rest in the asymmetrical knot.[131] Also, almost all of the Bakhtiyari rugs that I have seen have had two wefts, but in this book there is a rug woven by that tribe (No. 23) that has only one weft (all of the other factors, including colour, point to its being of Bakhtiyari origin). Possibly a weaver from another area (such as Hamadan or Malayer) where single-wefting is characteristic may have woven this rug. Moreover, because of the movement of rugs and the borrowings that weavers make from each other, specific designs and pictorial subjects cannot always be conclusive evidence in tracing the origins of a rug. Therefore, to establish these factors it is necessary to have a wide familiarity with both typical structural elements of rugs from different regions, and also possible exceptions.

Colour is another important factor in differentiating between rugs of various regions. This, too, is a matter of cumulative experience of a wide variety of rugs at first hand. Because of the particular properties of plants in different parts of Iran and the variation in the ingredients and traditional formulas used in dyeing wool, natural dyestuffs give a characteristic colouring to the rugs of each district. For example, the colour red (when dyed with natural dyestuffs) and its variations are derived all over Iran today from the root of the madder plant (*Rubia tinctorum*), *runas* in Persian. But in each district the manner in which madder is used differs. In some regions the water in which the wool is dyed is warmed by fire and in others this is accomplished by the heat of the sun over a period of several days. Different temperatures of the dye bath and varying lengths of time the wool is left in the dye bath, as well as the mineral content of the water in different regions all cause variations in the shades of colours. Also, the use of different mordants to fix the colour on the wool, as well as the way the mordants are employed, affect shades of a given colour. Mordants used in Iran include *zaj* (alum). There are two different types of alum: *zaj-i safid* (white alum, potassium aluminium sulphate) and *zaj-i siyah* (black alum, which has a ferrous content). Other substances used as mordants are *jawhar-i limu* (citric acid), *dugh* (whey) and *qarah qorut* (dried black curds). In some areas the mordant is placed in the water at the same time as the dyestuff and wool, while in others the wool is first saturated in a warmed solution of the mordant in water, and after one or two days the dyestuff is added to it. In some regions this process is reversed; that is, the wool is first saturated in the dyepot for one or two days, and then mordanted. It is natural that such different methods should affect the shades of a given colour in different regions.

The preparation of yellow dyes differs in the various regions of Iran. For example, grape leaves are used in the villages of the Bakhtiyari for the preparation of yellow dyes. The Qashqa'i tribes, which have less access to grape leaves, sometimes utilise willow leaves and various desert plants for yellow, while many others use weld *Reseda Lutuola* (or, in Persian *isparak*).

In most villages and tribal groups green is obtained by first dying the wool yellow and then giving it to the professional indigo dyer (*abi-kar*, literally 'blue worker') who specialises in dyeing wool blue, which is a more intricate process than using other natural dyestuffs. But the Qashqa'i tribes, in order to dye wool green, buy wool already dyed blue from the bazaar and place it for a long time in whatever solution they use to produce yellow. Also the different reactions of the wool of different regions to dyes can cause regional variations in shades of a given colour. It is because of these special characteristics that some rug experts are able to recognise the provenance of a rug through its colours (if it has been woven with natural dyestuffs), even if its design or structure are less helpful.

In identifying the origins of the rugs in this book I have utilised both the elements of structure and colour. The various aspects of my methods of identification of subject as well as provenance are explained below.

## Subject depicted

Fortunately the subjects of many of the pictorial rugs are identified by inscriptions on them. In cases in which the subjects were not immediately clear I have been able to identify them with the help of photographs, block-printed curtains, illustrated books and paintings. However I must confess that in certain instances (among them rug No. 96) I have not yet succeeded in identifying the subject.

## Local weaving practices observed

In addition to examining the structural characteristics and colours, I made numerous field trips to various parts of Iran in search of information as to where the pictorial rugs were woven. In most cases, the weaving methods used in the rugs in this book are still being employed in most of these regions, but the passing of time has in some cases reduced the possibility of discovering precisely where these were woven. The provenances indicated in this book are, therefore, subject to a certain amount of imprecision. This lack of absolute certainty is due also to the fact that many of the districts or tribes have been made up of various different elements. The districts of Ferahan and Darjazin, for example, each include several villages, while the Kashkuli and Shish Boluki clans of the Qashqa'i tribe are themselves made up of different groups.

## Date of weaving

Fortunately many pictorial rugs are dated, and

the dates in most cases seem reliable. These dated rugs have been useful guides when dealing with examples lacking such information woven into them. Some dates in rugs are less reliable, however, because rug inscriptions and dates are reversed in mirror image because they were woven by copying from the backs of other rugs used as models. (When one rug is copied from another, the back is used so that the knots of each colour can be counted more easily).

Many pictorial rugs are woven in pairs. In such cases the inscription on one of the two rugs is sometimes in reverse if the weaver has copied the inscriptions from the back of the first rug, which thus serves as a cartoon for the weaver. Also there are rugs that are copies of earlier dated pieces. In the rugs in this book I have pointed out those that seem to include dates copied from earlier rugs. Rugs without dates have been attributed to either the first, middle, or last third of the relevant century.

The various aspects of the notes on structural analysis will be discussed below.

## Size

Pictorial rugs have been made in various dimensions to correspond to the ways in which they were intended to be used. Most are of the *daw zar'i* size (approximately 1 by 2 metres), while a considerable number have been woven in the *zar-u nim* size (approximately 1 by 1.5 metres). Some fall into the *pushti* category (less than 1 by 1 metres). A small number are called *kinarah* (approximately 1 by 4 metres).

## Direction of spin of wool

All the fibres of a rug—which may be wool, cotton or silk (or goat hair, which tribal weavers sometimes use for warps or side finishes)—are first spun, and single strands are then plied together. The direction of spin of the hand spindle is either clockwise or counter-clockwise. If the direction of spin is clockwise, the fibres are spun with a twist slanting down from left to right, as in the middle section of the letter 'S' (Ill. 1), thus the spin is designated as 'S'; while a spin in the opposite direction is identified by the letter 'Z' (Ill. 2), because the slant in the opposite direction is that of the mid-section of that letter. At certain times in history, and in certain places, the direction of spin (Z is more common than S) and ply (which would be in the opposite direction to that of the spin) seems to have some relevance in determining the provenance of a woven product, so it should be observed in studying the rugs. The direction of spin and ply and the number of single strands plied together are indicated in the structural analyses by a notation such as Z2S, meaning that two Z-spun single strands are S-plied.

## Ply

For greater strength, two or more single strands of spun fibres are twisted together. The twisting, or plying, of strands is normally in the opposite direction from the spin of the single strand, since the plied yarn is thus less likely to untwist (see Ills. 3,4).

The yarn used for the pile is usually more loosely plied than the warp and weft that compose the foundation structure of the rug and therefore need to be tightly plied for strength, whereas it is desirable that the yarn for the pile be fluffier than the warp and weft, therefore the threads of spun fibres used for the pile are not as tightly plied as the two structural components of a rug. Since the short pieces of wool of individual knots are not usually long enough to exhibit the direction (S or Z) of ply, but rather lie parallel to each other, I have indicated this effect by the term 'loosely plied'. Others have introduced the term 'winder ply', referring to the winding instrument used in plying the strands of spun fibres together. In general, wool spun in one direction can be assumed to be plied in the opposite direction, since the fibres so plied adhere together better than if plied in the direction of spin. In the technical notes following the general discussion of each rug I have thus indicated for the pile the direction of spin only, since the direction of ply is not easily discernible in the short piece of wool of the knot.

## Warp

Warp yarns of cotton, wool, silk or sometimes, goat hair are attached to the warp beams at either end of the loom in a vertical direction and together with the wefts form the basic foundation of each rug.

## Weft

The wool, cotton or silk yarns are woven in a transverse direction over and under the warps. One or more shoots of weft may be passed after each transverse row of knots to secure them in place and to create, with the warp, the foundation of the rug.

## Knots

These are formed of wool, cotton or silk yarns that are fastened to the warps in horizontal rows to create pile. As each knot is made, the weaver cuts the yarn used for it before making the next knot beside it. The knots of rugs in Iran are of two basic types: symmetrical knots (Turkish or Ghiordes) and symmetrical knots (Persian or Sennah). Each of the above types also has several variations (ills. 5-14). The type of knot is recorded in the structural analyses as part of the description of the pile. The knot count is recorded separately as, for example, 8V x 8H = 64 sq. in., meaning 8 vertical knots multiplied by 8 horizontal knots for the count in a square inch. The count per square decimetre is also given.

## Symmetrical knot

The yarn is wrapped over two warps and its ends are pulled up between those two warps. As is apparent from its name, this knot has a symmetrical construction. When the two ends of the yarn come up between two warps that are on one level, the knot is called symmetrical (1) (Sy1, ill. 5) If the right side of the knot is wrapped around one of the alternate warps that is slightly or completely depressed as compared with the warp around which the left side is wrapped, this type is called symmetrical (2) (Sy2, ill. 6). If the left side of the knot is wrapped around one of the alternately depressed warps, this type of knot is called symmetrical (3) (Sy3, ill. 7).

## Asymmetrical knot

The yarn of this type of knot is also wrapped around two warps, with this difference that one warp is completely encircled while the other is only three-fourths surrounded, or, as some describe it, 'open'. If the right warp of a knot is completely encircled by the yarn (and the warp on the left only partly encircled or, as some describe it, 'open'), the knot is called asymmetrical (1) (As1, ill. 8). If the left warp is completely encircled (and the warp on the right, 'open'), the knot is called asymmetrical (2) (As2, ill. 9). In both cases the warps are on one level. If, however, alternate warps are depressed and the right side of the knot completely encircles the depressed warp, the knot is termed (3) (As3, ill. 10). If the left side of the knot completely encircles the depressed warp, the knot is termed asymmetrical (4) (As4, ill. 11).

## Straight and undulating warps and wefts

A difference in the relative warp levels of the two halves of the knot may be seen on the back of the rug (see ills. 16, 17 and 18). This characteristic of weave can help in identifying the provenance of a rug. In rugs with the warps on one level only (the knots would be either Sy1, As1 or As2) and two or more passes of weft after each row of knots, the warps lie straight and all wefts undulate (see ills. 5, 8 and 9). However, in single-wefted rugs the wefts lie straight and the warps tend to undulate (ills. 12, 13, 14 and 15).

There is limited variation in the structure of single-wefted rugs, both from the point of view of the possible relative positions of warps and wefts and type of knot: only Sy4, As5 and As6 (ills. 12, 13 and 14) are possible and Sy2, Sy3, As3 and As4 are not possible.

With warps that have a degree of depression (and are not on one level as is the case with Sy1, As1 and As2—Ills. 5, 8, 9) there is always more than one weft, and the knot types possible are Sy2, As3 and As4 (Ills. 6, 7, 10, 11).

## Flat (*takht*), semi-depressed (*nim-lul*) and depressed (*lul*) warps

As discussed above, when the warps lie on one level, the knots are either Sy1, As1, As2, Sy4, As5 or As6. When this is the case both halves of the knot are seen on the back of the rug. Such a rug structure is called in Persian *takht-baft* or *takht* (flat) (Ills. 15, 16). When the warps do not lie on one level but rather are alternately depressed, the knots are Sy2, Sy3, As3 or As4 (Ills. 17, 18). In rugs with semi-depressed warps, the half of the knot on the lower warp will appear on the back of the rug to be smaller than the other. This structure is called semi-depressed, or in Persian *nim-lul* (Ill. 17). In rugs in which alternate warps are fully depressed, that is, on two levels, only one of the two halves of the knot can be seen on the back of the rug. This type of structure is called depressed, or *lul-baft* or *lul* (Ill. 18).

Rugs with flat warps (*takht*) and Sy1, As1, or As2 knots tend to be looser and more supple than rugs with depressed warps (*lul*), which have Sy2, Sy3, As3, or As4 knots. The latter type of rug is so stiff that when harshly folded it can crack and tear (examples of this type include some Saruq and Bijar rugs). Such rugs must be rolled rather than folded when taken up. As will be seen below, flat, semi-depressed and depressed warps can also affect the number of knots a rug can have.

## Knot density

The fineness of the weave of a rug is calculated on the basis of the number of knots per square inch or decimetre. Normally the density of knots in rugs with depressed warps (*lul*) is greater than the ones with flat warps, that is, warps on one level (*takht*). For example, if three rugs all of which are of the same size and material, and have the same kind and number of warps, wefts and knots, differ only in that they are woven with either flat (*takht*, warps on one level), semi-depressed (*nim-lul*, warps on two levels), or fully depressed (*lul*, warps on two levels, one warp completely hidden behind the other), the density of knots in each can be expected to be proportionally greater in the rug with fully depressed warps, and less so in the example with semi-depressed warps. The density of knots in a rug with flat warps (*takht*) is nearly half of that in a rug with depressed warps (*lul*) and two-thirds of that in a rug with semi-depressed warps.

Another important factor that affects fineness of weave as well as stiffness in rugs with depressed warps (*lul*) is the very strong beating down of the wefts with heavy metal beaters after each row of knots in made. There are two reasons for this very forceful beating: first, to secure the knots and, second to achieve an equal number of vertical and horizontal knots. (This is desirable in some designs, and particularly in rendering a design from a cartoon without distortion). The more firmly the weft is beaten down, the more compact and finer the weave.

Among the rugs that do not have an equal number of horizontal and vertical knots, the heavily wefted (sometimes as many as eight wefts), loosely-woven tribal rug of Fars province in southern Iran known as *gabbeh* is a notable exception.[132] In such rugs the horizontal knot count is far greater than the vertical. Rugs with cotton warps can stand up to heavier beating than rugs with wool warps. In comparing two rugs (one with cotton warp, the other wool warp) both with the same degree of warp depression, and a similar relationship in their vertical and horizontal knot counts, the rug with the cotton warp will usually be found to be stiffer and less flexible than the rug with wool warps.

Perhaps another reason for this variation in suppleness and stiffness between rugs with cotton warps and those with wool warps lies in different types of loom. In setting up a loom, warps cannot be pulled with the same very tight and even tension on the nomads' looms (which usually do not have nuts and bolts that would enable the loom structure to be tightened more effectively than the nomads' more simple loom, which sometimes has to be disassembled while a rug is in progress when it is time to migrate seasonally), or even on some village looms, as they can be on city or town (and some village) looms that have nuts and bolts and are permanently fixed in place.

## Pile height

For this book, where possible I have measured the pile of the rug as it was originally trimmed by the weaver. In the case of worn rugs, the pile of the best section was measured. Tribal and village weavers generally leave longer pile in the rugs they make for their own daily use.

## Texture

By texture I mean the impression gained when one handles the rug. The first attribute of texture taken into consideration is the feeling that comes from moving the hand over the front surface of the rug, for instance whether the pile feels silky, soft, or coarse. The quality of wool used for the pile in the rug is a particularly important aspect of the texture. The second attribute of a rug's texture is the thickness of the rug, which depends on the diameter of the yarn, the density of the knots, and the height of the pile. The third attribute of the texture considered in this book is the stiffness or flexibility of the rug.

## End finishes

The two ends of a rug are finished in order to protect the first and last rows of knots and prevent their coming out during use and cleaning.

1. Decorated plain weave

Many rugs illustrated in this book are woven with either balanced plain weave (Ill. 19) or weft-faced plain weave (Ill. 20) (sometimes with other decoration) at both ends, although one or both end finishes may be worn away. In balanced plain weave, the warp and weft are both seen (Ill. 19). In weft-faced plain weave, the wefts entirely cover the warps (Ill. 20). Occasionally one or more rows of weft twining (usually in coloured wool that contrasts with the plain weave) are woven into these ends (Ills. 23, 24). This weft twining may be in one or more rows in which the slant of the weft twining is in one direction (Ill. 23) or in pairs of rows in which the slant is reversed in alternate rows, producing a countered effect (Ill. 24). Another way of decorating a plain-weave end that is seen in some of the south Persian rugs in this book is a 'checkerboard' design, usually woven in blue and

*Kings, Heroes and Lovers*

white, which is one form of complementary-weft weave, specifically a complementary-weft weave with variable interlacing arranged to form a diamond-like pattern on a rectangular ground (Ill. 22).

2. Warp ends

In addition to the way the flat-woven end finishes are handled by weavers in different regions, the treatment of the warp ends that form a fringe at either end of the rug can offer help identifying the origin of a rug as well. Three types of warp end treatment appear in the rugs in this book (Illus. 25, 26, 27).

3. Plain weave folded under

In some rugs the plain weave section at one or both ends of the rug, which may be decorated with weft-twining (see Ills. 23, 24), is partly turned under and sewn in place (Ill. 28). If only one end of the rug is treated this way, the warp ends at the other form one of the types of fringe shown in Ills. 25, 26 and 27. This kind of end finish is mainly found in the multiple-wefted *gabbeh* rugs of Fars province, such as rugs Nos. 35, 83 and 86.

**Side finishes**

Weavers in different parts of Iran finish the two sides (selvages) of the rug during the weaving process in ways that are traditional to their own regions. The purpose of the side finish, like that of the ends, is to make the rug stronger and more durable. In Persian the general term for side finish is *shirazeh*. In Persian proverbs the word *shirazeh* is used metaphorically in relation to life. When someone reaches a dead end, it is said, 'the *shirazeh* of his life has come apart'. This proverb reflects the importance that the side finish has in the prolonged life of a rug and indicates that without the proper side finish the rug will come apart. (It has also been suggested that the term *shirazeh* comes from the name of the capital of Fars, Shiraz). The finishing of the two sides of the rug is also called in Persian *kinarah-bafi* (literally, edge weave). There are five types of side finishes found in the rugs discussed in this book. The side finish may be done in one or more colours, and with either the structural weft of the rug or with yarn unrelated to the foundation structure. Wool or silk yarn or strands made of goat hair is wrapped around one or more groups of several warps at both sides of the rug. After weaving one or several rows of knots and wefts the weaver wraps the group, or groups, of warps at each side of the work. The wrapping of the side finishes of city rugs and most village rugs usually consists of parallel wrapping in one colour; whereas tribal rugs, especially those from Fars province, usually have more than one colour in the wrapping as the side finish, whether it is parallel or crossed.

1. Parallel wrapping, on one level

In many rugs the wrapping of the warps at the sides of the rug is done in parallel fashion, in one or more colours (Ill. 29).

2. Parallel wrapping, one colour over another

In a variation of parallel wrapping one colour yarn is wrapped over the other, rather than beside it on the same level (Ill. 30).

3. Chevron, or crossed, wrapping

In this type of side finish, which is usually done in two contrasting colours, the way the yarn is wrapped, at a slant, creates a chevron effect as the yarn crosses over and under the two groups (or 'cords') of warps (Ill. 31).

4. Chevron, or crossed, wrapping over more than two warps

This variant of chevron, or crossed, wrapping is formed around three or more groups (or 'cords') of warps (Ill. 32) and is frequently seen in Baluchi rugs (in which goat hair is often used for the side finish) and occasionally in some Caucasian rugs, such as rug No. 85.

5. Selvage made with the structural ground weft

Some rugs are finished with a simple wrapping over and under two or more groups of warps at each side (after each row of knots), using the structural weft that forms the foundation of the rug (Ill. 33), rather than the supplementary, non-structural yarns used for the four types of side finish described above.

Very few of the kinds of rugs discussed in this book have sides finished in this manner; only on example (from the Caucasus) is illustrated (rug No. 93).

**Colours**

With few exceptions all of the pictorial rugs illustrated in this book have wool coloured with natural rather than synthetic dyes. The exact date of the first use of chemical dyes in Iran is not known. According to various reports synthetic dyes must have entered Iran before the 1890s, when Nasir al-Din Shah (and his successor Muzaffar al-Din Shah, in 1900) took steps to prevent their use in Iran, as they were found to be inferior to natural dyes in many ways, including colour fastness. According to existing reports,[133] however, synthetic dyes were used in only some towns and did not reach the villages and tribes as soon as they did the towns and cities. (I can attest to the fact that in some of the villages, among them ones of the Chahar Mahal-i Bakhtiyari

Province, dyers refrain from using synthetic dyes and still colour their wool with natural dyestuffs in a traditional manner). Synthetic colours were introduced in the northwestern part of Iran, such as Tabriz, which are closer to Europe, earlier than in other parts of Iran. To my knowledge, synthetic dyes began to be used by villagers and nomads chiefly in the last fifty years and in most cases only more recently. It is noteworthy that only a relatively small number of pictorial rugs were woven in that period.

## The structural characteristics of *gabbeh* rugs

*Gabbeh* is a local term used in Fars for a group of pile rugs made in that region which are characterised by a distinctive structure and often a distinctive patterning as well. Very soft, flexible and thick, rugs of the *gabbeh* type are woven primarily for the personal use of the tribespeople themselves. Because of their long pile and resultant thickness, *gabbehs* are often mistakenly called *khersaks*, which are a thick, inexpensive type of carpet woven in most parts of Iran. Rugs known as *khersak* are the same as most other pile rugs structurally, but have a very low knot count and inferior grade of wool. *Gabbehs*, on the other hand, are normally made of a soft, better quality of wool, and can have knot counts as high as Kashan and Kerman carpets as well as medium and low ones.

Properly speaking, *gabbehs* are woven only by the Qashqa'i, Bakhtiari and Lors, and a few other tribal groups of Fars. These rugs can be divided into two distinct groups: the more common ones which have simple geometric patterns without flowers and leaves, and a few that depict lions. Two examples of the latter type are published here (Nos. 83 and 85). Another pictorial *gabbeh* is No. 35. The structural aspects of the second group of *gabbehs*, which includes those that depict lions, are explained below.

*Weft*
The most salient characteristic of the *gabbeh* is the number of wefts between two rows of knots. Sometimes there are as many as sixteen shoots. The large number of wefts in some cases creates a space of about one centimetre of plain weave between two rows of knots. As long as the *gabbeh* is not badly worn these wefts lie hidden below the long pile, but once the pile is worn down they soon become visible.

*Knot size and pile length*
The size of the knots in *gabbehs* can differ widely, but whether a rug is finely or coarsely woven, the pile is always long. This is because there is very little, if any, trimming of the pile once the knots are tied. As a consequence, the pile is sometimes as much as four centimetre in length, long enough to cover numerous wefts with ease.

*End and side finishes*
The ends of *gabbehs* that depict lions differ from the ends of *gabbehs* with geometric designs. In the latter the two ends are finished in balanced plain weave, but in the former there are four to six centimetre of balanced plain weave, and half or less of this plain-weave area is turned under and sewn in place (Ill. 28). Sometimes one end is finished in this way and the other one is finished by gathering and knotting the warp ends into groups (Ill. 26). On one or both ends two-strand weft-twining (plain or countered) in two colours is also seen (Ills. 23, 24).

*Kings, Heroes and Lovers*

**Fig. 1** Carpet depicting Jamshid Jam, Saruq, inscribed *Part of the story of Jamshid Jam from Jahan Boro 1323* (1905 AD). Cotton warp and weft, wool pile; 5ft 7.25in by 3ft 3.75in. The figure described here as the legendary, prehistoric king Jamshid Jam is actually Xerxes I (r. 486-465 BC) depicted twice in mirror image for symmetry. *Private collection*.

**Fig. 2** Relief from a gateway at Persepolis (5th century BC) depicting Darius I (r. 522-486 BC).

**Fig. 3** Woodblock-printed (*qalamkar*) curtain, depicting some of the early kings of Iran. Isfahan, late nineteenth century. Cotton, 5ft 3in by 3ft 7.25in. *Collection of the Iranian Embassy in Kabul, Afghanistan.*

**Fig. 4** Detail of fig. 3, Jamshid Jam.

Kings, Heroes and Lovers

**Fig. 5** Fath 'Ali Shah (r. 1797-1834) on the Peacock Throne with sons and courtiers, of a mural painting formerly in the Nigaristan Palace, Tehran. *Indian Office Library, London.*

**Fig. 6** Peacock Throne, 1799-1800. Length 9ft 4.2in; width 6ft 1.812in. *Gulistan Palace, Tehran.*

**Fig. 7** Nadiri Throne, late eighteenth-early nineteenth century. Height 7ft 4.5625in; width 3ft 1.375in depth 3ft 1.375in. *Bank Melli, Tehran*.

**Fig. 8** Marble Throne, c. 1804. Height to top of columns (not including statues), 7ft 8.5in; length 11ft 1.875in; width 9ft 9.31in. *Gulistan Palace, Tehran*.

**Fig. 9** Detail of the Marble Throne: demon under the throne (left). Height of demon, 3ft 4.55in.

*Kings, Heroes and Lovers*

**Fig. 10** Relief at Persepolis (c. 516-330 BC) depicting soldiers of Pars.

**Fig. 11** Detail of fig. 3, Hushang Shah.

**Fig. 12** Gravestone of a woman at Dargazin, dated 1223 (1808 (AD), depicted at the bottom is a rug on a loom flanked by scissors and a beating comb used by rug weavers.

*Kings, Heroes and Lovers*

**Fig. 13** Relief depicting Xerxes I (r. 486-465 BC) enthroned, on a gateway at the Palace of One Hundred Columns, Persepolis (c. 516-330 BC)

**Fig. 14** Engraving of a drawing of the relief illustrated in Fig. 13; drawing made c. 1670 at Persepolis, published in Jean Chardin, *Voyages de Monsieur le Chevalier Chardin en Perse et Autres Lieux de l'Orient* (Amsterdam, 1711, between pp. 112 and 113).

**Fig. 15** Engraving of a drawing of the relief illustrated in fig. 13; drawing by Fursat al-Dawlah-yi Shirazi, in *Athar-i 'Ajam* (Works of the Iranians), Bombay, 1892, p. 179.

**Fig. 16** Qashqa'i carpet depicting the relief depicted in fig. 13; carpet dated 1222 (1807 AD). *Private collection; photograph by courtesy of Lefèvre and Partners, London.*

Kings, Heroes and Lovers

**Fig. 17** Statue of Shapur I (r. 241-272 AD), second half of the third century AD, in the cave of Shapur in Tang-i Chugan near Bishapur, Iran. Originally over twenty-one feet high, before the statue was broken at the knee.

**Fig. 18** Engraving of a drawing of the statue illustrated in fig. 17; drawing by Fursat al-Dawlah-yi Shirazi, in *Athar-i 'Ajam* (Works of the Iranians), (Bombay, 1892), p. 296.

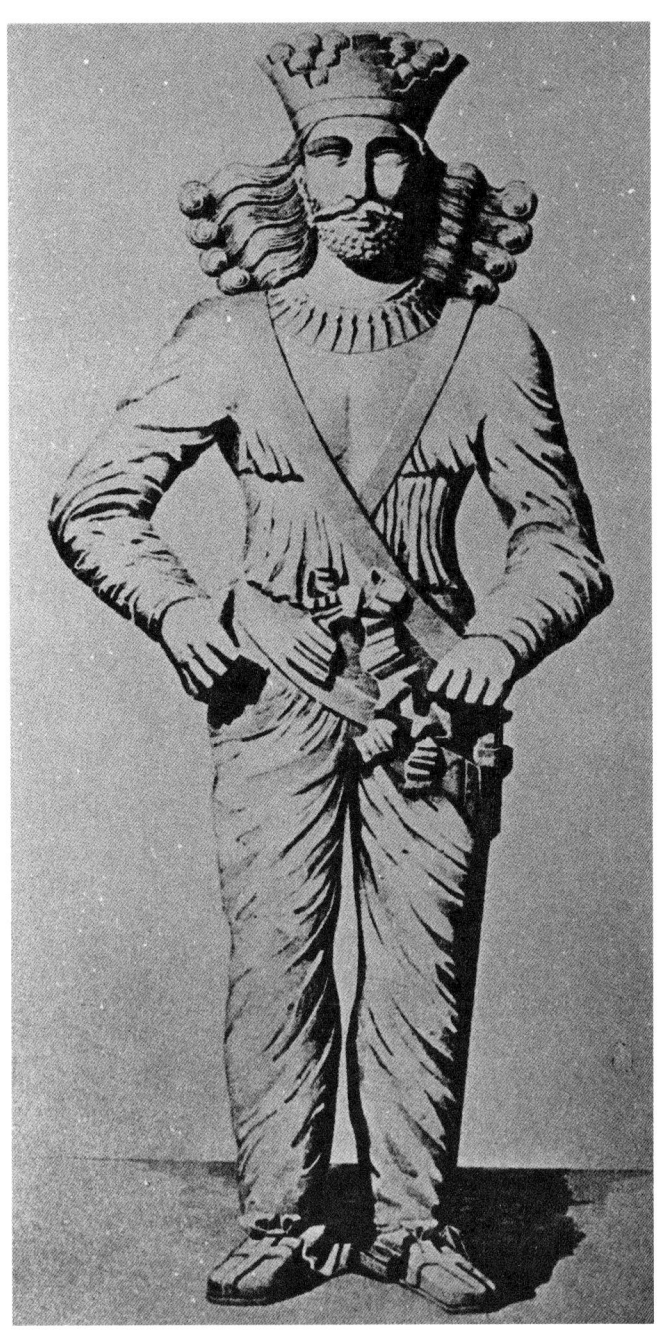

**Fig. 19** Engraving of a drawing by Charles Félix Marie Texier (1802-1872) of the statue of Shapur illustrated in Fig. 17; published in Texier, *L'Armenie, La Perse, et Mesopotamie, géographie, géologie, monuments anciens et modernes, histoire des moeurs et coutumes*, Paris, 1842- 1852, vol. II, p. 149.

**Fig. 20** Engraving of a drawing of Shapur I by Mirza Mutallib, published in Jalal al-Din Mirza, *Namah-yi Khusravan* (Book of Kings), Vienna, 1880, p. 266.

*Kings, Heroes and Lovers*

**Fig. 21** Shah 'Abbas I (r. 1588-1629), engraving by C. Heath after a painting attributed to Muhammad Zaman; published in Sir John Malcolm, *The History of Persia*, London, 1815, vol. I, facing p. 525.

**Fig. 22** Carpet depicting Nadir Shah (r. 1736-1747), inscribed *Nadir Shah*, Hamadan, mid-nineteenth century. Cotton warp and weft, wool pile; 10ft 2in by 5ft 4.25in. *Private collection*.

**Fig. 23** Fath 'Ali Shah (r. 1797-1834), attributed to 'Abdallah Khan, early nineteenth century, oil on canvas, 7ft 7in by 3ft 9in *Victoria and Albert Museum, London.*

**Fig. 24** Fath 'Ali Shah, hand-coloured engraving by W. T. Fry after a sketch from life by Sir Robert Ker Porter, published in Porter, *Travels in Georgia, Persia, Armenia, Ancient Babylonia, &.&. During the Years 1817, 1818, 1819 and 1820* (London, 1821, 1822), Vol. I, frontispiece. *Photograph by courtesy of the New York Public Library.*

*Kings, Heroes and Lovers*

**Fig. 25** Muhammad Shah (r. 1834-1848). Late nineteenth-century photograph of an oil painting inscribed: 'Image of the auspicious (or blessed) His Imperial Majesty the King of Kings, world under his protection, Muhammad Shah Qajar at the age of 39, 1261 (1845 AD)' *Private collection*. (Whereabouts of painting unknown).

**Fig. 26** Nasir al-Din Shah (r. 1848-1896).

**Fig. 27** Muhammad 'Ali Shah (r. 1907-1909).

**Fig. 29** Ahmad Shah (r. 1909-1924).

**Fig. 28** Carpet depicting Ahmad Shah (r. 1909-1924), Baluch of Khurasan province, mid-twentieth century; cotton warp and weft; wool pile; 4ft by 3ft 6.5in. *Private collection*.

*81*

*Kings, Heroes and Lovers*

**Fig. 30** Reza Shah (r. 1925-1941), 1921-1925, photographed while Reza Khan was an officer in the armed forces.

**Fig. 31** Woodblock-printed (*qalamkar*) curtain depicting Reza Shah (r. 1925-1941,) Tehran, early twentieth century. Cotton, 8ft 6.375in by 4ft 3.2in. *His Excellency Reza Khan, head of the army and armed forces and head of the cabinet and minister of war, may his fame last forever*, inscribed at upper right. *Private collection*.

82

**Fig. 32** Carpet depicting a seated army officer, Hamadan, Inscribed: *Aqa Mahmud Khan/Mahmud Khan Yadigar Fakhr al-Dawlat/1363 sannah* (the memory of Fakhr al-Dawlat in the year 1944). Cotton warp and weft, wool pile, 6ft 5.5in by 4ft 0.75in. *Private collection*.

**Fig. 33** *The Demon Akvan throws Rustam into the sea*, miniature painting from the *Shahnamah* (of Firdawsi) by Muhammad Juki, Herat, c. 1440. *Royal Asiatic Society, London*.

**Fig. 34** *The Demon Akvan throws Rustam into the sea*, lithograph in an edition of the *Shahnamah* by Firdawsi published in Bombay in 1890, vol. II, p. 199.

*Kings, Heroes and Lovers*

**Fig. 35** Carpet depicting figures from the story of Khusraw and Shirin from the *Khamseh* by Nizami; Qashqa'i, mid-twentieth century. Wool warp, weft, and pole; 6ft by 3ft 10in. *Private collection.*

**Fig. 36** Carpet depicting figures from the story of Khusraw and Shirin from the *Khamsah* by Nizami; Qashqa'i, mid-twentieth century. Wool warp, weft, and pile; 6ft 0.5in by 4ft 3in. *Private collection.*

**Fig. 37** Cartoon for a carpet depicting scenes from the story of Khusraw, Shirin and Farhad. *Top left:* Farhad carving the mountain. *Top right:* Khusraw going to visit Shirin in the castle in Kermanshah that Khusraw had built for her. *Below:* Khusraw comes upon Shirin bathing in a stream. Kashan(?), mid-nineteenth century. Watercolour and ink on paper, all lines of the squared paper drawn by hand; 7ft 2.5in by 5ft 5in. *Private collection.*

**Fig. 37a** Detail of Khusraw from upper right section of fig. 37.

**Fig. 37b** Detail of Shirin from fig. 37.

*Kings, Heroes and Lovers*

**Fig. 38** *Khusraw observes Shirin bathing in a stream*, miniature painting from the story of Khusraw and Shirin from the *Khamsah* by Nizami; Herat; sixteenth century. *Metropolitan Museum of Art, New York City; gift of Alexander Smith Cochran, 1913.*

**Fig. 39** *Khusraw observes Shirin bathing in a stream*, lithograph in an edition of the *Khamsah* by Nizami published in Tehran in 1896, p. 82.

*Figures*

**Fig. 40** Wood-block-printed curtain (*qalamkar*) depicting Khusraw observing Shirin bathing in a stream, Isfahan, early twentieth century. Cotton, 5ft 10.5in by 4ft 0.75in. *Collection of Manijeh and Parviz Tanavoli.*

**Fig. 42** *Shirin finds Farhad dead*, lithograph in an edition of the *Khamsah* by Nizami published in Tehran in 1869.

**Fig. 41** *Shirin visits Farhad*, lithograph in an edition of the *Khamsah* by Nizami published in Tehran in 1896, p. 138.

**Fig. 43** *Majnun surrounded by animals in the wilderness*, lithograph in an edition of the *Khamsah* by Nizami published in Tehran in 1879.

*Kings, Heroes and Lovers*

**Fig. 44** Woodblock-printed curtain depicting Layla visiting Majnun from the story of Layla and Majnun in the *Khamsah* by Nizami, Isfahan, early twentieth century. Cotton, 7ft 10.5in by 4ft 5.125in. *Tanavoli collection*.

**Fig. 45** Composite camel, Khurasan, Sabzavar, c. 1580. Painting on paper, 11.125 by 7in. *Fogg Art Museum, Harvard University, Cambridge, Massachusetts*.

**Fig. 46** Composite camel, by Sattar-i Tabrizi, mid-nineteenth century. Pen and ink with some gilt trim, 10.625 by 7.5in. *Private collection*.

**Fig. 47** Carpet depicting Hazrat 'Ali (Muhammad's son-in-law) and his two sons: kneeling at the left, Hasan, and, at the right, Husayn. Standing at the right is a dervish ('Ali's groom Qanbar?) wearing the dervish cap with twelve vertical folds (*taqiyah*) and carrying a beggar's bowl (*kashkul*). The figure standing at the left is Salman-i Farsi (also called Salman-i Pak, Salman the Pure), the first Iranian to convert to Islam and one of Muhammad's companions. Across his knees 'Ali holds his two-pronged sword, which he named *Zu'l-Fiqar*. Qum, mid-twentieth century. Cotton warp and weft; wool pile; 2ft 2.5in by 2ft 4.5in. *Private collection.*

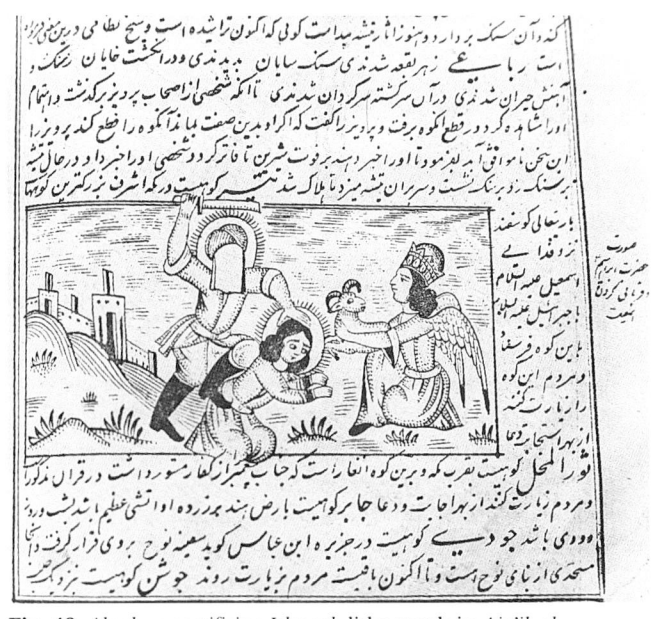

**Fig. 48** *Abraham sacrificing Ishmael*, lithograph in *Aja'ib al-Makhluqat* (The Wonders of the Creation) by Zakariya ibn Muhammad ibn Mahmud, Tehran, 1866, p. 102.

**Fig. 49** *Gabriel on a composite horse*, by Ramazan 'Ali, 1708. Watercolour, 7.875 by 5.125in. *Private collection.*

**Fig. 50** *Mary and Jesus*, signed *Muhammad Nabi Qaydari*. Reverse painting on glass (*shamayil*), Iran, early twentieth century, 1ft 5.5in by 1ft 1.75in. *Tanavoli collection.*

*Kings, Heroes and Lovers*

**Fig. 51** Carpet depicting Ahmad Shah of Iran (r. 1909-1924) and two rulers or diplomats of Turkey and Russia; Karabagh, southern Caucasus, early twentieth century. Wool warp, weft, and pile; 7ft 6.5in by 4ft 10in. *Private collection*.

**Fig. 52** Carpet depicting horses and dogs; Karabagh, southern Caucasus, late nineteenth or early twentieth century. Wool warp, weft, and pile; 6ft 2in by 4ft 3in. *Private collection*.

*Kings, Heroes and Lovers*

**Fig. 53** *Lady offering sweetmeats*, attributed to Muhammad, second quarter of the nineteenth century, Iran. Oil on canvas, 4ft 9in by 2ft 10.25in. Victoria and Albert Museum, London.

**Fig. 54** Stone lions marking graves in Bakhtiyari cemetery at Avargan, nineteenth century.

Kings, Heroes and Lovers

**Fig. 55** Dervish carrying axe (*tabarzin*) and bowl (*kashkul*), photographed in Iran c. 1920.

**Fig. 56** Tile mural depicting dervishes, 1917-1920, at the Takiyah Mu'avin al-Mulk in Kermanshah, where *ta'ziyah* ceremonies were held. Height 10ft 8.75in; width 9ft 0.625in.

**Fig. 56a** Detail of fig. 56, a dervish with some of his characteristic paraphernalia.

94

*Figures*

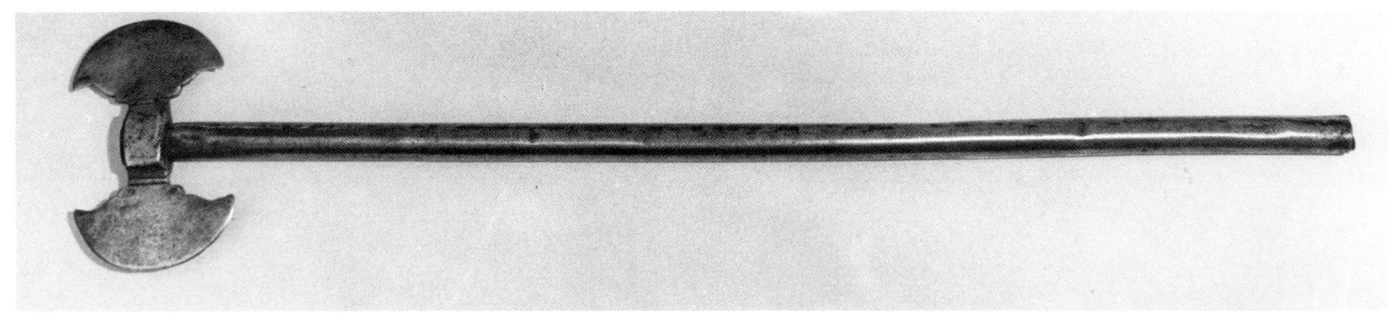

**Fig. 57** Dervish's axe (*tabarzin*), Iran, nineteenth century. Steel; length 2ft 3.5in, width 5.75in, depth 1.812in. *Tanavoli collection*.

**Fig. 58** Dervish bowl (*kashkul*), Iran, late eighteenth or early nineteenth century. Steel with relief cut and engraved; length 10.5in, height 5.75in, width 5.875in. *Tanavoli collection*.

**Fig. 60** *Fatima*, chromolithograph, Europe, early twentieth century.

**Fig. 59** Double-lobed coconut, known as *Coco de Mer* (from the species of palm called *Lodoicea sechellarum* or *Lodoicea maldivica*), Seychelles Islands, twentieth century; length 1ft 1in, width 1ft, depth 7in. Dervish bowls made from halves of these double-lobed coconuts are the prototypes for metal dervish bowls such as that illustrated in fig. 58. *Private collection*.

*Kings, Heroes and Lovers*

**Fig. 61** Saddle cover depicting European women, Kerman, mid nineteenth century; 3ft 3in by 2ft 11in. *Collection of Siawosch Azadi.*

**Fig. 62** Carpet depicting two deer, Qashqa'i, mid-twentieth century. Wool warp, weft, and pile; 6ft 5in by 4ft 5.5in. *Private collection.*

**Fig. 63a and b** Copper coin depicting Lion and Sun motif, Safavid dynasty; an Isfahan *folus* struck in the year 1124 (1712 AD); diameter 1.375in. *Tanavoli collection.*

*Figures*

**Fig. 64** Relief depicting a king slaying a lion, Hall of One Hundred Columns, Persepolis, 5th century BC.

**Fig. 66** Carpet depicting the relief illustrated in fig. 64, Qashqa'i mid-twentieth century. Wool warp, weft, and pile; 6ft 5in by 4ft 3in. *Private collection*.

**Fig. 65** Lithograph of the relief illustrated in fig. 64; drawing by Fursat al-Dawlah-yi Shirazi, in *Athar-i 'Ajam* (Works of the Iranians), Bombay, 1892, p. 177.

*Kings, Heroes and Lovers*

## Spin and ply directions

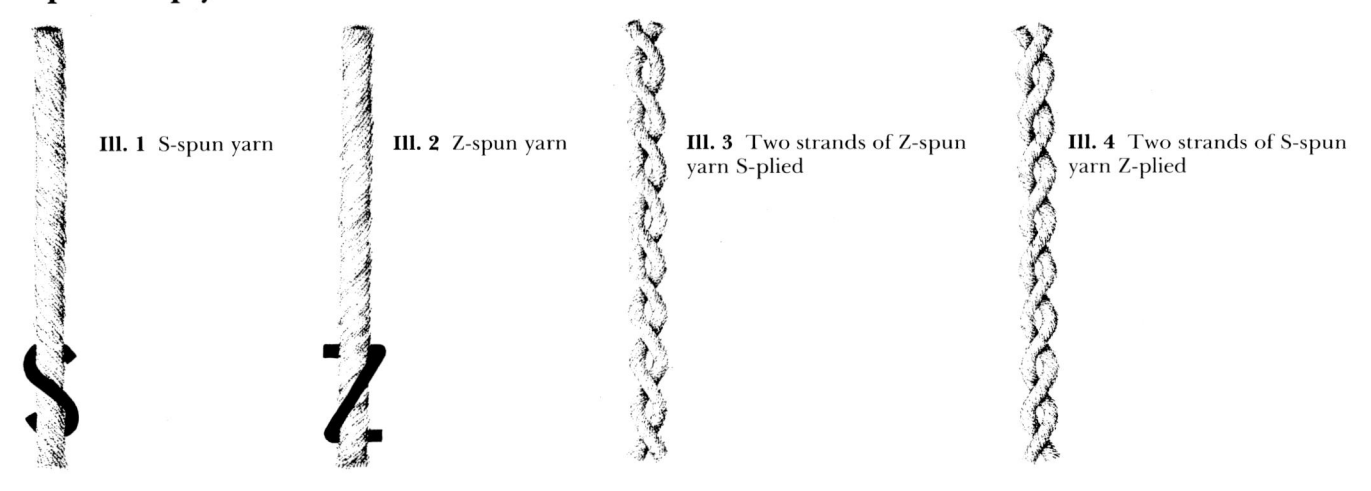

**Ill. 1** S-spun yarn

**Ill. 2** Z-spun yarn

**Ill. 3** Two strands of Z-spun yarn S-plied

**Ill. 4** Two strands of S-spun yarn Z-plied

## Knots

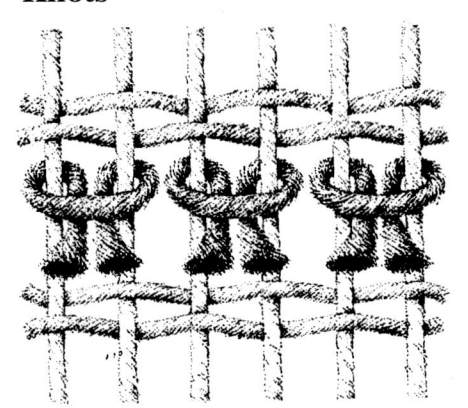

**Ill. 5** Sy1 (symmetrical knot, warps on one level, both wefts undulating)

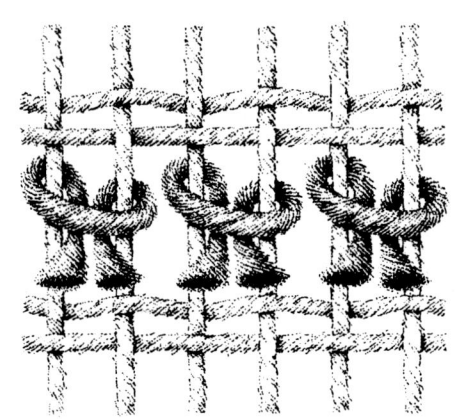

**Ill. 6** Sy2 (symmetrical knot, warps on two levels, right side of knot wrapped around depressed warp; one weft straight, one undulating)

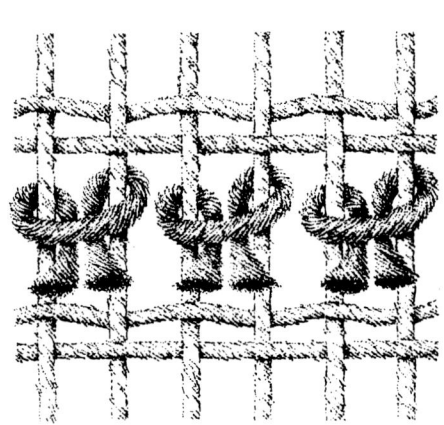

**Ill. 7** Sy3 (symmetrical knot, warps on two levels, left side of knot wrapped around depressed warp; one weft straight, one undulating)

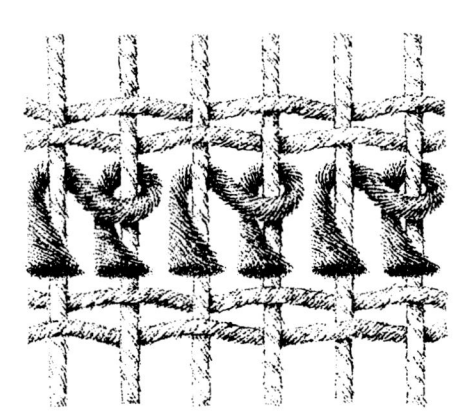

**Ill. 8** As1 (asymmetrical knot, open on the left, warps on one level; both warps undulating)

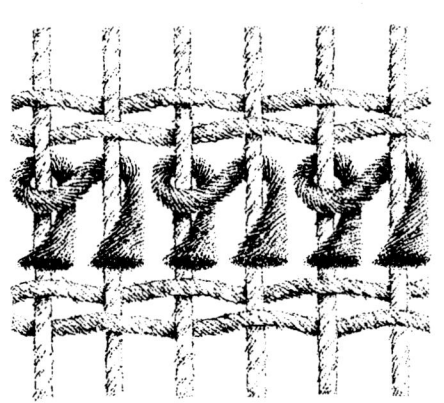

**Ill. 9** As2 (asymmetrical knot, open on the right, warps on one level; both warps undulating)

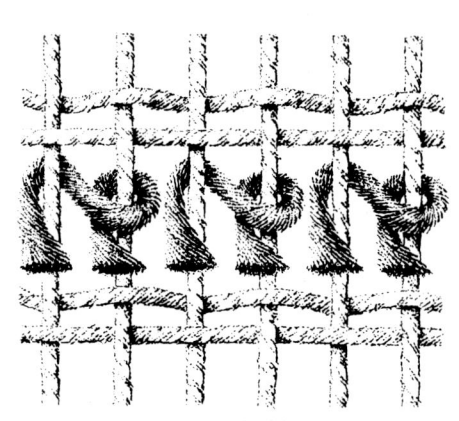

**Ill. 10** As3 (asymmetrical knot, open on the left, warps on two levels, yarn wrapped around depressed warp; one weft straight, one undulating)

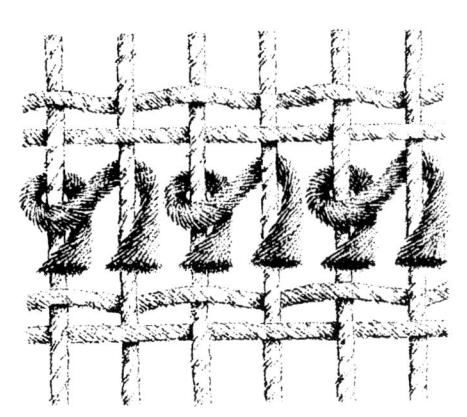

*Illustrations*

**Ill. 11** As4 (asymmetrical knot, open on the right, warps on two levels, yarn wrapped around depressed warp; one weft straight, one undulating)

**Ill. 12** Sy4 (symmetrical knot on undulating warps; single straight weft)

**Ill. 13** As5 (asymmetrical knot, open on the left, on undulating warps; single straight weft)

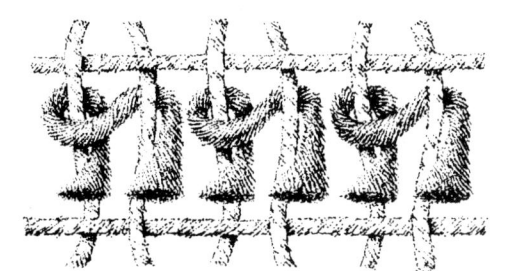

**Ill. 14** As6 (asymmetrical knot, open on the right, on undulating warps; single straight weft)

## Warp levels as seen on backs of rugs

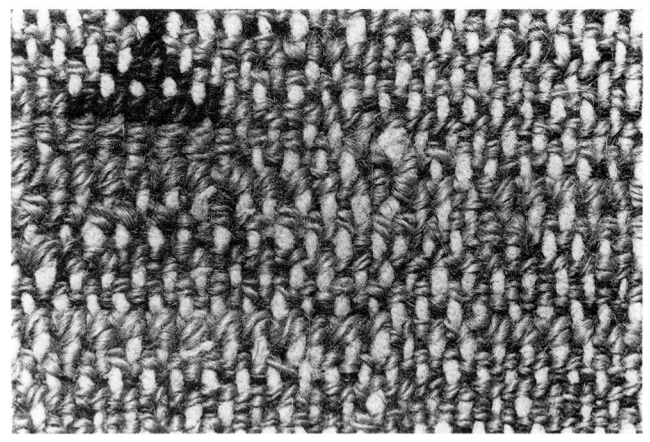

**Ill. 15** Detail of the back of a single-wefted rug with undulating warps, on one level

**Ill. 16** Detail of the back of a rug with warps on one level

**Ill. 17** Detail of the back of a rug with warps on two levels (semi-depressed)

*Kings, Heroes and Lovers*

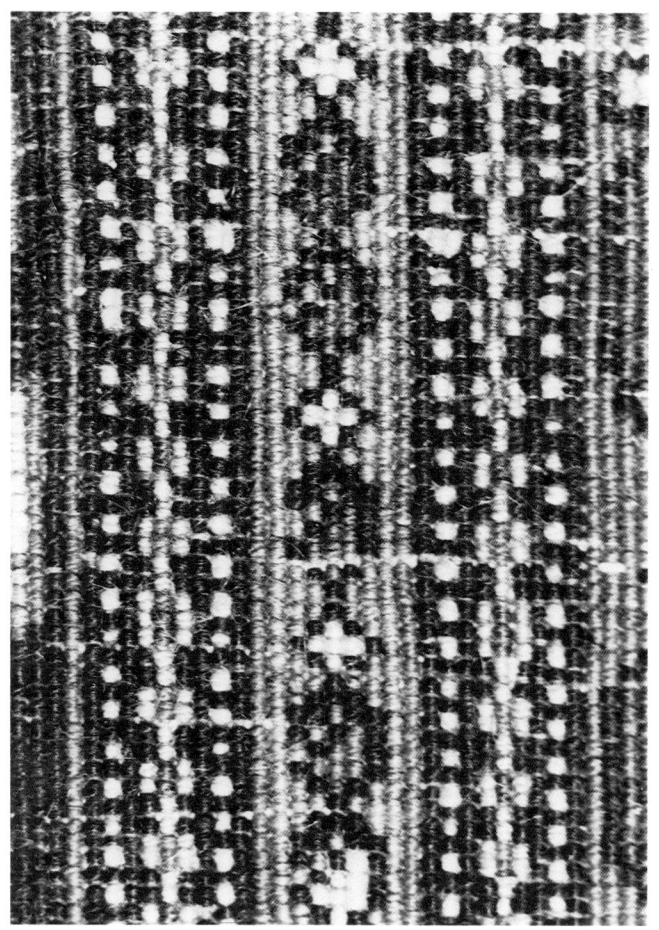

**Ill. 18** Detail of the back of a rug with warps on two levels (alternate warps are fully depressed behind the next)

# End finishes

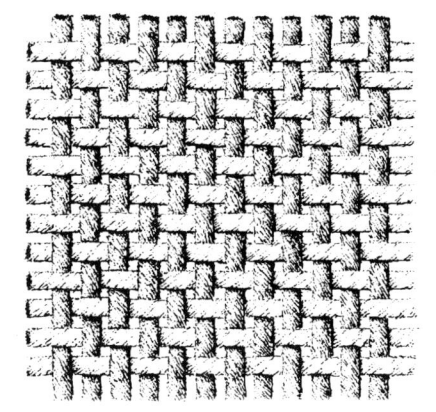

**Ill. 19** Balanced plain weave

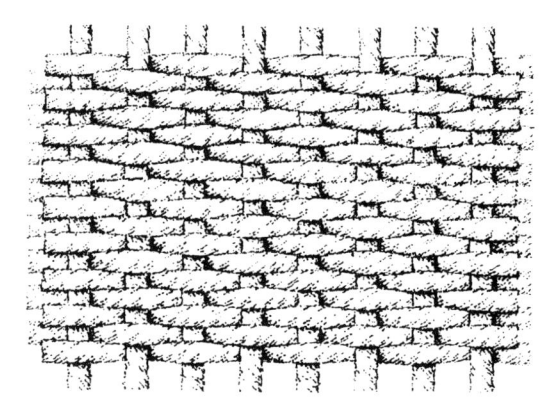

**Ill. 20** Loosely-packed weft-faced plain weave

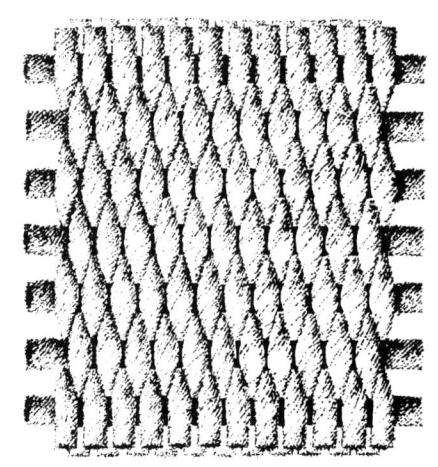

**Ill. 21** Tightly-packed warp-faced plain weave

*Illustrations*

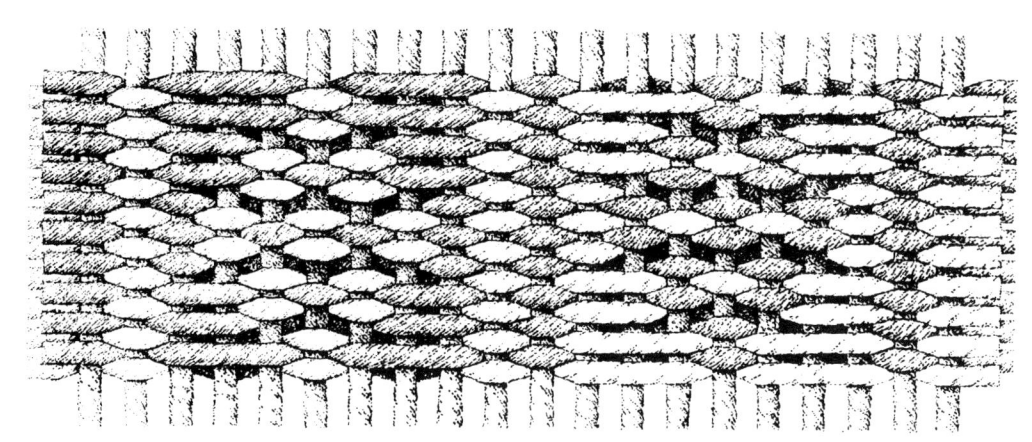

**Ill. 22** Two-colour complementary-weft weave with variable interlacing arranged to form a diamond-like pattern on a rectangular ground

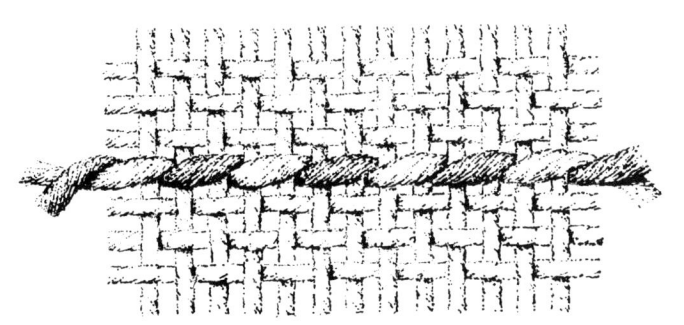

**Ill. 23** Two-strand weft twining (on balanced plain weave)

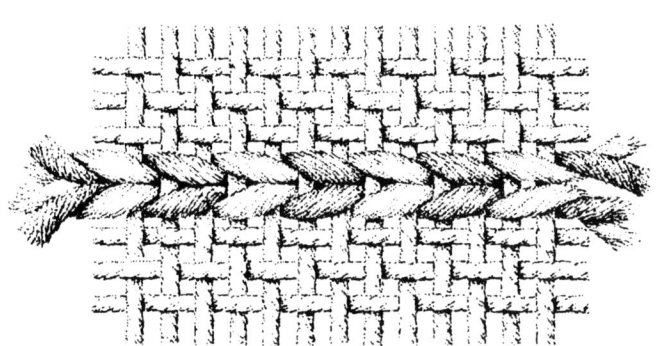

**Ill. 24** Two-stand countered weft twining (on balanced plainweave)

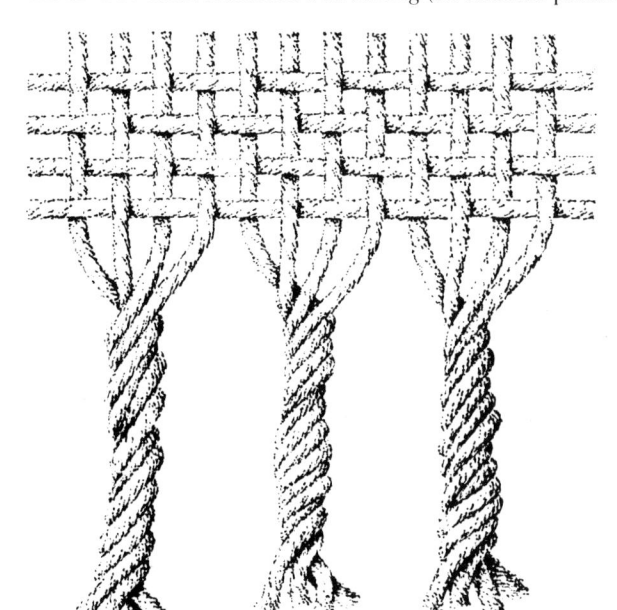

**Ill. 25** Fringe of twisted groups of warp ends

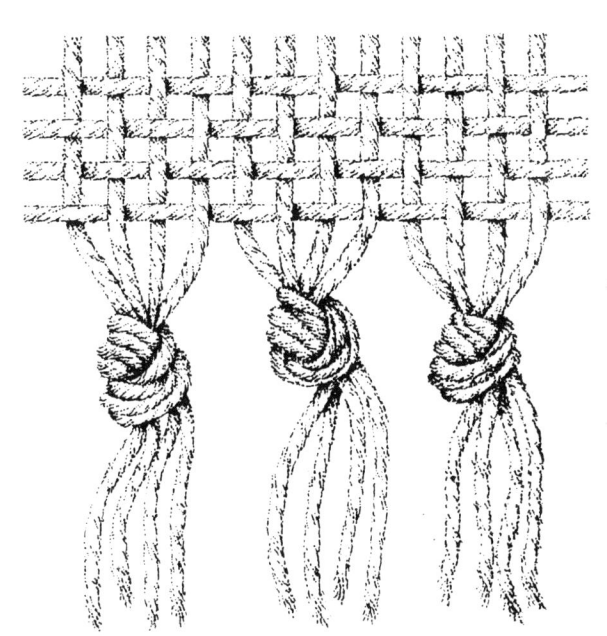

**Ill. 26** Fringe of knotted groups of warp ends

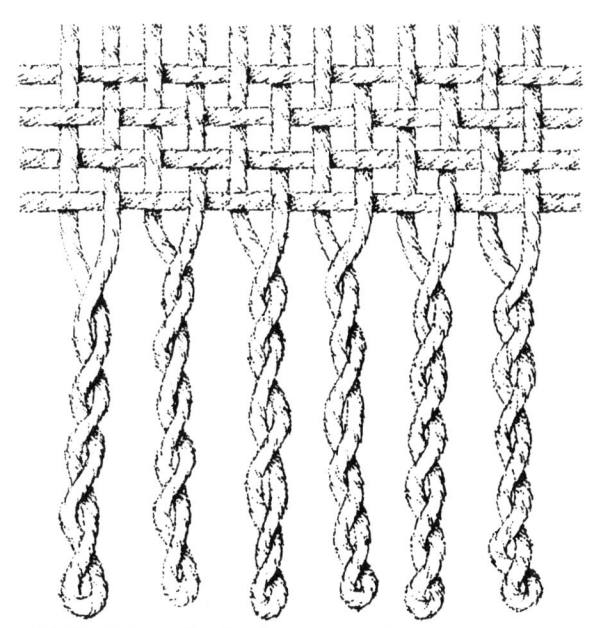

**Ill. 27** Fringe of twisted uncut warp loops

101

*Kings, Heroes and Lovers*

**Ill. 28** Balanced plain weave turned back and sewn down (often used in *gabbah* rugs of Fars Province)

## Side finishes (selvages)

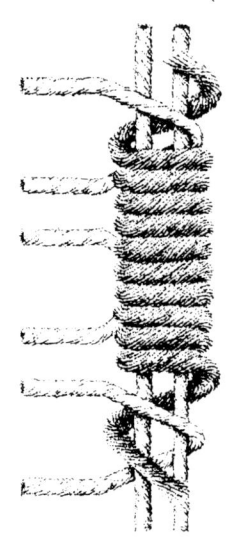

**Ill. 29** Parallel wrapping, on one level

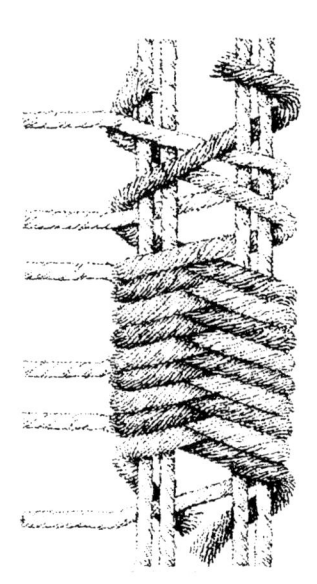

**Ill. 31** Chevron wrapping, over two groups (or 'cords') of warps

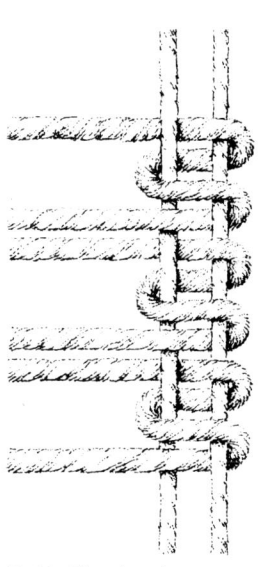

**Ill. 33** Simple selvage made with the structural wefts of the rug

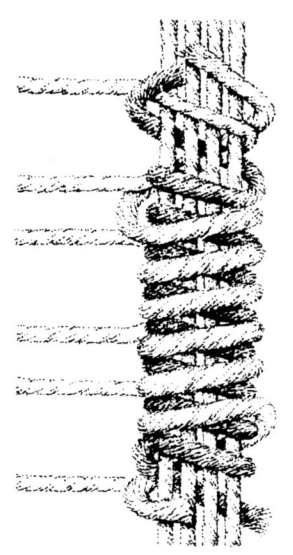

**Ill. 30** Parallel wrapping, one colour over another

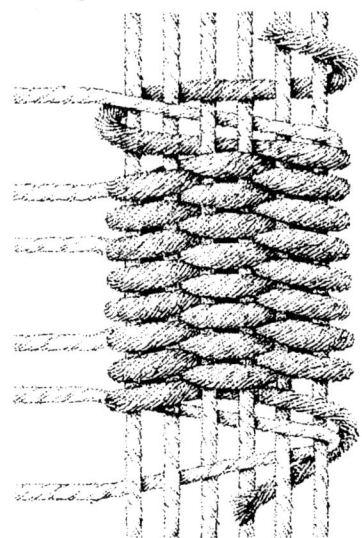

**Ill. 32** Chevron wrapping over more than two groups (or 'cords') of warps

*THE PLATES*

*Kings, Heroes and Lovers*

**1**

**Hushang Shah**
**Hamadan area**
**Inscription: *Hushang Shah***
**Mid-19th century**

In the use of the length of this *miyan farsh* (the long middle carpet in the traditional Iranian arrangement of four rugs used together), the design differs from that of others of the Hushang Shah group. Instead of being ranged in one row, soldiers are found in three horizontal rows. While similar, the various figures are not identical. The soldiers depicted here are reminiscent of some of the figures in the reliefs at Persepolis (see fig. 10 and p. 18). For a discussion of the throne on which the king sits, see p. 17 infra. The border used in this rug is commonly found in the Hamadan and Malayir areas. For general information about Hushang Shah as well as the production of rugs depicting this legendary ruler, see p. 15 infra.

*Sizes:* 11ft 3.25in x 5ft 1.75in
   (344 x 157cm)
*Warp:* cotton, Z5S, undyed, undulating, 1 level
*Weft:* cotton, Z6S, undyed, 1 shoot, straight
*Pile:* wool, Z2 loosely plied, Sy1, 0.25in (3mm)
*Knot count:* 8V x 8H = 64 per sq. in. (32V x 32H = 1024 per sq. dm.)
*Texture:* fairly soft, fairly thin, very flexible
*Sides:* wool, pale brown, parallel wrapping around 4 warps
*Ends:* missing
*Colours* 10, blue-black, blue, red, pink, orange, yellow, dark reddish brown, dark brown, light brown, ivory

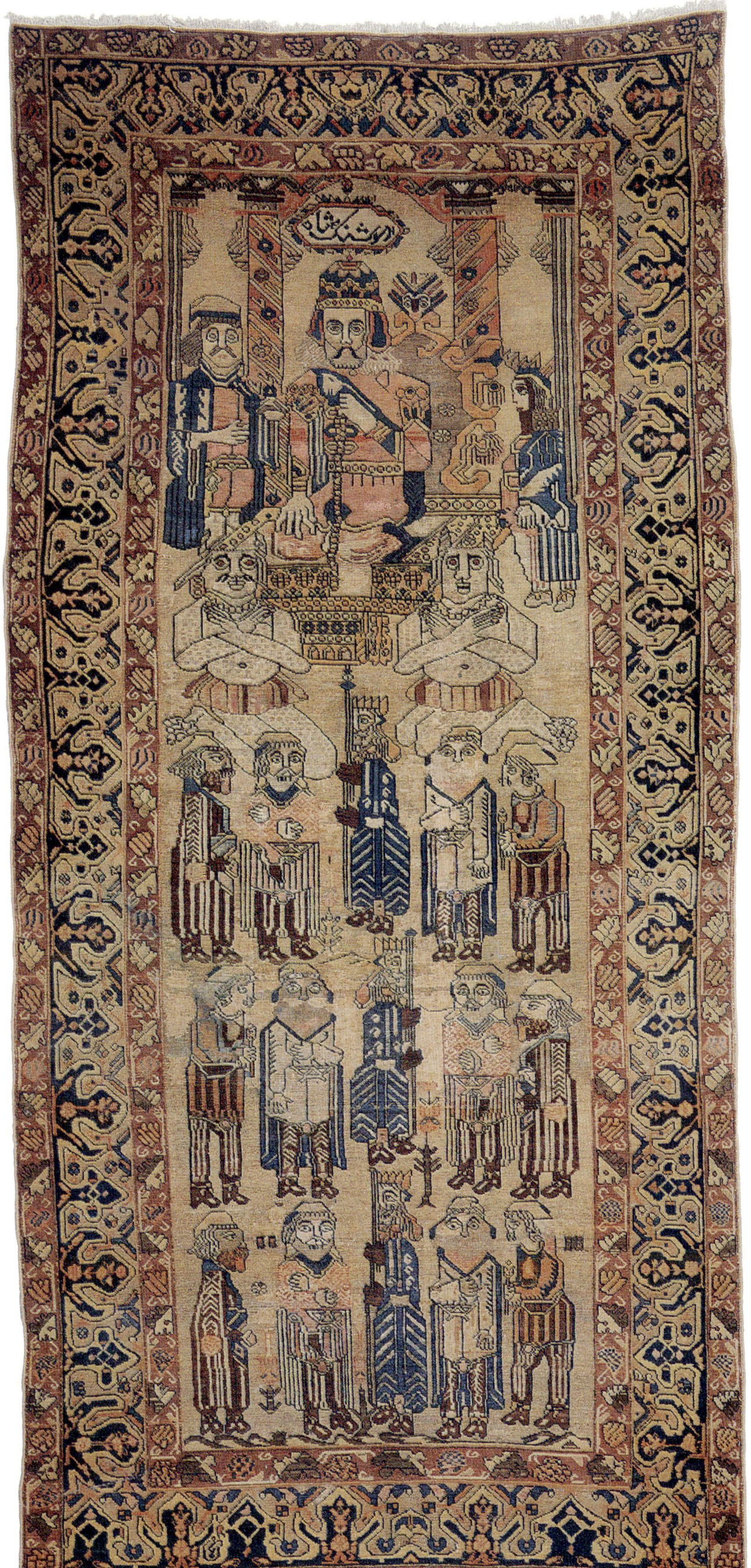

*Kings, Heroes and Lovers*

2

**Hushang Shah and European Diplomats**
**Hamadan area: Afshars of the Khamsah region between Hamadan and Zanjan**
**Inscription:** *Hushang Shah, Order of Isma'il Khan Afshar 1230 (1815 AD)*

So unexpected and intriguing are the men depicted at the top of this rug that our attention is drawn almost more to them than to the story centering on Hushang Shah, to whom is dedicated here one of the oldest and most imaginative rugs depicting this hero. (See p. 14 for a discussion of this legendary king.) From the attire of the men at the top it can be surmised that they are European diplomats. The cylindrical hats, striped pants, and the narrow, drawnout moustaches are among the characteristic signs of European ambassadors and diplomats in the art of the Qajar period. At first, the juxtaposition of these men together with Hushang Shah, a king of ancient times, seems incongruous, but the formal appearance of the diplomats and their disposition can only signify an official audience with the king. (The sources of the throne depicted here are discussed on p. 17 infra.) It is only the imagination of the weaver or the person who commissioned the rug that brought figures from two very different periods together in one scene and succeeded in creating one of the most interesting weavings of its time. The inscription on this rug indicates that this rug was commissioned by Isma'il Khan of the Afshar tribe.

Since part of this tribe is settled in villages in the Khamsah region between Hamadan and Zanjan it is possible that the rug was woven in one of those Afshar villages. (See p. 53 for information about the various regions of Iran where Afshar groups are found.)

*Size:* 7ft 11in x 4ft 10.25in (241 x 148cm)
*Warp:* cotton, Z3S, undyed, straight, 1 level
*Weft:* cotton, Z6S, undyed, 1 to 2 shoots, some shoots combine strands of cotton and blue wool, undulating
*Pile:* wool, Z2 loosely plied, Sy1, 0.03-0.0625in (1mm)
*Knot count:* 15V x 8H = 120 per sq. in. (60V x 32H = 1920 per sq. dm.)
*Texture:* fairly coarse, thin, fairly flexible
*Sides:* wool, pink, parallel wrapping around 4 warps
*Ends:* missing
*Colours* 13, blue-black, dark blue, blue, olive green, red, light red, orange, yellow, dark reddish brown, brown, light brown, buff, ivory

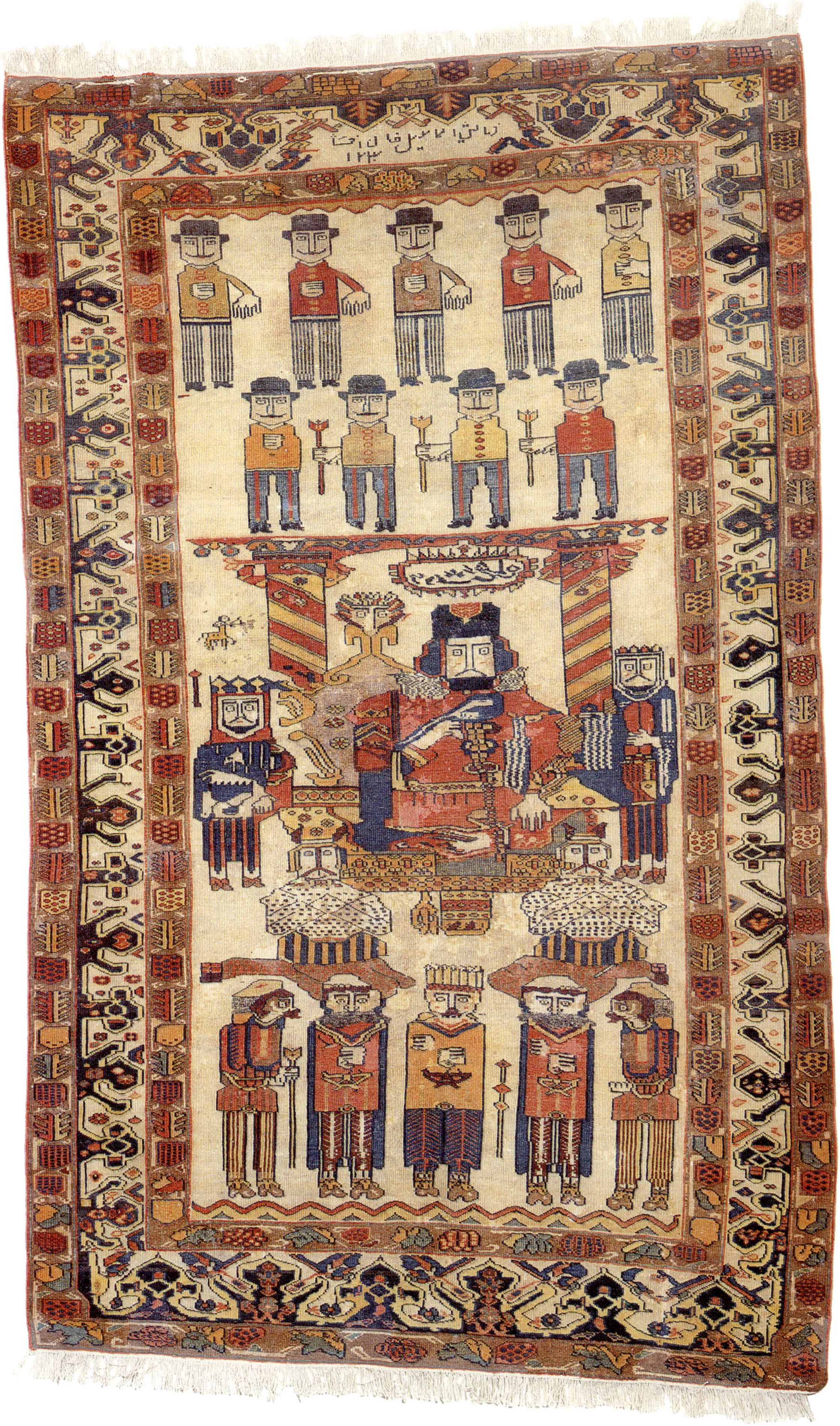

**3**

**Hushang Shah**
**Hamadan area**
**Inscription: *Hushang Shah***
**Late 19th century**

From the point of view of design and colour this is one of the most successful renditions of the Hushang Shah scene. The weaver, seeking variety and innovation, has creatively used colour and line particularly skilfully, as is evident in the corners and at the sides. Traditional proportions of the design are altered and exceptional power is achieved. There is a special harmony among all the elements and figures of the rug. The dark blue field, which inclines toward brown at the bottom, helps to show the various shapes and colours to best advantage. (For Hushang Shah, see p. 15, and p. 18 in particular regarding the throne depicted here, and p. 18 for a discussion of the figures of the two demons at the foot of the throne).

*Size:* 5ft 11.25in x 4ft 4.5in (181 x 133cm)
*Warp:* cotton, Z5S, undyed, undulating, 1 level
*Weft:* cotton, Z5S, undyed, 1 shoot, straight
*Pile:* wool, Z2 loosely plied, Sy1, 0.25in (3mm)
*Knot count:* 10V x 9H = 90 per sq. in. (40V x 36H =1440 per sq. dm.)
*Texture:* fairly soft, thin, fairly flexible
*Sides:* wool, undyed brown, parallel wrapping around 4 warps
*Ends:* 0.75in (2cm) weft-faced plain weave, undyed cotton
*Colours* 10, black, blue-black, blue, light blue, red, pink, brown, light brown, ochre, ivory

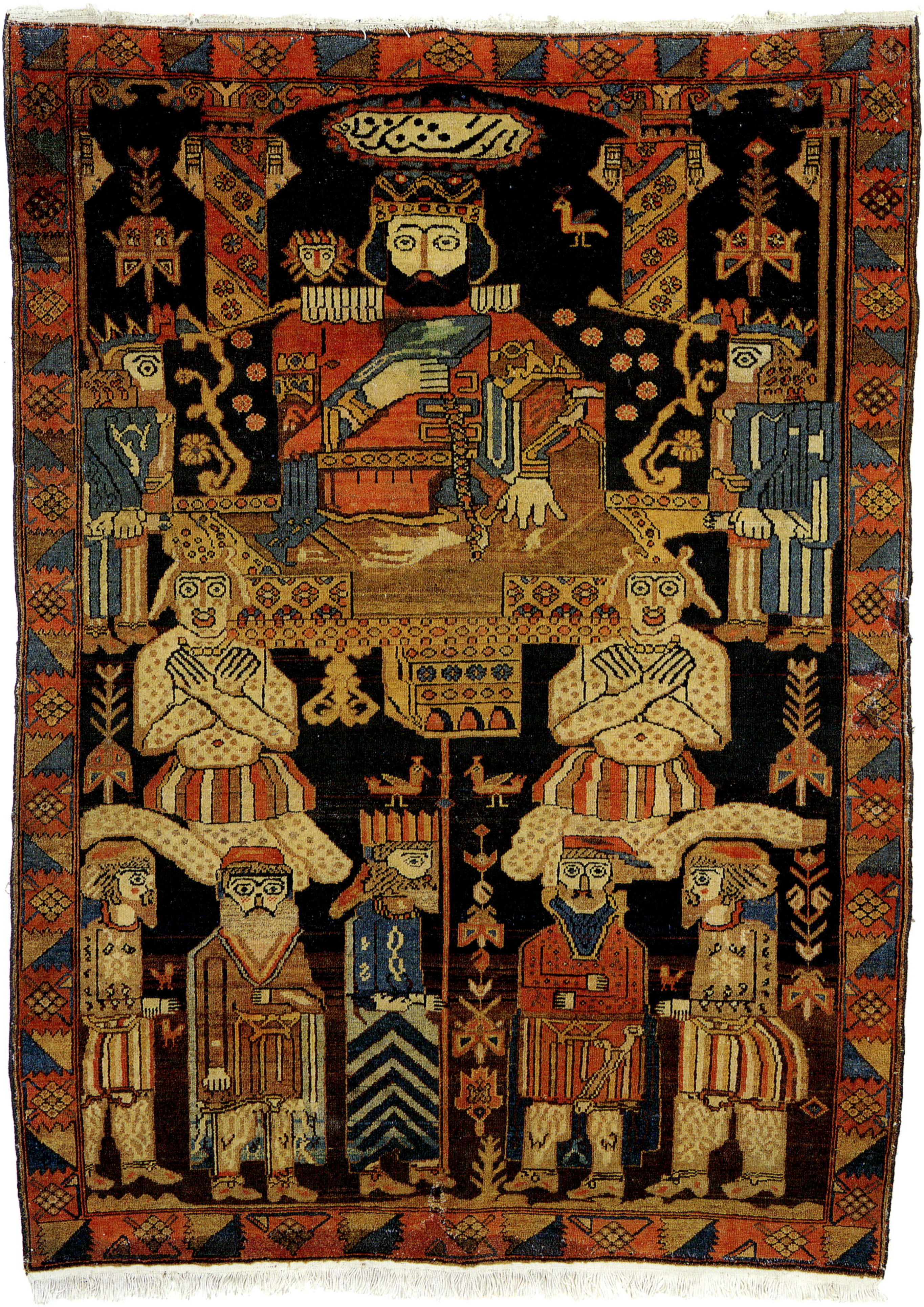

## 4

**Hushang Shah**
**Dargazin area**
**Inscription:** ***Hushang Shah***
**Early 20th century**

The Hushang Shah of this rug reminds one of some of the religious folk-art reverse paintings on glass devoted to the holy imams who are pictured in a similar kneeling position with both hands grasping a sword which rests on their knees (cf. fig. 47, a rug possibly based on such a folk painting).

If the over-all effect is highly colourful, the reason perhaps lies in the extensive use of two colours—red and light blue—which give a lively, happy quality to the rug. The clothing depicted here is extremely simplified and is given variety by means of different colours. Normally shown in profile, the centre figure of the bottom row in this case is seen straight on, but his clothes lack the symmetry of the others (notice the clothes of the vizier shown in profile on the shah's right) and indicate a change from the prototype. (For a general discussion of Hushang Shah, see p. 15, and for details about the throne depicted here, see p. 18).

*Size:* 6ft 7in x 4ft 4in (200 x 132cm)
*Warp:* cotton, Z5S, undyed, undulating, 1 level
*Weft:* cotton, Z4S, undyed, 1 shoot, straight; in the upper part: occasionally, cotton, Z3S, and wool, Z2S; at the very top: cotton, Z2S, and wool, Z2S
*Pile:* wool, Z2 loosely plied, Sy1, 0.25in (3mm)
*Knot count:* 9V x 9H = 81 per sq. in. (36V x 36H = 1296 per sq. dm.)
*Texture:* fairly soft, thin, stiff
*Sides:* wool, brown, remains of parallel wrapping around 6 warps
*Ends:* lower: 0.75in (2cm) weft-faced plain weave, undyed cotton
upper: remains of weft-faced plain weave, undyed cotton
*Colours* 8, blue-black, blue, very light green, red, orange, brown, light brown, white

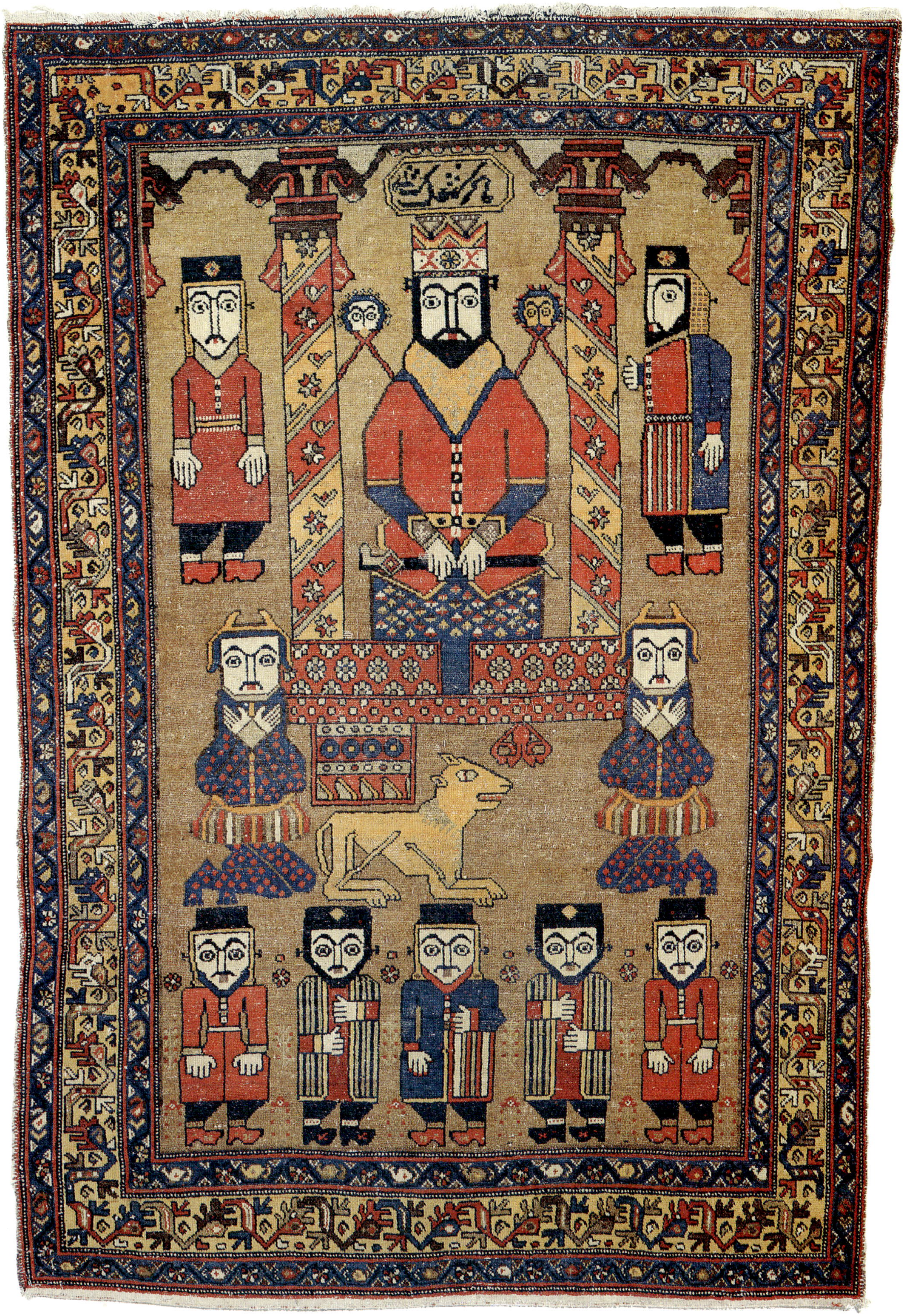

*Kings, Heroes and Lovers*

**5**

**Hushang Shah**
**Hamadan area or Zarand area**
**Dated: *[in the] year 1312* (1894 AD)**

As mentioned in the introduction, the weavers of pictorial rugs often drew inspiration from other rugs, but made minor changes reflecting their own interpretations of a design. For example, the striped coats of some of the soldiers in the lower part of rug no. 4 have, in rug no. 5, lost their character as articles of clothing and suggest shield-like objects that the vizier and soldiers are holding in front of them. Furthermore, the two motifs resembling branches of red roses seen above the shoulders of Hushang Shah are found in other Hushang Shah rugs in a variety of forms such as the sun, the finials of the shah's throne, and at times even the epaulets of the king's uniform. Below the throne is the lion-and-sun motif that has long been associated with Iran (see pp. 59, 60). (For Hushang Shah, see p. 15 and about the throne seen here, p. 18.)

*Size:* 6ft 0.75in x 4ft 0.5in (205 x 123cm)
*Warp:* cotton, Z6S, undyed, undulating, 1 level
*Weft:* cotton, Z6S, undyed, 1 shoot, nearly straight
*Pile:* wool, Z2 loosely plied, Syl, 0.1875in (4mm)
*Knot count:* 11V x 8H = 88 per sq. in. (44V x 32H = 1408 per sq. dm.)
*Texture:* soft, thick, flexible
*Sides:* wool, dark red, parallel wrapping around 4 warps
*Ends:* lower: 0.75in (2cm) weft-faced plain weave, undyed cotton
upper: 0.375in (1cm) weft-faced plain weave, undyed cotton
*Colours* 12, black, dark blue, blue, dark red, red, deep pink, orange, yellow, buff, dark brown, light brown, white

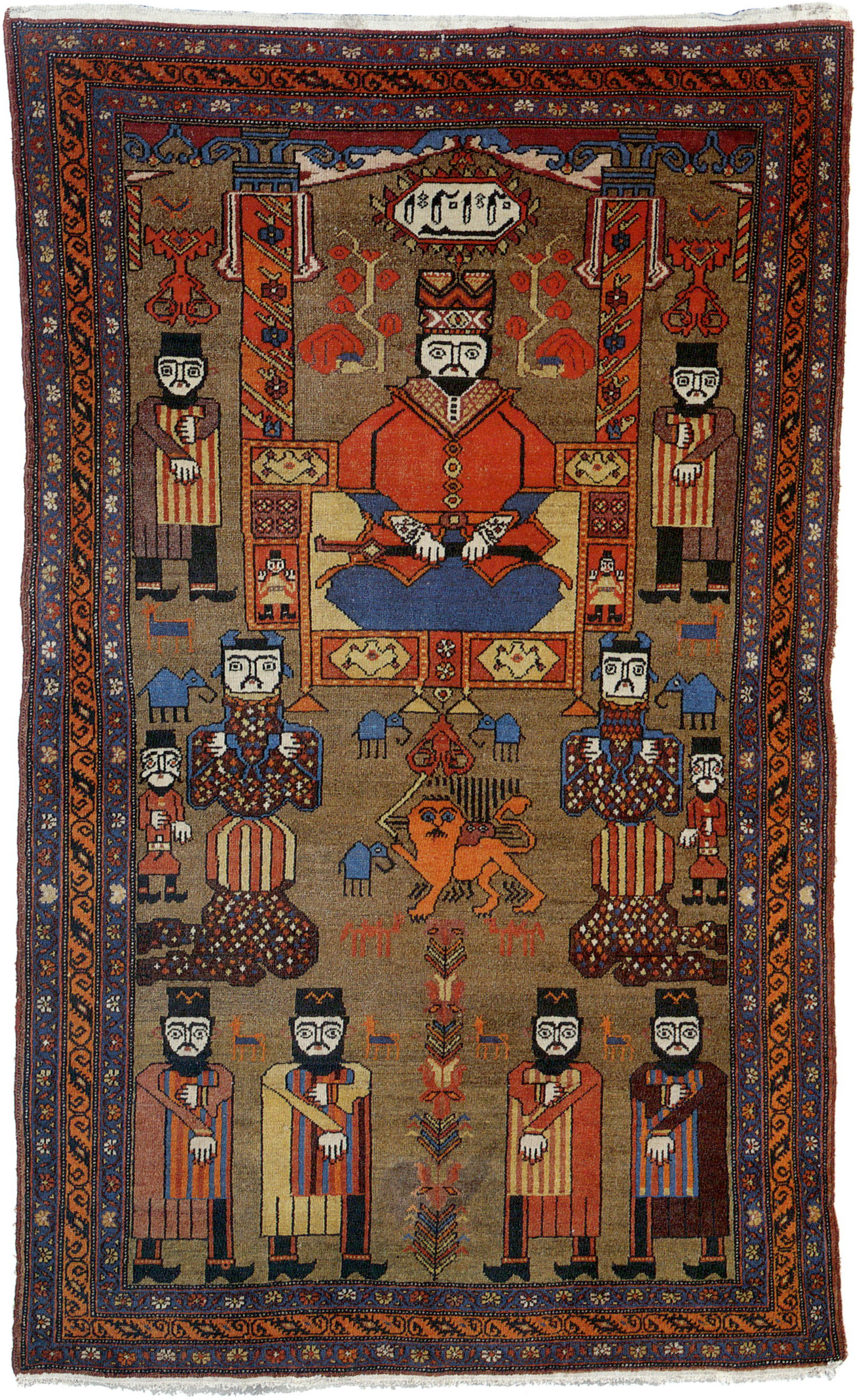

**6**

**Hushang Shah**
**Hamadan area**
**Inscription:** *Hushang Shah*
**Dated:** *1301 (1883 AD)*

Hushang Shah is depicted here in a squarish shape. He sits in a fashion reminiscent of the Buddha. His throne room is reduced to a coloured band underneath him and at each side. (For a discussion of the sources for the throne depicted here, see p. 18.) Also greatly simplified are the tiny suns above his shoulders which appear as Xs and flowers. The sun behind the lion (see p. 59, 60) in the centre of the rug is also affected by the weaver's tendency to simplification and stylization. Despite its age, the rug remains in excellent condition. (For general information about Hushang Shah, see p. 15 infra.)

*Size:* 6ft 8.25in x 4ft (204 x 122cm)
*Warp:* cotton, Z5S, undyed, undulating, 1 level
*Weft:* cotton, Z5S, undyed, 1 shoot, straight
*Pile:* wool, Z2 loosely plied, Sy1, 0.0625in (2mm)
*Knot count:* 10V x 9H = 90 per sq. in. (40V x 36H = 1440 per sq. dm.)
*Texture:* fairly soft, thin, flexible
*Sides:* wool, brown, remains of parallel wrapping around 4 warps
*Ends:* missing
*Colours* 10, Black, dark blue, light blue, red, orange, very dark brown, dark brown, light brown, buff, white

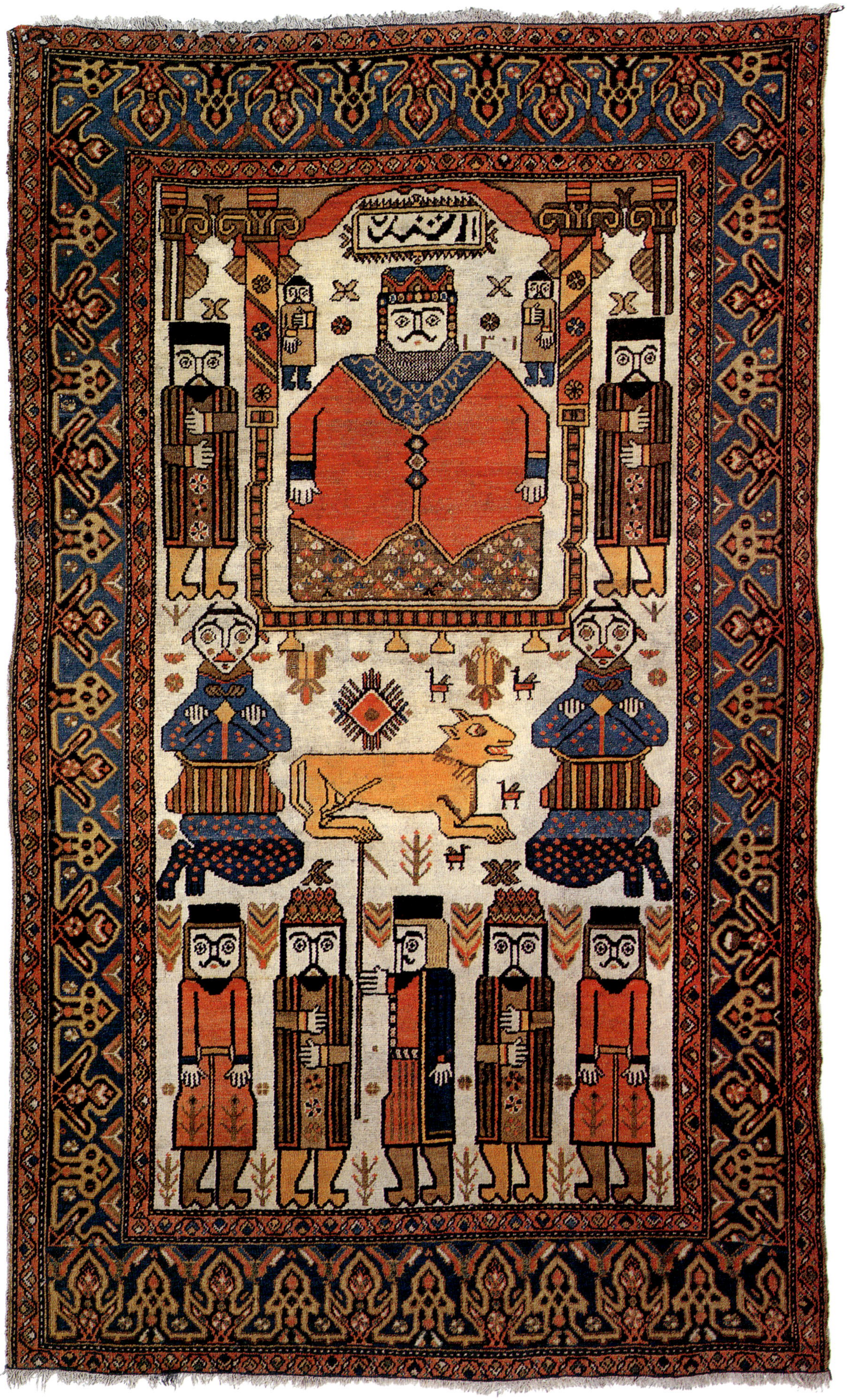

*Kings, Heroes and Lovers*

**7**

**Hushang Shah
Hamadan area
Inscription: *Hushang Shah*
Early 20th century**

A comparison of the various Hushang Shah rugs is interesting in that it reveals the different perceptions and sensitivities of their individual creators. The weaver of this particular rug may have used no. 6, or one very like it, for a model. The treatment of the suns with faces above Hushang Shah's shoulders as well as the one above the lion (see pp. 59,60) in the middle of the rug should be noticed. Usually the sun is depicted as a woman in Iranian art. Those, depicted here, however, each has a moustache. For a discussion of Hushang Shah, see p. 15 infra

*Size:* 6ft 7.5in x 4ft 2.5in (202 x 128cm)
*Warp:* cotton, Z6S, undyed, undulating, 1 level
*Weft:* cotton, Z4S, undyed, 1 shoot, straight
*Pile:* wool, Z2 loosely plied, Sy1, 0.1875in (4mm)
*Knot count:* 9V x 9H = 81 per sq. in. (36V x 36H = 1296 per sq. dm.)
*Texture:* fairly soft, fairly thick, flexible
*Sides:* not original
*Ends:* missing
*Colours* 11, black, blue-black, blue, green, light green, dark red, pink, yellow, brown, light brown, ivory

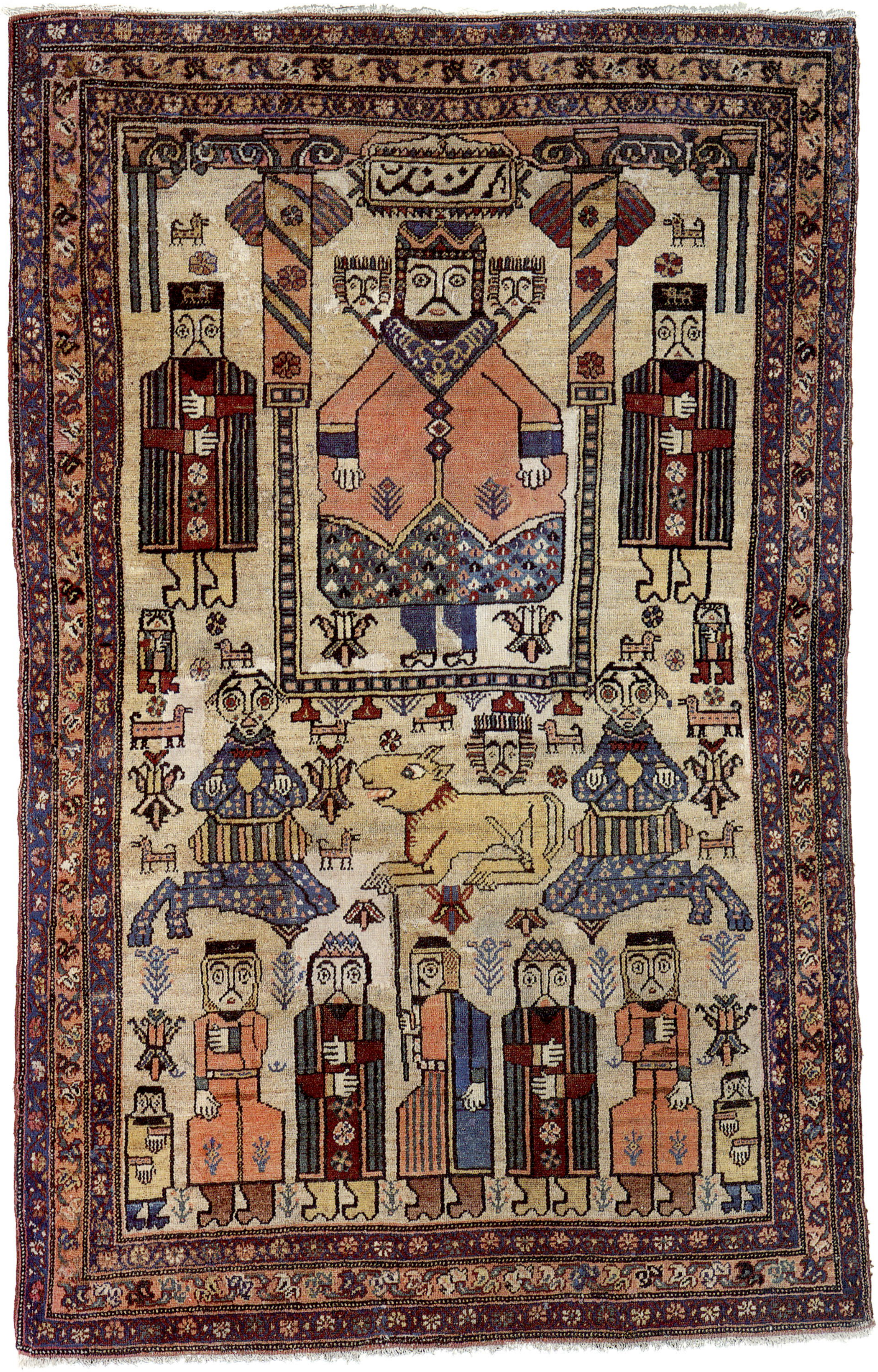

**8**

**Hushang Shah
Hamadan area
Inscription: *Hushang Shah*
Early 20th century**

Occasionally an element of variety in the Hushang Shah rugs occurs in the otherwise standard repertoire of depictions of this figure in rugs. The new element might even be the dimensions of the rug or, as in the case of this small piece, the substitution of a part of the picture for the whole. Here the weaver has shown only Hushang Shah and none of the usual surrounding figures. The way the king sits is like the pose of the main figure in the rug illustrated in fig. 47. That pose is the classic one used in portrayals of 'Ali, the Prophet Muhammad's son-in-law. Hushang Shah in rug no. 8 (like 'Ali in the rug illustrated in fig. 47) holds a sword, although it is somewhat hard to distinguish because of the lack of contrast in the colours of the sword and its background. The empty space on either side of Hushang Shah is filled with floral designs, spiral columns, and curtains. (For Hushang Shah, see p. 15 infra.)

*Size:* 3ft 8.5in x 2ft 8in (113 x 81cm)
*Warp:* cotton, Z5S, undyed, undulating, 1 level
*Weft:* cotton, Z5S, undyed, 1 shoot, straight
*Pile:* wool, Z2 loosely plied, Sy1, 0.25in (3mm)
*Knot count:* 10V x 10H = 100 per sq. in. (40V x 40H = 1600 per sq. dm.)
*Texture:* fairly soft, fairly thin, flexible
*Sides:* wool, undyed brown, parallel wrapping around 4 warps
*Ends:* 0.75in (2cm) weft-faced plain weave, undyed cotton
*Colours* 8, blue-black, dark blue, light green, red, pink, orange-yellow, dark brown, ivory

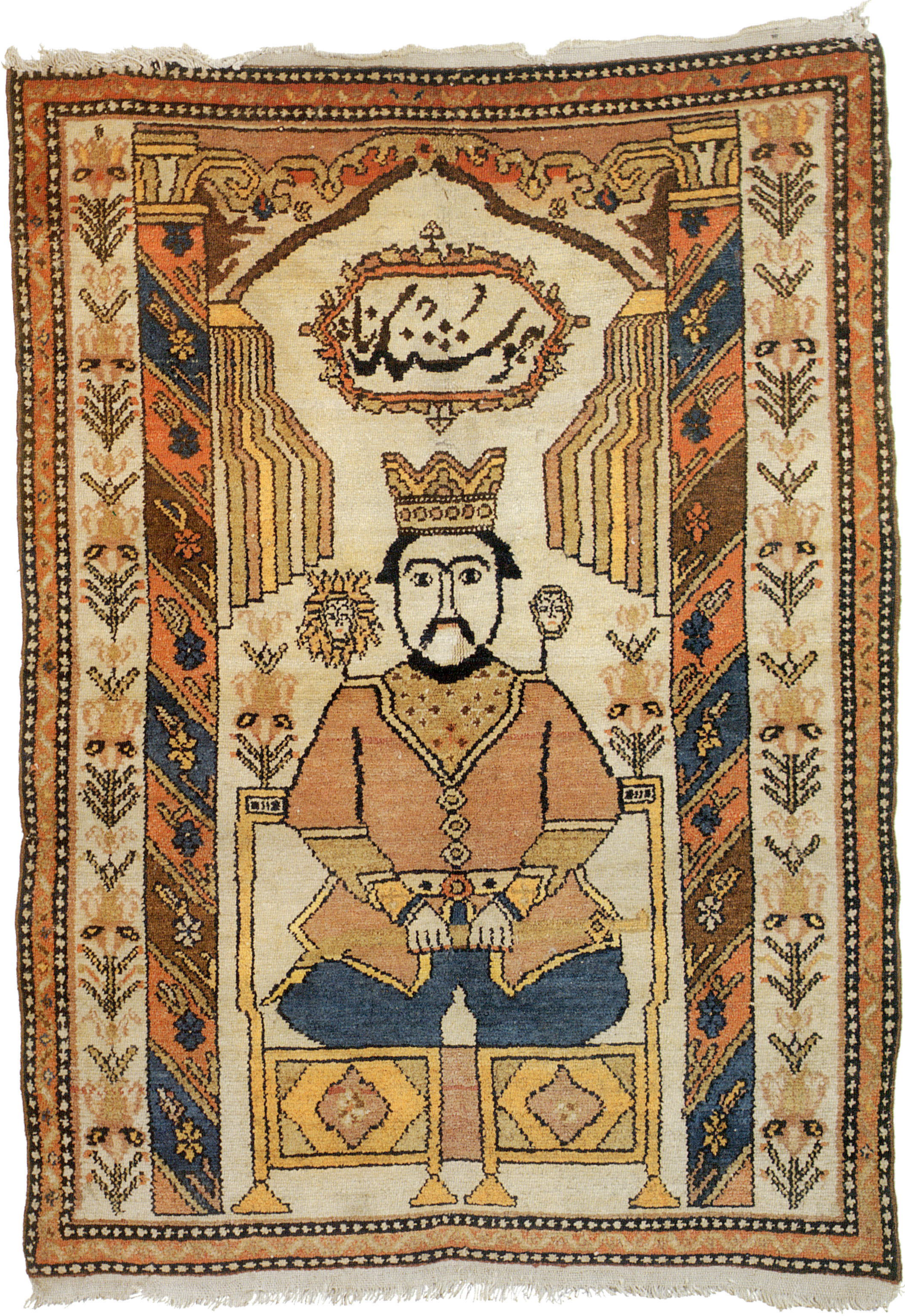

**9**

**Hushang Shah**
**Malayir area**
**Inscriptions:** *Hushang Shah,*
  *Ghaffar, work of Farza*
**Late 19th century**

The Hushang Shah of this rug closely resembles that of rug no. 10. The ruler seated on his throne is flanked by two of his viziers. The four men at the top must be the soldiers seen in other Hushang Shah rugs. They are wearing clothes typical of the Qajar period, which is also true of the two viziers and of Hushang Shah himself. Despite the age of the rug, the colours are still bright and alive. The side borders are missing but the field remains intact. Hushang Shah, with one arm placed on his knee and the other raised upwards, is the only figure that does not appear with a symmetrical counterpart. Even the writing in the centre and the bottom is bilaterally symmetrical. The inscription 'work of Farza' may designate the weaver or the person who had the rug woven or provided the cartoon. (For Hushang Shah, see p. 15 infra.)

*Size:* 4ft 9.125in x 2ft 9in (145 x 84cm)
*Warp:* cotton, Z4S, undyed, undulating, 1 level
*Weft:* cotton, Z3S, undyed, 1 shoot, straight
*Pile:* wool, Z2 loosely plied, Sy1, 0.03-0.0625in (1mm)
*Knot count:* 10V x 9H = 90 per sq. in. (40V x 36H = 1440 per sq. dm.)
*Texture:* coarse, fairly thin, flexible
*Sides:* not original
*Ends:* missing
*Colours* 8, blue-black, blue, red, pink, brown, light brown, buff, ivory

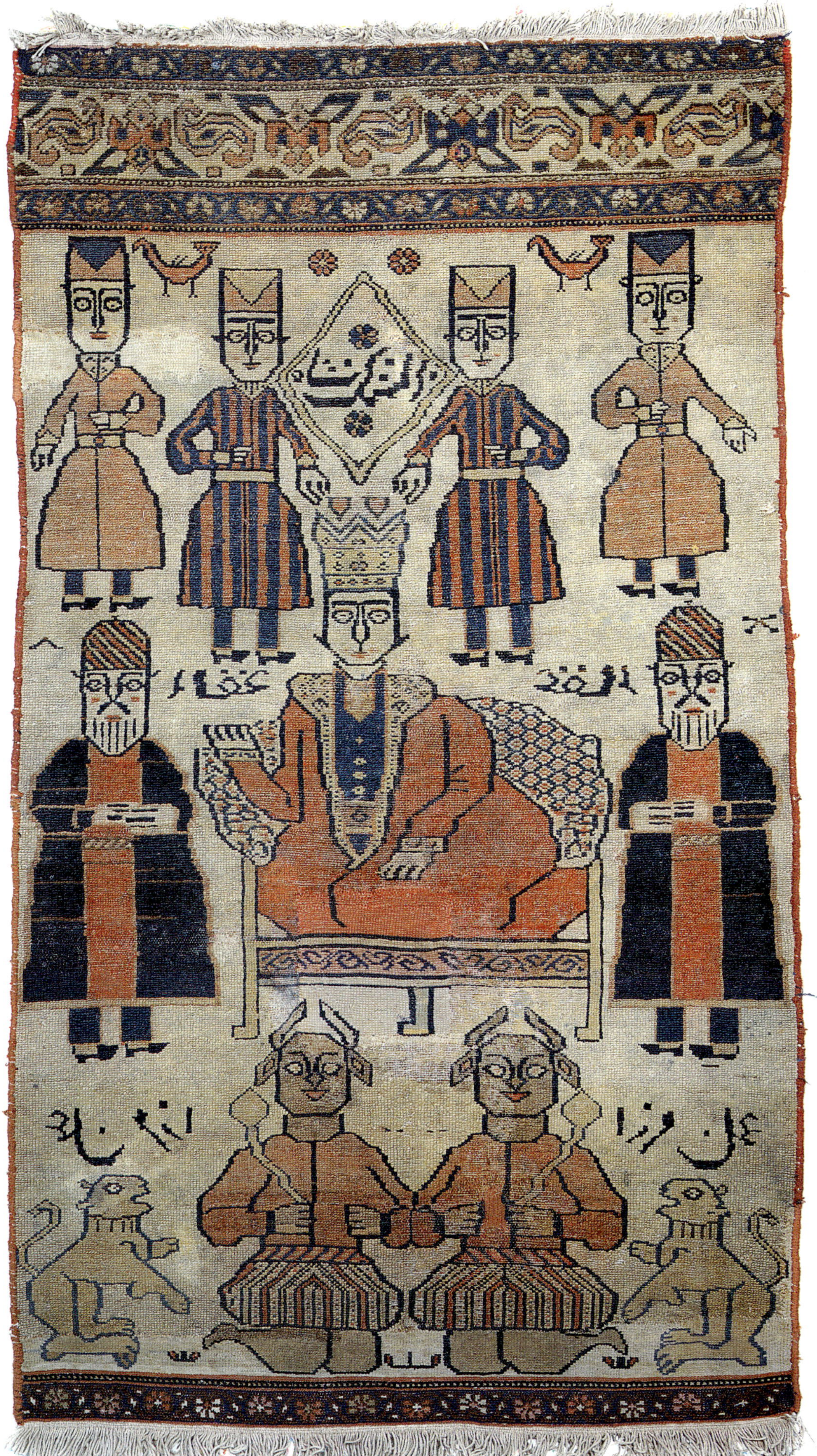

*Kings, Heroes and Lovers*

**10**

**Hushang Shah**
**Malayir area**
**Inscription:** ***Hushang Shah***
**Mid-19th century**

This rug exhibits a different expression of the Hushang Shah theme. From the point of view of both form and space this example is noteworthy. Hushang Shah's court has been reduced to a throne and cushion with nothing remaining of the audience hall, columns, curtains, and soldiers. All that is shown are the shah and his two viziers who have childlike faces and clothing typical of the Qajar period. Their youthful faces seem to be echoed in the happy, laughing faces of the demons who look more like slave boys at the Qajar court than frightening monsters. The lions on either side of the demons have been transformed into small playful creatures. All these elements have produced a happy scene of the Hushang Shah story enacted by children. (For Hushang Shah, see p. 15 infra.)

*Size:* 3ft 4.25in x 2ft 9in (102 x 84cm)
*Warp:* cotton, Z4S, undyed, undulating, 1 level
*Weft:* cotton, Z2S, undyed, 1 shoot, straight
*Pile:* wool, Z2 loosely plied, Sy1, 0.0625in (2mm)
*Knot count:* 11V x 10H = 110 per sq. in. (44V x 40H = 1760 per sq. dm.)
*Texture:* coarse, thin, very flexible
*Sides:* not original
*Ends:* missing
*Colours* 9, black, blue, dark brown, red, pink, light orange, light yellow, light brown, ivory

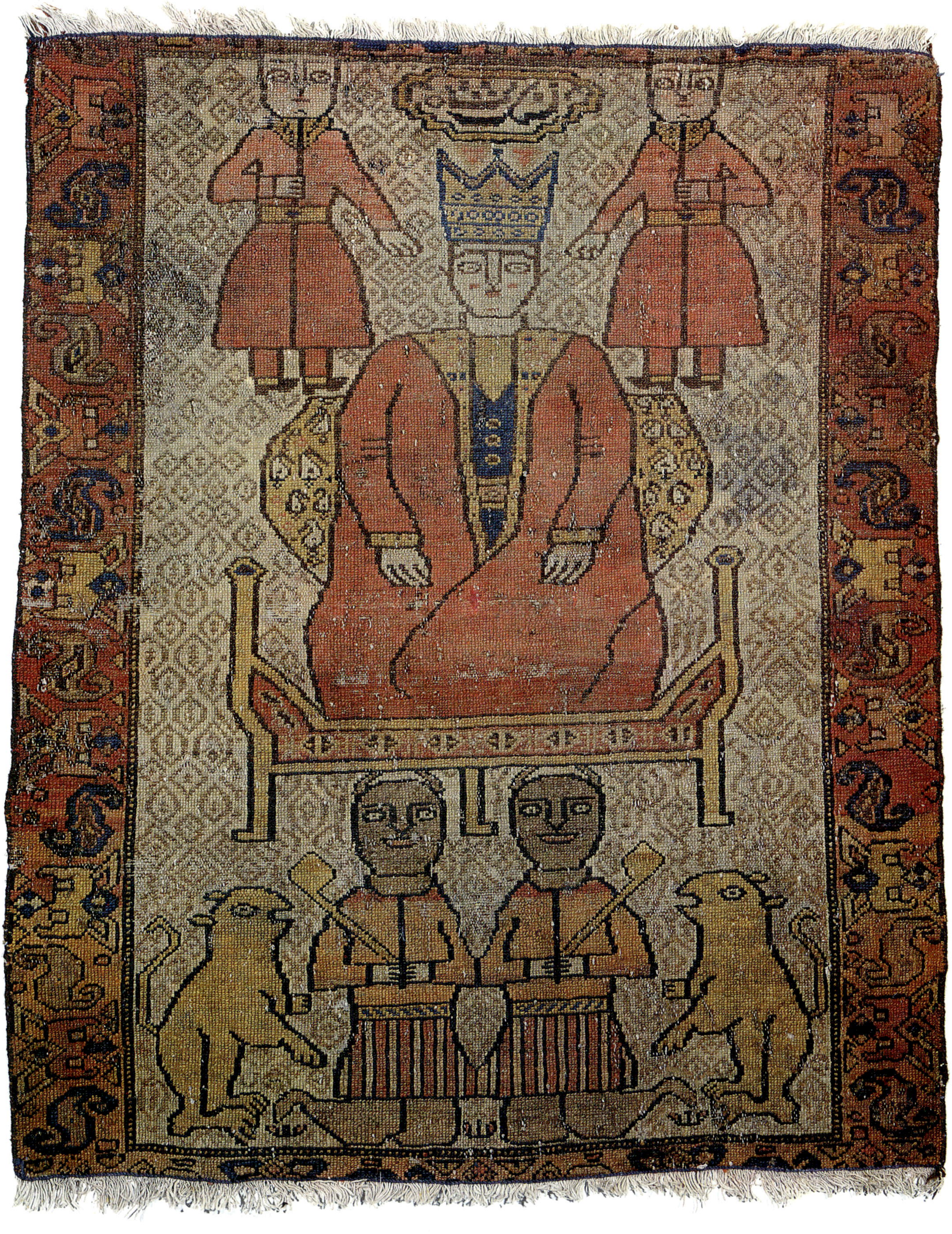

*Kings, Heroes and Lovers*

**11**

**Hushang Shah
Qashqa'i
Inscription: *Hushang Shah [in mirror image]*
Late 19th century**

Although the subject of Hushang Shah has been popular with rug weavers of the villages of western Iran, especially in the province of Hamadan and the Malayir area, it was seldom depicted by nomadic weavers. This is the only example of this subject made by Qashqa'i weavers that I have seen. It is, however, one of the finest examples of Qashqa'i weaving, with respect to quality of wool, dyes, and fineness of weave (knot count). Although the rendering of the king's head is similar to that in a *qalamkar* curtain (see fig. 11, and p. 10), there are some indications that the subject of this rug was taken from a city rug, possibly an example from Kerman. Among these indications is the tendency of the weaver to give a naturalistic appearance to the portrait by shading to give an effect of depth and by curvilinear outlines. These are features of city weaving but not of nomadic or village work. Also, on the left side (below the centre) there is a medallion with the picture of an Iranian hero (possibly Suhrab, see p. 31), and on the right side, half way up, a hunting dog is depicted running after a mountain goat. These, too, are so naturalistically portrayed that they seem to indicate that the weaver used a city rug as a model. In any case, even a cursory look at the rug shows the weaver's success in giving the subject a Qashqa'i character. The figures of the soldiers at the bottom, like those in rug no. 1, are reminiscent of reliefs at Persepolis (see fig. 10), which the Qashqa'i pass during their biannual migrations. (For Hushang Shah, see p. 15 infra.)

*Size:* 7ft 10.5in x 4ft 11in (240 x 152cm)
*Warp:* wool, Z2S, undyed ivory, straight, semi-depressed
*Weft:* wool, Z2S, undyed ivory, 2 shoots: the first straight, the second undulating
*Pile:* wool, Z2 loosely plied, Sy2, 0.0625in (2mm)
*Knot count:* 15V x 12H = 180 knots per sq. in. (60V x 48H = 2880 per sq. dm.)
*Texture:* very soft, very thin, flexible
*Sides:* wool, red and blue, parallel wrapping around 5 warps
*Ends:* lower: 3.125in (8cm) balanced plain weave, undyed wool, decorated with 1 row of weft twining
upper: 0.375in (1cm) balanced plain weave, undyed wool, with warp ends twisted in bunches with the ends knotted
*Colours* 10, very dark blue, dark blue, dark green, dark brown, light brown, red brown, dark pink, dark yellow, yellow, ivory

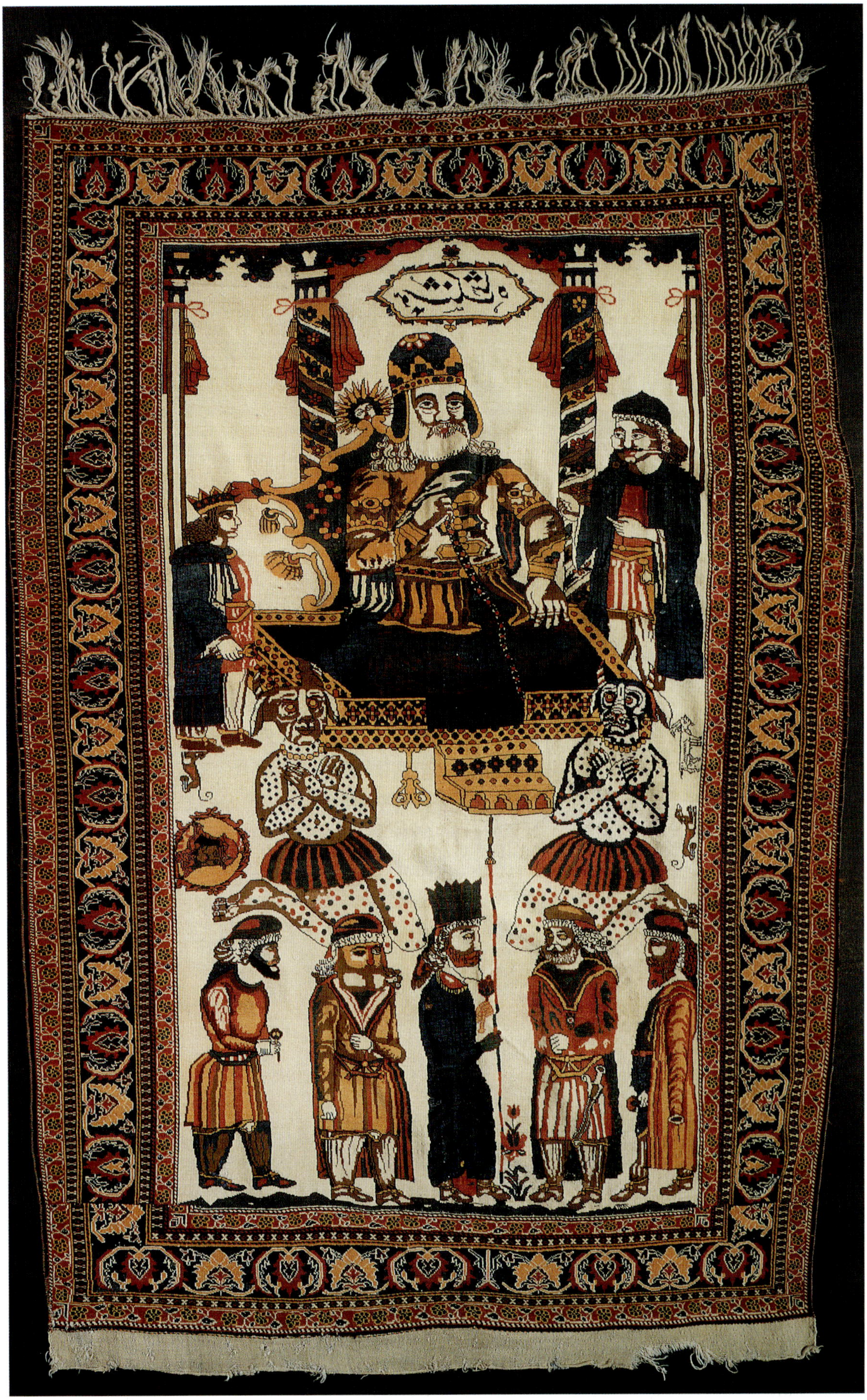

## 12

**Hushang Shah**
**Baluch of Khurasan**
**Inscription:** *Hushang Shah*
**Early 20th century**

This rug is an example of outstanding quality in Baluch weaving. It is in perfect condition and looks as if it had just been removed from the loom. It was apparently always treated with special care and received little, if any, use on the floor and was only hung on a wall or used as a curtain. Everything about it is of excellent quality: pure, soft wool; clear, bright colours; and masterfully regular weave. For symmetry the weaver repeated the lower row of soldiers at the top. (The soldiers are similar to those in rugs nos. 1 and 11, all based on reliefs at Persepolis, seen in fig. 10.) Such successful repetition is seen in some of the other long Hushang Shah rugs. The reversed inscription 'Hushang Shah' indicates that this was copied from the back (where it would read more clearly) of another Hushang Shah rug. Camels, human figures, birds, plants, and other motifs in the field add to the appeal of this rug. (For Hushang Shah, see p. 15 infra.)

*Size:* 8ft 6.5in x 4ft 7in (260 x 140cm)
*Warp:* wool, Z2S, undyed, ivory, straight, semi-depressed
*Weft:* wool, Z2S, undyed dark brown, 2 shoots: the first straight, the second undulating
*Pile:* wool, Z2 loosely plied, As3, 0.25in (7mm)
*Knot count:* 10V x 9H = 90 per sq. in. (40V x 36H = 1440 per sq. dm.)
*Texture:* soft, thin, very flexible
*Sides:* wool, dark pink and green, 2 'cords,' each wrapped around 4 warps
*Ends:* 1.1875in (3cm) weft-faced plain weave, wool; red, green, blue; warp ends knotted in groups
*Colours* 8, blue-black, dark blue, dark green, dark red, light red, dark brown, mustard, ivory

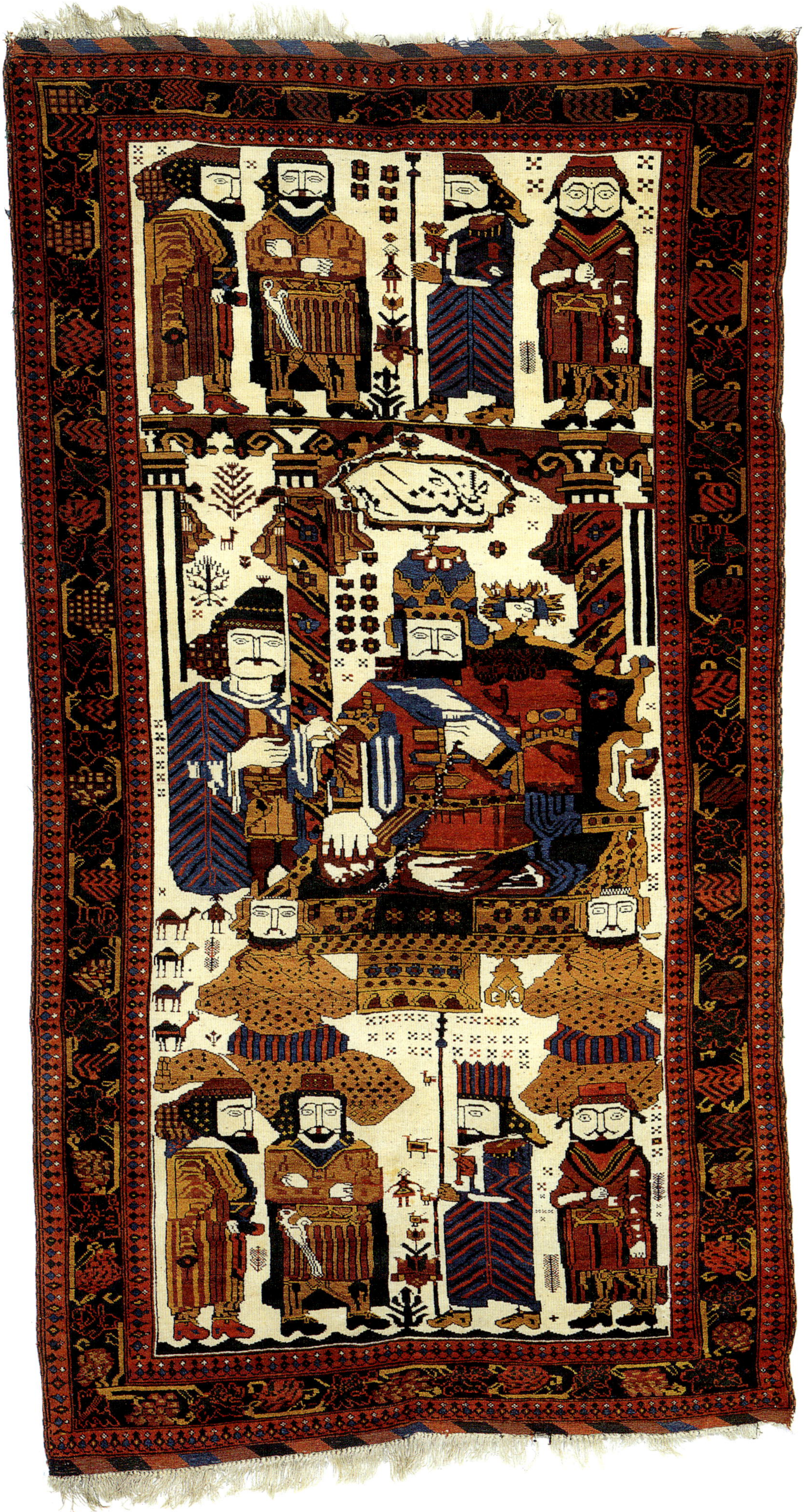

*Kings, Heroes and Lovers*

**13**

**Xerxes I**
**Qashqa'i**
**Inscription:** *Jan Khan Qashqa'i*
**Early 19th century**

Based on a scene carved in relief in stone at the entrance of the Palace of One Hundred Gates at Persepolis, Xerxes I sits on the royal throne (see figs. 13-16). At the top of the rug the name Jan-i Khan Qashqa'i is written. Jan-i Khan in the year 1234 (1819 AD), by order of Fath 'Ali Shah, became the first official Il Khan (overall chief) of the Qashqa'i tribe in Fars province (see p. 19 infra). While the stone relief prototype is uncoloured, wherever possible the weaver gave colour to the forms in her rug. For example, in the upper part, where the *farvahar* (winged symbol of Ahura Mazda, the central figure in the pantheon of Zoroastrian gods) design is found, all twelve colours seen in this weaving are employed; or again, each fold of the clothes of each one of the four small figures immediately under the king is done in a different colour. From every point of view, and especially from that of the virtuosity of the colours, this rug is a valuable example of early Qashqa'i weaving. Some of the colours, such as the bright red that appears in small amounts here and there, reach a brightness that is seldom achieved with natural dyestuffs. However, there is no doubt that none of the colours of this rug is synthetic, for the date of entry of synthetic dyes into Iran is well known to have been during the reign of Nasir al-Din Shah and the weaving of this rug precedes this date by a large margin. (For Xerxes I, see p. 19.)

*Size:* 6ft 8in x 4ft 7.5in (203 x 141cm)
*Warp:* wool, Z2S, undyed ivory, nearly straight, semi-depressed
*Weft:* wool, Z1, red; 2 shoots: the first straight, the second undulating
*Pile:* wool, Z2 loosely plied, As2, 0.0625in (2mm)
*Knot count:* 12V x 12H = 144 per sq. in. (48V x 48H = 2304 per sq. dm.)
*Texture:* very soft, very thin, very flexible
*Sides:* wool, green and red, parallel wrapping around 6 warps
*Ends:* missing
*Colours* 12, blue-black, dark blue, light blue, dark green, light green, olive green, dark red, flame red, dark brown, chocolate brown, buff, ivory

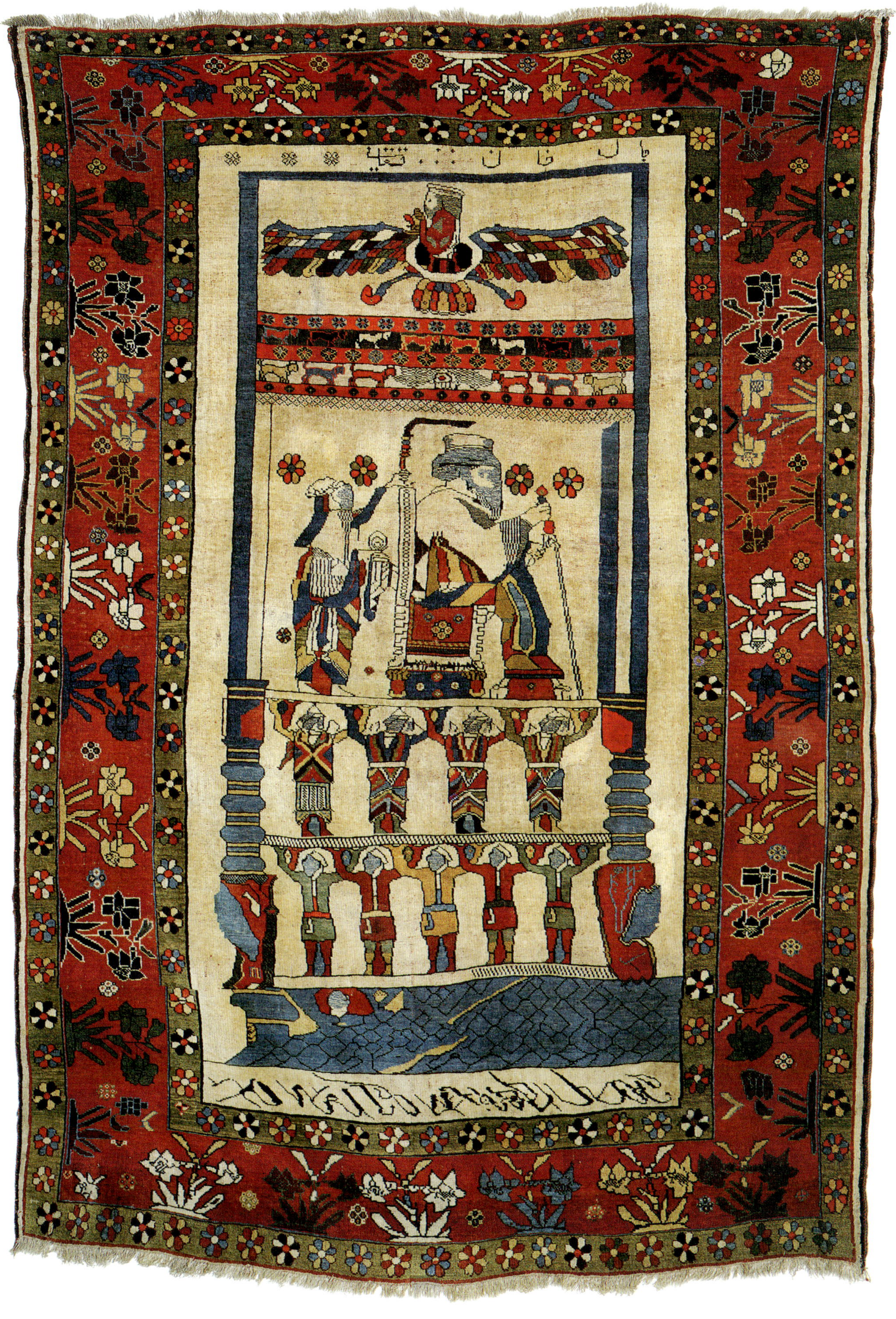

*Kings, Heroes and Lovers*

**14**

**Shapur I**
**Jozan**
**Inscription:** *Shapur*
**Late 19th century**

The centrally placed figure in this rug bears a striking resemblance to the large statue of Shapur I in the cave of Shapur near Kazerun, in southern Iran (see figs. 17, 18, 19; for information about Shapur I, see p. 21 infra). This resemblance is seen not only in a comparison of certain details of both (such as the hair, crown, and placement of the arms) but also in the monumentality and dignity that both share. Furthermore, pleasant, attractive colours greatly enhance the appearance of this rug. This is probably the most successful execution of the Shapur motif I have seen. Quite justifiably, the weavers of Jozan enjoy the reputation of producing the finest rugs in the Arak area. Geographically, Jozan is considered to be part of the Malayir province, but its proximity to Saruq helps give its rug designs a great similarity to those of the better-known Saruq region. Contrary to what earlier authors have written, I have found from analysing the knots used in older pictorial rugs from those two villages that it is inaccurate to attribute rugs to one or the other village solely on the basis of whether they have symmetrical or asymmetrical knots. This example, from Jozan, has symmetrical knots; but nos. 17 and 38, which also have symmetrical knots, are from Saruq. Although more Saruq rugs are woven with asymmetrical knots, certain pictorial rugs with symmetrical knots have colours, materials, and structure (apart from the type of knot) characteristic of Saruq as distinguished from typical Jozan products.

*Size:* 5ft 0.25in x 3ft 7.75in (153 x 111cm)
*Warp:* cotton, Z6S, undyed, straight, 2 levels
*Weft:* cotton, 2 shoots: the first, Z8S, undyed, straight; the second, Z3S, blue, undulating
*Pile:* wool, Z2 loosely plied, Sy2, 0.25in (3mm)
*Knot count:* 19V x 13H = 47 per sq. in. (76V x 52H = 3952 per sq. dm.)
*Texture:* very soft, thin, very stiff
*Sides:* wool, dark blue, parallel wrapping around 4 warps
*Ends:* missing
*Colours* 15, blue-black, dark blue, light blue, turquoise, dark green, jasper green, orange-red, dark pink, dark orange, orange, lemon yellow, black-brown, chocolate brown, buff, white

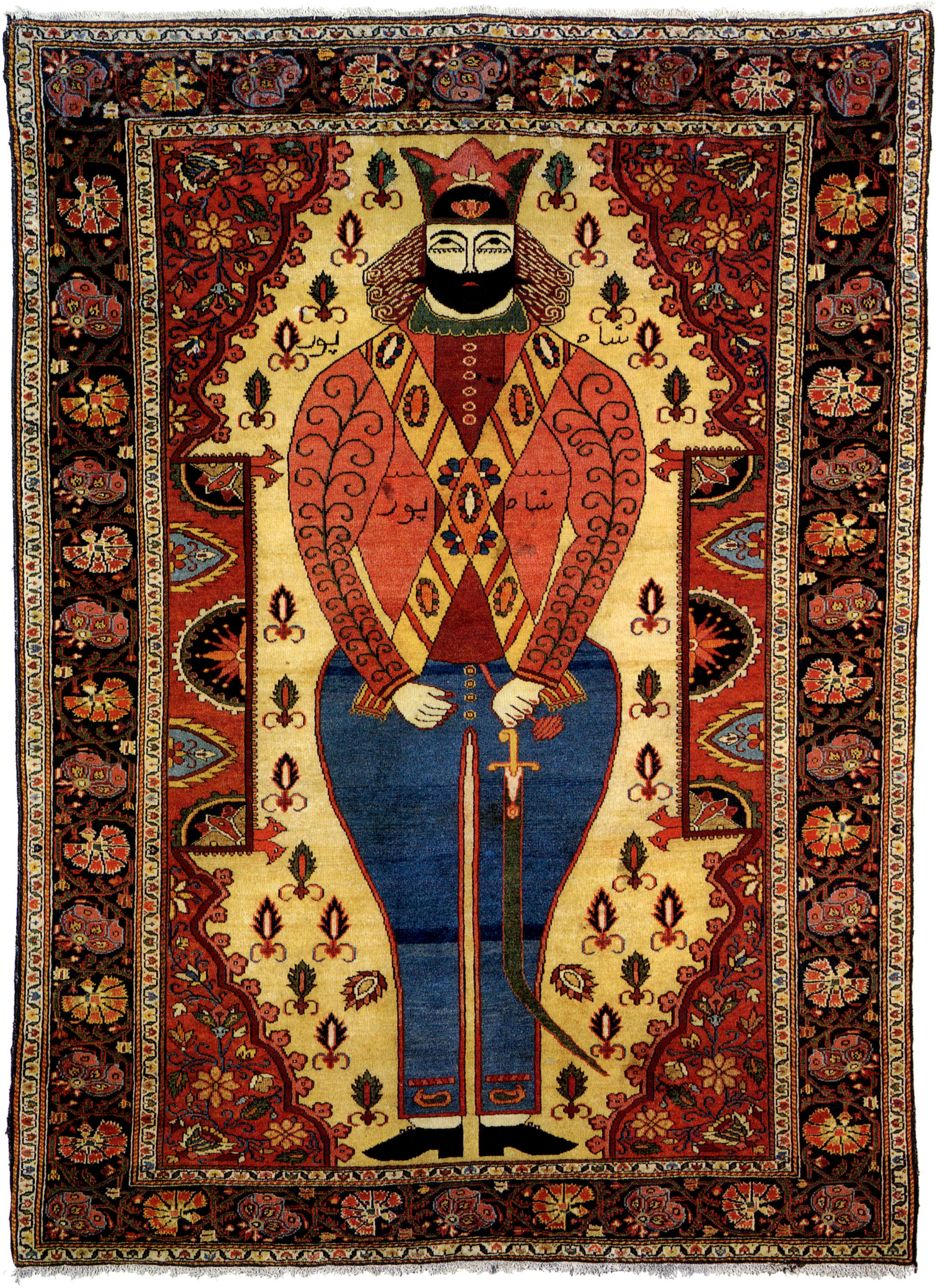

## 15

**Shapur I**
**Saruq**
**Early 20th century**

This is yet another example of the wide range in treatment of a single subject and composition of which weavers of the Arak area are capable. At first sight this rug appears to differ considerably from the other Shapur rugs, but after careful comparison one can relate it to the others and to the original inspiration—the mental image of Shapur of which each weaver has a different perception. (For Shapur I, see p. 21 infra.)

Weavers occasionally alter certain parts of a design to such a degree that they affect the appearance of the entire figure. For example, the weaver of this particular rug, in order to show the shah's hair more clearly, depicts it as resting on his shoulders in wide bands, at the ends of which are circles to convey the idea of curliness. Although this handling of the hair tends to emphasize that feature over the size of his body, the figure has a marked degree of monumentality, which gives a special quality to the small rug.

*Size:* 2ft 6.75in x 1ft 10.5in (78 x 57cm)
*Warp:* cotton, Z15S, undyed, straight, 2 levels
*Weft:* cotton, Z7S, undyed, 2 shoots: the first straight, the second undulating
*Pile:* wool, Z2 loosely plied, As3, 0.25in (3mm)
*Knot count:* 15V x 13H = 195 per sq. in. (60V x 52H = 3120 per sq. dm.)
*Texture:* soft, thin, stiff
*Sides:* wool, red, parallel wrapping around 4 warps
*Ends:* missing
*Colours* 10, blue-black, dark blue, light blue, olive, red, dark pink, dark orange, mustard yellow, brown, white

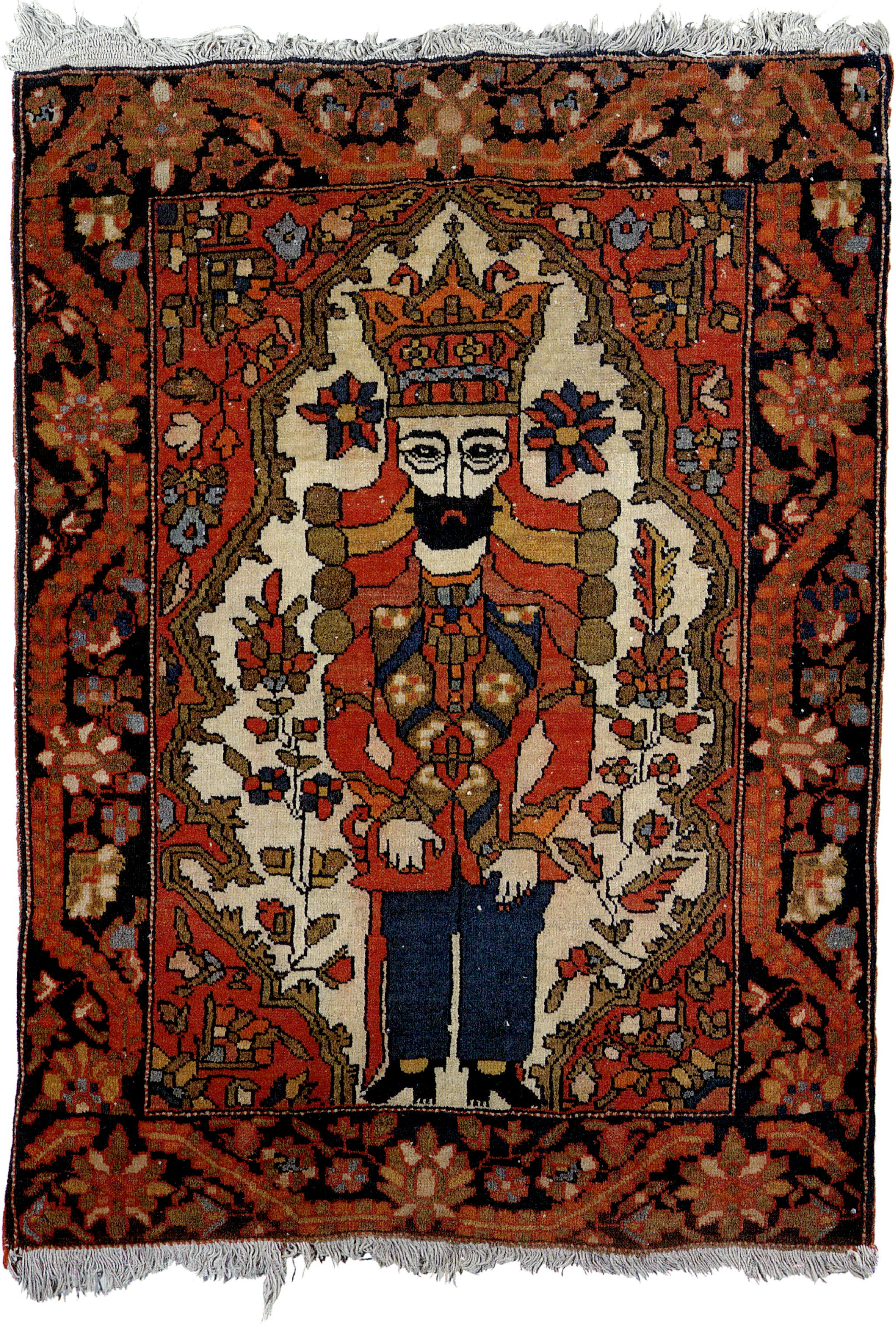

*Kings, Heroes and Lovers*

**16**

**Shapur**
**Saruq**
**Inscription:** *Shapur, ordered by Habibullah, 1296 (1879 AD)*

This is the only rug in this collection in which Shapur is seen seated. Interestingly enough, he is seated in a kneeling position, in the style of a Muslim caliph resting against a cushion rather than standing, as the pre-Islamic Sasanian monarch Shapur is usually shown in rugs. (The over-all composition may have been inspired by the drawing showing Shapur seated, in Jalal al-Din Mirza's *Namah-yi Khusrawan* [Book of Kings] published in Vienna in 1880, see fig. 20.) Also, his beard and crown closely resemble those of Shapur as shown in other rugs depicting this king. (The bulb-shape centre of Shapur's crown in the statue in fig. 17 has large corrugations shown in such a way as to suggest that this part of the crown was made of fabric.) It would seem that when the weaver reached the crown and found it rather like a dome of a mosque, she placed two minarets on either side of it and on each minaret seated a bird. (For Shapur I, see p. 21 infra.)

The rug was ordered by a man named Habibullah. Given the age of this rug indicated by its legible date it is possible that it was made for the Habib al-Sultan of rug no. 40. Rigid symmetry in the field is alleviated by the use of two cypress trees on one side and a weeping willow on the other.

*Size:* 2ft 0.5in x 2ft 5.5in (62 x 75cm)
*Warp:* cotton, Z14S, undyed, straight, 2 levels
*Weft:* cotton, Z14S, undyed, and Z5S, light blue, 2 shoots: the first straight, the second undulating
*Pile:* wool, Z2 loosely plied, As4, 0.25in (6mm)
*Knot count:* 16V x 18H = 288 per sq. in. (64V x 72H = 4608 per sq. dm.)
*Texture:* soft, fairly thin, very stiff
*Sides:* wool, black, parallel wrapping around 3 warps
*Ends:* lower: 0.75in (2cm) weft-faced plain weave, undyed cotton, decorated with one row of weft twining in green and red wool
upper: 0.75in (2cm) weft-faced plain weave, undyed cotton, decorated with 1 row of weft twining in pink and very light green wool
*Colours* 9, black, blue-black, dark blue, blue green, light green, deep red, pink, dark brown, ivory

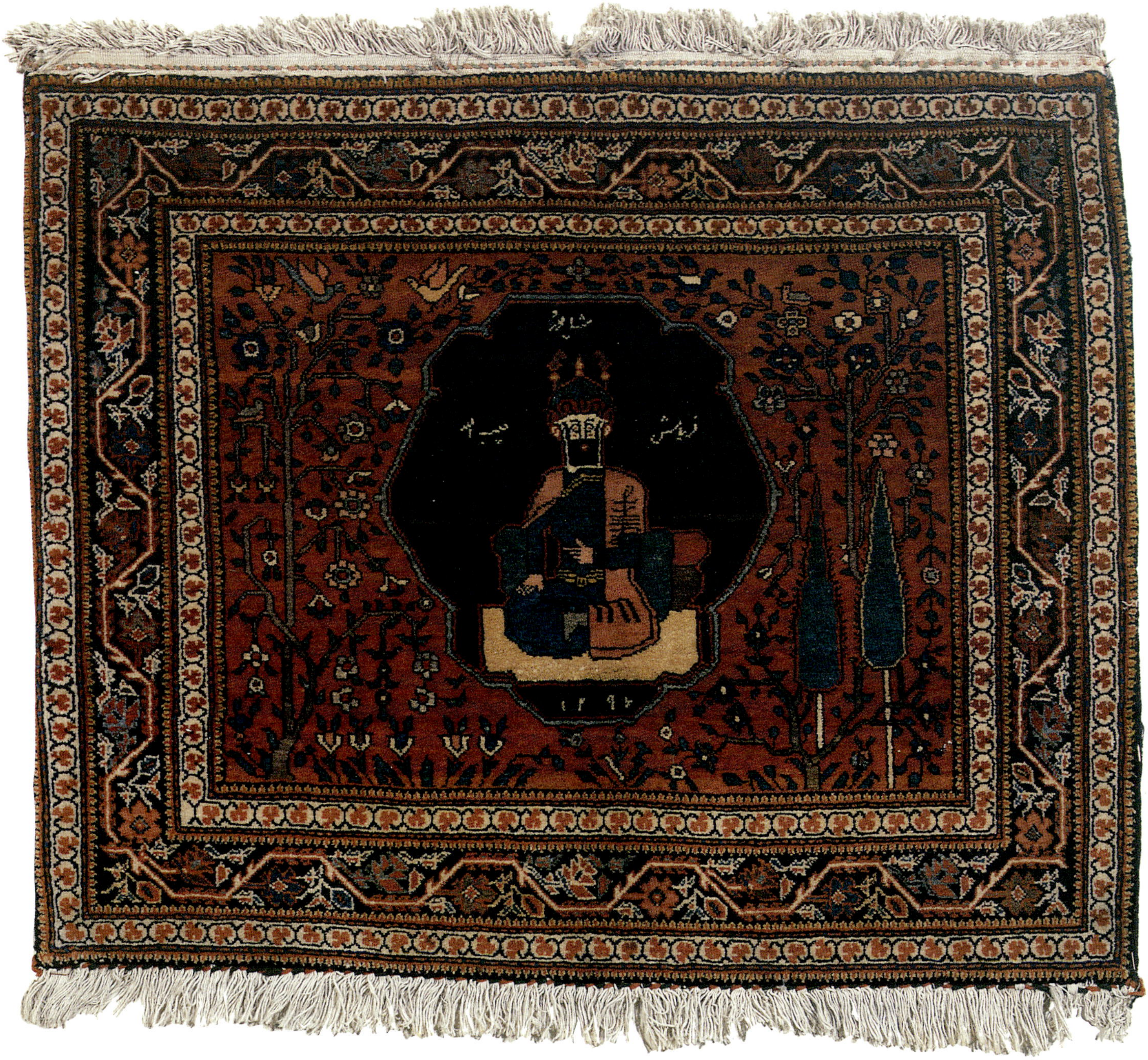

*Kings, Heroes and Lovers*

**17**

**Shapur I**
**Saruq**
**Inscription:** *Shapur, Shah 'Abbas, designed [by] Muhammad 'Ali the Carpet Designer [in the] year 1331 (1913 AD)*

Very surprisingly we encounter the name of Shah 'Abbas at the bottom of the rug under the feet of the king. The figure here bears no resemblance to the Safavid ruler Shah 'Abbas I and can only be the Sasanian monarch Shapur (cf. figs. 17-19), whose name appears in the open space under both arms. Perhaps the weaver really wanted to weave the likeness of Shah 'Abbas but had to settle for Shapur for lack of a portrait of Shah 'Abbas. Besides containing the features characteristic of other rugs depicting Shapur, this one is marked by a very engaging face as well. (See discussion of symmetrical knots in Saruq rugs in the entry for rug no. 14; see also rug no. 38. For Shapur I, see p. 21 infra.)

*Size:* 4ft 9in x 3ft 4.5in (144 x 103cm)
*Warp:* cotton, Z16S, undyed, straight, 2 levels
*Weft:* cotton, Z12S, undyed, 2 shoots: the first straight, the second undulating
*Pile:* wool, Z2 loosely plied, Sy2, 0.25in (3mm)
*Knot count:* 15V x 15H = 225 per sq. in. (60V x 60V = 3600 per sq. dm.)
*Texture:* soft, thin, very stiff
*Sides:* wool, undyed ivory, parallel wrapping around 4 warps
*Ends:* lower: 1.1875in (3cm) weft-faced plain weaver, undyed cotton, decorated with one row of weft twining in yellow and orange wool
upper: missing
*Colours* 14, blue-black, blue, light blue, green, very light green, dark red, red, pink, orange, yellow, dark brown, brown, light brown, ivory

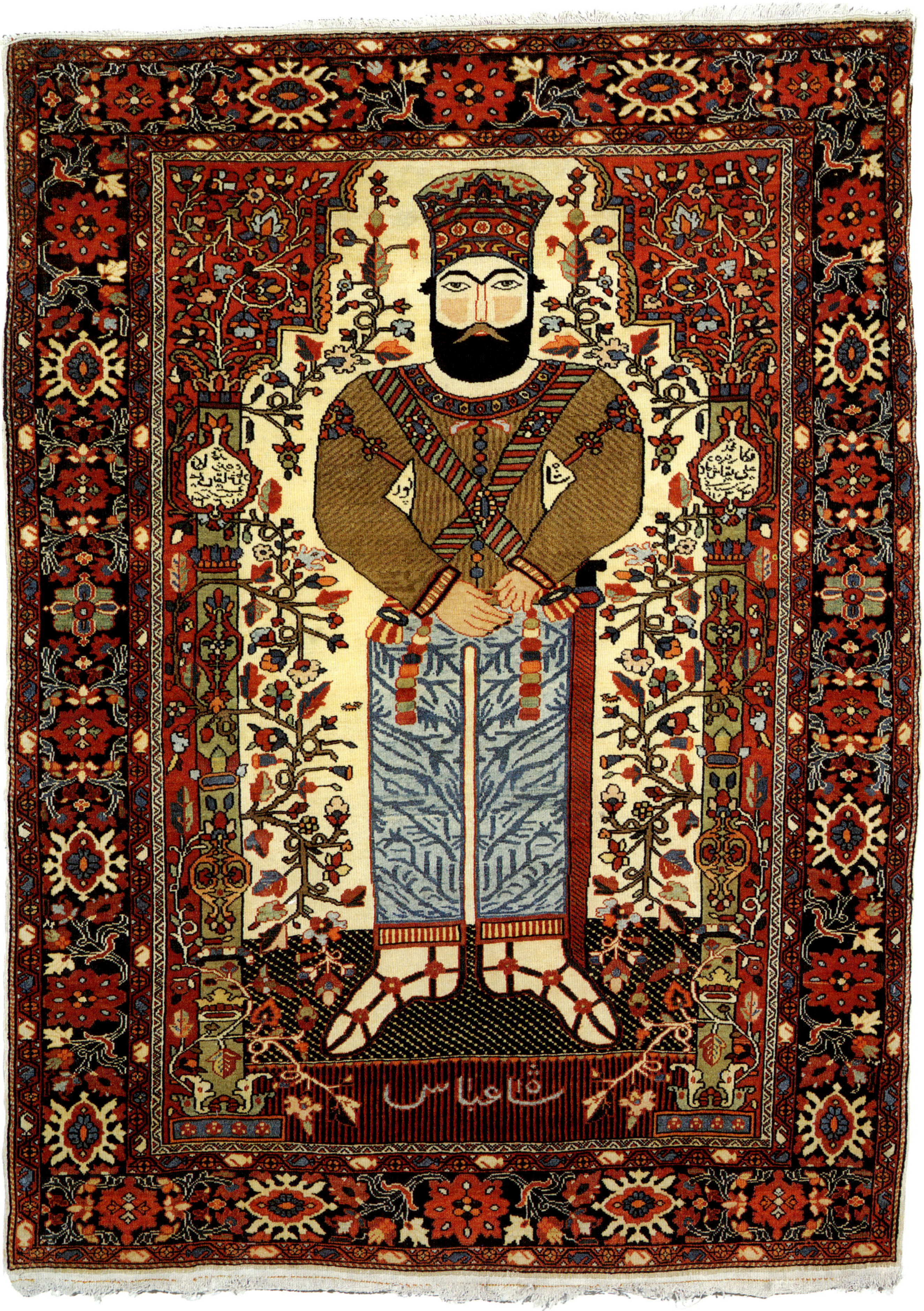
شاه عباس

## 18

**Shapur I**
**Saruq**
**Inscription:** *Shapur*
**Early 20th century**

The considerable similarity between this rug and rug no. 19 raises a significant problem, which is related to the individual interpretations by their weavers. While both weavers generally followed one model and subject, they each used different details, which gives each rug an individual character despite the similarity of the main subject. Although both rugs were woven in the same area and during the same period, there are variations in such details as the faces, crowns, shoes, and patterns in the clothes.

Shapur's face in this rug exhibits a special beauty. the weaver has given a greater emphasis to his face by showing his large eyes, long eyelashes, rosy cheeks, small mouth, and full beard. Furthermore, the weaver has skilfully chosen the colour blue to show the moustache (on a dark blue beard) to better advantage. (For Shapur I, see p. 21 infra.)

*Size:* 6ft 2in x 4ft (188 x 122cm)
*Warp:* cotton, Z14S, undyed, straight, 2 levels
*Weft:* cotton, Z14S, 2 shoots, undyed except about 19.75in (50cm) at the top of the rug, which are dyed blue; the first shoot straight, the second undulating
*Pile:* wool, Z2 loosely plied, As3, 1.1875in (3mm)
*Knot count:* 17V x 16H = 272 per sq. in. (68V x 64H = 6152 per sq. dm.)
*Texture:* very soft, thin, very stiff
*Sides:* wool, deep pink, parallel wrapping around 4 warps
*Ends:* missing
*Colours* 15, blue-black, dark blue, green, turquoise green, light turquoise, olive, light olive, red, pink, dark brown, reddish brown, orange, mustard yellow, yellow, ivory

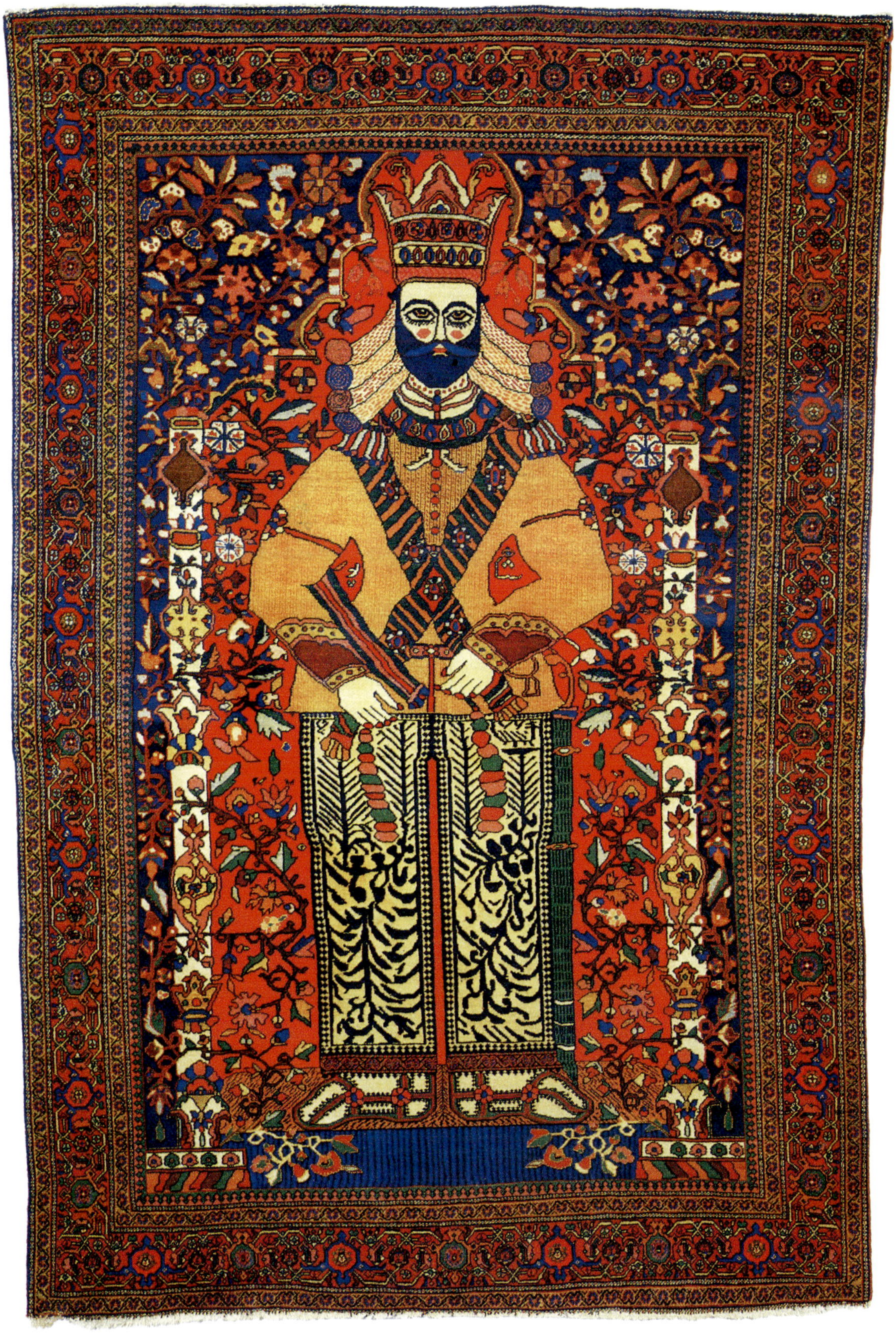

Kings, Heroes and Lovers

**19**

**Shapur I**
**Saruq? Bijar?**
**Inscription:** *Shapur, designed [by] Muhammad 'Ali . . . [remainder illegible] 1333 (1915 AD)*

Although at first sight the figure of Shapur seen here resembles the portrayals of Shapur of some other rugs, especially no. 17, there is in fact a difference in conception and feeling here that distinguishes this example from the rest. This is one of the most successful rugs depicting this ruler, an example that contains great richness of colours and skilful drawing of design. Notice in Shapur's clothes the degree of abstraction that the play of lines reaches and the delicacy with which branches of flowers enter the stripes under his feet.

It is not impossible that this rug was copied from one like no. 17, because it bears a signature similar to that of no. 17, but less legible. There are, however, many differences between the two. Among them is a discrepancy in *Size:* this carpet is larger than the other by about one-fourth. (For Shapur I, see p. 21 infra.)

*Size:* 6ft 6in x 4ft 3.25in (198 x 130cm)
*Warp:* cotton, Z14S, undyed, straight, 2 levels
*Weft:* cotton, Z10S, undyed; Z4S, blue, 2 shoots: the first undyed, straight; the second blue, undulating
*Pile:* wool, Z2 loosely plied, As4, 0.1875in (4mm)
*Texture:* soft, thin, very stiff
*Sides:* wool, dark blue, parallel wrapping around 4 warps
*Ends:* missing
*Colours* 16, blue-black, dark blue, turquoise, light blue, emerald green, light green, dark olive green, deep red, bright red, orange, yellow, pink, dark brown, light brown, buff, ivory

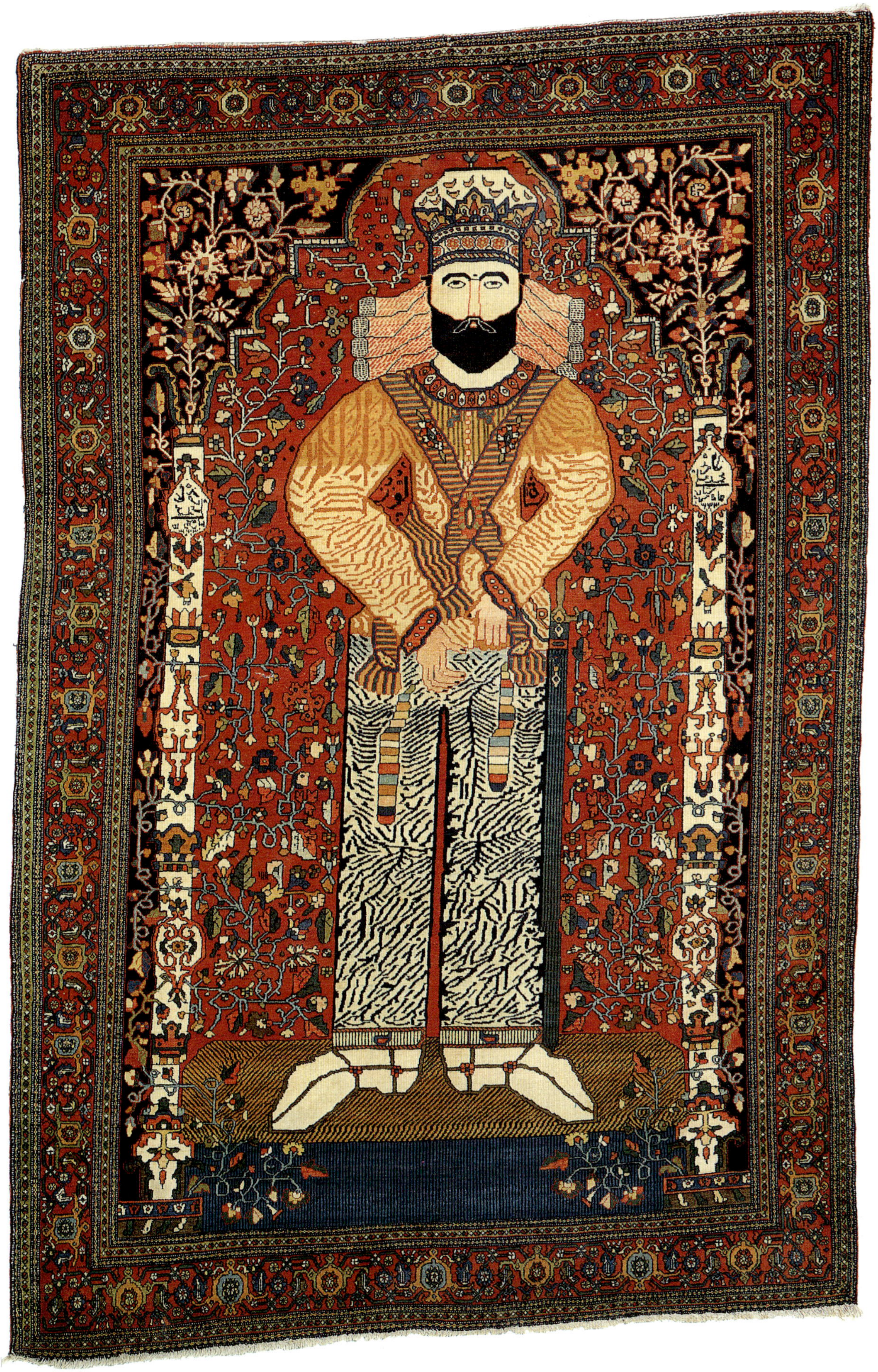

**20**

**Shapur I**
**Saruq**
**Inscription: *Shah***
**Early 20th century**

Despite the weaver's efforts to impart a royal aura to this figure, the result suggests a rustic playing the role of a shah. Even the long hair and royal crown do not dispel this impression. On the other hand, the weaver included details not found in other Shapur rugs. Among these are pockets and buttons on the trousers, fingernails, teeth, and even coloured eyes. (For Shapur I, see p. 21 infra.)

*Size:* 6ft 2.75in x 4ft 2in (190 x 127cm)
*Warp:* cotton, Z3S, undyed, straight, 2 levels
*Weft:* cotton, Z2S, pale blue, 2 shoots: the first straight; the second undulating
*Pile:* wool, Z2 loosely plied, As4, 0.25in (3mm)
*Knot count:* 12V x 12H = 144 per sq. in. (48V x 48H = 2304 per sq. dm.)
*Texture:* soft, thin, stiff to very stiff
*Sides:* not original
*Ends:* missing
*Colours* 10, blue-black, blue, light blue, light green, red, pink, brown, light brown, buff, ivory

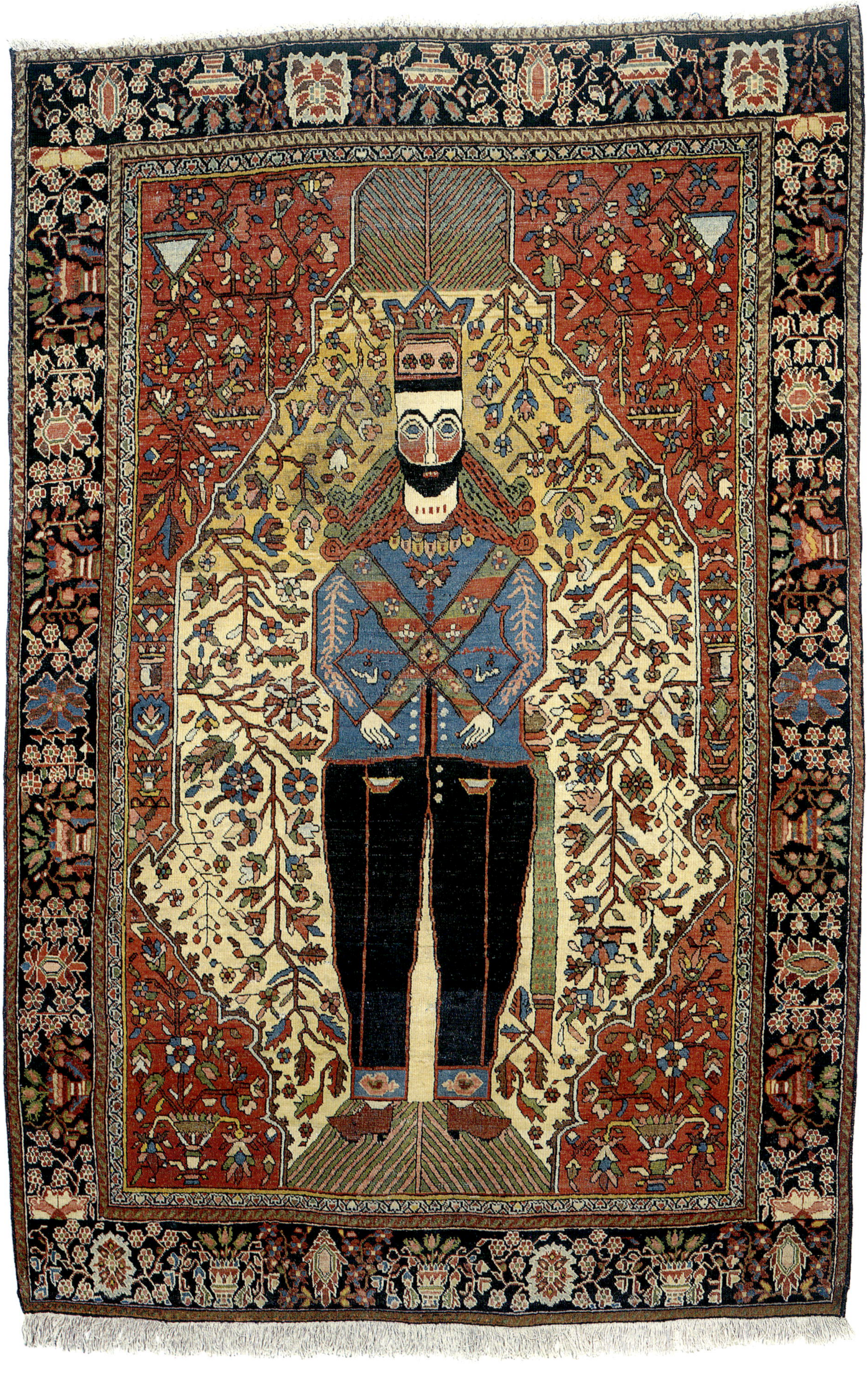

## 21

**Shapur I**
**Ferahan area**
**Early 20th century**

This rug and no. 22 were woven in very small dimensions and each has a character all of its own. All of the features of larger Shapur rugs are to be found in these two. Here spandrels, or cornerpieces, are also seen in the four corners, creating a lozenge-shaped 'medallion' which frames the central figure. With careful attention the viewer can find many similarities in the figures of each of these two rugs, each of which also has a distinct personality. In this example, which is the smaller rug, curls and twists are more common and are even used at the ends of the hair which resembles long ribbons hanging down on either side of the head. The weaver of the larger one (no. 22) was far less successful in showing the king's hands than in portraying the face, or perhaps chose to emphasize the face in favour of the tiny hands. (For Shapur I, see p. 21 infra.)

*Size:* 1ft 9.25in x 1ft 9.5in (55 x 55cm)
*Warp:* cotton, Z8S, undyed, straight, semi-depressed
*Weft:* cotton, Z8S, undyed (some dyed light blue), 1 and 2 shoots: the first almost straight, the second undulating
*Pile:* wool, Z2 loosely plied, Syl, 3 0.0625in (4mm)
*Knot count:* 12V x 11H = 132 per sq. in. (48V x 44H = 2112 per sq. dm.)
*Texture:* soft, thin, fairly stiff
*Sides:* not original
*Ends:* missing
*Colours* 8, blue-black, turquoise blue, sky blue, olive green, dark pink, pink, brown ivory

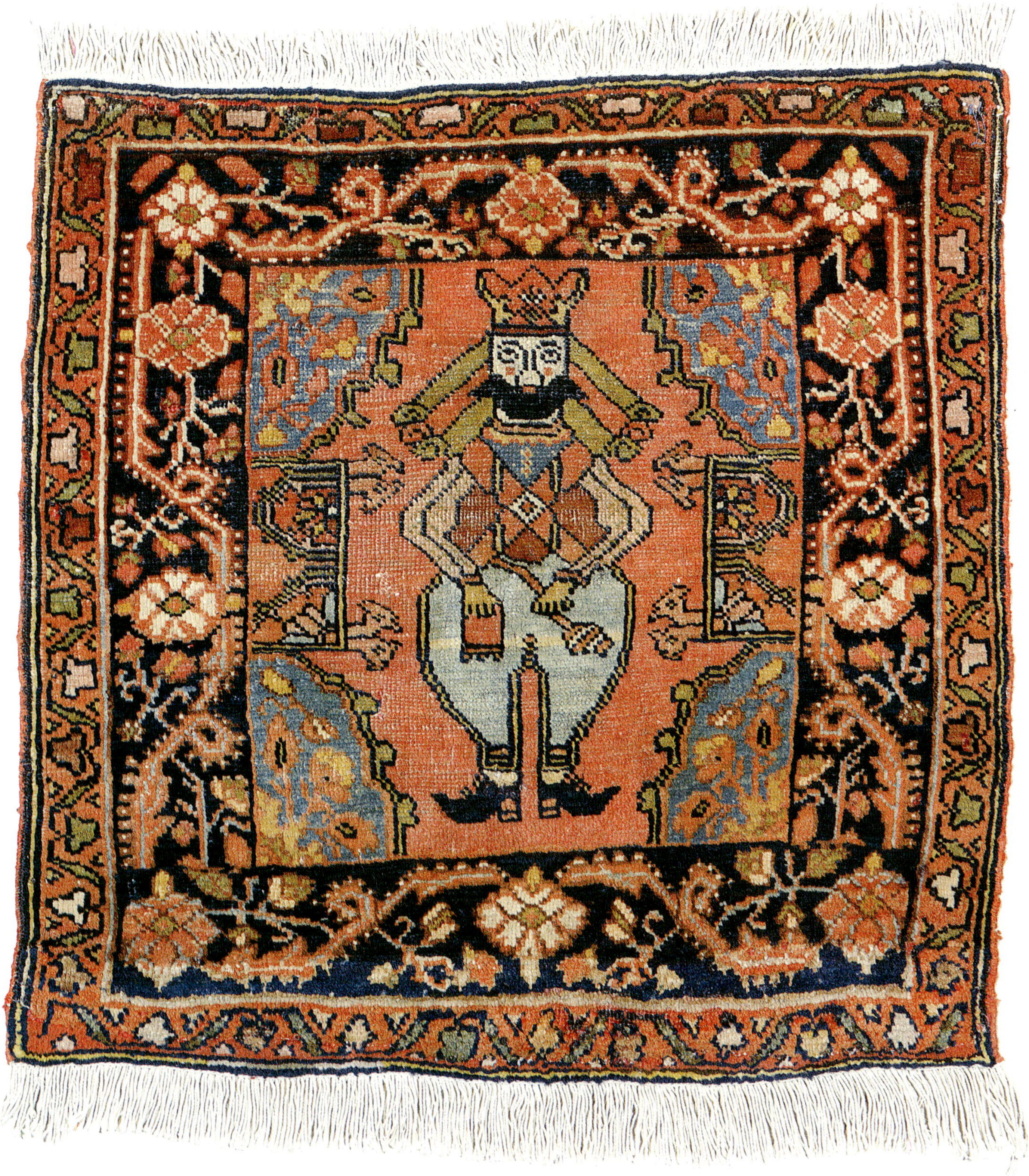

*Kings, Heroes and Lovers*

**22**

**Shapur I**
**Ferahan area**
**Early 20th century**

This is a different version of the same subject as that of no. 21, woven in the same area.

*Size:* 2ft 4.25in x 1ft 9in (72 x 53cm)
*Warp:* cotton, Z4S, undyed, straight, semi-depressed (almost 2 levels)
*Weft:* cotton, Z3S, 2 shoots: the first undyed, straight; the second blue, undulating
*Pile:* wool, Z2 loosely plied, Sy3, 0.25in (3mm.)
*Knot count:* 15V x 12H = 180 per sq. in. (60V x 48H = 2880 per sq. dm.)
*Texture:* soft, thin, fairly stiff
*Sides:* not original
*Ends:* 0.375in (1cm) weft-faced plain weave, undyed cotton
*Colours* 9, blue-black, blue, olive, pink, light orange, dark brown, light brown, buff, ivory

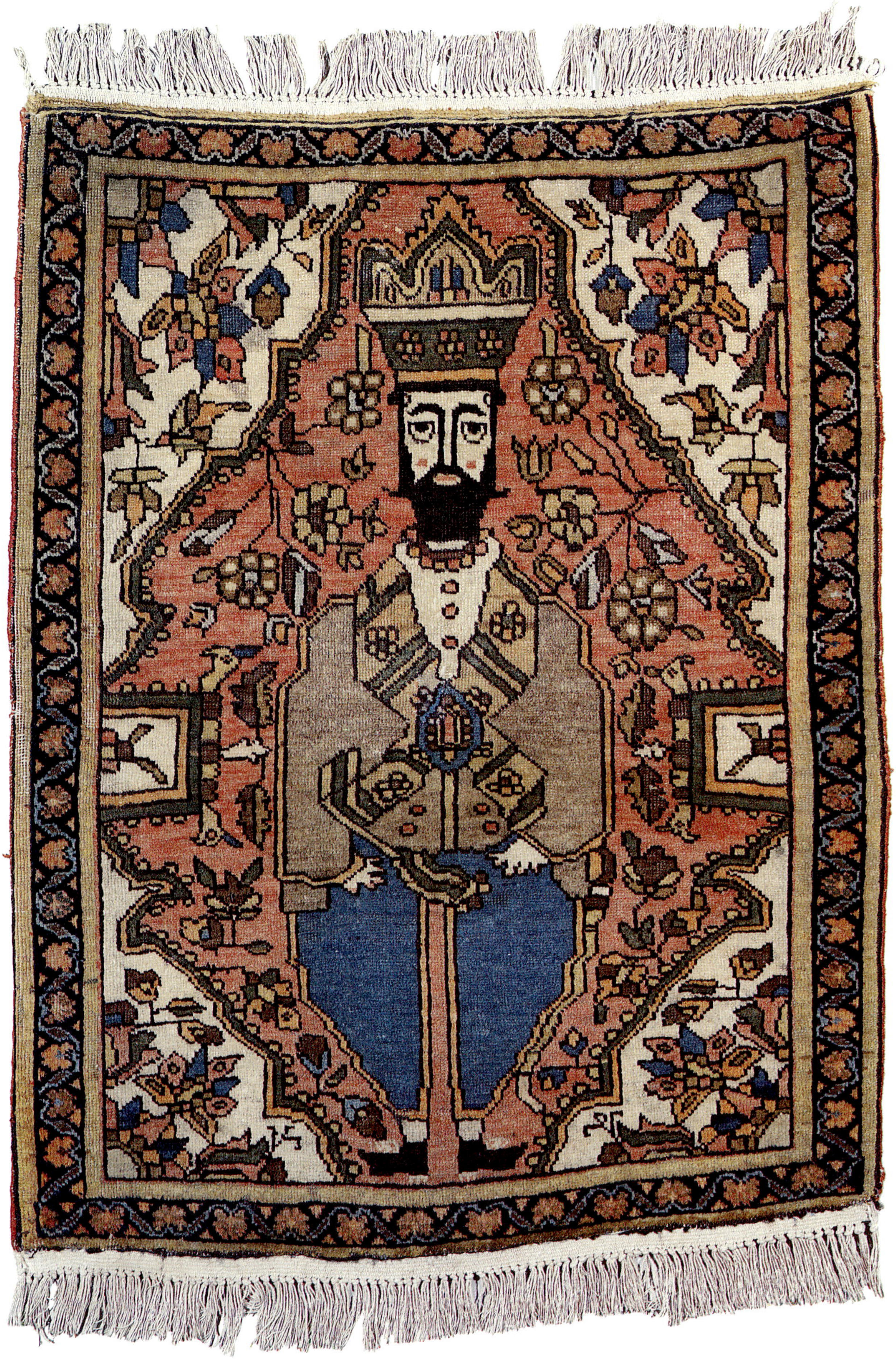

**23**

**Shah 'Abbas I**
**Bakhtiyari villages of province of Chahar Mahal-i Bakhtiyari**
**Possibly village of Saman**
**Inscription:** *Ordered by Mir Latif Khan Shohrati, Shah 'Abbas 1340 (1921 AD)*

The source of inspiration for the picture of this rug is a painting from the Safavid period (see p. 29 and fig. 21). The original painting was taken out of Iran in the early nineteenth century and later became known in Iran through its publication in history books and its appearance on post cards. The weaver of this rug tried to show details as precisely as possible, but when it came to the background she chose to show scenes from her own region. The building on the right is reminiscent of some of the residences of the Bakhtiyari khans. Many of these large residences are still seen in villages of the Bakhtiyari province. Behind the shah's head is a suggestion of the dun-coloured mountains and plains of the Bakhtiyari region, and, at the far left, the trees, birds, and flowers of that area. (For Shah 'Abbas I, see p. 24.)

*Size:* 2ft 8in x 4ft 0.3in (81 x 122cm)
*Warp:* cotton, Z3S, undyed, undulating, 1 level
*Weft:* cotton, Z3S, undyed, 1 shoot, straight
*Pile:* wool, Z2 loosely plied, Sy1, 0.0625in (2mm)
*Knot count:* 11V x 12H = 132 per sq. in. (44V x 48H = 2112 per sq. dm.)
*Texture:* soft, fairly thin, very flexible
*Sides:* wool, purplish red, remains of parallel wrapping around 3 warps
*Ends:* missing
*Colours* 12, black, blue-black, blue, turquoise blue, dark green, olive green, purplish-red, dark pink, brown, mustard yellow, buff, ivory

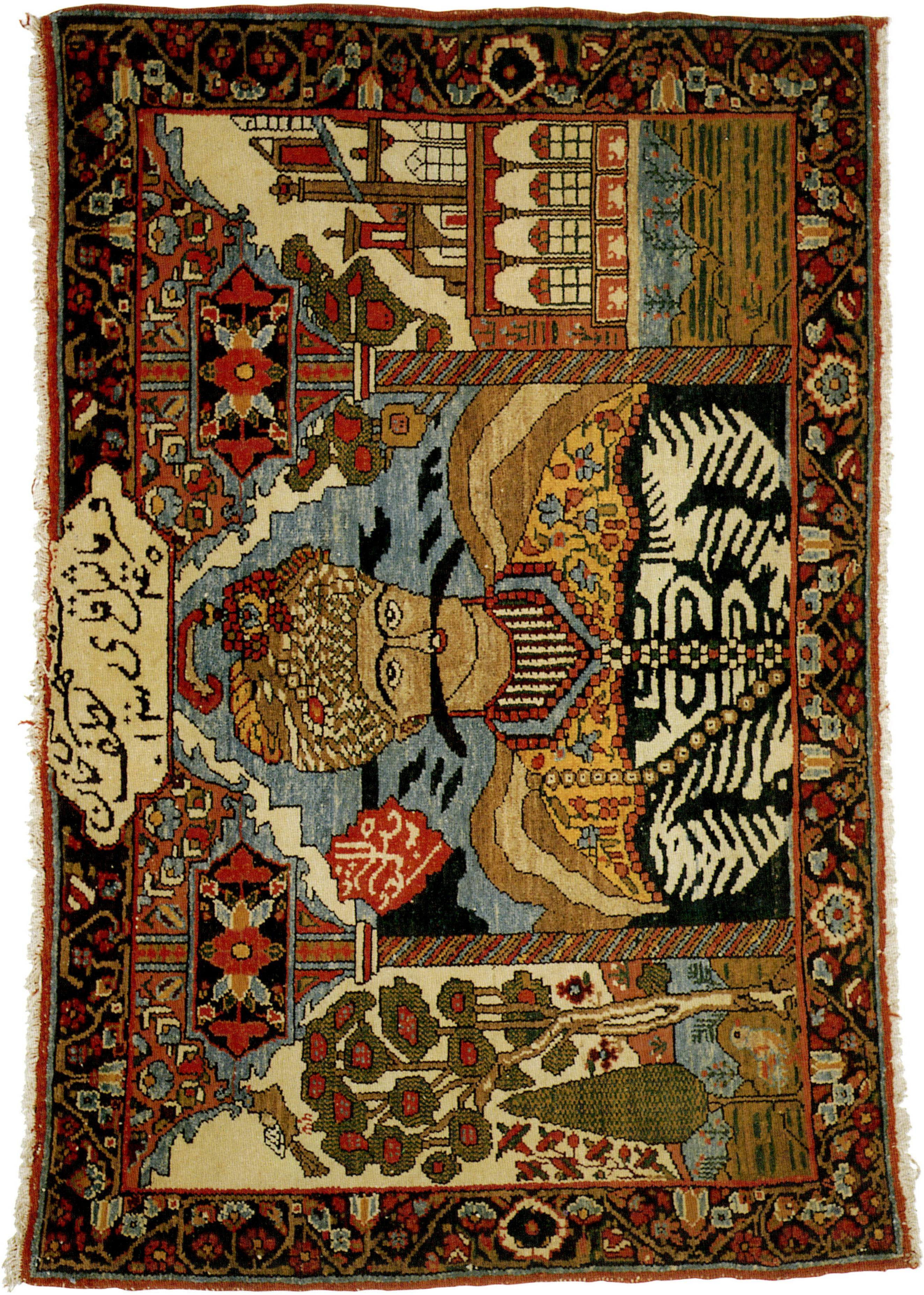

*Kings, Heroes and Lovers*

**24**

**Nadir Shah**
**Isfahan**
**Inscription: *Portrait of Nadir Shah***
**Late 19th century**

In addition to being a good example of the structural characteristics of Isfahan rugs of the end of the last century, this rug is also representative of many of the artistic conventions of that time. Among these are the use of natural elements (flowers, plants, and birds) to fill empty spaces, the placement of the main figure under an elaborate arch decorated with flowers, and the inclusion of a chair at the far left (which was one of the signs of status in that age; traditionally, people in that part of the world sat on the floor not on chairs).*

Here we see Nadir Shah depicted with the characteristics mentioned in the section of the text devoted to Nadir Shah (p. 25). His four-peaked hat, coat, armbands, jewel-studded sword, high boots, and masculine face and physique are well drawn by a masterful and experienced rug designer. The weaver in turn, following the cartoon, executed this design well. Particularly noteworthy are the effects of shading to indicate roundness in the man's arms, legs, and body.

Here, too, the weaver has skilfully carried out the designer's intent. In most areas light and dark shades of the main colour were used. Only in the boots was a suggestion of cross-hatching used to indicate shading for a three-dimensional effect. This is probably the beginning of the use of shading in pictorial rugs.

* Samuel R. Peterson, 'Chairs and Change in Qajar Times,' in Michael E. Bonine and Nikki R. Keddie, eds., *Modern Iran, The Dialectics of Continuity and Change*, Albany, 1981, pp. 383-446.

*Size:* 7ft 0.75in x 4ft 6.25in (215 x 138cm)
*Warp:* cotton, 4(Z3S)Z undyed, straight, 2 levels
*Weft:* cotton, 2 shoots: the first undyed, straight; 4(Z3S)Z; the second light blue, undulating, 2(Z3S)Z
*Pile:* wool, Z2 loosely plied, As3, 0.0625in (2mm)
*Knot count:* 16V x 18H = 288 per sq. in. (64V x 72H = 4608 per sq. dm.)
*Texture:* velvety, very thin, fairly stiff
*Sides:* wool, red, parallel wrapping around 4 warps
*Ends:* 0.75in (2cm) weft-faced plain weave, undyed cotton, decorated with 1 row of weft twining in yellow and red wool; at the top all warps are tied in bunches
*Colours* 19, blue-black, dark blue, blue, light blue, dark green, green, turquoise, olive green, red, dark pink, pink, yellow, aubergine, dark brown, brown, light brown, mustard, buff, ivory

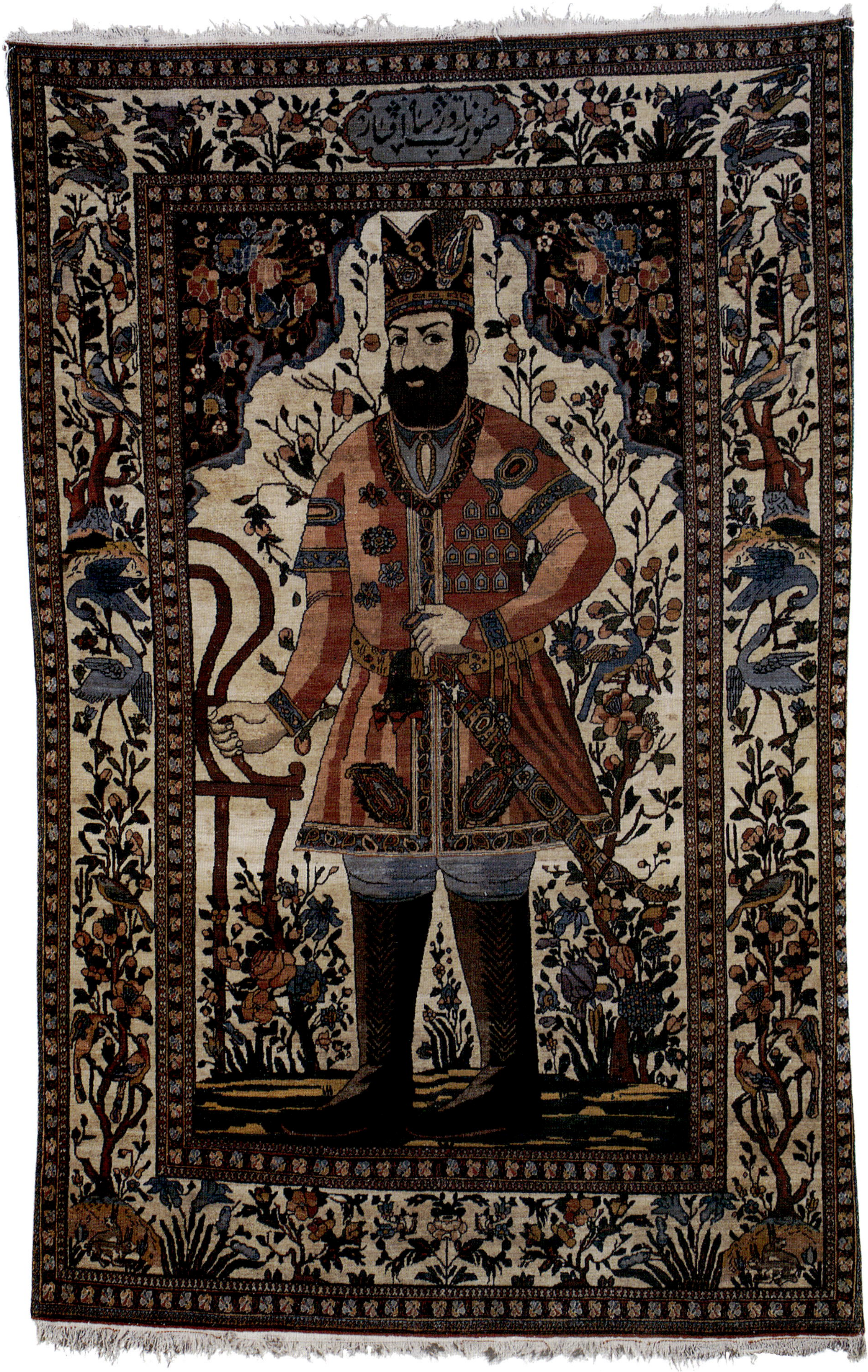
صورت نادرشاه افشار

## 25

**Fath 'Ali Shah**
**Kashan**
**Inscription: al-Sultan Fath 'Ali Shah Qajar**
**Late 19th century**

In the section of the text on Fath 'Ali Shah his attractive appearance and his elegant court are discussed (see p. 25 and figs. 23, 24). Most of what has been said about this shah is also seen in this rug: his marble-like skin, attractive eyes, long beard decorated with jewels, sumptuous clothes covered with indescribable jewels, and suggestions of his splendid court. These details that appear in this rug—which is executed with lustrous wool pile, a very fine weave, and delicate pastel colours—add to its magnificence and regal quality.

This is one of the type of rug known as 'Mohtasham' (rugs woven in Kashan at the end of the last century with merino wool from Australia are called 'Mohtasham'). From all points of view, these rugs are among the most desirable of Kashan rugs. Various things have been said about Mohtasham. Many have thought him to be a famous Kashan merchant who at the end of the last century imported great quantities of machine-spun merino wool from Manchester, in Great Britain, for use in his textile mill. When his factory went bankrupt he is said to have used this wool for rug weaving. This opinion agrees with what people knowledgeable in the rug field have said and also with what Cecil Edwards has written in his book (*The Persian Carpet*, p. 334). Regarding the way in which merino wool was employed in Kashan rugs, Edwards and the above-mentioned statement are in complete accord. The only point of difference is that Edwards mentions a man named Hajji Mullah Hassan instead of Mohtasham. It is not improbable that Hajji Mullah Hassan was also known as Mohtasham.

*Size:* 6ft 3.25in x 4ft 6.25in (191 x 138cm)
*Warp:* cotton, 3(Z4S)S, undyed, fairly straight, semi-depressed
*Weft:* cotton, Z5S, blue, 2 shoots: the first straight, the second undulating
*Pile:* wool, Z2 loosely plied, As3, 0.0625in (2mm)
*Knot count:* 19V x 18H = 345 per sq. in. (76V x 72H = 5472 per sq. dm.)
*Texture:* velvety, very thin, flexible
*Sides:* wool, reddish purple, parallel wrapping around 4 warps
*Ends:* 0.75in (2cm) weft-faced plain weave, undyed cotton, warp ends tied in bunches, lower end decorated with weft twining in pink and undyed ivory wool
*Colours* 9, blue-black, blue, light turquoise, green, light green, pink, light brown, buff, ivory

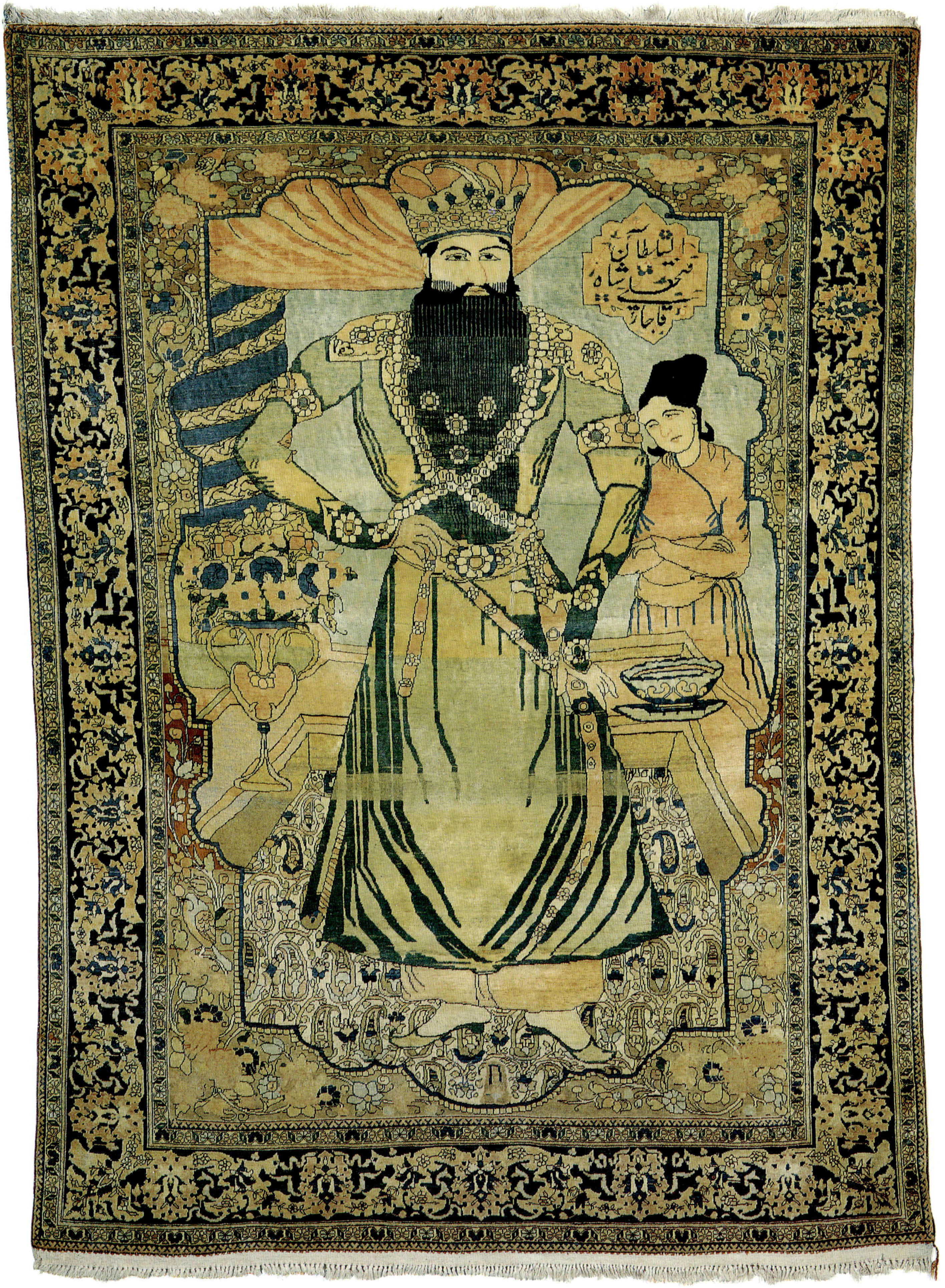
السلطان فتحعلی شاه قاجار

*Kings, Heroes and Lovers*

**26**

**Muhammad 'Ali Mirza Dawlatshah (?) and A Qajar Princess (?)**
**Bijar area**
**Early 19th century**

This small rug is one of the masterpieces of Iranian weaving of the early nineteenth century, a period when the art of Iran again reached a point of great fruitfulness during the Zand and Qajar dynasties, with production centred in the palace workshops (see p. 8). Once more painters produced many works centering on kings and their offspring, but this time not as miniature painting illustrating books so much as large oil paintings (with, for the first time in the Islamic era in Iran, large-scale figures), many of which have survived down to the present day.

This new painting style, however, is rarely reflected in rug weaving. The present example is the only one of its kind that I have ever seen. The subject of the rug probably commemorates the betrothal of a Qajar prince. All of the features of the rug, such as its age, style, and where it was woven, as well as aspects of the young women's clothes (including her head scarf and belt, which resemble those of Kurdish girls in western Iran) seem to relate the rug to Prince Muhammad 'Ali Mirza Dawlatshah, one of the two eldest sons (by different wives) of Fath 'Ali Shah, and governor of Kermanshah. Muhammad 'Ali Mirza considered himself superior to 'Abbas Mirza, the crown prince, and laid claim to the monarchy.

The beauty of the features of the young woman's face was carefully depicted by the weaver: large almond-shaped eyes, eyebrows that meet over the nose (a stylized convention of beauty in Persian art), long eyelashes, pink cheeks, beauty marks which were part of the make-up of that period, as well as the presence of fine details such as the teeth which are done with extreme delicacy, and the elegant decoration of her long tresses all contribute to her attractiveness and appeal. Without doubt the weaver was familiar with all of the features considered beautiful in her own day and used them in the faces of the young prince and princess.

*Size:* 3ft 11in x 3ft 9.5in (119 x 115cm)
*Warp:* cotton, Z6S, undyed, straight, 2 levels
*Weft:* cotton, Z2S, undyed, and wool, Z3S undyed light brown; 2 shoots: the first wool, straight; the second cotton, undulating
*Pile:* wool, Z2 loosely plied, Sy3, 0.0625in (2mm)
*Knot count:* 19V x 16H = 340 per sq. in. (76V x 64H = 4864 per sq. dm.)
*Texture:* very soft, thin, very stiff
*Sides:* wool, dark red, remains of parallel wrapping around 4 warps
*Ends:* missing
*Colours* 10, blue-black, blue, emerald green, green, crimson, red, pink, brown, light brown, ivory

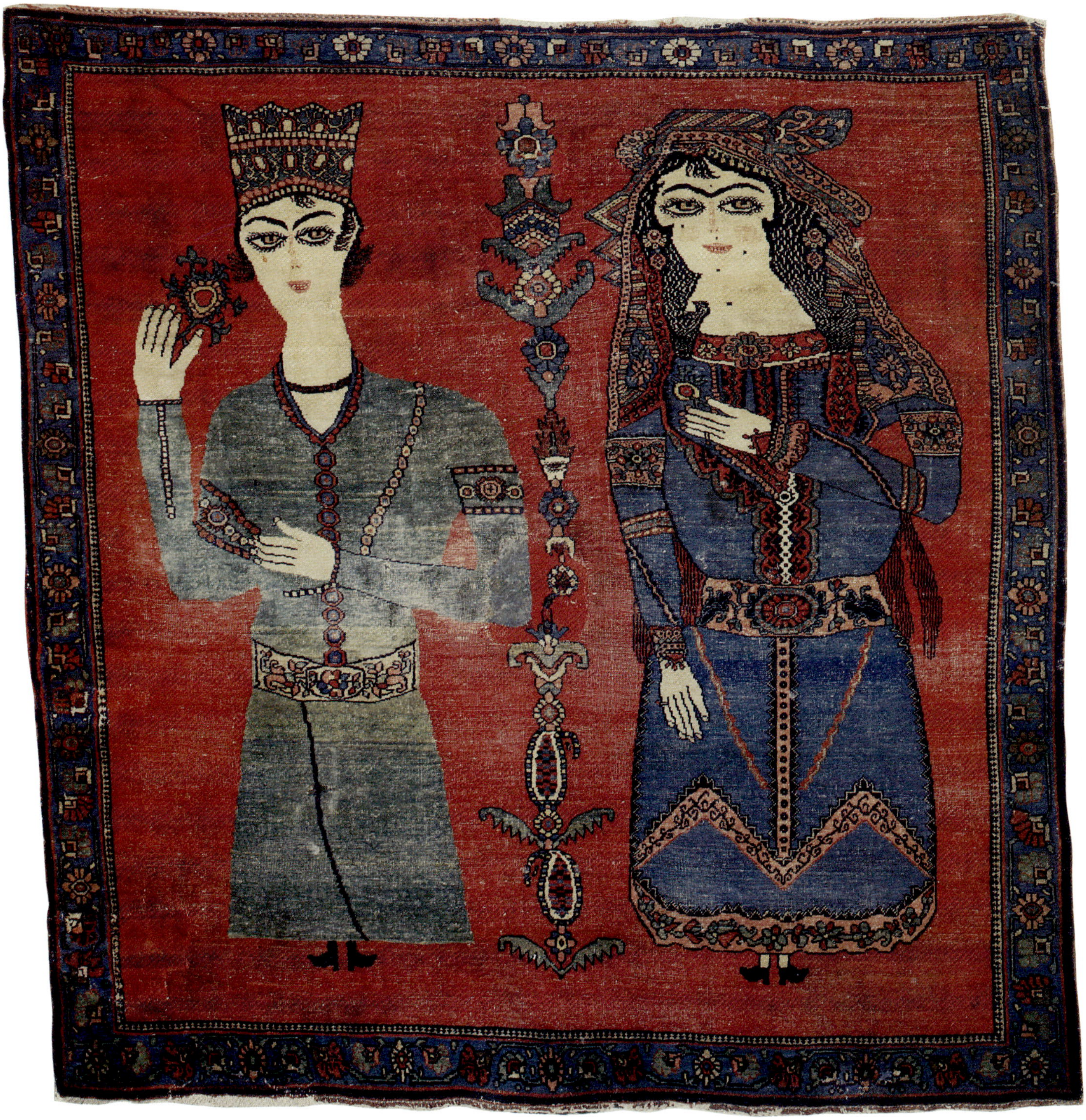

*Kings, Heroes and Lovers*

**27**

**Muhammad Shah
Kerman
Mid-19th century**

The royal personage seated in a chair depicted in this rug, with a servant nearby holding a water pipe, might be taken for Nasir al-Din Shah, who is portrayed in the next four rugs, except that the latter did not wear a beard. The figure seated in a chair here, at first glance, bears a slight resemblance to the tiny seated figure of Nasir al-Din Shah in rug no. 29, but this rug no. 27 probably shows Muhammad Shah, who did wear a beard. He was a grandson of Fath 'Ali Shah (who is seen in rug no. 25) and came to the throne after Fath 'Ali Shah's death in 1834. Muhammad Shah was succeeded after his death in 1848 by his son Nasir al-Din Shah. If this rug does portray Muhammad Shah, it is the only one known of that subject. The shah, reflecting a fashionable status symbol of the time this rug was woven, is shown seated on a chair (see rug no. 24 and note). Typical of hierarchical pictorial tradition, the king is significantly larger than his respectful servant, who offers him the water pipe. The rug is a high-quality example of Kerman weaving. (For Muhammad Shah, see p. 26.)

*Size:* 6ft 11.5in x 4ft (212 x 122cm)
*Warp:* cotton, Z5S, undyed, straight, depressed
*Weft:* cotton, Z2S, 2 shoots: the first undyed, straight; the second dyed beige, undulating
*Pile:* Z2 loosely plied, As3, 0.25in (3mm)
*Knot count:* 15V x 17H = 250 per sq. in. (61V x 69H = 4209 per sq. dm.)
*Texture:* soft, thin, rather stiff
*Sides:* wool, dark blue, parallel wrapping around 4 warps
*Ends:* remains of balanced plain weave
*Colours* 13, blue-black, blue, light blue, light green, grey-green, dark brown, yellow-brown, beige, red, pink, orange, yellow, ivory

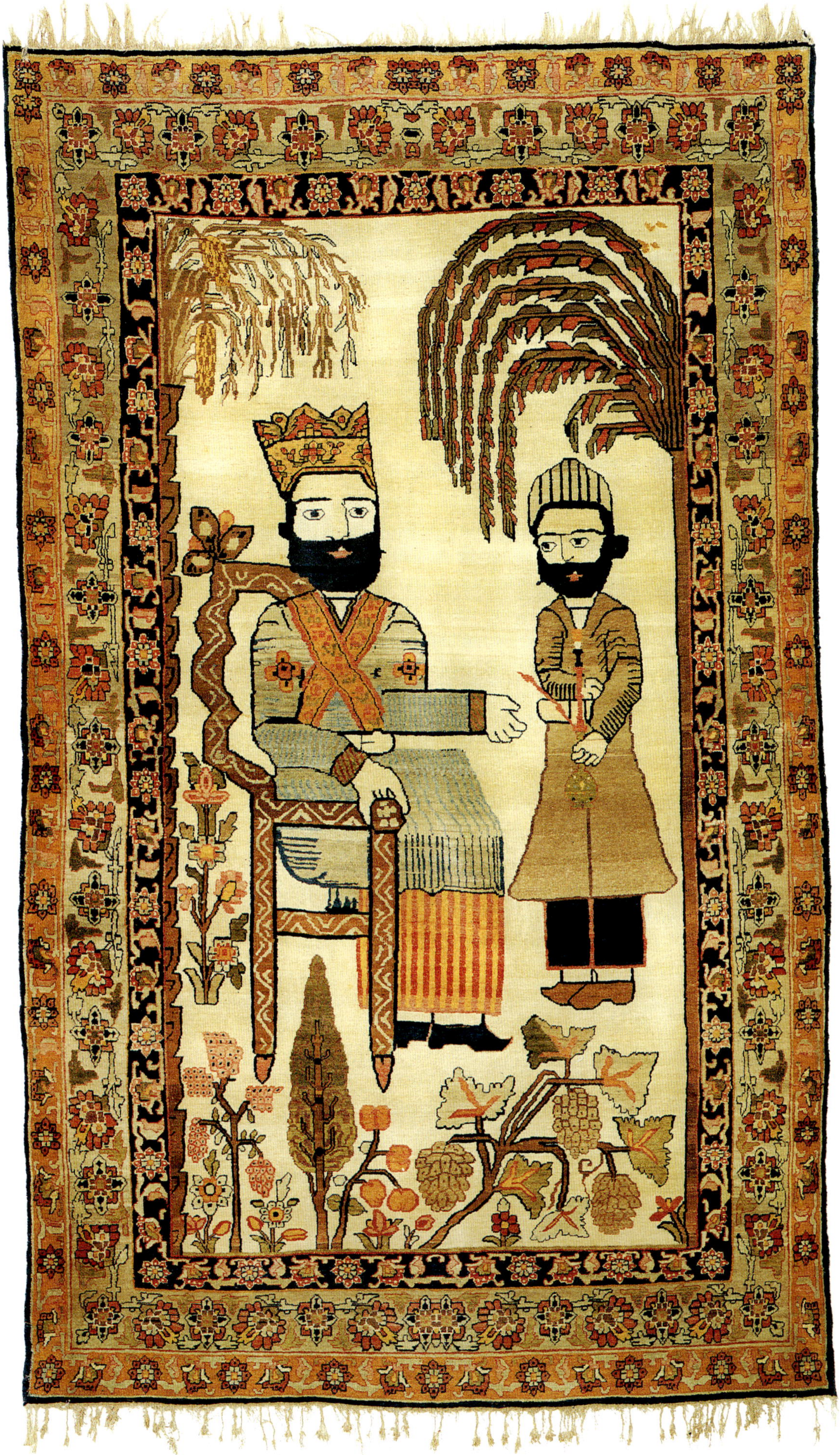

## 28

**Nasir al-Din Shah**
**Dorokhsh**
**Late 19th century**

Here the weaver has repeated a small portrait of Nasir al-Din Shah (see fig. 26) many times, instead of the more usual practice in rugs depicting kings of showing one large portrait. The weaver has avoided monotony by reversing the direction of alternate busts, and by varying the colours in the background. The composition of the rug, with many small portrait busts in a grid-like arrangement, is reminiscent of *qalamkar* curtains such as fig. 3. The repetition in this rug of a portrait of one man is similar to the work of certain late twentieth-century painters such as Andy Warhol.

Dorokhsh, in eastern Iran, has been up to recent times one of the important rug weaving centres of Iran. Rugs from this district are especially famous for their designs and colours. This is the only pictorial rug from Dorokhsh that I have ever seen. This village was situated in eastern Iran on the edge of the desert about forty-five miles northeast of Birjand. Due to earthquakes in recent years Dorokhsh is now abandoned and its name has been omitted from recent maps. Cecil Edwards, who visited this village in 1948, mentions that there were twenty rug looms in Dorokhsh at that time and about 120 in the surrounding area (Edwards, *The Persian Carpet*, pp. 171-172). (For Nasir al-Din Shah, see p. 26.)

*Size:* 7ft 3.5in x 4ft 6in (222 x 137cm)
*Warp:* cotton, Z3S, undyed, straight, 2 levels
*Weft:* cotton, Z3S, undyed; 2 shoots: the first straight, the second undulating
*Pile:* wool, Z2 loosely plied, As4, 0.25in (3mm)
*Knot count:* 25V x 18H = 450 per sq. in. (100V x 72H = 7200 per sq. dm.)
*Texture:* very soft, thin, very flexible
*Sides:* wool, dyed tan, parallel wrapping around 4 warps
*Ends:* missing
*Colours* 7, blue-black, blue, olive, light red, dark brown, light brown, ivory

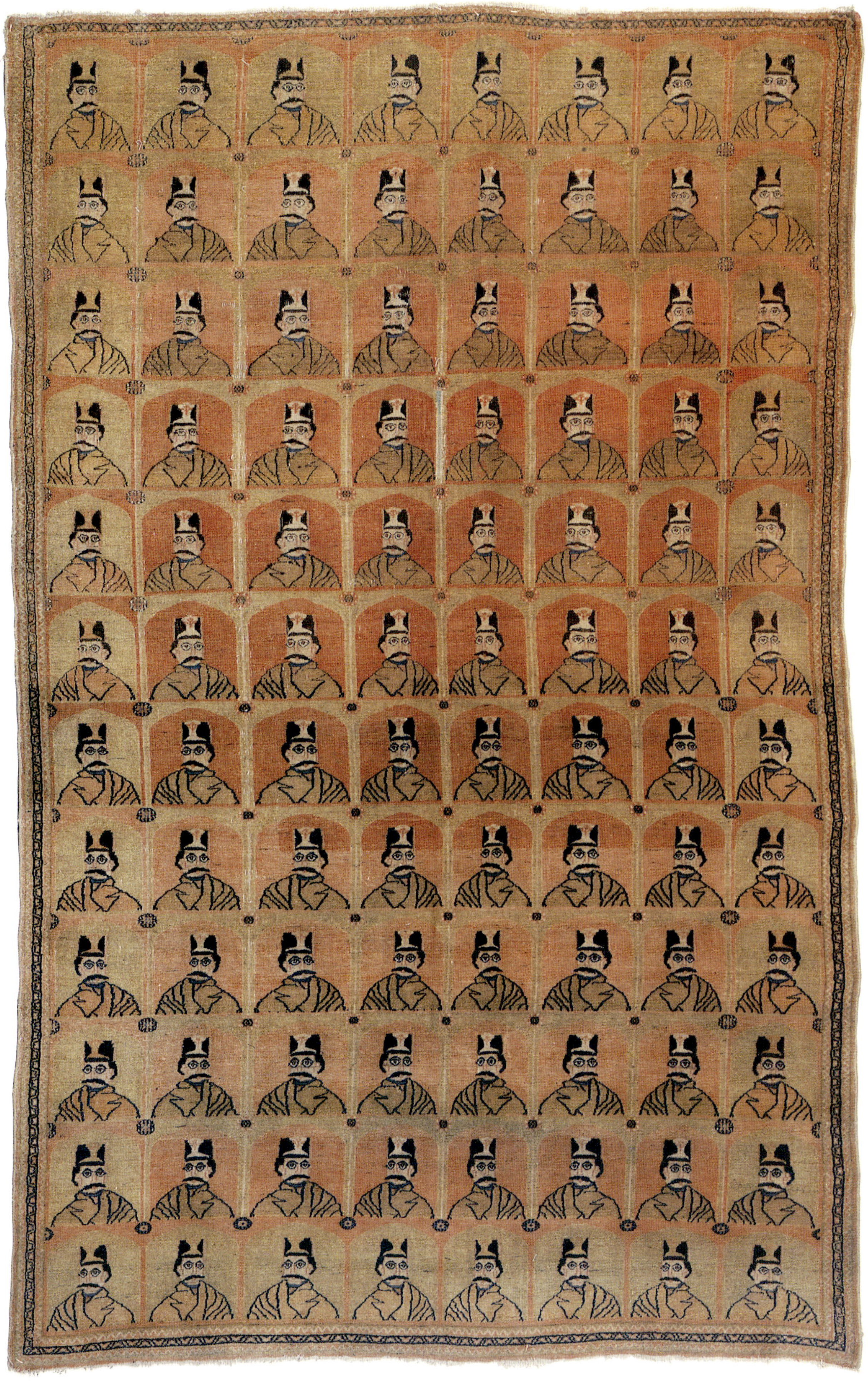

## Kings, Heroes and Lovers

**29**

**Nasir al-Din Shah**
**Malayir**
**Dated:** *1301 (1883 AD)*

This rug, like no. 28, is also an overall repeat pattern portraying Nasir al-Din Shah, who is seen here forty-two times, seated in a chair under a tree, in offset rows, sometimes in a reversed position. The colour changes in costume and foliage, using all twelve colours in this rug, give a lively appearance to the repetitive layout. Perhaps the weavers of this and the previous rug were both working from small photographs, but realized the concept of a royal portrait in a rug by repetition rather than by enlargement. Photographs were made of Nasir al-Din Shah in the late-nineteenth-century fashionable pose seated in a chair under a tree, sometimes with a water pipe, as seen in the fourth row from the top in this rug. At the sides of the carpet are a few small figures of male servants, echoing the convention of the smaller figure in rug no. 27. As the face of the king in the present rug is younger than the ruler was when this rug was woven (about thirty-seven), a photograph of the shah when he was younger may well have been used by the weaver. The figures in the second row from the bottom, with a moustache, most closely resemble Nasir al-Din Shah. He is similarly portrayed in rugs nos. 28, 30, and 31. (For Nasir al-Din Shah, see p. 26.)

*Size:* 3ft 9in x 3ft 3.5in (114 x 100cm)
*Warp:* cotton, Z4S, undyed, undulating, 1 level
*Weft:* cotton, Z4S, undyed, 1 shoot, straight
*Pile:* wool, Z2 loosely plied, Sy1, 0.03in (1mm)
*Knot count:* 13V x 11H = 143 per sq. in. (51V x 44H = 2244 per sq. dm.)
*Texture:* coarse, thin, flexible
*Sides:* missing
*Ends:* missing
*Colours* 12, dark blue, light blue, green, light green, dark brown, light brown, red, pink, yellow, mustard, ivory, white (cotton)

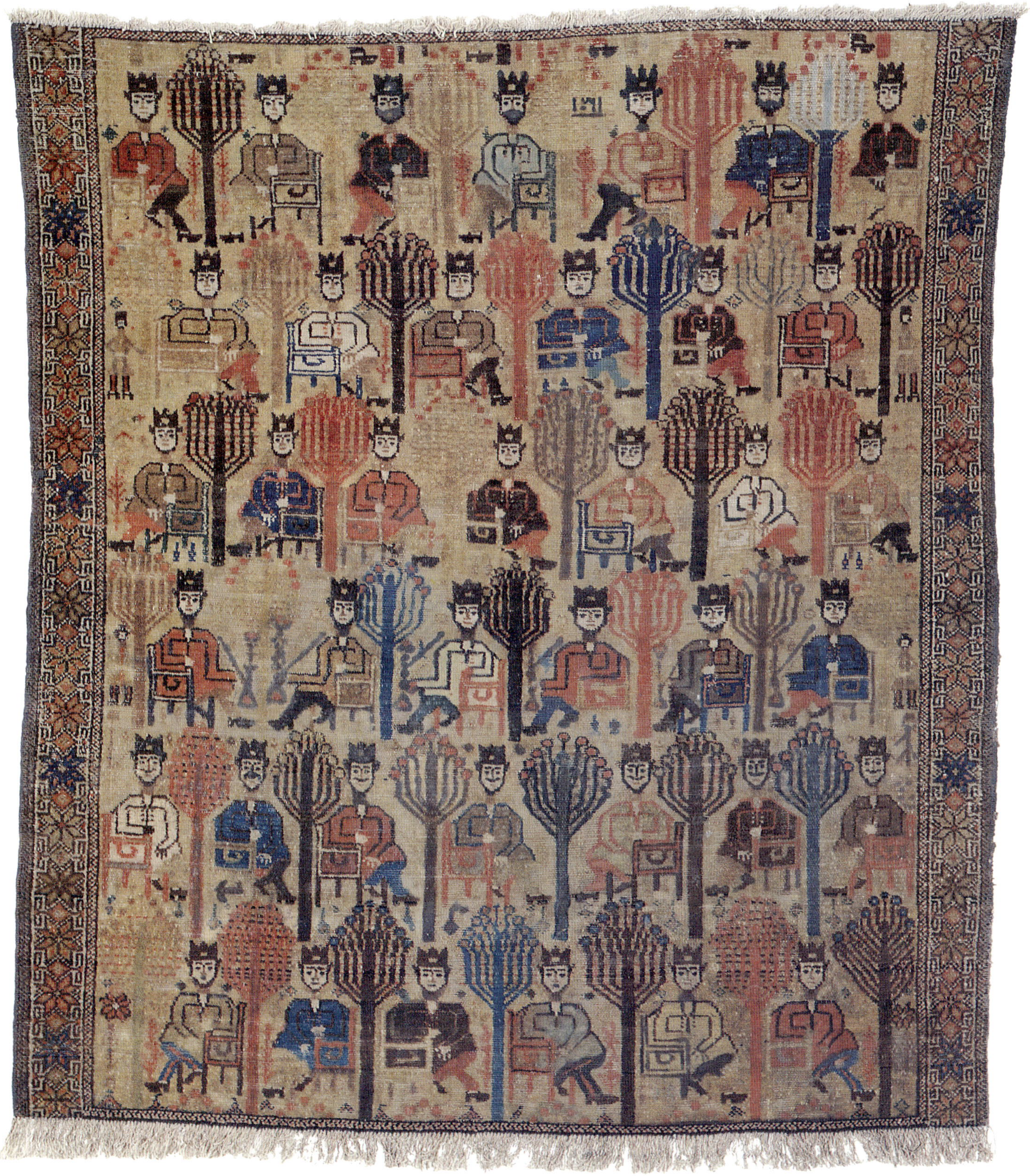

## 30

**Nasir al-Din Shah**
**Hamadan area**
**Early 20th century**

In spite of the fact that there are hundreds of photographs and paintings from the second half of the nineteenth century, when Nasir al-Din Shah ruled Iran, the image of this monarch was rarely woven into a rug. This stands in sharp contrast to the situation under Ahmad Shah, who during his much shorter reign was a favourite subject for rug weavers in most parts of Iran.

This small rug is one of the very few that can be said to portray Nasir al-Din Shah. It was very likely copied from a painting or a photograph (see fig. 26) and bears a reasonable likeness to him. A lion-and-sun motif (the national symbol of Iran;, see p. 58, 60) occupies each of the lower corners. The suggestion of shadows is an effect copied from the painting or photograph used as a model. The four-legged animal directly below the image of the shah lends a touch of the charm of folk art to this otherwise formal portrait. (For Nasir al-Din Shah, see p. 26.)

*Size:* 2ft 1.5in x 1ft 11.5in (65 x 60cm)
*Warp:* cotton, Z3S, undyed, undulating, 1 level
*Weft:* wool, Z2S, ivory, 1 shoot, straight
*Pile:* wool, Z2 loosely plied, Sy1, 0.25in (3mm)
*Knot count:* 11V x 12H = 132 per sq. in. (44V x 48H = 2112 per sq. dm.)
*Texture:* fairly coarse, thin, flexible
*Sides:* wool, brown, remains of parallel wrapping around 3 warps
*Ends:* missing
*Colours* 8, blue-black, blue, light olive, pink, brown, light brown, buff, ivory

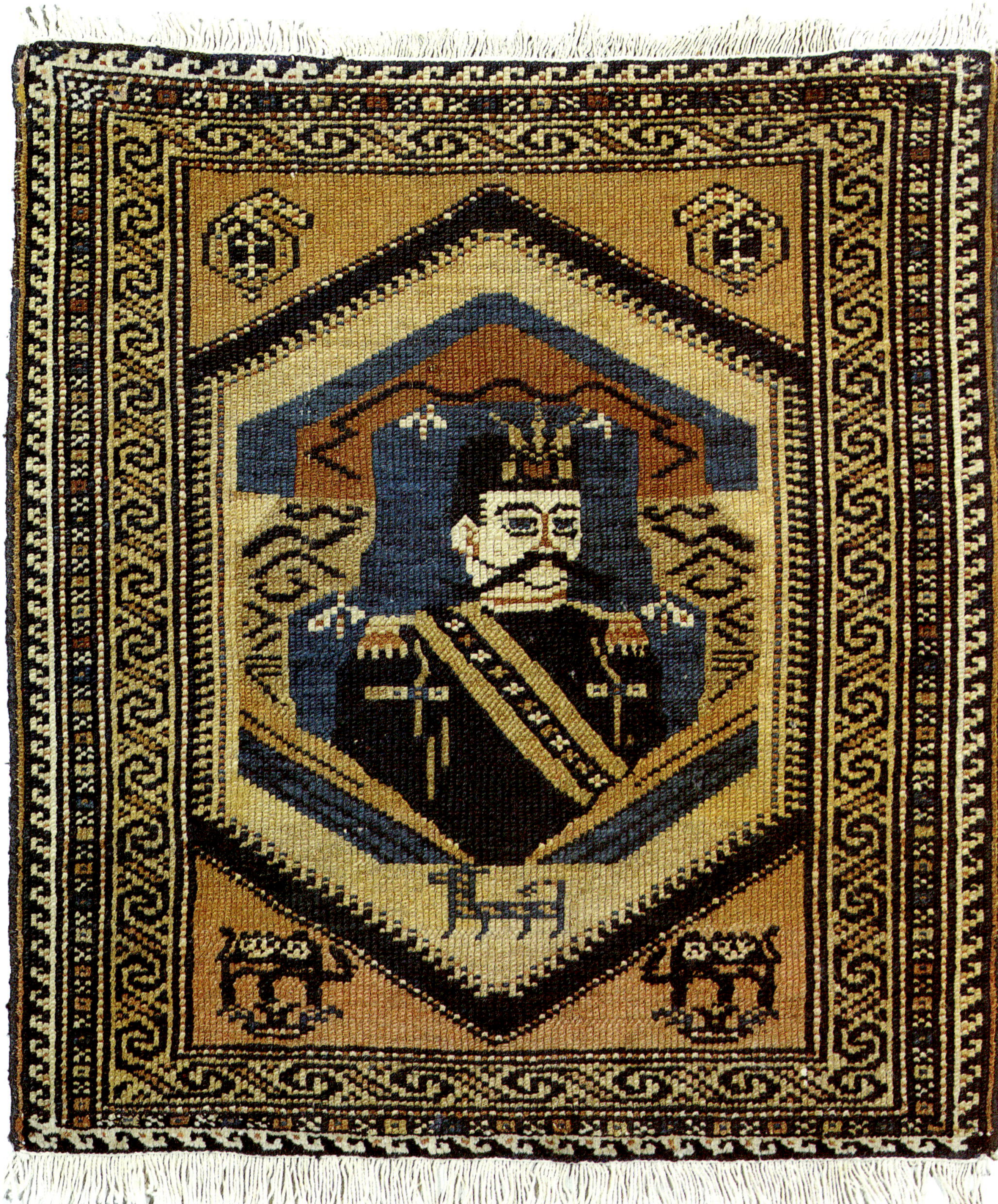

## Kings, Heroes and Lovers

**31**

**Nasir al-Din Shah?**
**Taleqan area, between Qazvin and Tehran**
**Inscription:** *illegible*
**Early 20th century**

The subject of this rug is a horseman pursuing a small animal in a forest. From the rider's clothes it can be assumed that he is an official or a monarch. His hat with its aigrette remind us of those worn by Nasir al-Din Shah.

The treatment of the horse's legs is unusual. The hind legs appear firmly planted while the front part of the animal, from the head and neck to the feet, exhibits motion and speed. The strange seated posture of the rider (particularly the position of the arms) is also noteworthy. It must be admitted that, despite the weaver's lack of familiarity with the art of figure portrayal, she succeeded in making her intention clear, which is not an easy task when a rider on horseback in the heart of thick forest is to be shown. (For Nasir al-Din Shah, see p. 26.)

*Size:* 6ft 5.5in x 4ft 6.25in (197 x 138cm)
*Warp:* cotton, Z5S, undyed, undulating, 1 level
*Weft:* wool, Z2S, undyed ivory to dark brown, 1 shoot, straight
*Pile:* wool, Z2 loosely plied, Sy1, 0.375in (1cm)
*Knot count:* 9V x 7H = 63 per sq. in. (36V x 28H = 1008 per sq. dm.)
*Texture:* soft, thick, fairly stiff
*Sides:* wool, dark brown, parallel wrapping around 6 warps
*Ends:* 1.1875in (3cm) weft-faced plain weave, undyed cotton
*Colours* 7, blue-black, dark blue, green, brownish red, lemon yellow, dark reddish brown, ivory

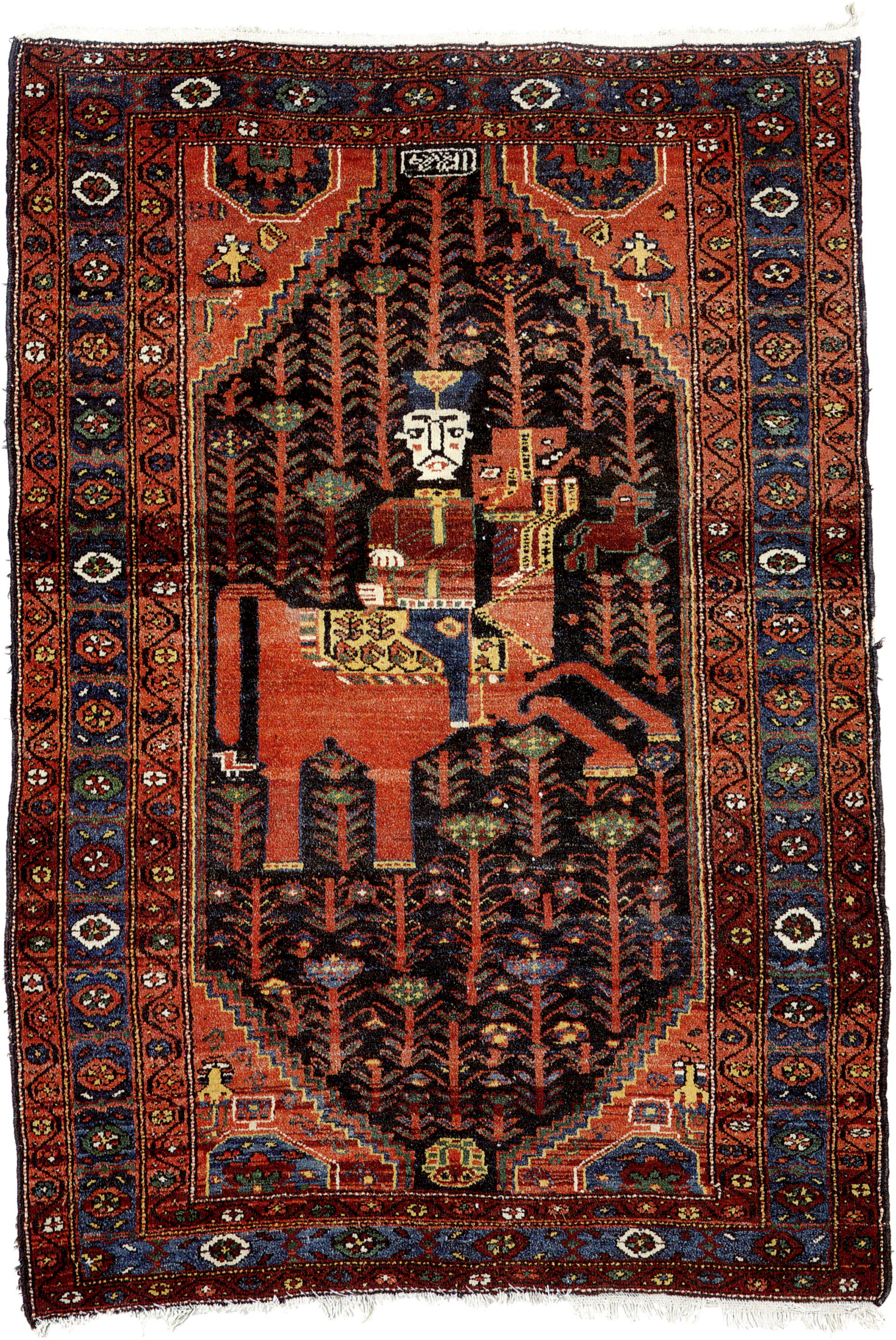

# Kings, Heroes and Lovers

**32**

**A Qajar Shah (Muhammad 'Ali Shah?)**
**Zanjan area**
**Early 20th century**

This rug probably depicts Muhammad 'Ali Shah. However, since Muhammad 'Ali Shah was a tyrant and opponent of the constitutional movement and freedom, and attacked the parliament, as well as the people, with cannon on many occasions, it seems unlikely that his portrait would appear on a rug, unless, of course, it was woven at the order of one of his supporters.

In any case the rug dates to the short reign of either Muhammad 'Ali Shah (r. 1907-1909) or Ahmad Shah (r. 1909-1924), the last Qajar monarch. None of the traditional features of rug designing has been altered by the placement of the bust of the shah in the middle of the central medallion in this rug. The weaver was so faithful to the traditions of her craft that the bust of the shah, at least from the shoulders down, suggests the form of an almost completely regular hexagon. If the head of the shah were removed, the remaining portion of the body would not be recognized as such, since the shah's insignia, medals, and ornamental braids are executed as traditional rug patterns (see fig. 27). (For Muhammad 'Ali Shah, see p. 27.)

*Size:* 5ft 8.5in x 3ft 0.5in (173 x 93cm)
*Warp:* 3 strands of undyed cotton plied with 1 strand of undyed brown wool, Z4S, undulating, 1 level
*Weft:* wool, Z3S, undyed brown, 1 shoot, straight
*Pile:* wool, Z2 loosely plied, Sy1, 0.0625in (2mm)
*Knot count:* 10V x 7H = 70 per sq. in. (40V x 28H = 1344 per sq. dm.)
*Texture:* coarse, fairly thin, flexible
*Sides:* wool, undyed brown, remains of parallel wrapping around 4 warps
*Ends:* missing
*Colours* 8, blue, light blue, light green, pink, dark brown, brown, buff, ivory

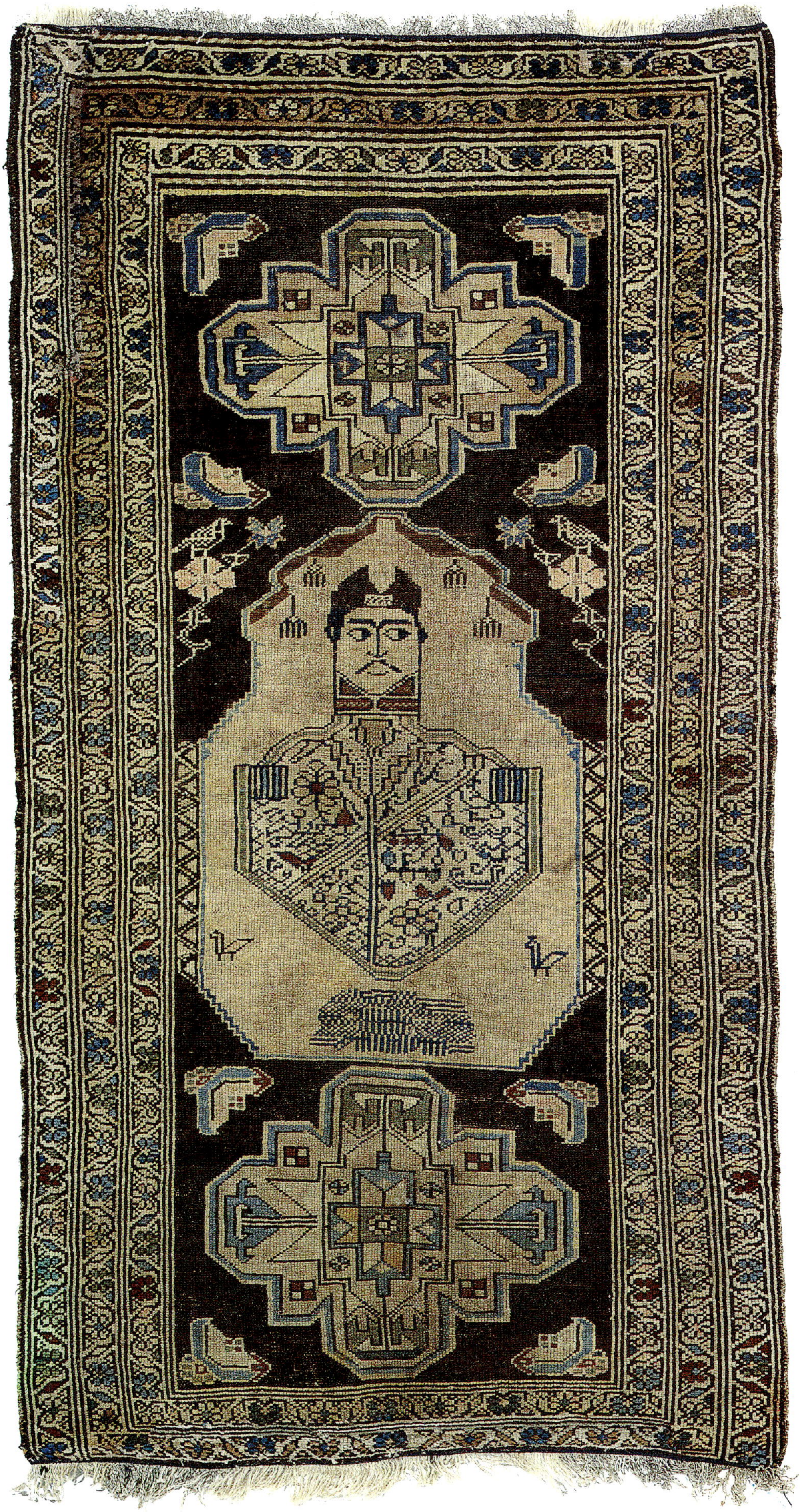

*Kings, Heroes and Lovers*

**33**

**Ahmad Shah**
**Malayir area**
**Inscription at top of rug:** *People, make way so our dear one can pass, so the shah of Iran [Ahmad Shah], the moon of Caanan [symbolising the Biblical figure Joseph] can pass*
**Inscription in cartouches above and below the portrait:** *Shahanshah of Iran*
**Early 20th century**

From both the point of view of proportions and colour the face seen here is one of the most charming of the rugs depicting Ahmad Shah. The frame of different borders and corner pieces holds the young shah as it would a jewel. The dark pink field, like a translucent ruby, helps to set off the central figure.

Very probably this rug was copied from an official photographic portrait of Ahmad Shah (see fig. 29). The weaver's efforts to show the shah in correct proportions and the details of his clothes met with great success. (For Ahmad Shah, see p. 28.)

*Size:* 3ft 7.5in x 2ft 10.75in (110 x 88cm)
*Warp:* cotton, Z4S, undyed, undulating, 1 level
*Weft:* cotton, Z4S, light brown, 1 shoot, straight
*Pile:* wool, Z2 loosely plied, Sy1, 0.25in (3mm)
*Knot count:* 9V x 8H = 72 per sq. in. (36V x 32H = 1152 per sq. dm.)
*Texture:* soft, thin, fairly stiff
*Sides:* wool, red, chevron wrapping around 6 warps
*Ends:* lower: 0.75in (2cm) balanced plain weave, undyed cotton
upper: 1.1875in (3cm) balanced plain weave, undyed cotton, decorated with 1 row of weft twining in red and green wool
*Colours* 10, blue-black, dark blue, turquoise, green, red, yellow, dark brown, reddish brown, light brown, ivory

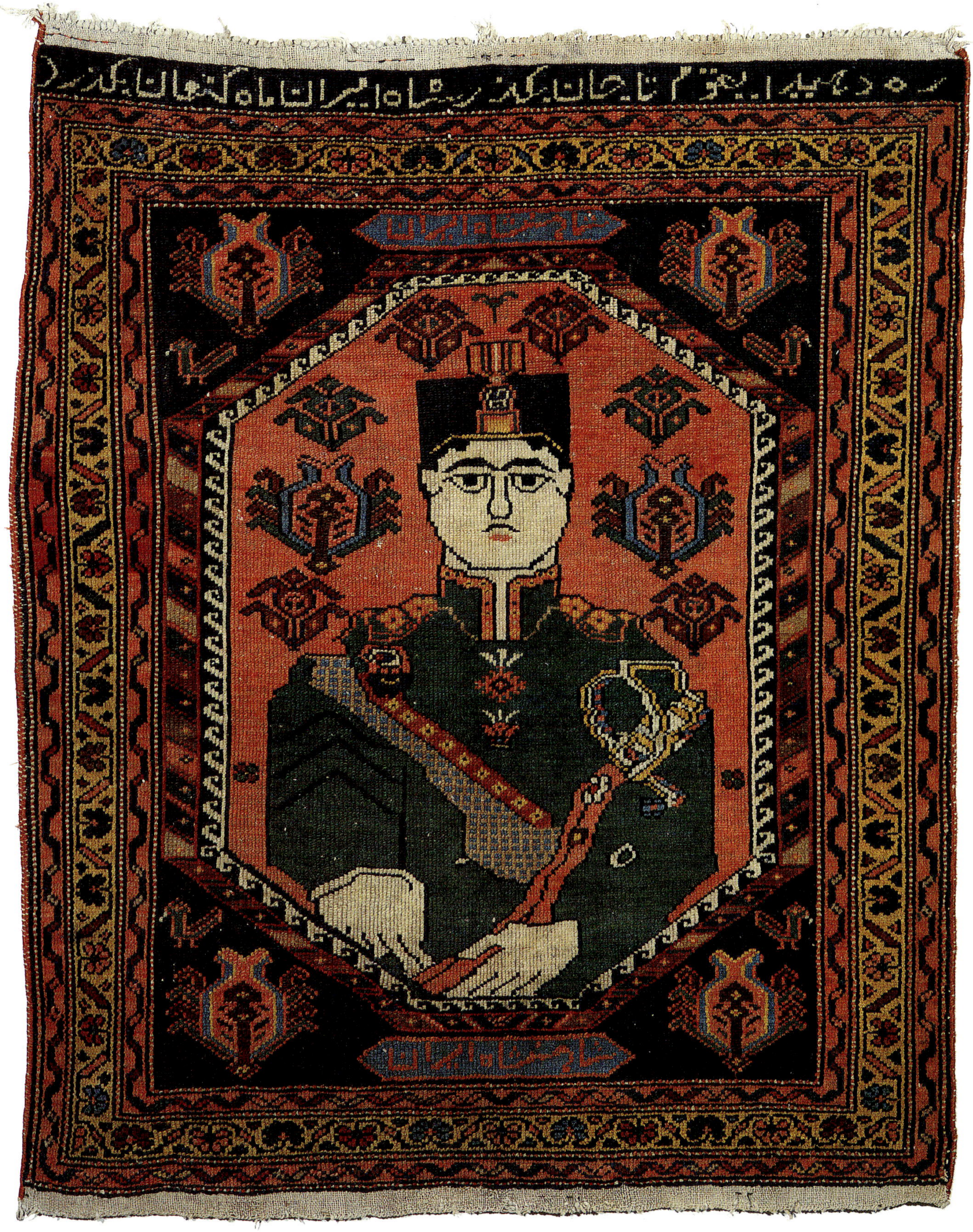

## 34

**Ahmad Shah**
**Hamadan area**
**Inscription:** *illegible inscriptions in the upper right hand corner*
**Dated:** *1342 (1923 AD)*

This rug was woven during the last years of the reign of Ahmad Shah (r. 1909-1924), when most of his authority had been taken from him and he lived abroad. But in spite of this, Ahmad Shah provided a subject for many weavers during those years and even after his reign had ended.

Here the bust of Ahmad Shah (see fig. 29) is framed in a medallion called *qab-i ayinah* (mirror frame). Above the shah's head is a dark blue curtain that has been pulled to each side. Tassels hang down from it on either side of his head. Curtains included at the top of some paintings and *qalamkar* curtains were a feature of art of the Qajar period (see fig. 31). Above and below the central medallion, among the many small animals and birds, are the busts of two men which represent two portraits of the person who originally ordered and owned the rug. (For Ahmad Shah, see p. 28.)

*Size:* 7ft 10.5in x 5ft 1.5in (240 x 156cm)
*Warp:* cotton, Z6S, undyed undulating, 1 level
*Weft:* cotton, Z3S, undyed, 1 shoot, straight; some rows have two shoots: 1 cotton and 1 wool, Z4S loosely plied, undyed ivory; the first straight, the second undulating
*Pile:* wool, Z2 loosely plied, Sy1, 0.1875in (4mm)
*Knot count:* 8V x 9H = 72 per sq. in. (32V x 36H = 1152 per sq. dm.)
*Texture:* soft, fairly thick, very flexible
*Sides:* wool, undyed dark brown, parallel wrapping around 5 warps
*Ends:* lower: missing
upper: 0.375in (1cm) weft-faced plain weave, undyed cotton, decorated with 1 row of weft twining in red and light olive wool
*Colours* 9, blue-black, olive, blue, light olive, brownish red, pink, orange, mustard yellow, ivory

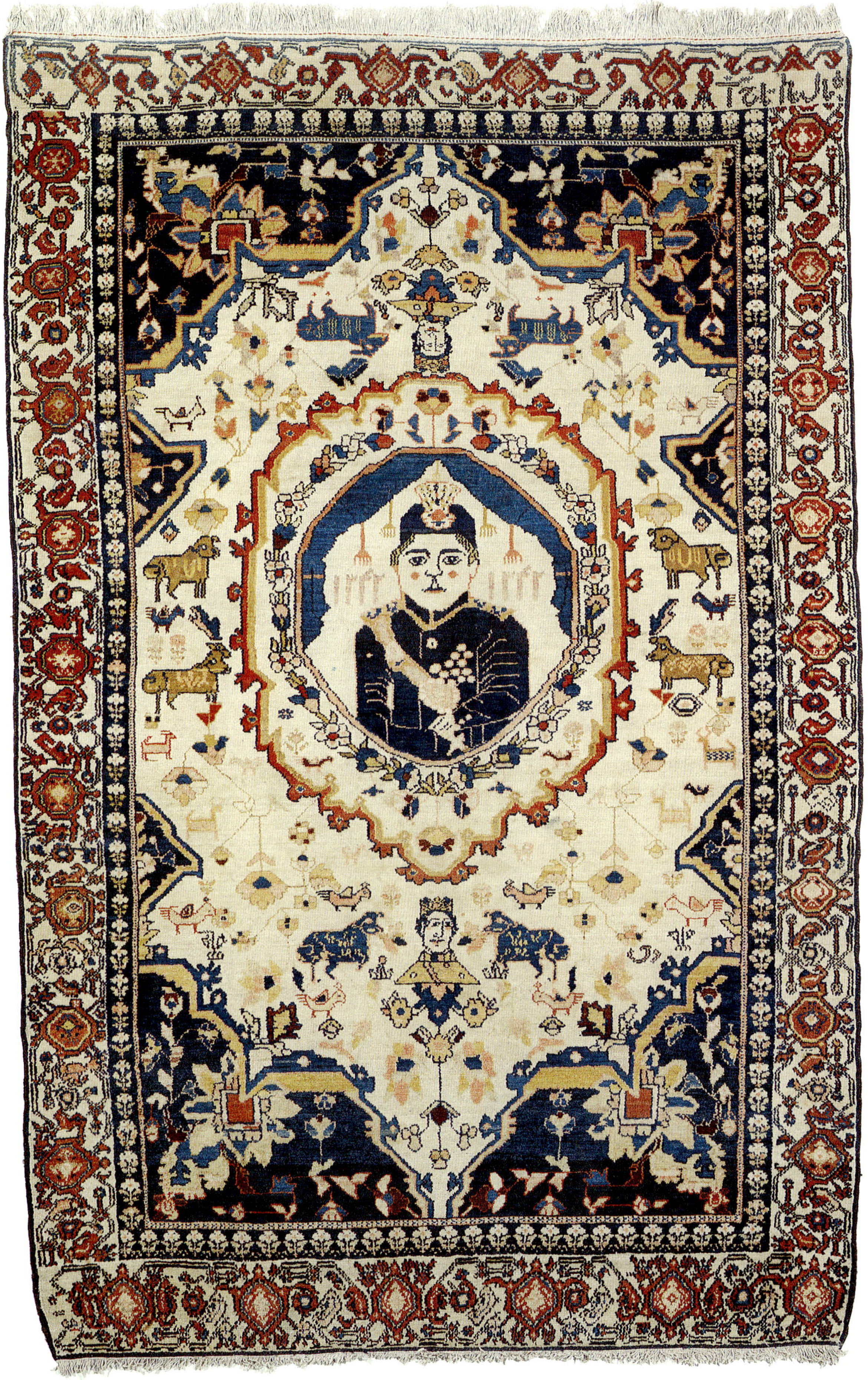

# Kings, Heroes and Lovers

**35**

**Ahmad Shah**
**Safi Khani subtribe of the Qashqa'i**
**Early 20th century**

This figure was probably based on one of the official photographs of Ahmad Shah (see fig. 29). The weaver tried her best to follow the model faithfully, and for a tribal craftswoman unfamiliar with naturalism in art did a very good job in reproducing the soft, curved outlines of the figure in the photograph in rug knotting. This is especially true since the rug is of the *gabbeh* type, which means that it is loosely woven, with long pile and numerous wefts between each row of pile knots (see p. 67). Placing the figure on a plain ground has helped to show it to best advantage. (For Ahmad Shah, see p. 28.)

*Size:* 6ft 3.25in x 4ft 5.25in (191 x 135cm)
*Warp:* wool, Z2S, undyed brown, straight, 1 level
*Weft:* wool, Z2S loosely plied, brown, 3 to 5 shoots, undulating
*Pile:* wool, Z2 loosely plied, Sy1, 0.375in (1cm)
*Knot count:* 6V x 7H = 42 per sq. in. (24V x 28H = 672 per sq. dm.)
*Texture:* soft, thick, very flexible
*Sides:* wool, undyed brown, parallel wrapping around 4 warps
*Ends:* missing
*Colours* 10, blue-black, turquoise blue, dark green, green, bright red, pink, yellow, brown, buff, ivory

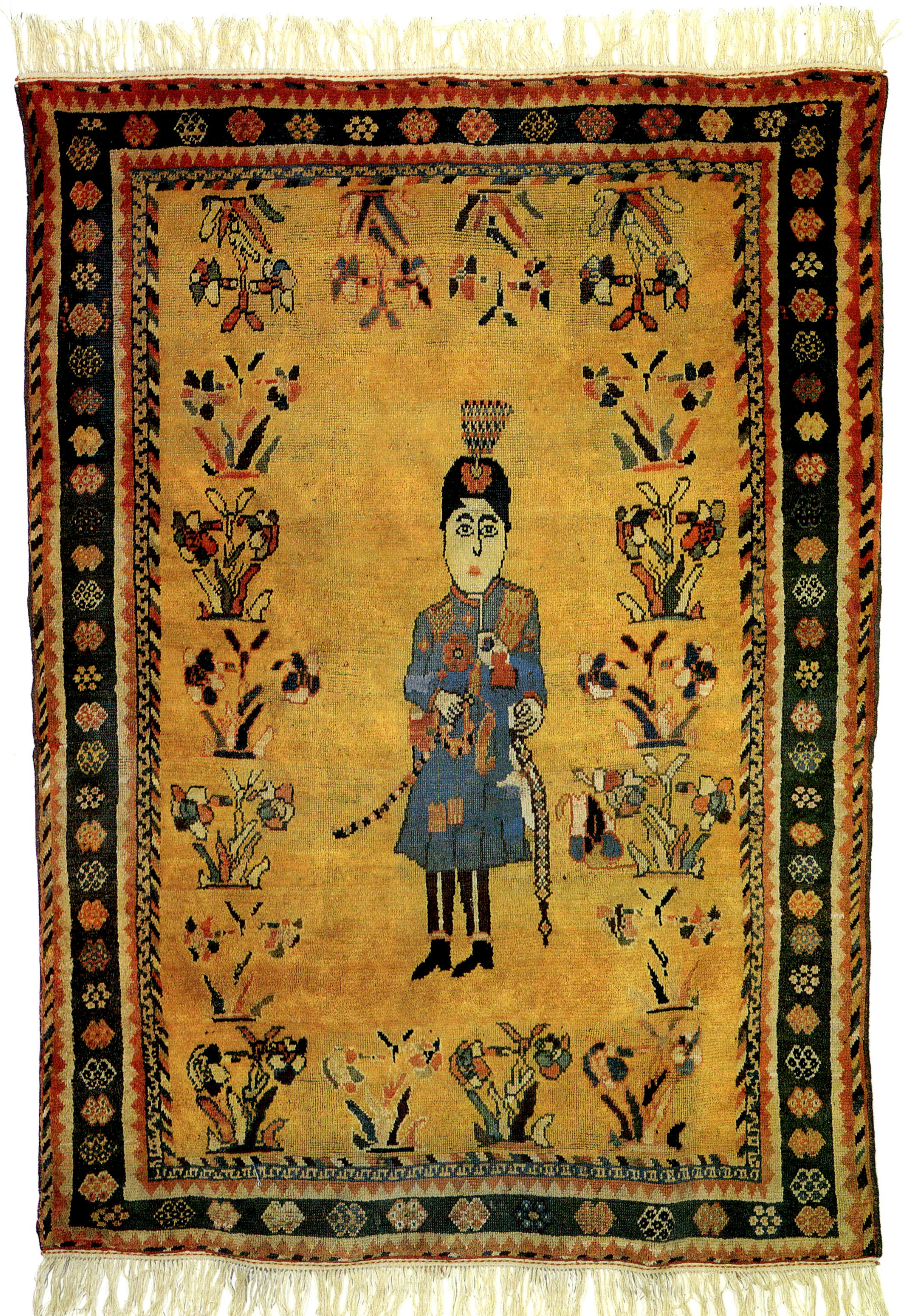

## 36

**Reza Shah**
**Abadeh area**
**Early 20th century**

The considerable similarity that exists between the central figure here and some photographs of Reza Khan (later Reza Shah, r. 1925 to 1941) while he was an officer of the armed forces from 1921 to 1925 (see fig. 30) helps to identify the subject and age of the rug.

The design of the rug is based on common Abadeh patterns, with Reza Khan's figure in place of the central medallion. Outwardly it might seem that there is not a sufficient connection or congruity between the rug design and its dominating figure, or even that the figure was almost cut out of a photograph and placed on top of an existing rug. But the weaver exhibited subtle skill in carrying out the pattern of this rug. The delicate designs in the various parts of the clothing have helped to reduce the differences between the two areas: a military figure so realistically portrayed and the traditional abstract motifs in the background. These two seemingly incompatible elements are thus brought into harmony. (For Reza Shah, see p. 28.)

*Size:* 7ft 1.5in x 4ft 8.25in (217 x 143cm)
*Warp:* cotton, Z12S, undyed, straight, semi-depressed (almost 2 levels)
*Weft:* cotton, Z7S, blue; 2 shoots: the first straight, the second undulating
*Pile:* wool, Z2 loosely plied, As3, 0.1875in (4mm)
*Knot count:* 12V x 10H = 120 per sq. in. (48V x 40H = 1920 per sq. dm.)
*Texture:* soft, very thin, fairly flexible
*Sides:* wool, undyed ivory, blue-black, parallel wrapping around 12 warps
*Ends:* missing
*Colours* 9, blue-black, dark blue, light blue, turquoise blue, dark red, orange, dark brown, light brown, ivory

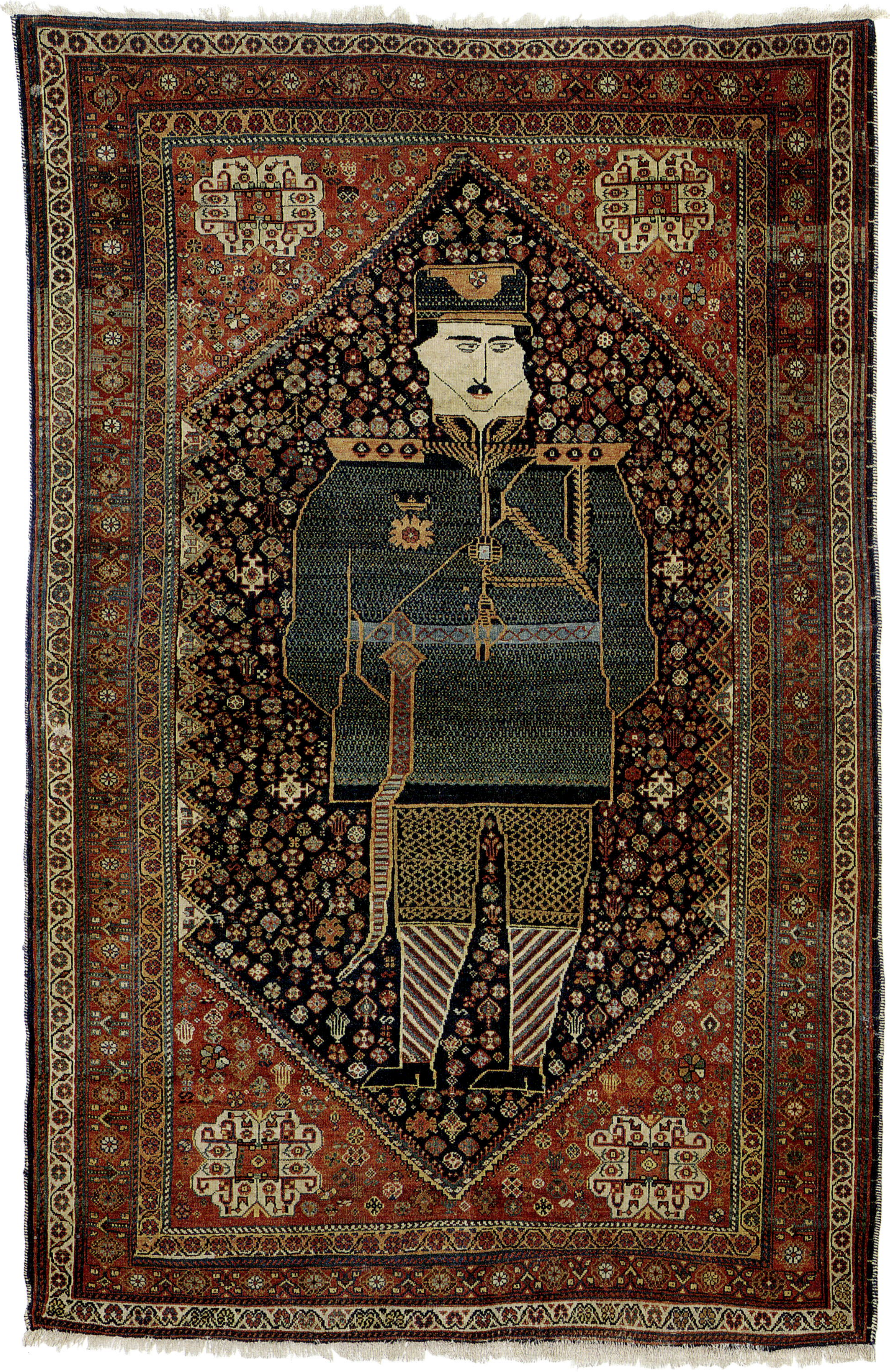

## 37

**Colonel Muhammad Taqi Khan**
**Kermanshah**
**Inscription:** *Colonel Muhammad Taqi Khan*
**Early to mid-20th century**

Without the inscription on this carpet, it might be taken for another interpretation of the rug in fig. 32, which depicts another army officer, or for the wood-block-printed curtain in fig. 31, which portrays Reza Khan (later Reza Shah) when he was an army officer. But the inscription here makes it clear that this rug portrays Colonel Muhammad Taqi Khan. Carpets with such figures were made at the beginning of this century, when posing in a chair was a fashion in photography (see rug no. 24 and note). Colonel Muhammad Taqi Khan was an officer when Reza Khan was a general and head of the army during the final years of the reign of the last Qajar ruler, Ahmad Shah, when the country was in great upheaval. After the coup d'état of 1921, first Sayyid Zia al-Din and then Qavam al-Saltanah served as prime minister and Reza Khan headed the army. Colonel Taqi Khan was asked to resign and to present himself to the capital. He not only disobeyed that order but rebelled against the central government, as did tribal chiefs and other local officials. But his resistance was short-lived; he was killed while fighting pro-government troops.

*Size:* 8ft 2in x 5ft 0.625in (249 x 154cm)
*Warp:* cotton, Z10S, undyed, undulating, 1 level
*Weft:* cotton, Z9S, blue grey, 1 shoot, straight
*Pile:* wool, Z2 loosely plied, Sy1, 0.1875in (5mm)
*Knot count:* 10V x 11H = 110 per sq. in. (40V x 44H = 1760 per sq. dm.)
*Texture:* soft, rather thick, fairly flexible
*Sides:* wool, blue-black, parallel wrapping around 6 warps
*Ends:* lower: 0.375in (1cm) balanced plain weave, undyed cotton
upper: long braided fringe of warps
*Colours* 11, blue-black, dark blue, light blue, light green, dark red, orange, brown, yellow, pink, ivory, white

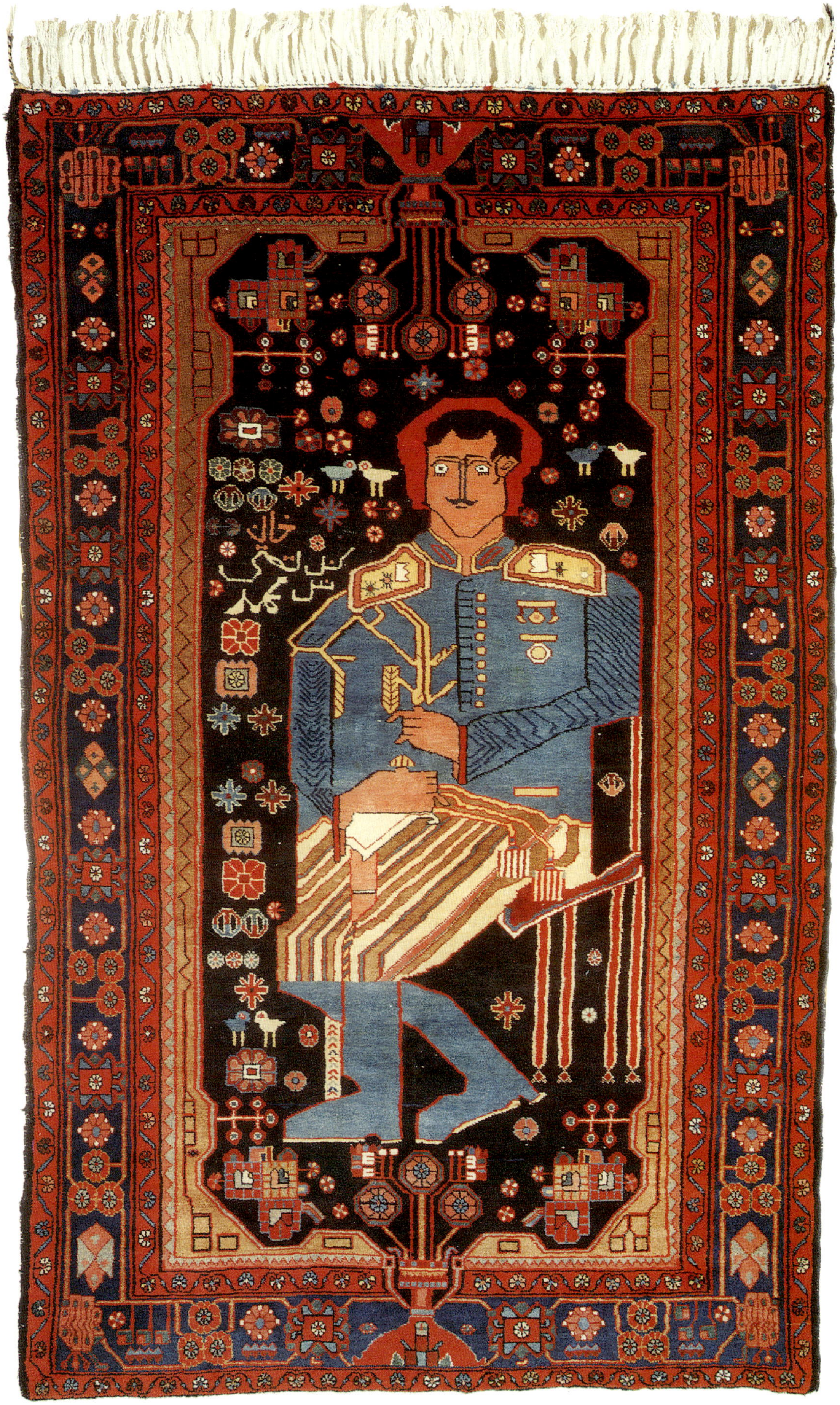

*Kings, Heroes and Lovers*

**38**

**Rustam**
**Saruq**
**Inscription:** ***Rustam-i Zal ('Rustam, Son of Zal'),***
***Muhammad 'Ali, the designer, [in the] year 1324 (1906 AD)***

Although Rustam, the peerless legendary champion of Iran, is a well-known figure in that country and stories about him are very popular (see p. 30 infra), pictures of him on rugs are not frequently encountered. Despite the fact that a given pictorial subject is often repeatedly woven in one year and one might expect to find a number of examples, the picture of Rustam was apparently rarely woven in Saruq (I have seen only two examples to date).

With the exception of the subject portrayed, everything else in this rug resembles the Shapur rugs of Saruq in general, and rug no. 17 in particular. It would appear that the same person designed this Rustam rug and Shapur rug no. 17, as is indicated in the inscriptions. (See the discussion of symmetrical knots in Saruq rugs in the entry for no. 14; see also no. 17.)

Many of Rustam's characteristic attributes described by Firdawsi in his *Shahnamah*, such as his helmet made from the skull of the White Demon, his mace with an ox or bull-like head at the top, his split beard, powerful arms, and leopard-skin tunic are clearly shown.

*Size:* 4ft 10.25in x 3ft 4.5in (148 x 103cm)
*Warp:* cotton, Z3S, undyed, straight, 2 levels
*Weft:* cotton, Z10S, undyed; 2 shoots: the first straight, the second undulating
*Pile:* wool, Z2 loosely plied, Sy2, 0.25in (3mm)
*Knot count:* 13V x 13H = 169 per sq. in. (52V x 52H = 2704 per sq. dm.)
*Texture:* soft, thin, stiff
*Sides:* wool, undyed dark brown, parallel wrapping around 4 warps
*Ends:* 0.75in (2cm) weft-faced plain weave, undyed cotton, decorated with 1 row of weft twining in brown and blue wool
*Colours* 13, blue, light blue, green, red, pink, orange, orange yellow, yellow, very dark brown, dark brown, brown, light brown, ivory

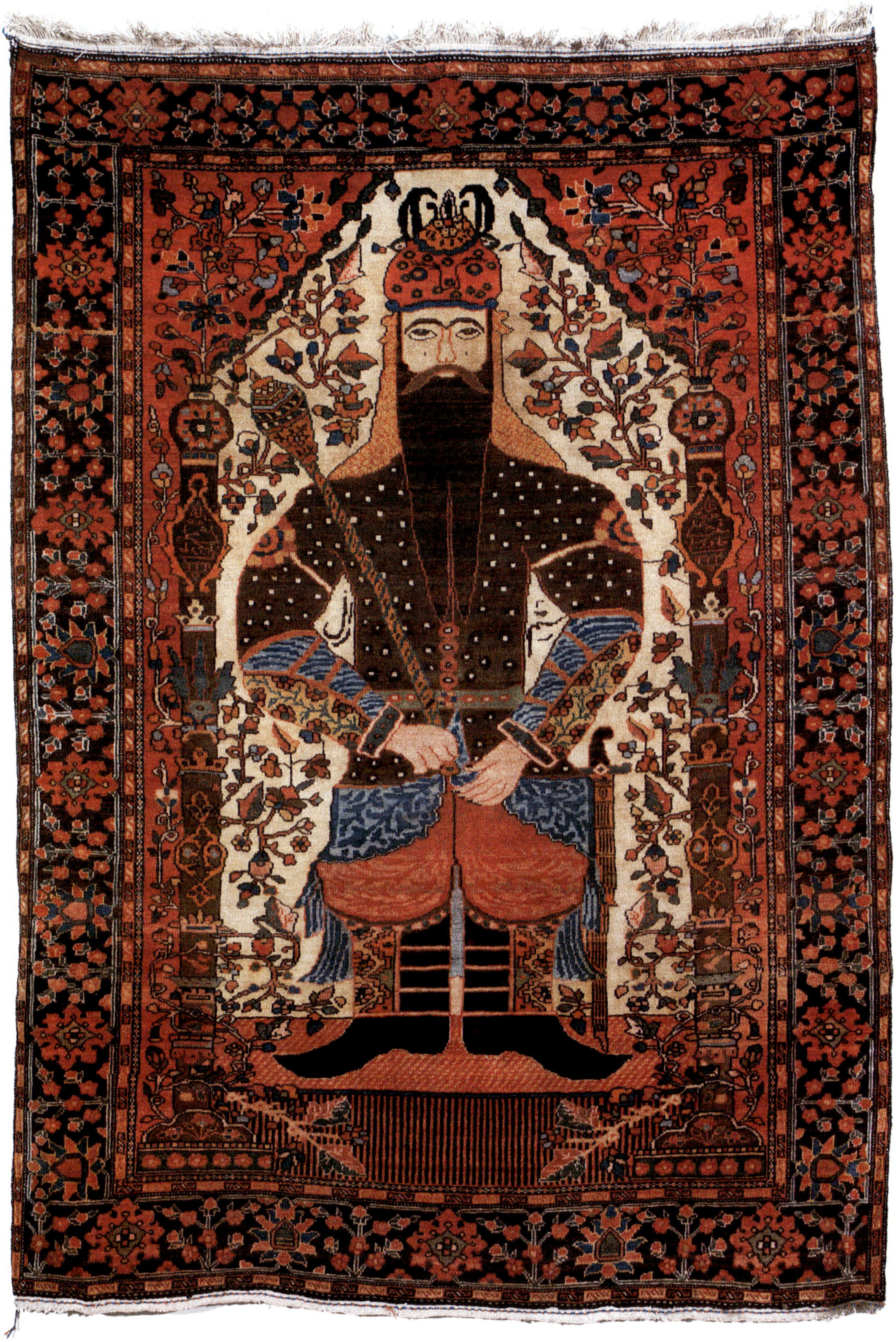

## 39

**Rustam and Suhrab**
**Karabagh region of the southern Caucasus**
**Inscription: *Suhrab (written in mirror image)***
**Early 19th century**

This small rug may have been woven by Armenians (see p. 47 infra), in spite of the fact the subject is drawn from the Persian national epic, and that the inscription is written in Persian. At the bottom of the rug the imaginative weaver has included a frolicking dog. The dog has nothing to do with the subject of this rug, and would be a highly unusual animal for a Persian rug weaver to add to this scene, since Muslims consider dogs unclean and Armenians do not.

The subject of this rug is Suhrab, who unwittingly fought his own father, Rustam, by whom he was killed (see the story of Rustam and Suhrab, p. 31). Here he and his father sit in chairs on either side of a tree. The weaver apparently wanted to create a peaceful scene from the Rustam-Suhrab story. The Rustam and Suhrab scenes usually depicted centre on the dramatic moment when Suhrab is killed by Rustam.

The two figures, with the exception of their faces, are nearly identical here and are balanced symmetrically, with one leg over the other, sword in hand, seated in battle dress. Only Rustam's split beard distinguishes him from his son.

Different shades of pink (which are characteristic of Karabagh rugs) on a dark brown field produce a special attractiveness in this rug. Although the two ends of the rug have been worn away, the main part of the rug has not been damaged.

*Size:* 3ft 11.25in x 2ft 9.5in (120 x 85cm)
*Warp:* wool, Z3S, undyed ivory to brown, straight, semi-depressed
*Weft:* 2 strands of undyed cotton, Z2S, and 1 strand of wool, Z1, twisted together as Z3S light orange; 2 shoots: the first straight, the second undulating
*Pile:* wool, Z2S, Sy2, 0.0625in (2mm)
*Knot count:* 6V x 7H = 42 per sq. in. (24V x 28H = 672 per sq. dm.)
*Textures:* fairly coarse, fairly thin, fairly flexible
*Sides:* not original
*Ends:* missing
*Colours* 8, red, pink, greenish yellow, yellow, dark brown, light brown, brownish grey, ivory

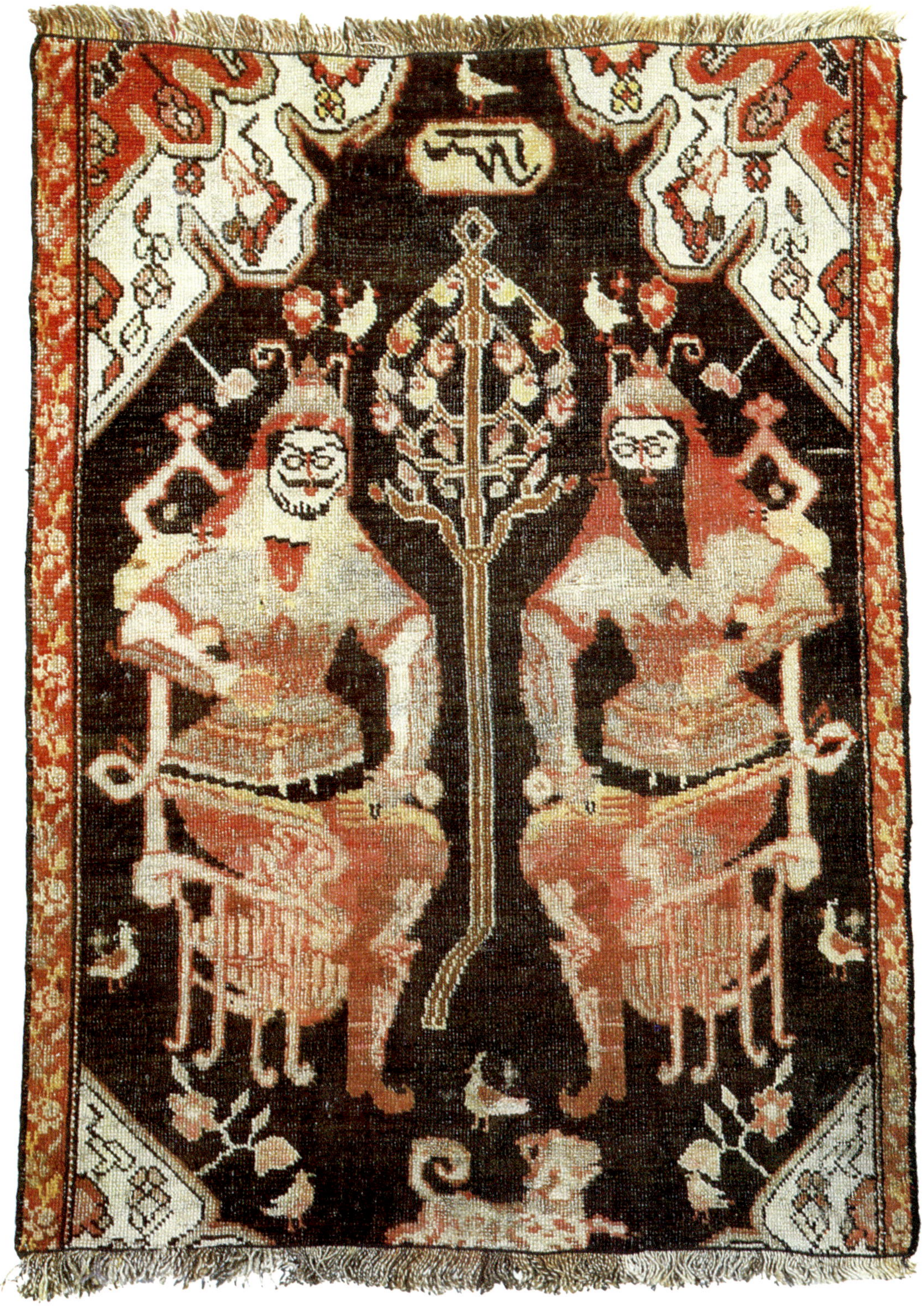

**40**

**Rustam and Akvan the Demon
Ferahan area
Inscription: *The order of His Excellency Habib al-Sultan (illegible) [in the] year 1214 (1799 AD)*
Late 19th century**

The story of Rustam and Akvan the Demon, while well known to Iranians (see p. 32), has been illustrated only infrequently in Iranian art. Examples of these illustrations are found in some of the manuscripts of the *Shahnamah*, such as the mid-fifteenth century manuscript known as the Muhammad Juki *Shahnamah* in the collection of the Royal Asiatic Society in London (see fig. 33). This scene is also depicted in a line drawing illustrating a nineteenth-century lithographed edition of the *Shahnamah* (see fig. 34). In the miniature painting in fig. 33 Rustam and Akvan the Demon are portrayed in a manner different from that seen in this rug. What helps make the woven version so effective is Rustam's horse, Rakhsh, and wooded area with birds and animals, which impart a lifelike quality to the picture. The simplification of some of the forms also makes the images more forceful. For example, the chunk of earth on which the sleeping Rustam is lying and being held up in the air by the Demon Akvan is a more or less regular polygon against which the thick neck and shoulders, weapons, and highly decorated clothes of the curled-up Iranian hero are skilfully contrasted. The use of dark blue for the chunk of earth serves as a good foil to set off the red shades of Rustam and symbolizes the sky as well. This rug must be over one hundred years old, not simply because of the date woven into it (dates woven into rugs are not always reliable), but also because of the lustre of the colours and erosion of the black. Another indication of its age is the title of the person who commissioned it: Sultan, an appellation for nobility that was used during the Qajar dynasty.

*Size:* 6ft 8in x 4ft 4in (203 x 132cm)
*Warp:* Cotton, Z11S, undyed, straight, semi-depressed (almost 2 levels)
*Weft:* cotton, Z14S, blue 2 shoots: the first straight, the second undulating
*Pile:* wool, Z2 loosely plied, As3, 0.0625in (2mm)
*Knot count:* 16V x 10H = 160 per sq. in. (64V x 40H = 2560 per sq. dm.)
*Texture:* fairly coarse, thin, fairly flexible
*Sides:* wool, very dark red, remains of parallel wrapping around 2 warps
*Ends:* missing
*Colours* 10, black (eroded), dark blue, blue, dark green, mustard, dark red, pink, chocolate, dark buff, ivory

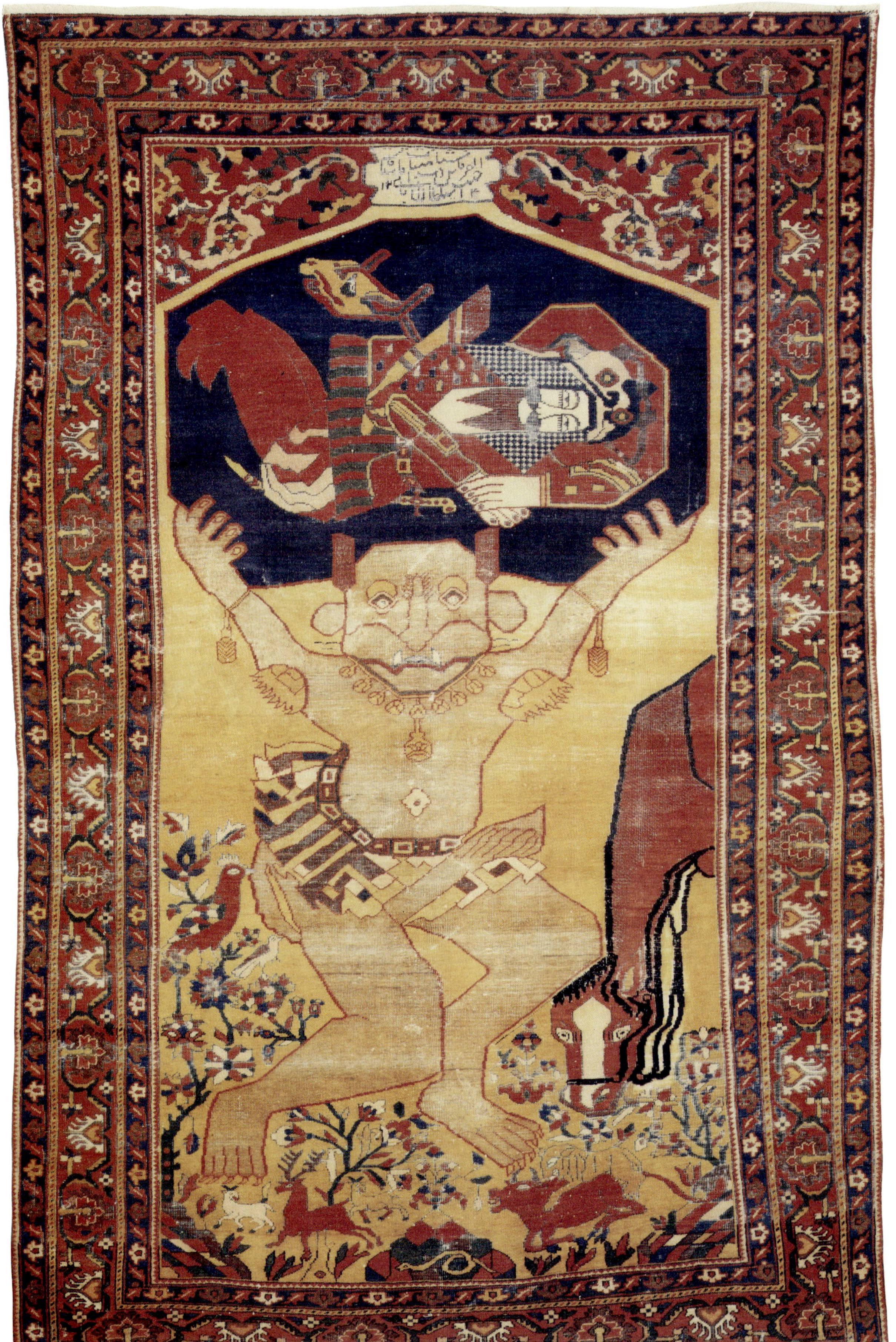

**41**

**Khusraw and Shirin
Firdows area
Inscription:** *illegible*
**Early 20th century**

What distinguishes this piece from other Firdows rugs depicting Khusraw and Shirin (see p. 35 infra) is the treatment of the upper section of the field. Why the weaver, who followed a more traditional portrayal of the figures at the bottom, did not do so at the top is unknown. In the upper section Khusraw is not seated on the horse; rather, his head and shoulders are seen above his steed. Unlike the other horses in this group of rugs depicting similar figures, the proportion of the head to the body is not naturalistic and instead of a mane the animal has long tresses like those of a human. Most interesting of all is Khusraw's attendant: his clothes are a mixture of an old traditional style and a police uniform of the present century.

At the bottom Shirin is shown seated, with an attendant standing on each side.

*Size:* 4ft 10in x 3ft 7.25in (147 x 110cm)
*Warp:* cotton, Z4S, undyed, straight, 1 level
*Weft:* cotton, Z3S loosely plied, grey brown, 2 shoots, both undulating
*Pile:* wool, Z2 loosely plied, As2 0.25in (6mm)
*Knot count:* 8V x 8H = 64 per sq. in (32V x 32H = 1024 per sq. dm.)
*Texture:* soft, thin, flexible
*Sides:* wool, undyed black, parallel wrapping around 7 warps
*Ends:* missing
*Colours* 10, blue-black, blue, dark green, emerald green, red, pink, orangish yellow, dark brown, light brown, ivory

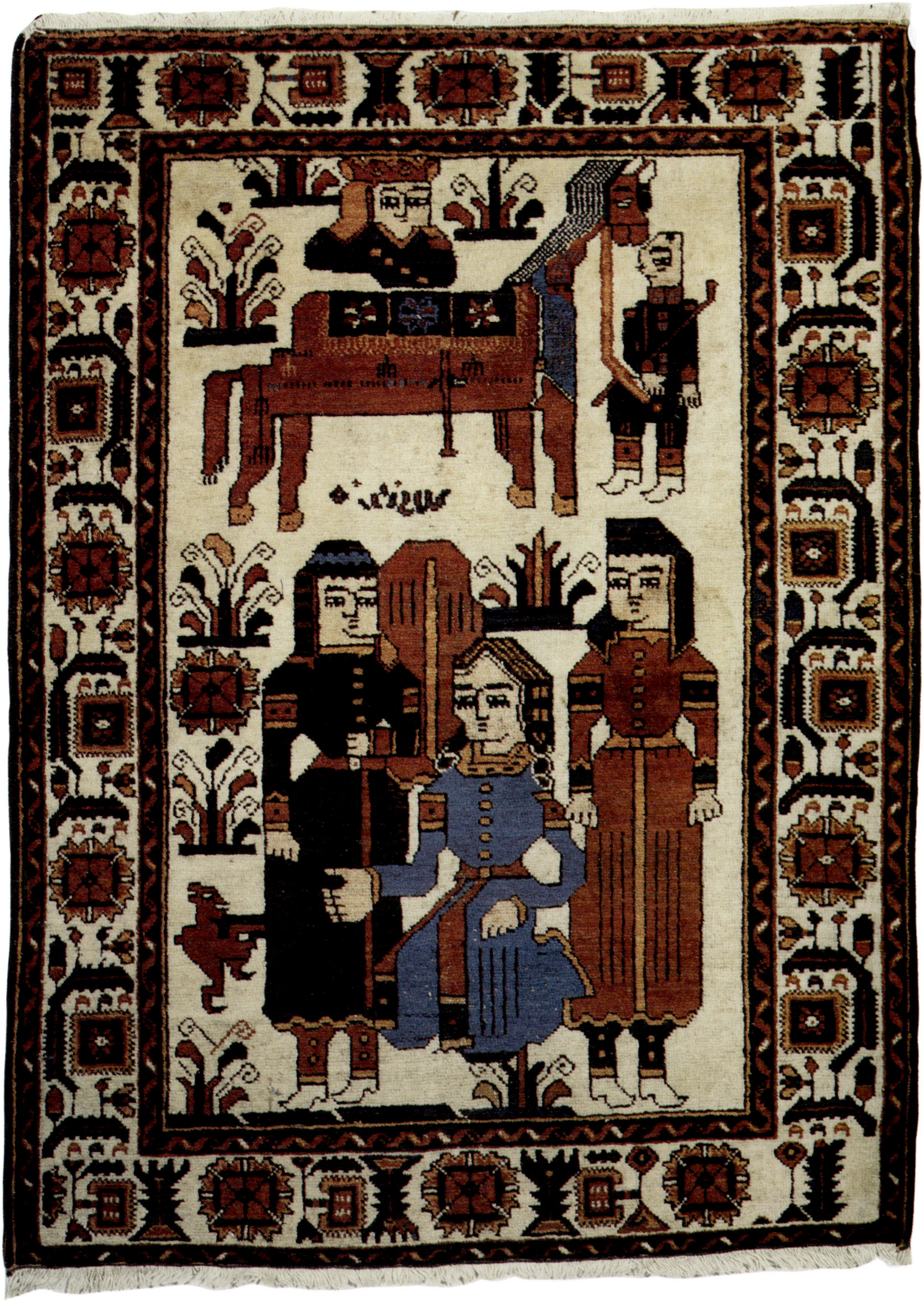

## 42

**Khusraw and Shirin Hunting a Wild Boar; Majnun and a Gazelle
Firdows area
Early 20th century**

Although the Khusraw and Shirin theme (see p. 35 infra) is one that has been utilized by rug weavers in most parts of Iran, it must be considered special to Firdows, since the majority that depict this story are from that area and rugs almost identical to this one are still being woven there today. Differences of colour do, however, distinguish the older examples from the new products. Various shades of green, for instance, are no longer found in Firdaws rugs as they once were.

The scene of Khusraw and Shirin hunting is portrayed in all its details at the top of the rug and is continued in the centre. Of interest is the way Khusraw is shown standing in his stirrups and leaning forward in order to cut off the head of the wild boar. Archers at the top and in the middle add to the excitement of the scene. The seated figure at the lower left corner is another representation of Shirin, flanked by two standing figures of women of her court (cf. the lower section of rug nos. 43, 44, 45).

Majnun's presence at the bottom of the rug is unexpected, since he is a character in a completely different story (see p. 37 infra.) Perhaps his well-known friendship with animals and desire to set captured gazelles free are responsible for his being included with the hunt scene above, especially as some of the hunters are taking aim at baby gazelles.

*Size:* 5ft 7.75in x 3ft 7.25in (172 x 110cm)
*Warp:* cotton, Z4S undyed, straight, 1 level
*Weft:* cotton, Z3S, light grey brown, 2 shoots, both undulating
*Pile:* wool, Z2 loosely plied, As2, 0.375in (10mm)
*Knot count:* 9V x 8H = 72 per sq. in. (36V x 32H = 1152 per sq. dm.)
*Texture:* soft, fairly thick, flexible
*Sides:* wool, red, parallel wrapping around 3 warps
*Ends:* 1.1875in (3cm) weft-faced plain weave, grey-brown cotton and red wool
*Colours* 9, blue-black, dark green, light green, red, dark pink, light blue, dark brown, light brown, ivory

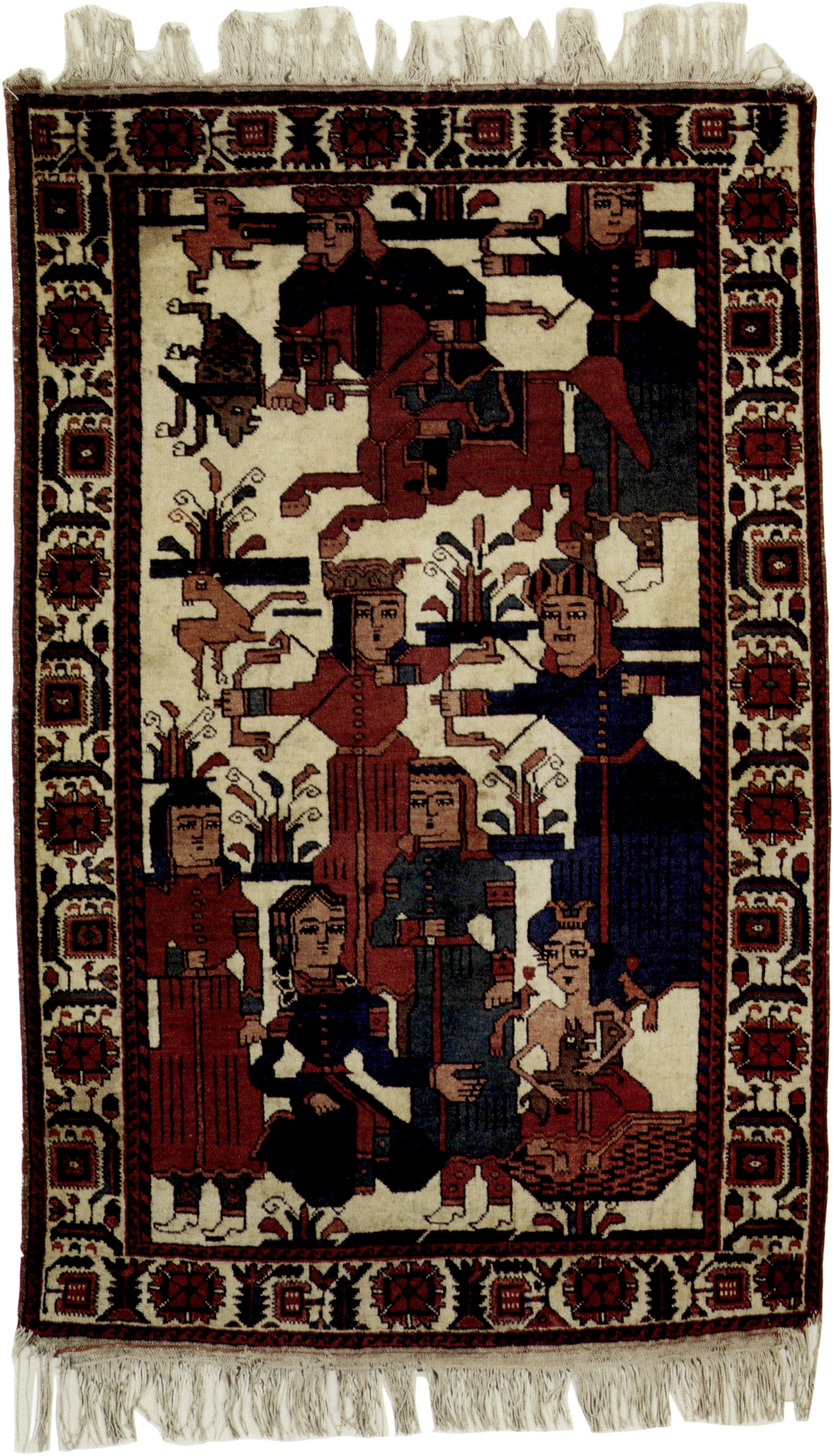

*Kings, Heroes and Lovers*

**43**

**Khusraw and Shirin
Nahavand area
Mid-20th century**

While most rugs depicting Khusraw and Shirin (see p. 35 infra) were woven in eastern Iran, an occasional example from western Iran turns up as well. Even a quick glance tells us that this Khusraw and Shirin rug must have been based on an eastern Iranian prototype, except for the animals placed in Khusraw's hunting ground. These consist of the lion-and-sun (see pp. 59, 60), the official emblem of Iran, seen in three places, and a lion attacking a gazelle, a type of motif common in sixteenth- and seventeenth-century Persian hunting carpets. The drawing of the horse's head is interesting.

*Size:* 6ft 3.5in x 4ft 4in (192 x 132cm)
*Warp:* cotton, Z5S, undyed, undulating, 1 level
*Weft:* cotton, Z13S, light blue, 1 shoot, straight
*Pile:* wool, Z2S, Sy1, 0.375in (1cm.)
*Knot count:* 8V x 8H = 64 per sq. in. (32V x 32H = 1024 per sq. dm.)
*Texture:* soft, very thick, fairly flexible
*Sides:* wool, dark brown, parallel wrapping around 4 warps
*Ends:* lower: 0.75in (2cm) weft-faced plain weave, undyed cotton
upper: 0.375in (1cm.) weft-faced plain weave, light blue cotton
*Colours* 10, blue-black, blue, brownish olive, light olive, bright red, orange, dark brown, brown, buff, ivory

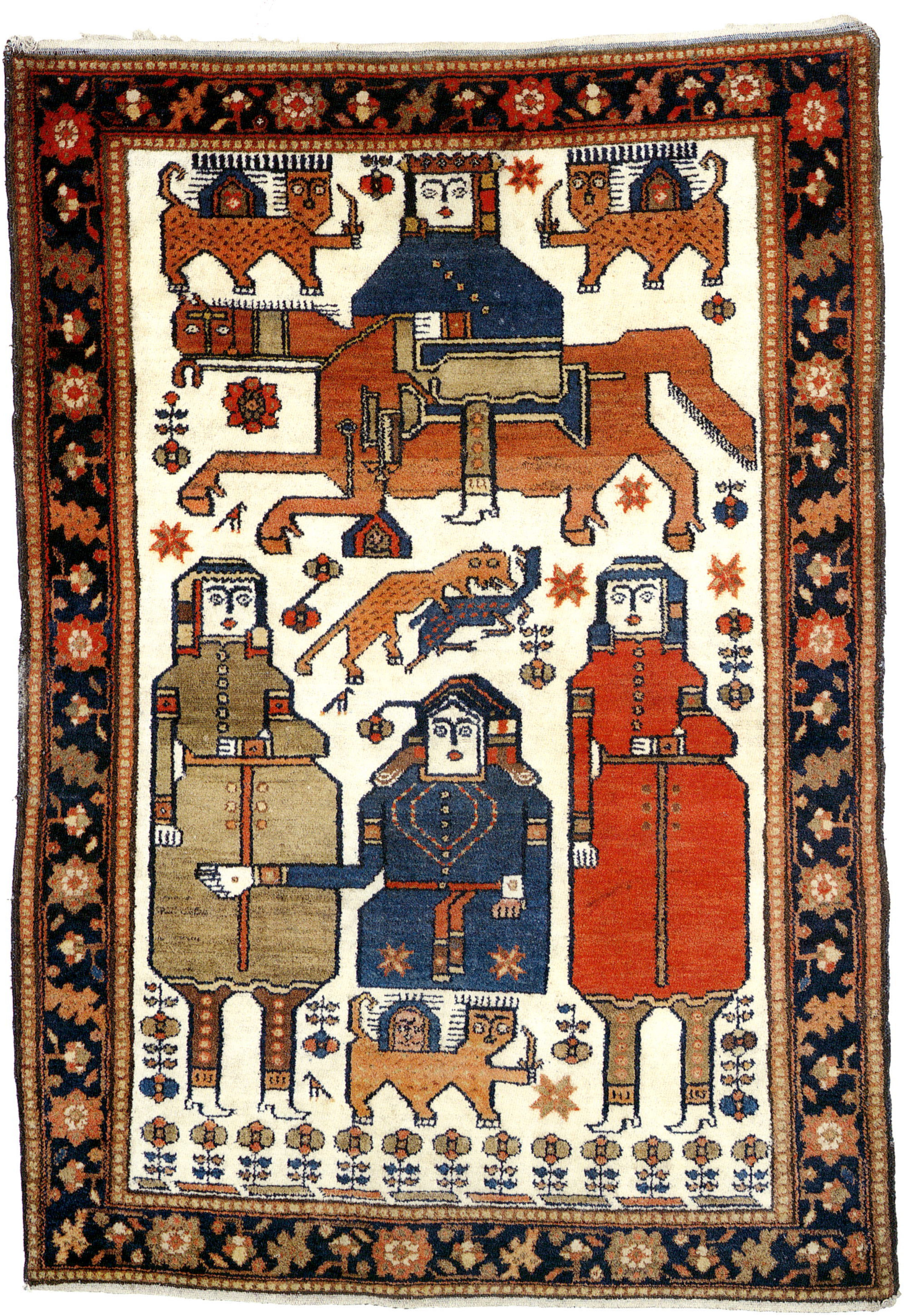

*Kings, Heroes and Lovers*

**44**

**Khusraw and Shirin**
**Baluch of the Zabul area**
**Mid-20th century**

The Khusraw and Shirin theme (see p. 35 infra) with its special arrangement of figures is seen quite often in Firdows rugs. Here we find the same subject portrayed in quite a new fashion by a weaver of the Zabul area. There are three sections, the uppermost of which shows Khusraw seated on a horse, in front of which stands an attendant or companion. In the centre is a row of four people who resemble other rows of human figures in Baluchi rugs (cf. rugs nos. 63, 64, 65, 66). These are all about the same height and size and only a change in the colour of their clothes distinguishes one from the other. At the bottom, Shirin is shown seated and flanked by two attendants.

As is frequently the case, small plant and animal forms fill the spaces between the large human and animal figures in the field.

*Size:* 6ft 3.25in x 3ft 4.25in (191 x 102cm)
*Warp:* wool, Z2S, undyed ivory, straight, 1 level
*Weft:* wool, Z2 loosely plied, undyed dark brown, 2 shoots, both undulating
*Pile:* wool, Z2 loosely plied, As1, 0.1875in (5mm)
*Knot count:* 10V x 8H = 80 per sq. in. (40V x 32H = 1280 per sq. dm.)
*Texture:* soft, fairly thin, very flexible
*Sides:* goat hair, undyed dark brown, 4 cables, each wrapped around 3 warps
*Ends:* 1.5625in (4cm) weft-faced plain weave, undyed wool, warps tied in groups
*Colours* 9, dark brown, dark green, light green, red, orange, dark purplish brown, orangish brown, light brown, ivory

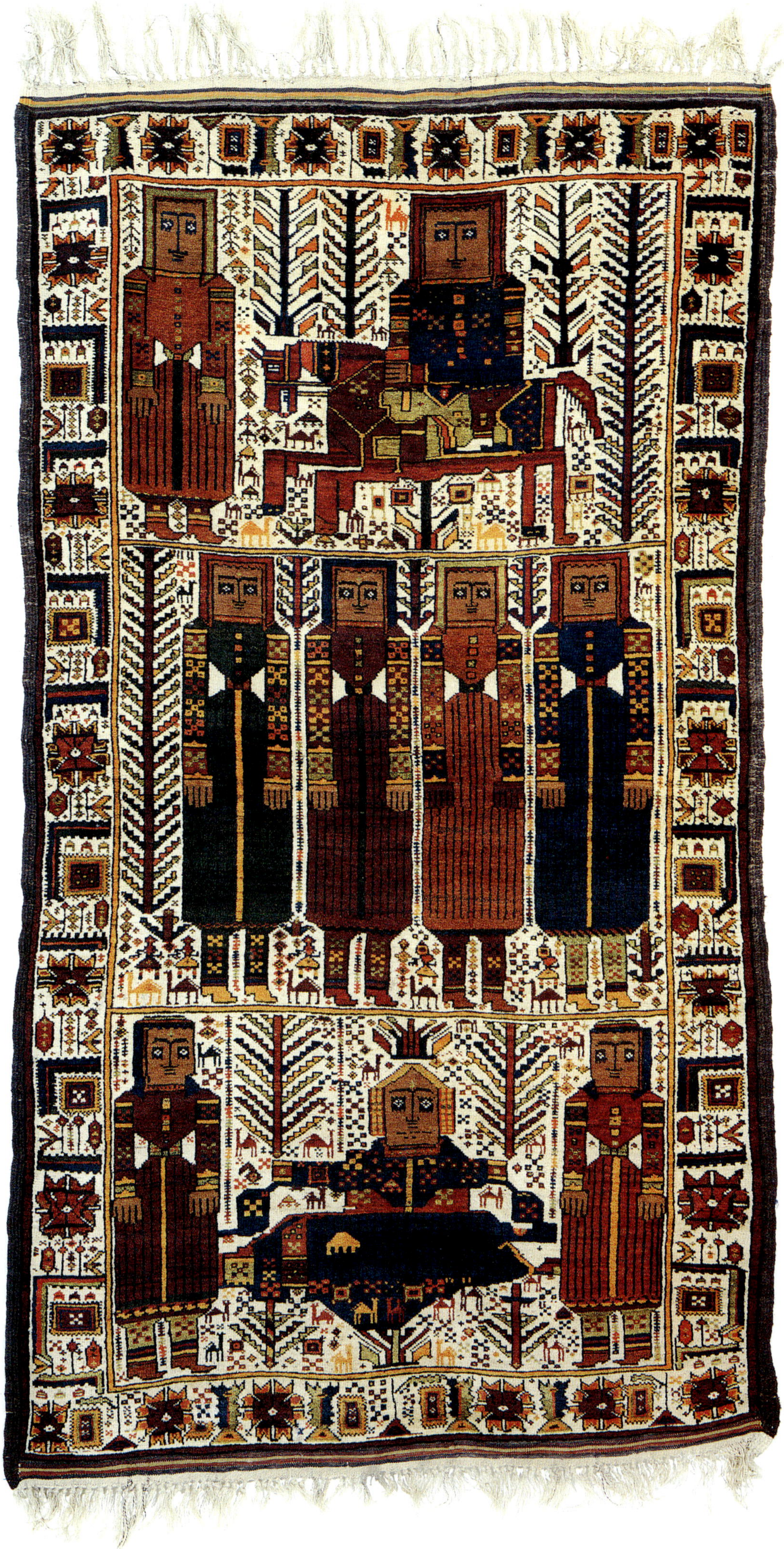

*Kings, Heroes and Lovers*

**45**

**Khusraw and Shirin
Rudehen area, near Tehran
Inscription: *Batul Ghani 1367
(1947 AD)***

This rug was discovered in the early 1970s in a teahouse in Rudehen, a village on the road between Tehran and Damavand. It was covering a raised wooden platform on which we were sitting and drinking tea. The rug was in bad shape. The present owner bought it from the owner of the teahouse and at the same time learned that it had been woven in the same village about twenty-five years earlier by Batul Ghani, the woman whose name appears on it. Originally it was one of a pair and was hung on the wall of the teahouse. Later, when colour photographs and posters became available, the rug was taken down and thrown over the raised platform of the teahouse.

The people of Rudehen speak a Turkic dialect and are known as 'Ali-Allahis. They immigrated to Rudehen in past centuries. In contrast to other Khusraw and Shirin rugs, this is woven with a dark ground which helps to set off the different forms and colours. (For a discussion of the story of Khusraw and Shirin, see p. 35 infra.)

*Size:* 5ft 11.75in x 4ft 7.5in (182 x 141cm)
*Warp:* cotton, Z3S, light brown, somewhat undulating, 1 level
*Weft:* wool, Z2S, undyed dark brown, 1 shoot, nearly straight
*Pile:* wool, Z2 loosely plied,سy1, 0.1875in (4mm)
*Knot count:* 7V x 5H = 35 per sq. in. (28V x 20H = 560 per sq. dm.)
*Texture:* fairly coarse, fairly thick, flexible
*Sides:* wool, undyed dark brown, parallel wrapping around 4 warps
*Ends:* 0.75in (2cm) weft-faced plain weave, wool, undyed dark brown
*Colours* 12, blue-black, green, emerald green, olive green, red, pink, orange, dark brown, brown, olive brown, blue grey, ivory

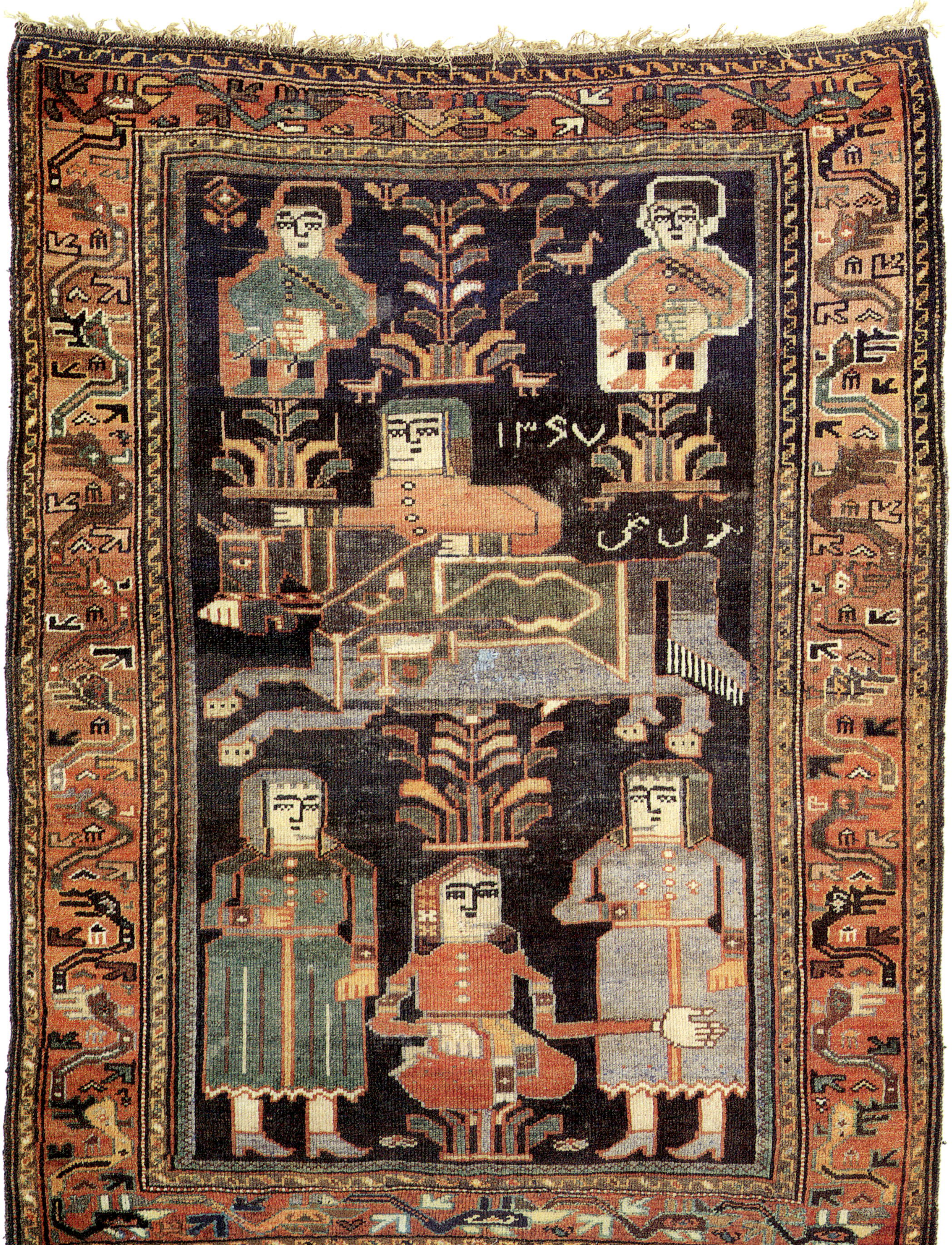

**46**

**Shirin Bathing at a Spring Observed by Khusraw**
**Province of Arak, village of Lilihan**
**Late 19th-early 20th century**

This famous scene is found in most illustrated books containing the story of Khusraw and Shirin. While this scene has been depicted in various different periods which differ in style, the general composition tends to be similar at all periods.

The major elements of the story of Khusraw and Shirin are summarized on p. 35 infra; this scene represents the first encounter between Khusraw and Shirin. The source of inspiration for this rug could have been a lithographed book illustration such as fig. 39 or a *qalamkar* curtain such as fig. 40, either of which would themselves have been based on a miniature painting similar to fig. 38. (This well-known scene is also depicted in the cartoon illustrated in fig. 37.)

This rug was woven in a village that for a long time was populated by Armenians. For a discussion of the Armenian contribution to pictorial rugs, see p. 47 infra.

*Size:* 3ft 0.5in x 2ft 8.75in (93 x 83cm
*Warp:* cotton, Z9S, undyed, undulating, 1 level
*Weft:* cotton, Z3S, buff; 1 shoot, straight
*Pile:* cotton, Z2 loosely plied, Sy1, 0.25in (3mm)
*Knot count:* 13V x 12H = 156 per sq. in. (52V x 48H = 2496 per sq. dm.)
*Texture:* soft, thin, very flexible
*Sides:* wool, black, parallel wrapping around 5 warps
*Ends:* 0.375in (1cm) weft-faced plain weave, undyed cotton
*Colours* 10, blue-black, blue, turquoise blue, dark green, red, pink, pale pink, mustard yellow, yellow, buff

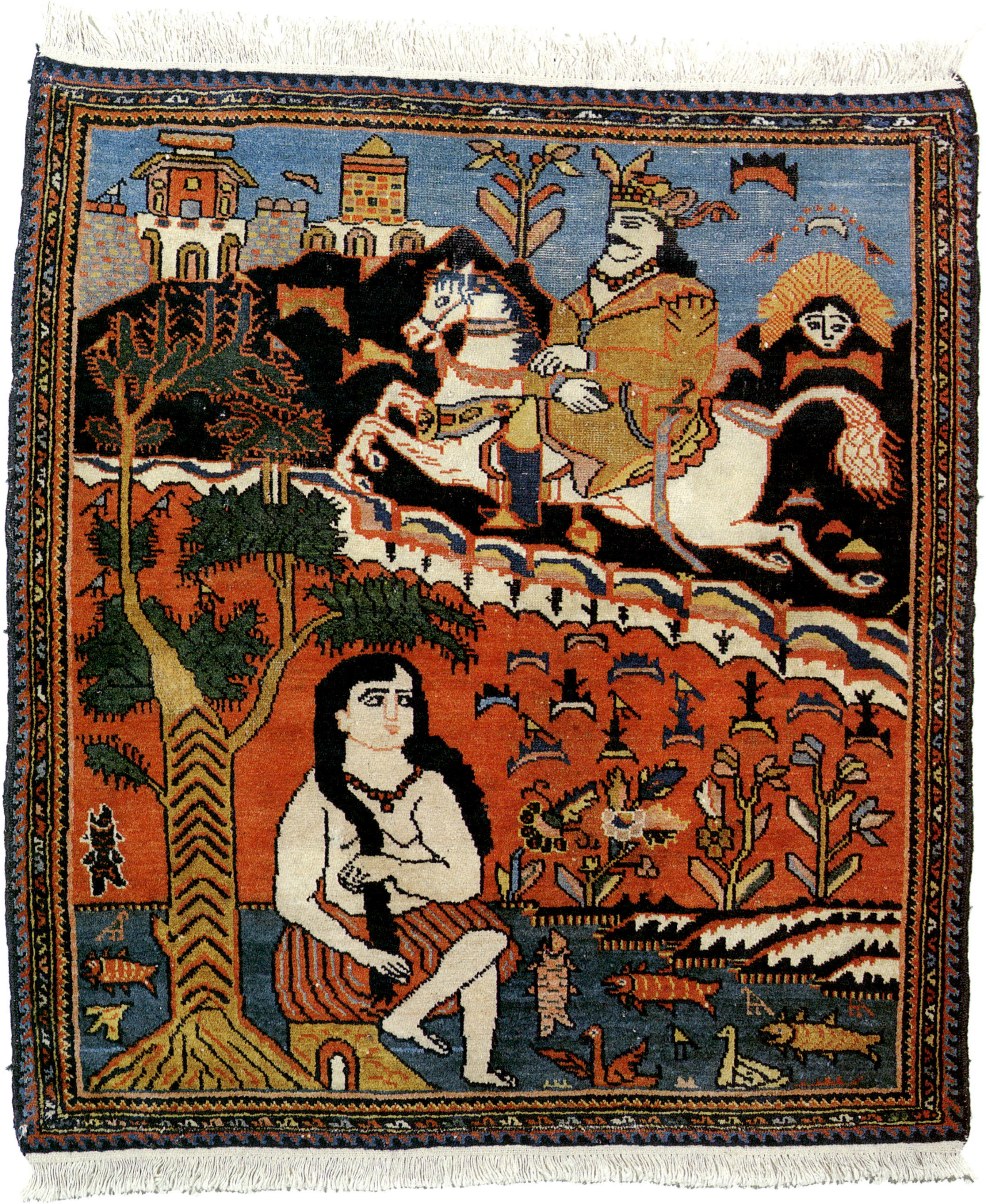

## 47

**Shirin Bathing at a Spring Observed by Khusraw**
**Shahreza area, possibly an Arab or Qashqa'i tribe**
**Mid-20th century**

Like most tribal pictorial rugs, this is characterized by departures from more traditional renderings of popular themes. Here in depicting a scene in the story of Khusraw and Shirin (p. 35 infra) the weaver uses a traditional general arrangement of a 'medallion' and 'cornerpiece' (see p. 12), but in a very individual way. The large figure of Khusraw on horseback dominates the field of the rug, as a medallion would in a traditional design. The corners are treated in an interesting way here. The upper corner decorations seem to suggest the convention of curtains in Qajar paintings and *qalamkar* curtains inspired by them, such as fig. 31. The lower corners are filled with figures of Shirin bathing, on the left, attended by a female companion on the right.

Rugs woven like this, with cotton wefts dyed blue and warps usually made of cotton, are known as Shahreza products in the bazaars in Iran. (Shahreza is 85 kilometres south of Isfahan.) Rugs like this, however, have not been produced in Shahreza and are probably the work of nomadic tribes (probably an Arab group) and also of villages in the general vicinity of Shahreza.

*Size:* 6ft 1.5in x 4ft 6.25in (187 x 138cm)
*Warp:* in parts of the two sides and in the centre: Z4S, undyed cotton, and groups of undyed cotton, Z2S, and undyed dark brown wool, Z1; the rest: wool, Z2S, dark brown, straight, 1 level
*Weft:* cotton, Z3S, blue, 2 shoots, both undulating
*Pile:* wool, Z2 loosely plied, As1, 0.5in (7mm)
*Knot count:* 8V x 7H = 56 per sq. in. (32V x 28H = 896 per sq. dm.)
*Texture:* soft, fairly thick, flexible
*Sides:* wool, dark brown, parallel wrapping around 10 warps
*Ends:* missing
*Colours* 8, black, dark blue, green, red, pink, orange, dark brown, ivory

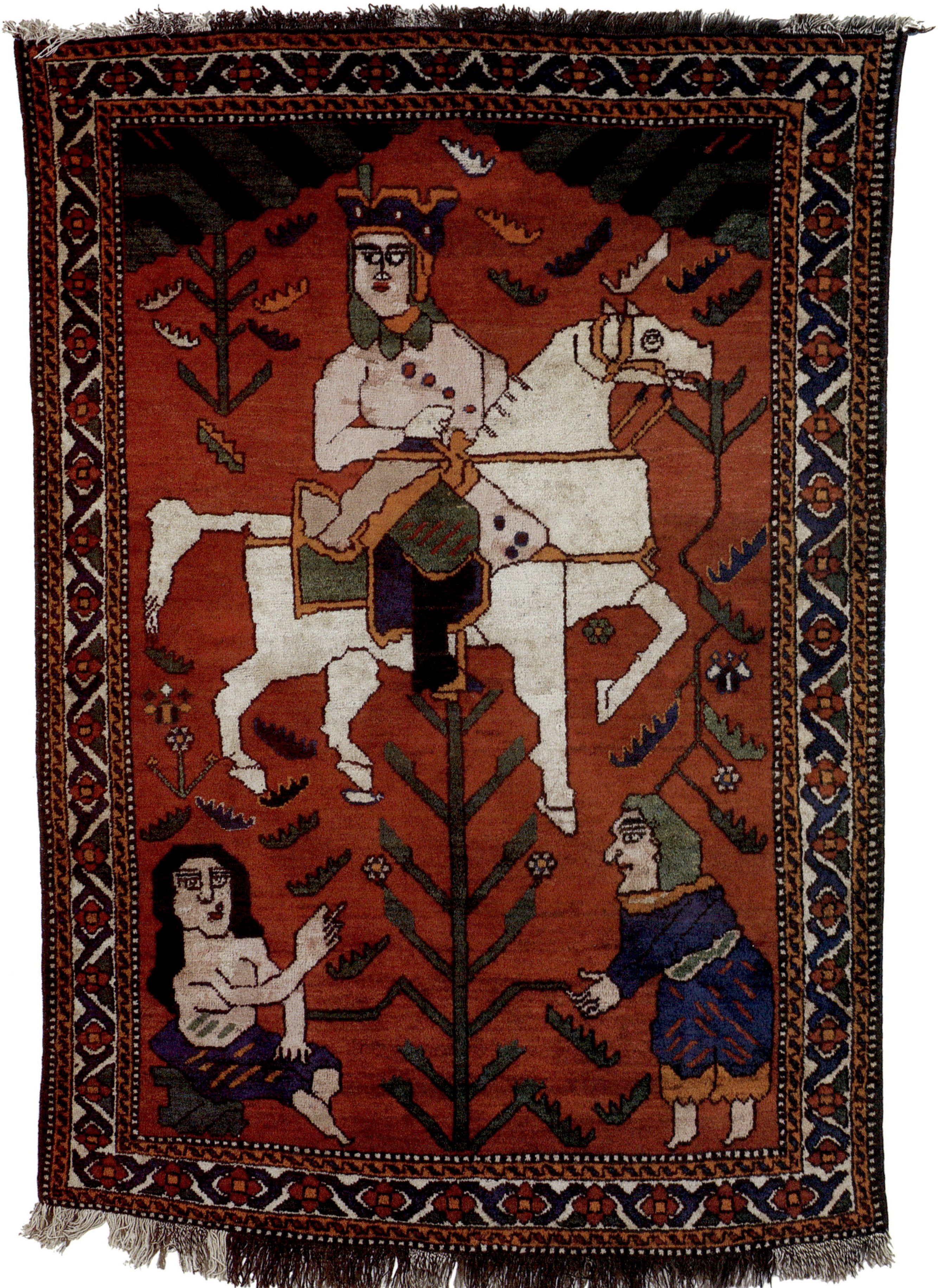

## 48

**Shirin and Farhad/Layla and Majnun**
**Hamadan area, possibly village of Kahak**
**Inscription:** *Farhad and Shirin/Layla and Majnun 1339 (1920 AD)*

From the point of view both of the subject matter and the composition and design, this rug is one of the most interesting examples of the pictorial type. Two famous love scenes are depicted on it: Shirin and Farhad (see p. 36) at the top and Layla and Majnun (see pp. 33, 37) at the bottom. Both relate to stories of the beloved coming to see her lover, one on horseback and the other on a camel. The former is Shirin, who is astonished to see Farhad and the mountain that he has carved (see fig. 41). The latter is Layla, who has come into the desert with her companions to see Majnun, who sits, thin and weak, with a baby gazelle on his knee and surrounded by tame and wild animals which have befriended him (see fig. 43). A variety of attractive motifs fill any spaces not taken up by these two scenes. There is a considerable power in the design of this rug, particularly in the faces. Each knot is used effectively to create particularly expressive faces on the human and animal figures. Some of these knots are even used to show fine details such as fingernails and eyebrows.

*Size:* 6ft 5in x 4ft 1.25in (196 x 125cm)
*Warp:* cotton, Z5S, undyed, undulating, 1 level
*Weft:* cotton, Z3S, undyed, 1 shoot, straight
*Pile:* wool, Z2 loosely plied, Sy1, 0.03-0.0625in (1mm)
*Knot count:* 9V x 8H = 72 per sq. in. (36V x 32H = 1152 per sq. dm.)
*Texture:* fairly coarse, thin, flexible
*Sides:* not original
*Ends:* lower: missing
upper: 1.5625in (4cm) weft-faced plain weave, undyed cotton
*Colours* 8, blue-black, blue, turquoise blue, very light green, dark red, dark brown, light brown, buff

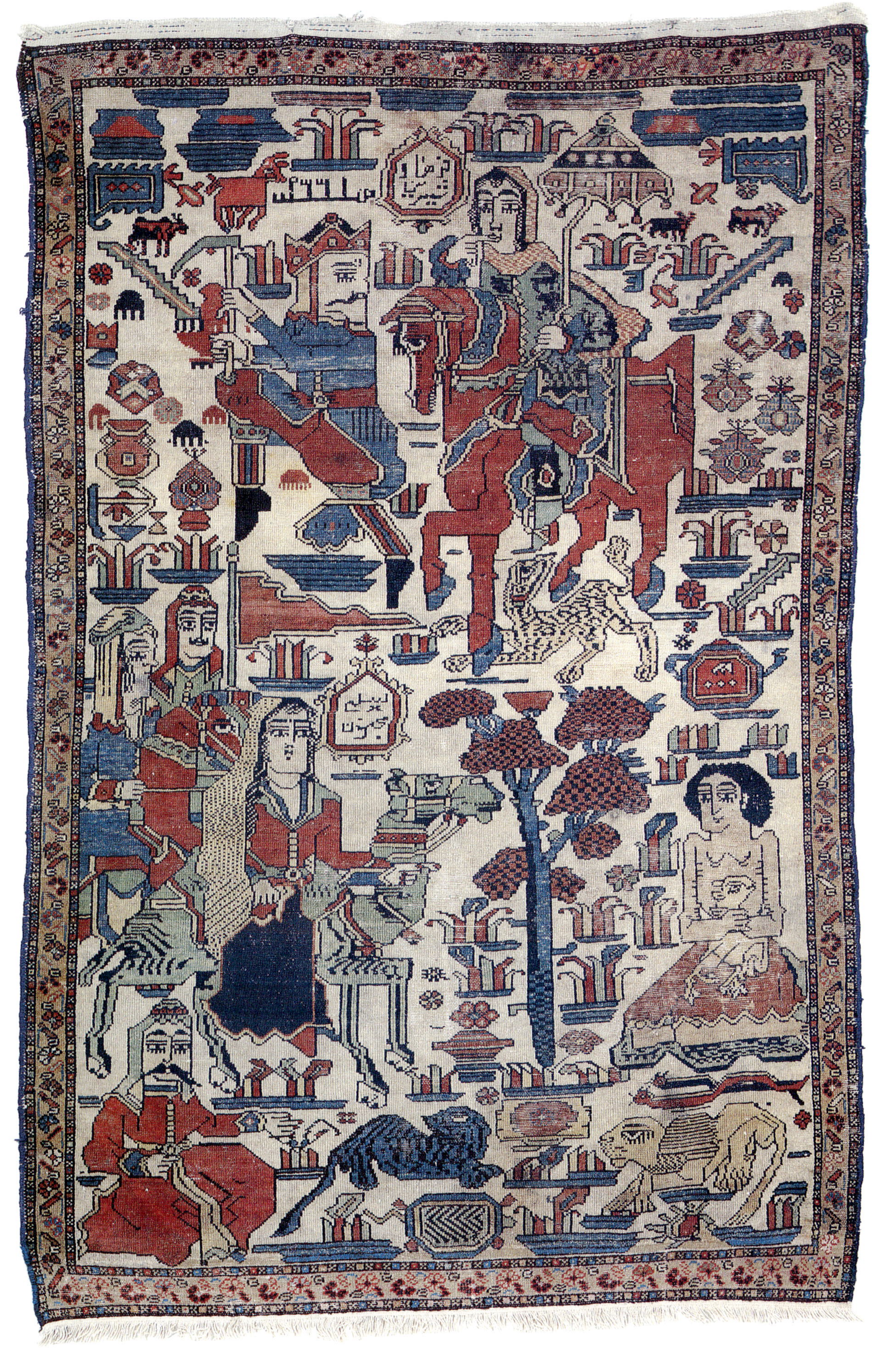

## 49

**Layla and Majnun**
**Hamadan area**
**Mid-20th century**

In this imaginatively depicted meeting of Layla and Majnun (see p. 37), she is looking out of a camel litter at her beloved. The camel, a somewhat unsuccessful combination of the traditional depiction of Layla's camel, anatomical parts from different animals (Majnun's friends), is covered here with various designs (see figs. 44, 45, 46 and p. 35). It is interesting to note how trees and birds appear to grow behind the head and above the tail of the camel and fill the rest of the background of the top half of the rug. One of the branches has even entered the empty white area of the camel litter, thereby adding a poetic quality to the rather primitively woven and designed rug.

*Size:* 7ft 0.25in x 4ft 1.25in (214 x 125cm)
*Warp:* cotton, Z6S, undyed, undulating, 1 level
*Weft:* cotton, Z8S, undyed, 1 shoot, straight
*Pile:* wool, Z2 loosely plied, Sy1, 0.375in (1cm)
*Knot count:* 8V x 8H = 64 per sq. in. (32V x 32H = 1024 per sq. dm.)
*Texture:* Soft, thick, fairly flexible
*Sides:* wool, dark pink, parallel wrapping around 11 warps
*Ends:* missing
*Colours* 11, dark blue, blue, light blue, red, dark pink, pink, light pink, dark brown, light brown, buff, white

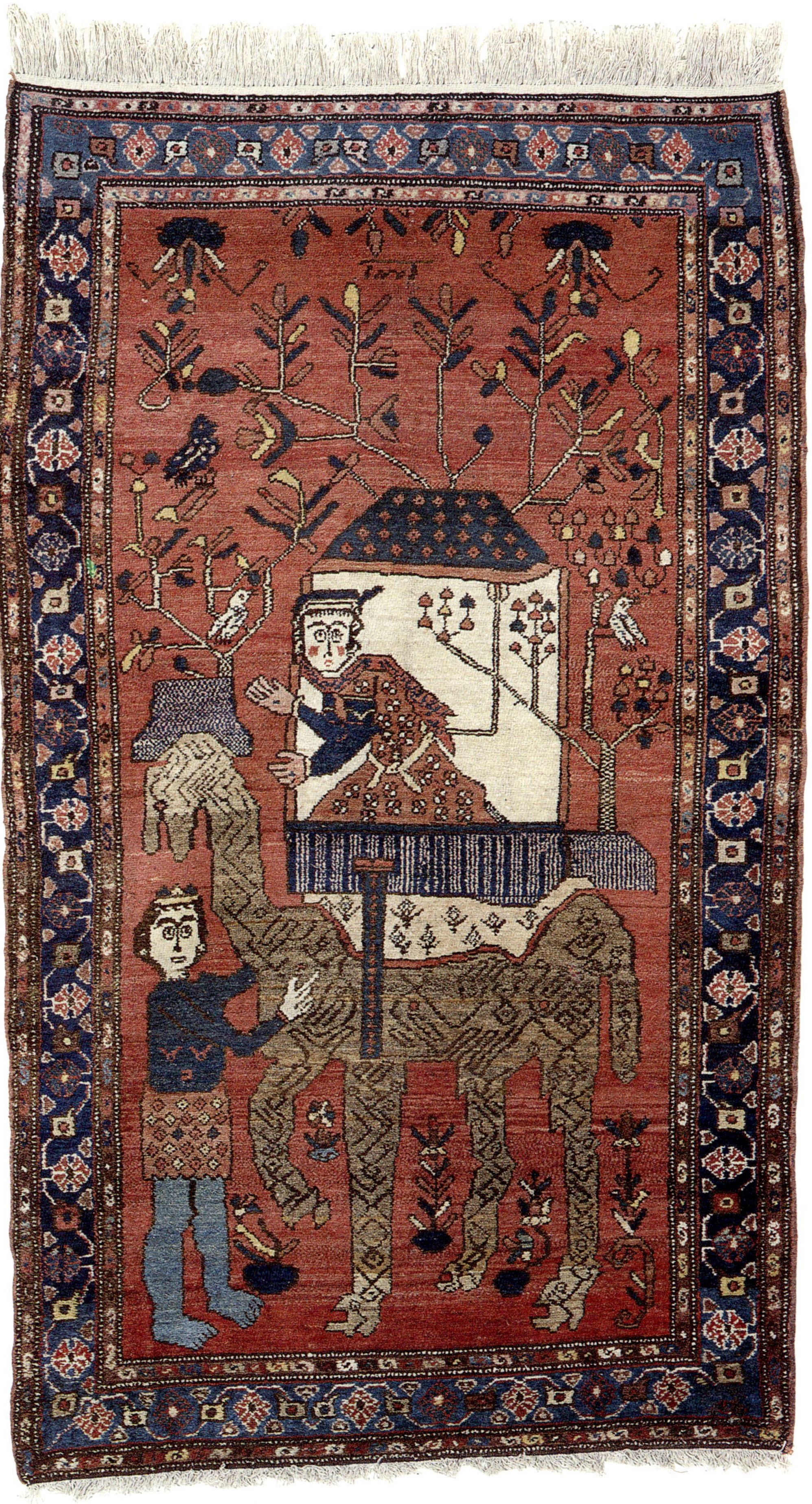

*Kings, Heroes and Lovers*

**50**

**Shirin and Farhad/Majnun
Saveh
Mid-20th century**

The two separate love stories of Layla and Majnun (p. 37) and of Shirin and Farhad (p. 35 infra) are brought to mind by this rug, the former because of the animals and birds scattered throughout and because of the figure in the upper left corner who seems clearly to be Majnun (see fig. 43). The two large figures at the right indicate that the weaver also had in mind the last scene of the Shirin and Farhad episode in the main story of Khusraw and Shirin. In this final scene of the episode involving Shirin and Farhad, the latter falls off the mountain and dies and Shirin grieves over him. These two figures are very similar to the figures of Shirin and Farhad in a depiction of this scene in a late 19th century lithograph (see fig. 42).

The lover and his beloved are attired in the style common among villagers in the Saveh region where the rug was woven. The weaver has reinforced the amorous nature of her subject by repeating the courtship of two pairs of birds at the top and bottom of the field. Of greatest interest is the unusual border of the rug which, with a regular rhythm and crispness of form, helps compensate for the lack of clarity in the story-telling content of the rug.

*Size:* 4ft 5.125in x 3ft 8.875in (135 x 114cm)
*Warp:* cotton, Z7S, undyed, undulating, 1 level
*Weft:* cotton, Z7S, undyed, 1 shoot, straight
*Pile:* wool, Z2 loosely plied, Sy1, 0.25in (3mm)
*Knot count:* 8V x 8H = 64 per sq. in. (32V x 32H = 1024 per sq. dm.)
*Texture:* soft, thin, flexible
*Sides:* wool, brown, parallel wrapping around 7 warps
*Ends:* missing
*Colours* 7, blue-black, brownish pink, dark brown, brown, light brown, buff, ivory

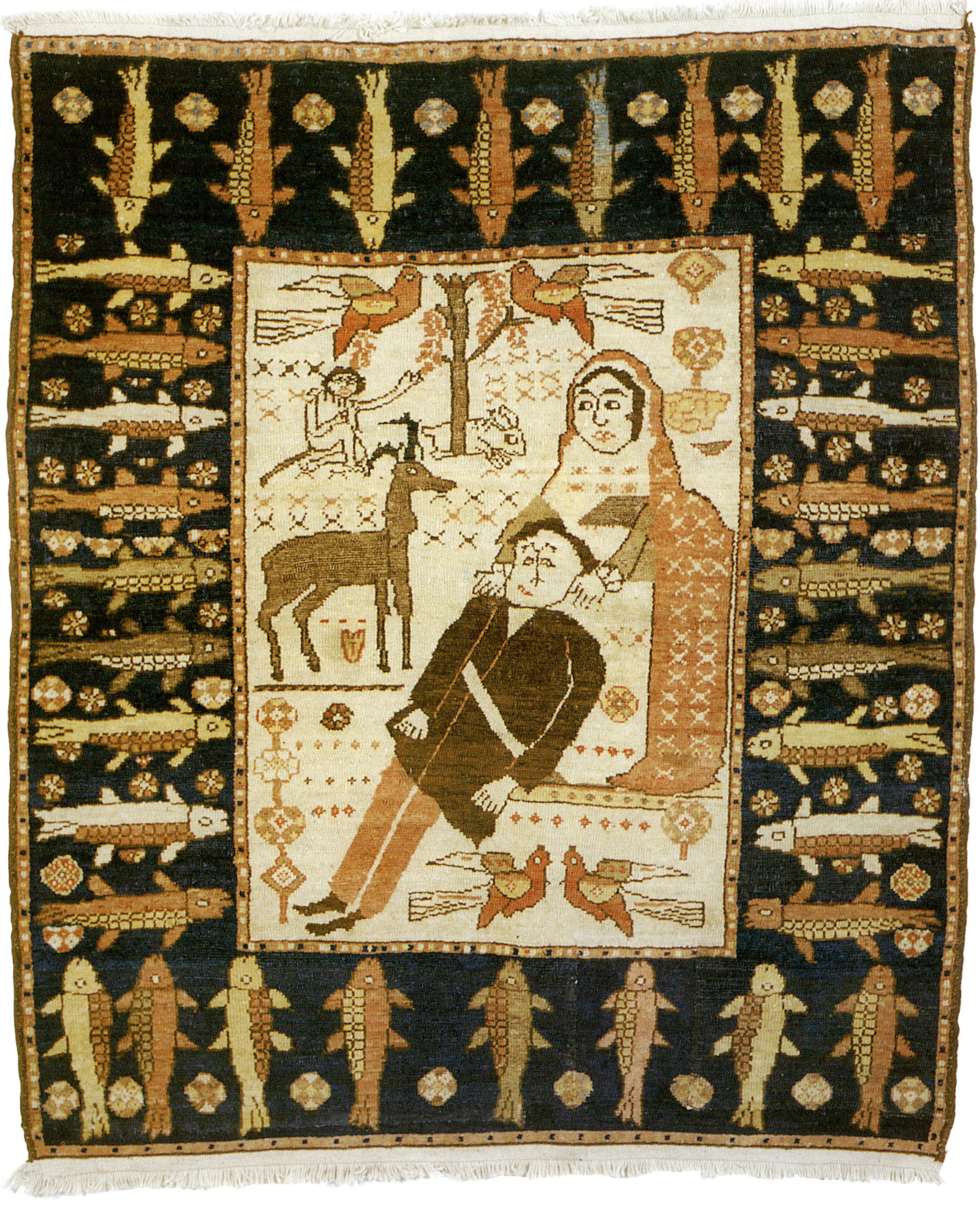

*Kings, Heroes and Lovers*

**51**

**Abraham Sacrificing His Son Ishmael**
**Province of Arak, village of Lilihan**
Inscription: *Abraham's Sacrifice of Ishmael, 1314 (1896 AD)*

On pp. 39-40 is a summary of the story of Abraham's sacrifice of his son Ishmael, as told in the Koran (Sura 37, verses 101-111) and in related books of commentary such as Mawlana Muhammad Jazayiri's *Stories of the Prophets*.

Nearly all of the major aspects of the story are shown in this rug. at the top of the scene is Hagar, Ishmael's mother, who is standing in the doorway of her house waiting for her son, and on the left is the Devil who apprehensively watches the sacrifice scene. On the right at the top is the winged and crowned figure of Gabriel who has brought a goat as a substitute sacrifice. A simple line drawing in an inexpensively produced book (such as fig. 48) may have served as a source of was woven (see also p. 47).

*Size:* 4ft 5.5in x 3ft 6in (136 x 107cm)
*Warp:* cotton, Z5S, undyed, undulating, 1 level
*Weft:* cotton, Z10S, undyed (the first few rows are dyed light blue, Z4S); 1 shoot, straight
*Pile:* wool, Z2 loosely plied, Sy1, 0.31in (8mm)
*Knot count:* 12V x 9H = 108 per sq. in. (48V x 36H = 1728 per sq. dm.)
*Texture:* soft, thick, very flexible
*Sides:* wool, red, parallel wrapping around 6 warps
*Ends:* 0.75in (2cm) weft-faced plain weave, undyed cotton
*Colours* 10, blue-black, blue, light blue, very light green, red, pink, brown, light brown, buff, ivory

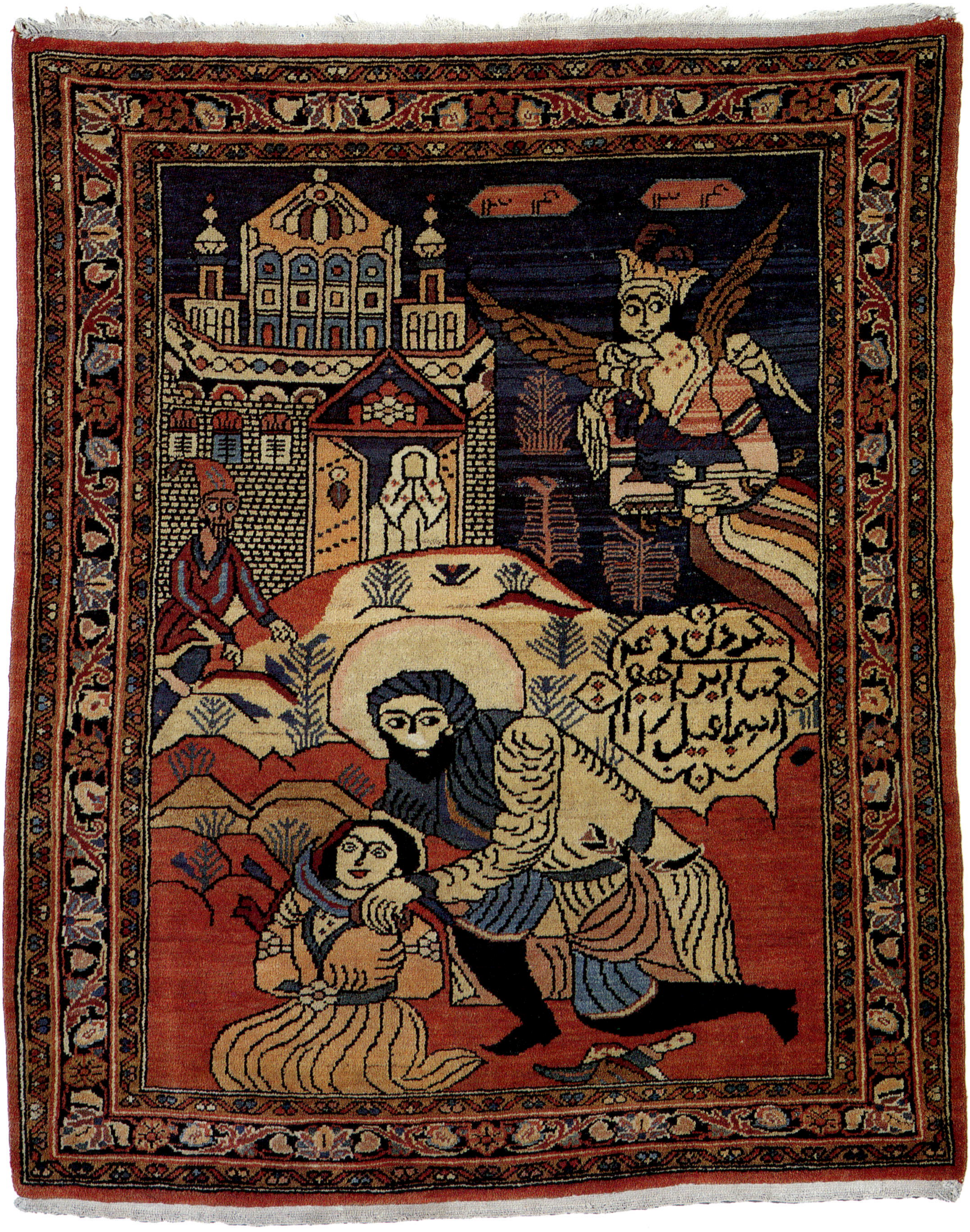

*Kings, Heroes and Lovers*

**52**

**Gabriel on a Camel
Baluch of the Zabul area
Inscription: *Muhammad [rest of inscription illegible]*
Mid-19th century**

As in the case of some other rugs, the scene depicted in this rug is composed of elements from several unrelated stories: the winged figure mounted on a camel and wearing a crown must be Gabriel, one of the angels close to God (see fig. 49). In Iranian stories Gabriel (see p. 40) usually has a crown and wings (note the appearance of Gabriel in rug no. 52). Moreover, the camel on which Gabriel is seated here greatly resembles Layla's camel (see p. 38 and rug no. 49 and figs. 44, 45, 46). In the orally transmitted stories about Layla and Majnun it is said that the group of animals that kept Majnun company in the desert assumed the form of a camel and brought Layla to see Majnun. Despite this, the religious elements found in the rug, such as the inscription and the picture of Gabriel (or another angel, as is apparent from the wings and crown) suggest a religious context.

Some of the strong and vivid colours, such as orange, yellow, and green, are among those often seen in older rugs from Zabul. These colours are less frequently encountered in weavings done in the last hundred years.

*Size:* 3ft 1.75in x 2ft 9in (96 x 84cm)
*Warp:* wool, Z2S, undyed ivory, straight, semi-depressed
*Weft:* wool, Z2S, very light green, 2 shoots: the first straight, the second undulating
*Pile:* wool, Z2 loosely plied, As3, 0.0625in (2mm)
*Knot count:* 16V x 13H = 208 per sq. in. (64V x 52H = 3328 per sq. dm.)
*Texture:* soft, very thin, very flexible
*Sides:* not original
*Ends:* not original
*Colours* 11, blue-black, blue, dark green, light green, red, orange, yellow, purple brown, dark brown, light brown, ivory

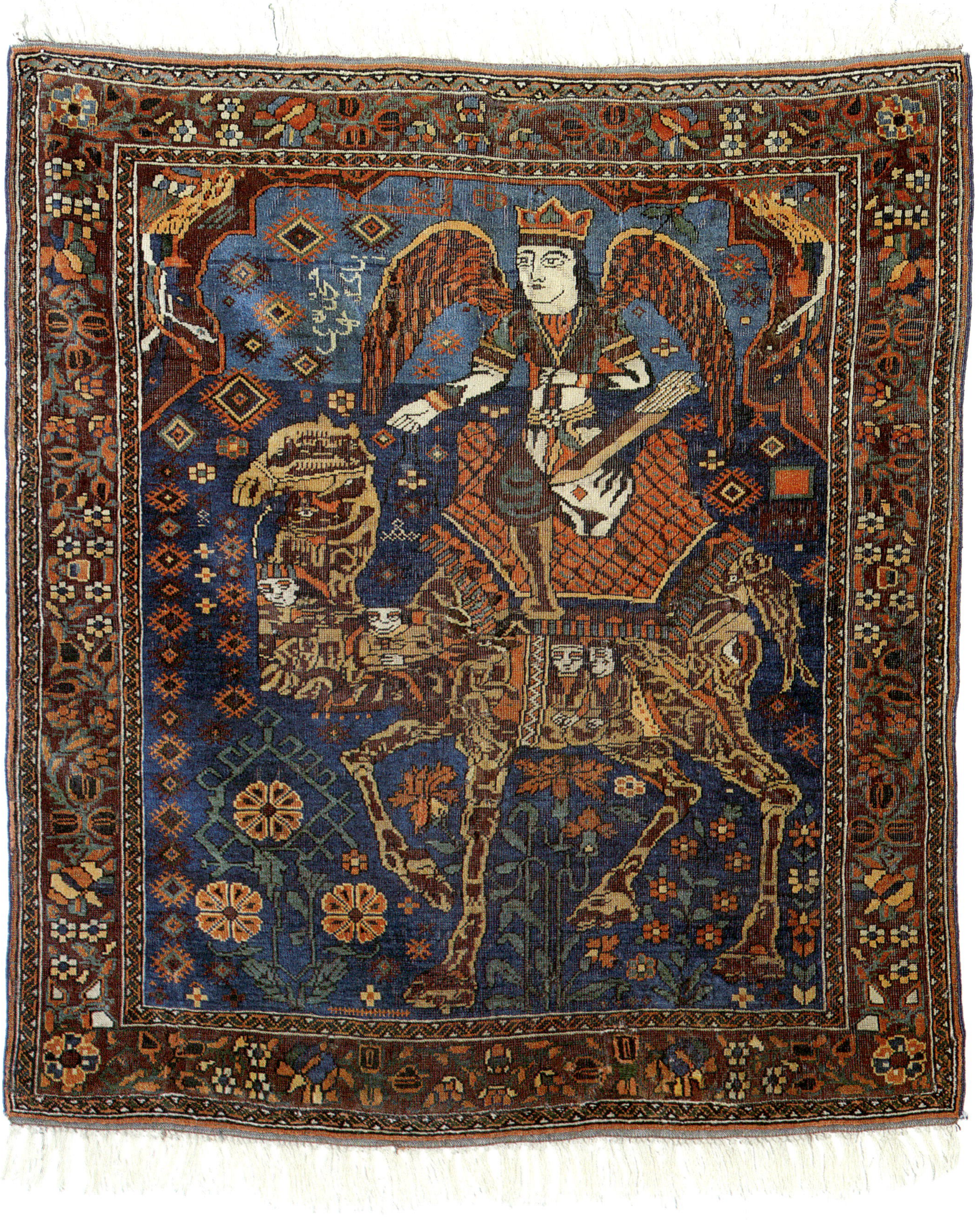

## 53

**Mary and Jesus**
**Baluch of the Zabul area**
**Early 20th century**

Although the existence of a Baluchi rug devoted to Mary and Jesus may seem surprising, it should not be forgotten that stories about both Mary and Jesus are included in the Koran, and this subject matter has from time to time inspired rug weavers and textile designers in Iran in general (see p. 40) and those of Tabriz and Kerman in particular. Rugs depicting the Madonna and Child exist that were woven during the last century in these areas, based on European paintings and Russian icons, which also inspired reverse paintings on glass done by Iranian folk artists (see fig. 50). One such weaving may possibly have played a role in the creation of the present Baluchi rug. The treatment of the figures, in their formal, stiff, frontal pose, is very reminiscent of Russian icons.

The weaver solved many of the inevitable problems of execution, such as the treatment of light and dark areas and folds in the clothing, by the use of stripes of different colours. The space around Mary's head has been filled with traditional motifs of tribal rug weaving such as tiny stylized birds, and the borders of the rug and around each panel are composed of traditional abstract motifs.

*Size:* 6ft 3in x 3ft 3in (190 x 99cm)
*Warp:* wool, Z2S, undyed, ivory, straight, very slightly depressed
*Weft:* wool, Z2S, undyed, brown, 2 shoots, both undulating
*Pile:* wool, Z2 loosely plied, As1, 0.0625in (2mm)
*Knot count:* 9V x 9H = 81 per sq. in. (36V x 36H = 1296 per sq. dm.)
*Texture:* soft, very thin, very flexible
*Sides:* wool, undyed dark brown, 2 cables, each wrapped around 4 warps
*Ends:* missing
*Colours* 8, medium blue, dark green, red, yellow, reddish brown, light brown, grey, ivory

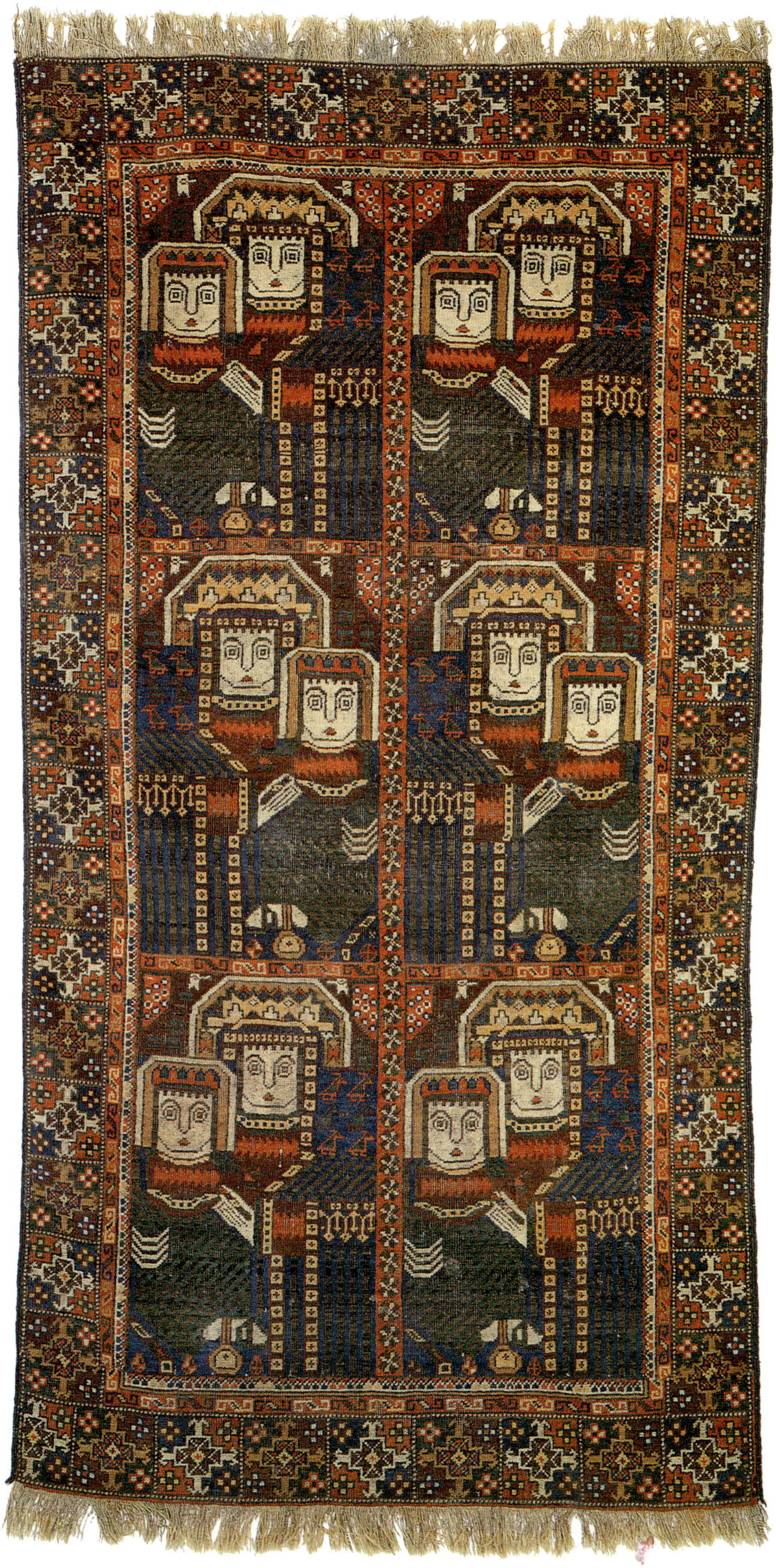

## 54

**Nur 'Ali Shah and Mushtaq 'Ali Shah**
**Kashan**
**Inscription:** *Portrait of Nur 'Ali Shah and Portrait of Mushtaq 'Ali Shah [poetry in the border translated on pp. 139-140] 1221 (1806 AD) (This date is given five times, once between the inscribed cartouches between the two men, and in four of the inscribed cartouches in the border)*

On p. 43 infra is an account of the lives of Nur 'Ali Shah (d. 1797) and Mushtaq 'Ali Shah, two dervishes of the Ni'matallahi order of Sufis, who caused an uproar at the end of the eighteenth century. The scene depicted here demonstrates how the dervish's paraphernalia was used (see figs. 55-58). Some of these objects are shown hanging on the wall in customary fashion, while others are held by Nur 'Ali Shah, the figure at the right (for an explanation of this paraphernalia, see p. 44 infra). Under the central arch at the top of this rug (which suggests a prayer niche) is a leopard skin hanging on the wall and a lantern suspended in front of it. Below the lantern hangs a dervish's trumpet fashioned from the horn of a buffalo or ram (some dervishes blow their horns under special circumstances when publicly condemning sin or when praying). Under the horn, also against the animal skin, a beggar's bowl is hung. At the left side of the rug Mushtaq 'Ali Shah's hat is seen in a niche above his head. Nur 'Ali Shah holds an axe and beggar's bowl while Mushtaq 'Ali Shah holds a dervish's string of prayer beads. On the chest of both is a flower which represents a dervish's seal, normally made of jasper. The weaver apparently intended to show the dervishes in a *khanaqah* (a building in which dervishes meet and carry out devotions). (For general information about dervishes and Sufism, see p. 42 infra.)

*Size:* 4ft 11.5in x 3ft 5.25in (151 x 105cm)
*Warp:* silk, Z3S, undyed, straight, 2 levels
*Weft:* undyed silk, Z4S, undyed, 2 shoots: the first straight, the second undulating
*Pile:* silk, Z2 loosely plied, As3, 0.375in (9mm)
*Knot count:* 24V x 21H = 504 per sq. in. (96V x 84H = 8064 per sq. dm.)
*Texture:* velvety surface, thin, stiff
*Sides:* silk, reddish purple, remains of parallel wrapping around 2 warps
*Ends:* 0.75in (2cm) weft-faced plain weave, undyed silk, decorated with one row of weft twining in reddish purple and green wool
*Colours* 8, turquoise blue, very light green, dark reddish purple, light reddish purple, black brown, grey brown, buff, ivory

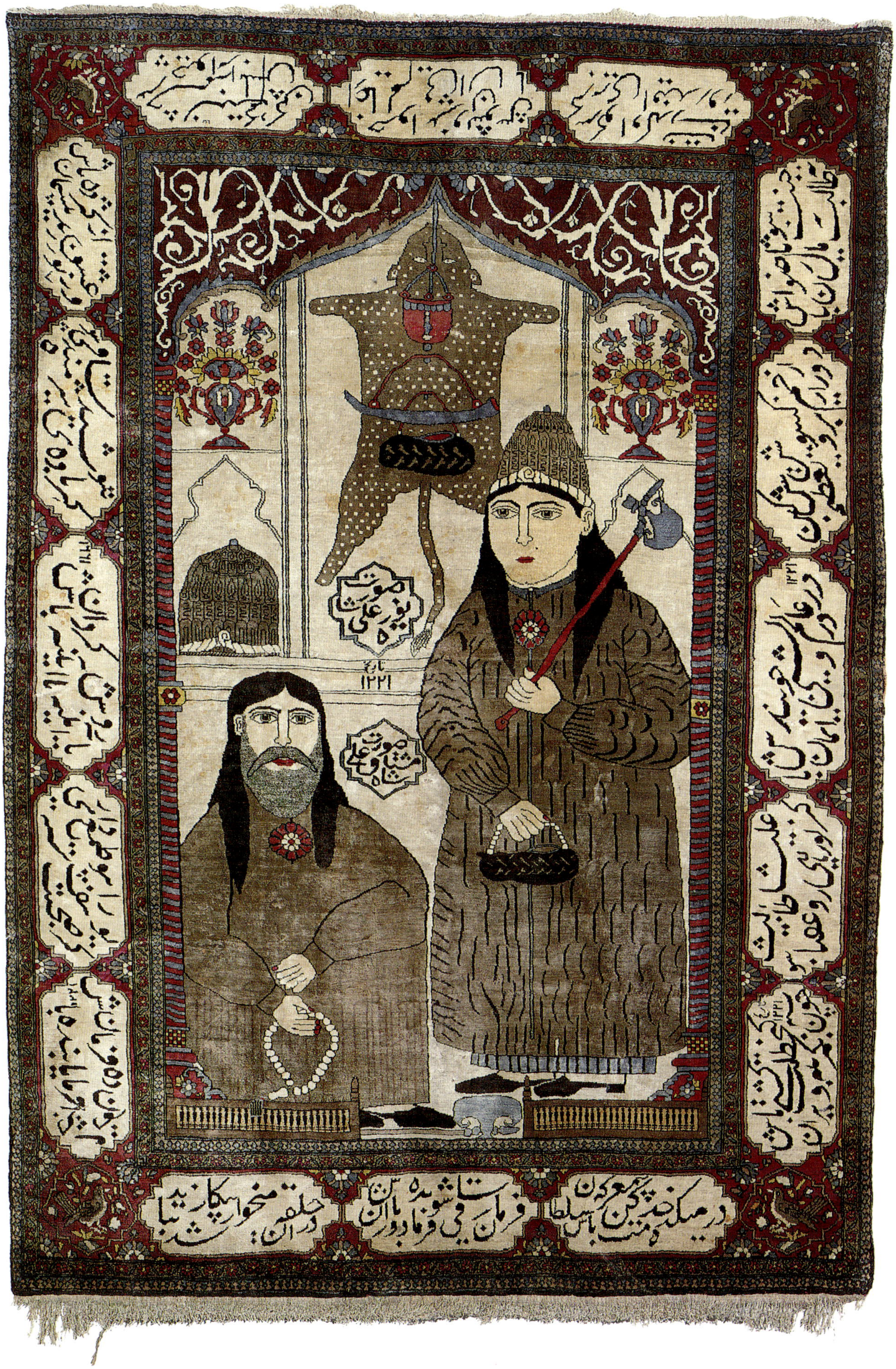
صورت نور علی شاه
تاریخ
۱۳۲۱
صورت مشتاق علی شاه

*Kings, Heroes and Lovers*

**55**

**Nur 'Ali Shah
Nahavand area
Inscription:** *see inscription on rug no. 54 (depicting Nur 'Ali Shah) where the inscription is more legible than it is here*
**Mid-20th century**

Of the famous dervishes of Iran, Nur 'Ali Shah has been the most popular among rug weavers (see p. 43 infra). He is known for having a beautiful face, something weavers have tried to capture in numerous examples woven with his portrait. In this rug we see Nur 'Ali Shah resting under a weeping willow tree at the edge of a spring in which ducks and fish are swimming. He is holding an axe in one hand and red apple in the other, while his dervish bowl and pouch are artistically used by the weaver as enriching elements of design against the plain garment he wears (see figs. 55-58 and p. 43 infra). The dark blue field of the rug gives the impression of a night-time scene, especially since the red outline around the dervish and weeping willow is like a halo of moonlight.

For general information about dervishes and Sufism, see p. 42 infra.

*Size:* 7ft 3.5in x 4ft 9in (222 x 145cm)
*Warp:* cotton, Z6S, undyed, undulating, 1 level
*Weft:* cotton, Z8S, light blue, 1 shoot, straight
*Pile:* wool, Z2 loosely plied, Sy1, 0.5in (12mm)
*Knot count:* 9V x 8H = 72 per sq. in. (36V x 32H = 1152 per sq. dm.)
*Texture:* soft, thick, flexible
*Sides:* wool, dark blue, parallel wrapping around 4 warps
*Ends:* lower: 0.375in (1cm) weft-faced plain weave, undyed cotton
upper: 1.5625in (4cm) weft-faced plain weave, undyed cotton, decorated with 2 rows of weft twining in red and yellow wool; worked into the weft-faced plain weave, close to the pile, are single Sy1 knots at 2-inch (5cm) intervals
*Colours* 12, blue-black, dark blue, blue, dark green, dark red, red, pink, orange, mustard yellow, light brown, olive brown, ivory

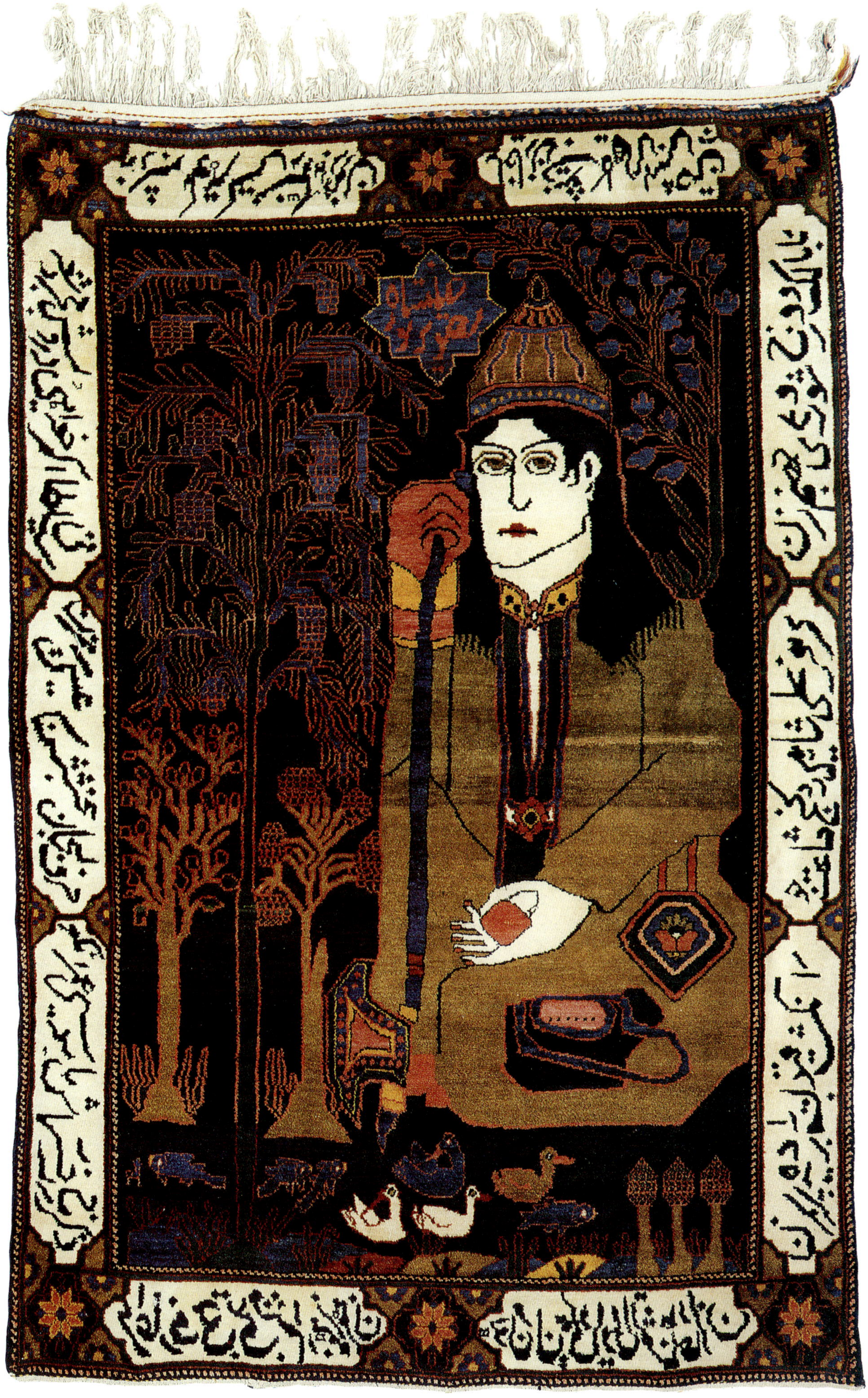

## 56

**Dervish Leopard Skin**
**Saruq**
**Inscription around edge of cap:** *Sufi poetry largely illegible*
**Late 19th century**

We encounter one of the masterpieces of Iranian rug weaving in this rug from Saruq. It is outstanding not only from the point of view of colour, weave, and composition but also because of the beautiful world created by the weaver, a floral world of bliss like the garden of paradise. Branches full of flowers and leaves extend everywhere. In such an aromatic and supernatural space are hung the accoutrements of a dervish. The multicoloured flowers and leaves of the garden have a mysterious effect on this ritual equipment and cause them to appear like heavenly instruments. It is interesting to note that the many colours used in the leopard skin, hat, and pouches with a checker-board pattern, are used to bind the intimate relationship with the flower-filled space that surrounds them, and finally the world that opens up to us within the arch, as if one were looking through a gateway into a garden. (For an understanding of the symbolic equipment of dervishes see figs. 55-58 and p. 44.

For general information about dervishes and Sufism, see p. 42 infra.)

*Size:* 6ft 4.5in x 4ft 0.5in (194 x 123cm)
*Warp:* cotton, Z10S, undyed, straight, 2 levels
*Weft:* 2 shoots: the first cotton, Z12S, undyed, straight; the second cotton, Z3S, light blue, undulating
*Pile:* wool, Z2 loosely plied, As3, 0.25in (3mm)
*Knot count:* 16V x 15H = 240 per sq. in. (64V x 60H = 3840 per sq. dm.)
*Texture:* soft, very thin, very stiff
*Sides:* wool, red, parallel wrapping around 4 warps
*Ends:* missing
*Colours* 16, blue-black, dark blue, blue, light blue, dark green, very light green, olive green, light olive green, red, dark pink, buff yellow, dark brown, brown, light brown, dark buff, ivory

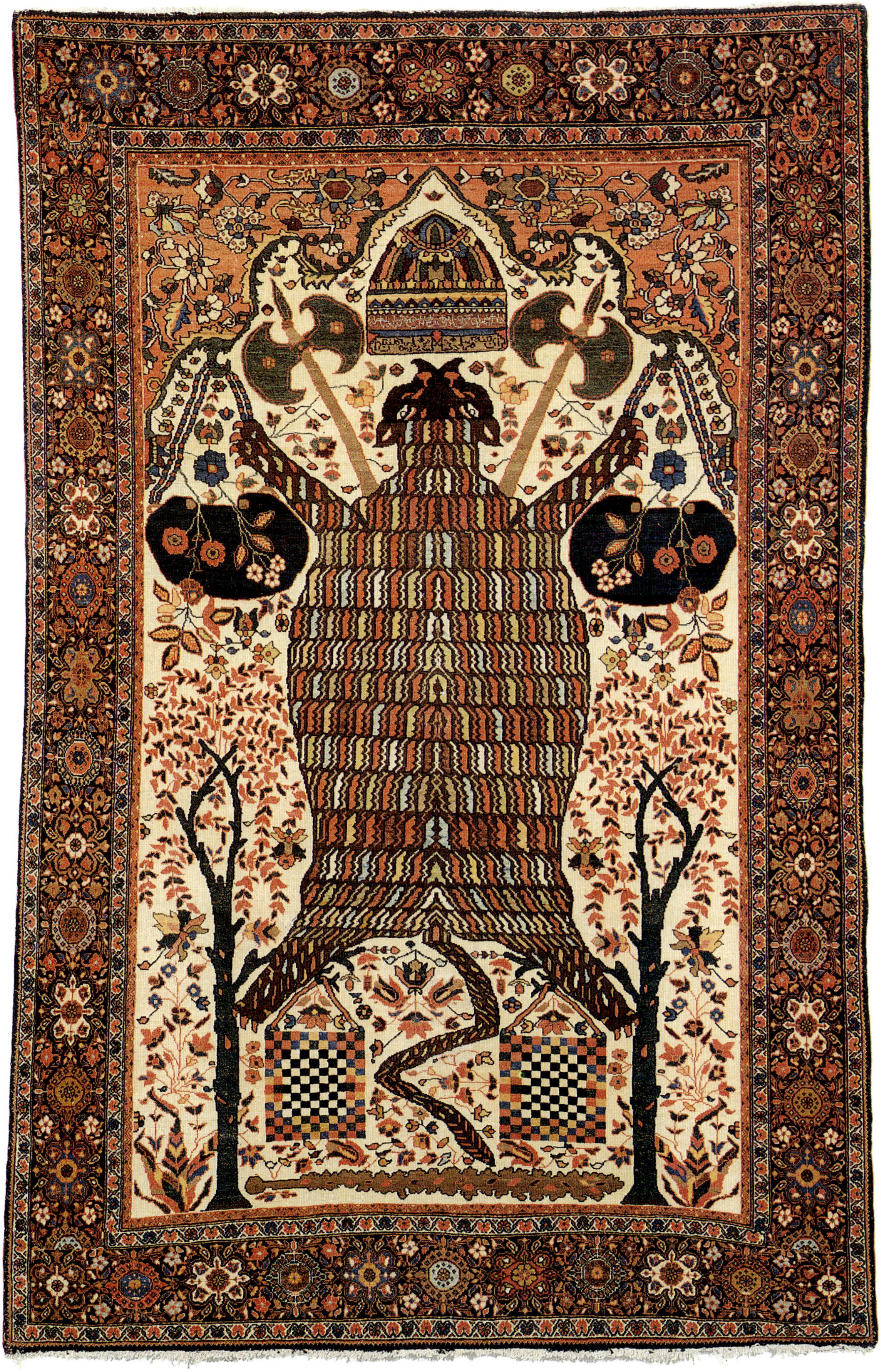

**57**

**Dervish Leopard Skin**
**Saruq**
**Inscription around edge of cap:** *Sufi poetry largely illegible*
**Late 19th century**

This pictorial rug with a midnight-blue field immediately suggests night time. This example and no. 56 make an interesting comparison, for both have practically the same subject and composition but different coloured backgrounds. Such a contrast creates two very different moods. The rug with the ivory background brings to mind the joy and happiness evoked by glowing colours that seem lit from within by their own inner source of light. The dark-blue background of the rug illustrated here, on the other hand, creates a mysterious atmosphere in which these possessions of a dervish are suspended against a midnight sky. Also, the leopard skin of this rug is less colourful than that of no. 56, and because of this it enhances the sense of peace and tranquillity which it conveys.

For an explanation of the symbolic equipment of dervishes see figs. 55-59 and p. 44. For general information about dervishes and Sufism, see p. 42 infra.

*Size:* 6ft 6in x 4ft 2.5in (198 x 128cm)
*Warp:* cotton, Z10S, undyed, straight, 2 levels
*Weft:* cotton, Z3S, light blue, and Z14S, undyed; 2 shoots: the first light blue, straight; the second undyed, undulating
*Pile:* wool, Z2 loosely plied, As3, 0.0625in (2mm)
*Knot count:* 14V x 15H = 210 per sq. in. (56V x 60H = 3360 per sq. dm.)
*Texture:* soft, very thin, very stiff
*Sides:* wool, dark blue, parallel wrapping around 4 warps
*Ends:* missing
*Colours* 12, blue-black, blue, turquoise, dark olive, light olive, red, pink, pale yellow, dark brown, brown, buff, ivory

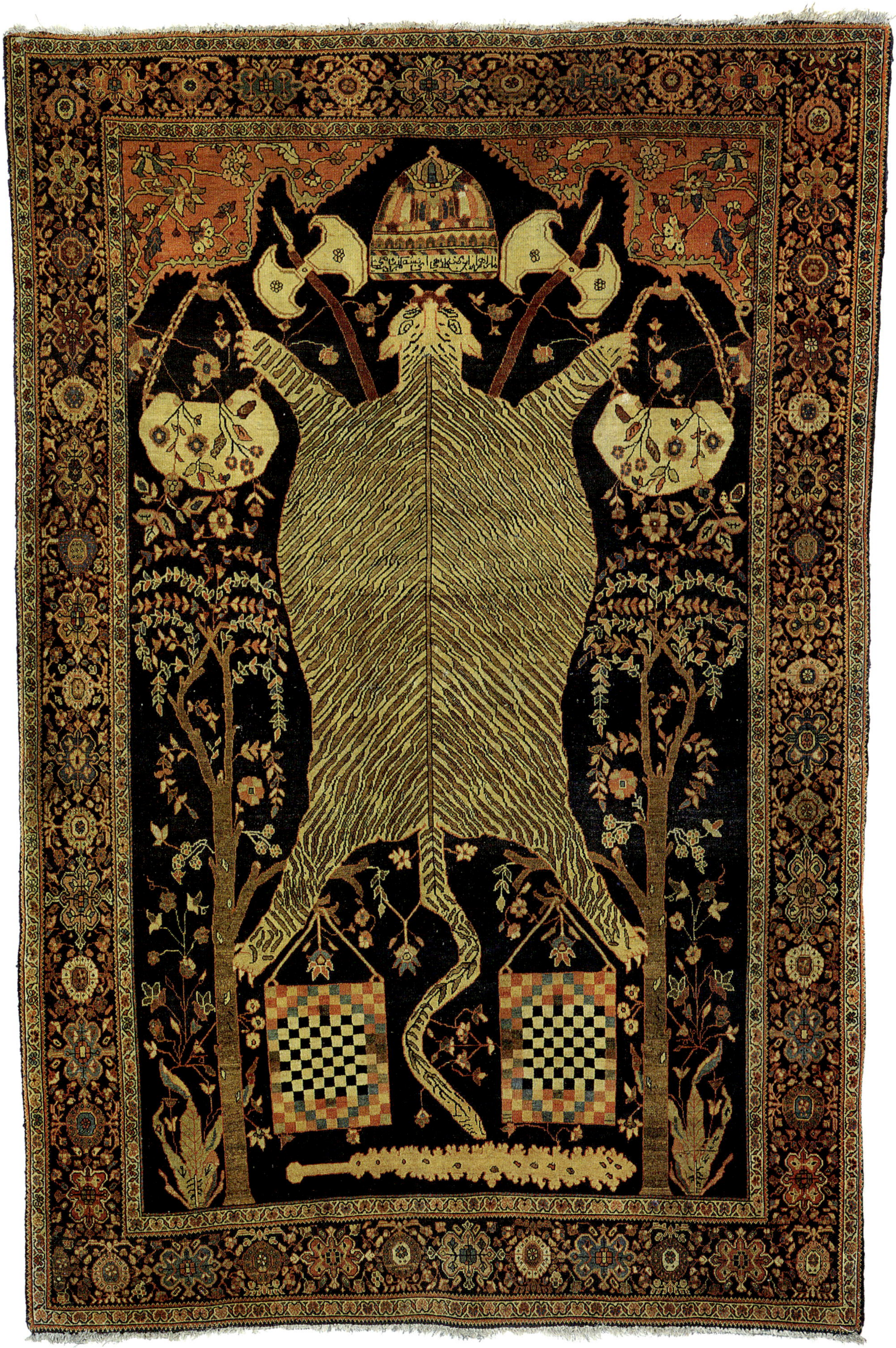

*Kings, Heroes and Lovers*

**58**

**Shaykh San'an**
**Shahsavan or Afshar of the Hamadan area**
**Inscription:** *Shaykh San'an*
**Early 20th century**

This rug illustrates a story that belongs to the mystical Sufi tradition of Iran. This tale comes from the allegorical poetic work *The Conference of the Birds* by Farid al-Din 'Attar (see p. 45 infra). The rug depicts various scenes and personalities from the story of Shaykh San'an and glimpses of life in Iran. Notice the concern expressed in the faces of Shaykh San'an's followers, seen standing on the left, for their spiritual guide and leader who has fallen in a state of helplessness at the feet of his beloved, a tall, haughty Armenian Christian girl who is giving the Shaykh some wine (which is forbidden to strict Muslims). At the top of the rug is a landscape of the city, its walls, and towers suggestive of a medieval European painting. The flock of pigs at the bottom is both unexpected and remarkable. Pigs are an animal considered unclean by Muslims, and the degree of thraldom to his Christian sweetheart is underlined by the shaykh's submitting to the indignity of tending pigs at the behest of her family. In contrast to the usual practice in most other pictorial rugs, the weaver here has made little effort to create symmetrical correspondences in the rug, but has nevertheless created a balanced and lively narrative scene. The *boteh* (paisley) motifs in a row along the top and bottom of this rug are reminiscent of *botehs* in similar locations in *qalamkar* curtains (fig. 44) which indicates the very probable type of source that inspired the weaver of this rug.

*Size:* 9ft 0.5in x 5ft 6in (275 x 168cm)
*Warp:* cotton, Z6S, undyed, undulating, 1 level
*Weft:* cotton, Z6S, undyed, 1 shoot, straight
*Pile:* wool, Z2 loosely plied, Sy1, 0.31in (8mm)
*Knot count:* 10V x 9H = 90 per sq. in. (40V x 36H = 1440 per sq. dm.)
*Texture:* soft, fairly thick, flexible
*Sides:* wool, orange, parallel wrapping around 4 warps
*Ends:* lower: remains of weft-faced plain weave, undyed cotton
upper: 0.75in (2cm) weft-faced plain weave, undyed cotton, decorated with one row of weft twining in light green and red wool; warp ends knotted in groups
*Colours* 13, dark blue, olive green, light green, dark red, red, light red, pink, orange, black brown, dark chocolate, light chocolate, buff, white

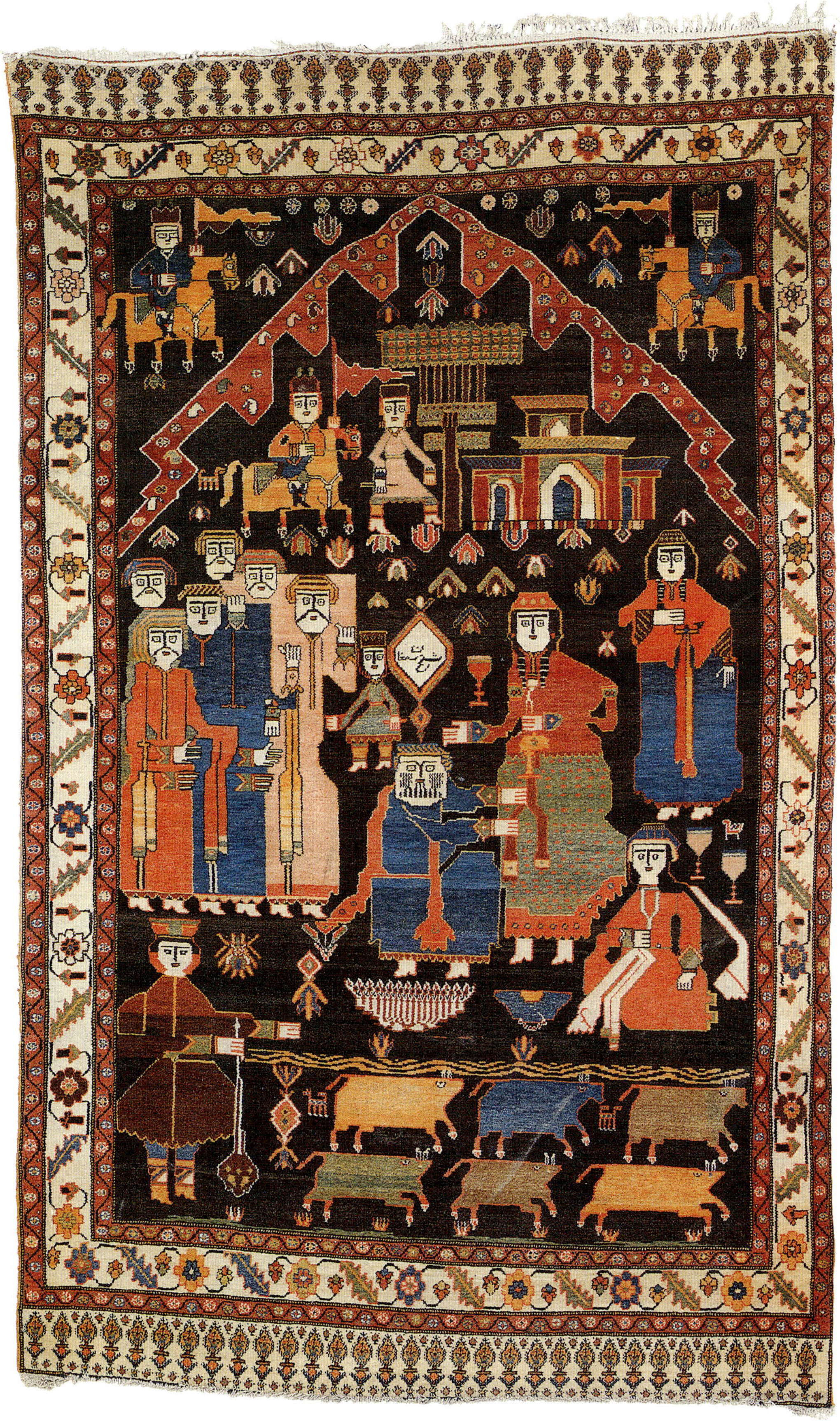

## 59

**Story of David of Sassoun**
**Karabagh region of the southern Caucasus**
**Inscription:** *(in Armenian) at the top: David M Arka (David and the King of Egypt); at the left, reading from top to bottom: N (possibly an abbreviation of Nakshetz, meaning designer of the rug), M (for either Mard, [March], or Mais, [May]), 10 (the day of the month), Verti Osepiantz and Arisag Osep (two names, which could possibly be those of either weaver or owner of the rug), 1916/T (the Armenian word Teev, which is a shortened form of dialect words Tvagan or Toovagan for 'year'). The word toward the lower right and the three letters in the lower part of the right-hand male figure have eluded interpretation.*
**Dated:** *1916*

This rug depicts figures from the Armenian national epic, a summary of which is given on p. 48 infra. The story and the rug are full of symbolism. The most interesting part of the picture here is in the centre of the rug, where the Egyptian king is seated and flanked by David's paternal and maternal uncles, who are dressed in tigerskin garments and who have raised their hands into the air. This part of the picture, which appears to have been woven from the imagination and without a cartoon, has a somewhat unnatural and confused aspect to it, whereas the horses in the four corners of the picture are characterized by fairly natural qualities and proportions. Possibly the weaver used a cartoon or model for the execution of the latter figures, or else she was simply more accustomed to depicting horses than human figures of this type. The way the horses are drawn represents the form favoured by the Armenian rug weavers of Karabagh. In this book we have included another Karabagh rug featuring a similar horse (fig. 52.)

The traditional medallion and 'cornerpiece layout is suggested by the over-all composition of this rug (see p. 12). (For Armenians and pictorial rugs, see p. 47 infra.)

*Size:* 6ft 8in x 3ft 11.75in (203 x 121cm)
*Warp:* wool, Z3S, undyed light grey to brown, straight, 1 level
*Weft:* wool, Z2S, undyed dark brown, 2 shoots, both undulating
*Pile:* wool, Z2 loosely plied, Sy1, 0.31in (8mm)
*Knot count:* 7V x 7H = 49 per sq. in. (28V x 28H = 784 per sq. dm.)
*Texture:* soft, fairly thin, fairly flexible
*Sides:* wool, undyed dark brown, remains of parallel wrapping around 2 warps
*Ends:* lower: remains of weft-faced plain weave, wool, undyed ivory, and wool dyed dark blue
upper: remains of weft-faced plain weave, wool, undyed light brown
*Colours* 12, black, dark purple, light purple, blue grey, dark green, light green, olive, purple red, red, pink, light brown, ivory

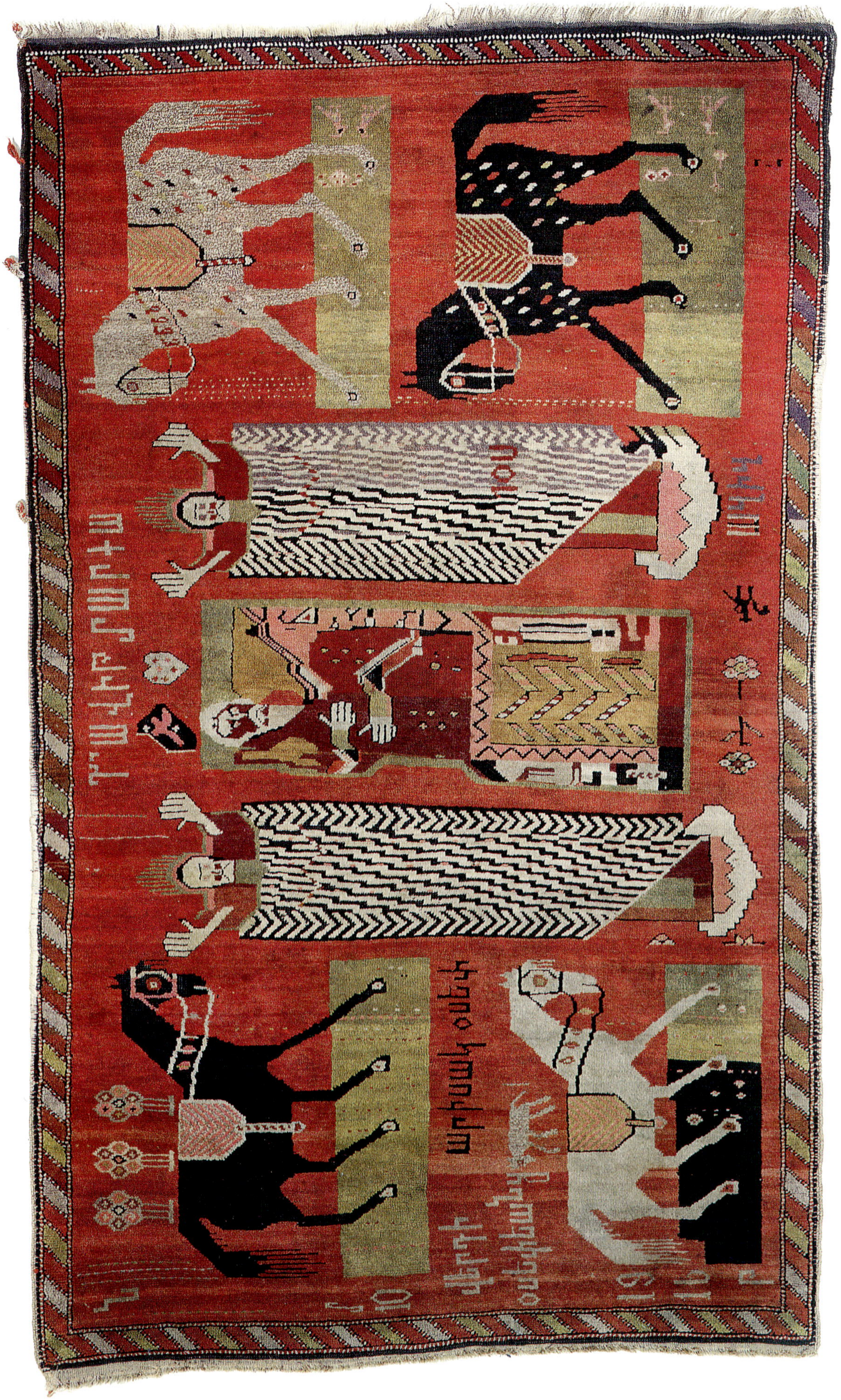

## 60

**Tribal Men**
**Firdows area, Arab tribes**
**Early 19th century**

Both from the point of view of weave and border design, this rug closely resembles Firdows rugs and must in fact be one of the older surviving Firdows pieces. Unlike those woven in Firdows in the last century it has a wool warp and weft instead of the now usual cotton ones. In order to show the human designs to better advantage the weaver employed a long, narrow, white ground in the centre. In addition to the two main male figures, six smaller ones and a number of goats and birds fill the empty spaces of the field. The fine, beautiful designs which are seen on the shirts and coats of the large figures are realistic renditions of decorative features seen in the traditional clothing of the district in which the rug was woven. Those various costume details have given these men greater individuality. The portrayals of the human figures here come entirely from the weaver's own rich imagination.

For a discussion of rugs depicting tribal people, see p. 50 infra.

*Size:* 4ft 11.75in x 3ft 3in (152 x 99cm)
*Warp:* wool, goat hair, Z2S, undyed ivory to dark brown, straight, 1 level
*Weft:* wool (also approximately 10 rows of undyed cotton), Z2S, loosely plied, undyed dark brown, 2 shoots, both undulating
*Pile:* wool, Z2 loosely plied, As1, 0.1875in (4mm)
*Knot count:* 10V x 6H = 60 per sq. in. (40V x 24H = 960 per sq. dm.)
*Texture:* soft, thin, very flexible
*Sides:* not original
*Ends:* missing
*Colours* 7, blue-black, dark red, orange, deep pink, dark brown, light brown, ivory

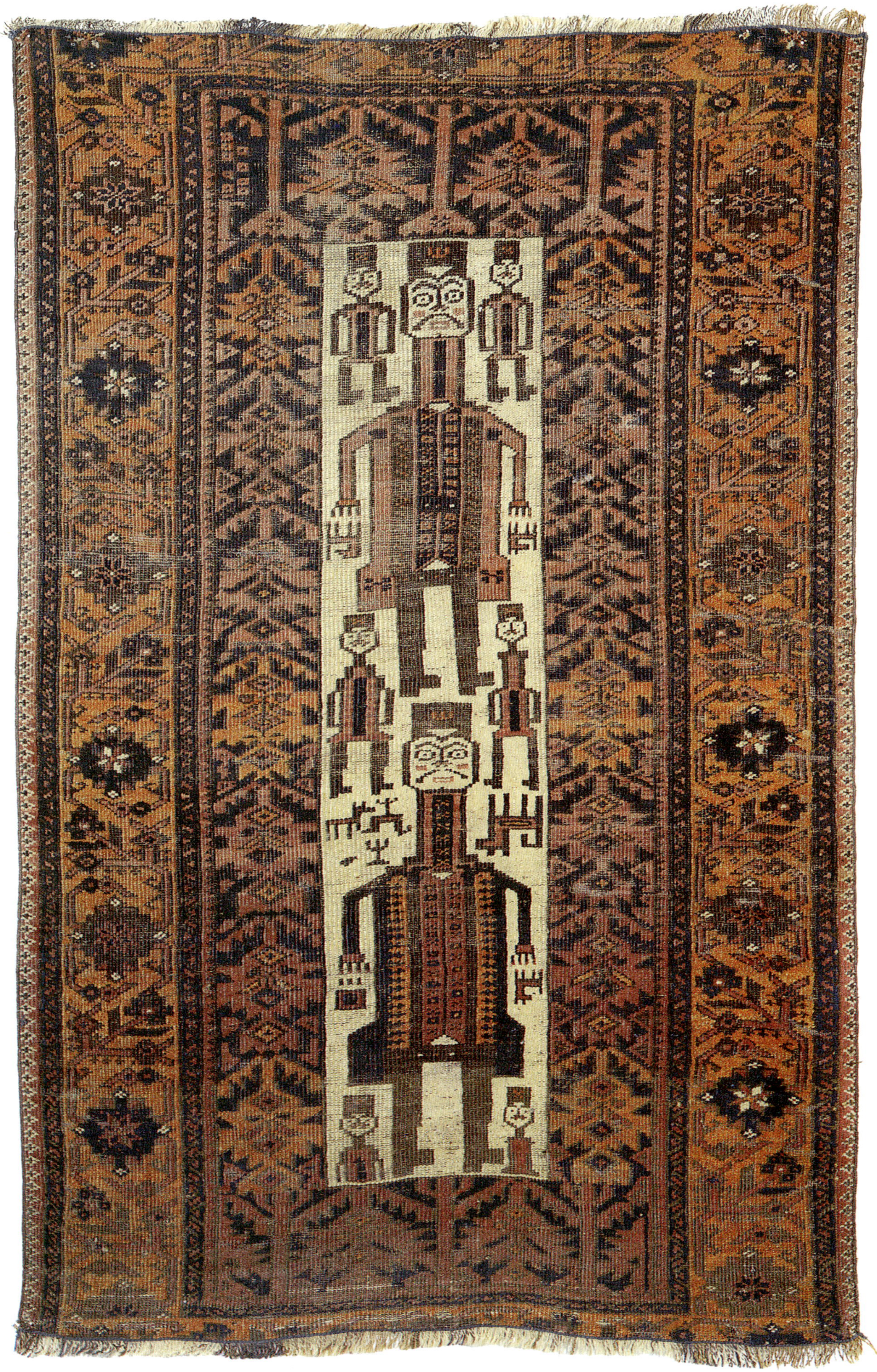

**61**

**Ahmad Shah? and a Tribal Chief (or Dervish?)**
**Qashqa'i**
**Inscription (in mirror image):** *Sultan Ahmad Shah Qajar [in the] year 1338 (1919 AD)*

The inscription at the top of this rug (which is reversed, thus suggesting that it was copied from the back of another rug by an illiterate weaver) provides a key to understanding the subject of rug no. 62 as well as of this one. Both were produced in southern Iran, but by different tribal groups. The two figures (the pair is repeated three times) of this Qashqa'i rug are more clearly differentiated from each other than those of the other related example (no. 62), and Ahmad Shah (with a stylized aigrette emerging from the top of his hat) and the tribal chief (the figure could, perhaps also be interpreted as a dervish because of his peaked cap) can easily be distinguished from each other.

For rugs depicting tribal people, see p. 50 infra.

*Size:* 6ft 2.75in x 3ft 10.5in (190 x 118cm)
*Warp:* wool, Z2S, undyed ivory, straight, 1 level
*Weft:* wool, Z1, brown, 3 to 4 shoots, all undulating
*Pile:* wool, Z2 loosely plied, Sy1, 0.31in (8mm)
*Knot count:* 7V x 7H = 49 per sq. in. (28V x 28H = 784 per sq. dm.)
*Texture:* soft, thick, fairly stiff
*Sides:* wool, yellow and blue, parallel wrapping around 3 warps
*Ends:* 1.5625in (4cm) weft-faced plain weave, wool, blue, yellow, half turned under and sewn down
*Colours* 11, blue-black, blue, light blue, dark green, light green, olive green, red, orange-yellow, dark brown, brown, ivory

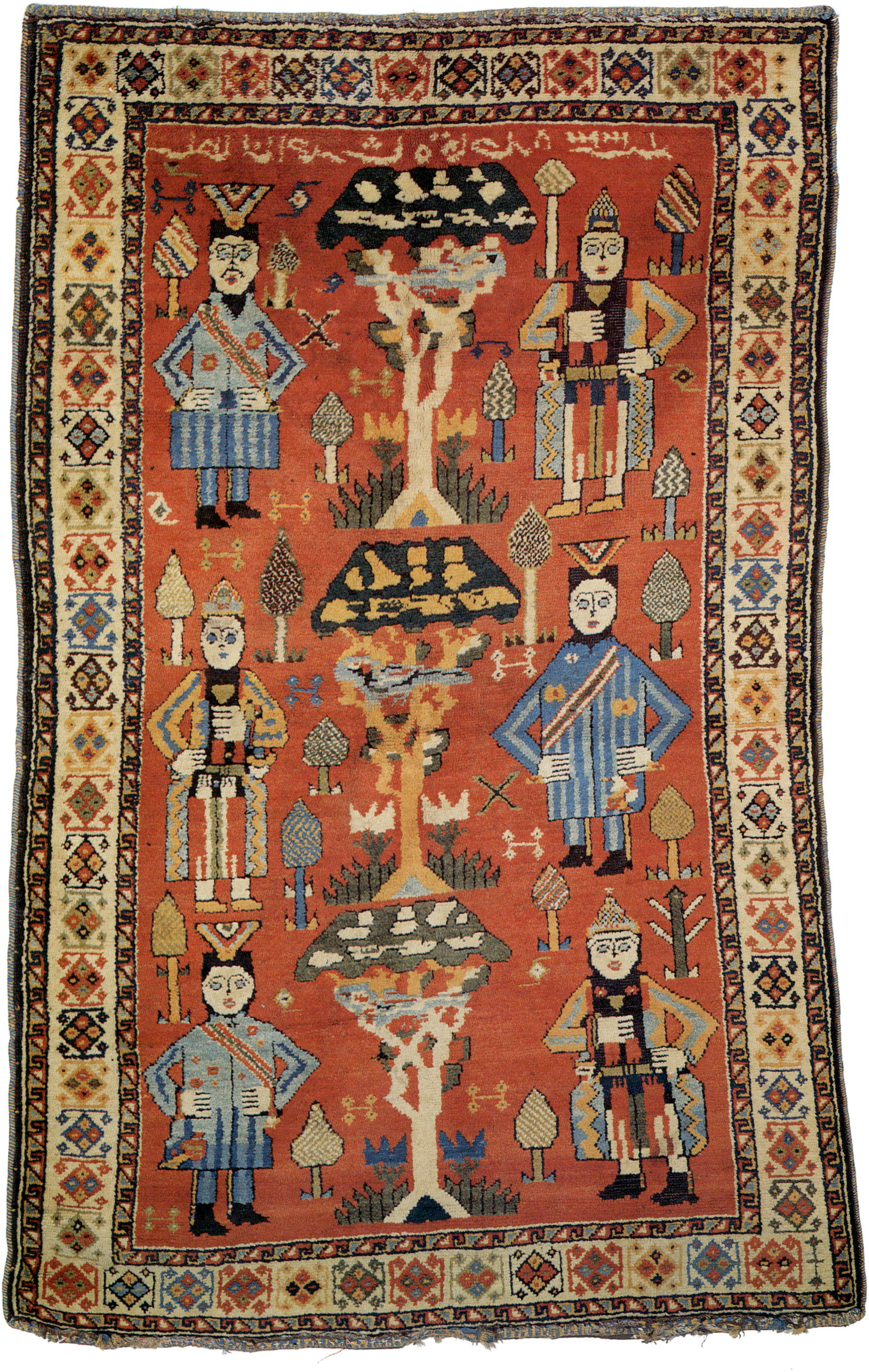

## 62

**Ahmad Shah? (Tribal Chief?)**
**Lori-Boyer Ahmad**
**Date:** *135(?) (c. 1931 AD)*

From the inscription on the Qashqa'i rug (no. 61) discussed earlier, we know that the figure repeated fourteen times in this example may also represent either Ahmad Shah (or possibly a tribal chief, but not a dervish). However, the stylization here is such that it would be difficult to make this association without the benefit of the other similar rug. How easy it would be to consider the figures simply anonymous tribesmen since in many ways they resemble people in the area where the rug was woven. This resemblance is especially close in the clothing, which is much more tribal than royal, and undoubtedly more familiar to the weaver than regal costume.

The other motifs, such as the trees, are also stylized. All the designs are placed harmoniously and skilfully in a simpler and more geometrical manner than is the case with no. 61. This gives the rug a tribal character.

For rugs depicting tribal people, see p. 50 infra.

*Size:* 8ft 4.75in x 5ft 1in (256 x 155cm)
*Warp:* wool, Z2S, undyed ivory to dark brown, straight, 1 level
*Weft:* wool, Z1, dark brown, 3 shoots, all undulating
*Pile:* wool, Z2 loosely plied, Sy1, 0.1875in (4mm)
*Knot count:* 7V x 6H = 42 per sq. in. (28V x 24H = 672 per sq. dm.)
*Texture:* soft, fairly thick, very flexible
*Sides:* wool, brown, chevron wrapping around 10 warps
*Ends:* lower: missing
upper: 1.1875in (3cm), countered weft-twining (*sumak* brocading), wool, undyed ivory, blue
*Colours* 9, blue-black, blue, dark green, green, light red, dark brown, light brown, mustard, ivory

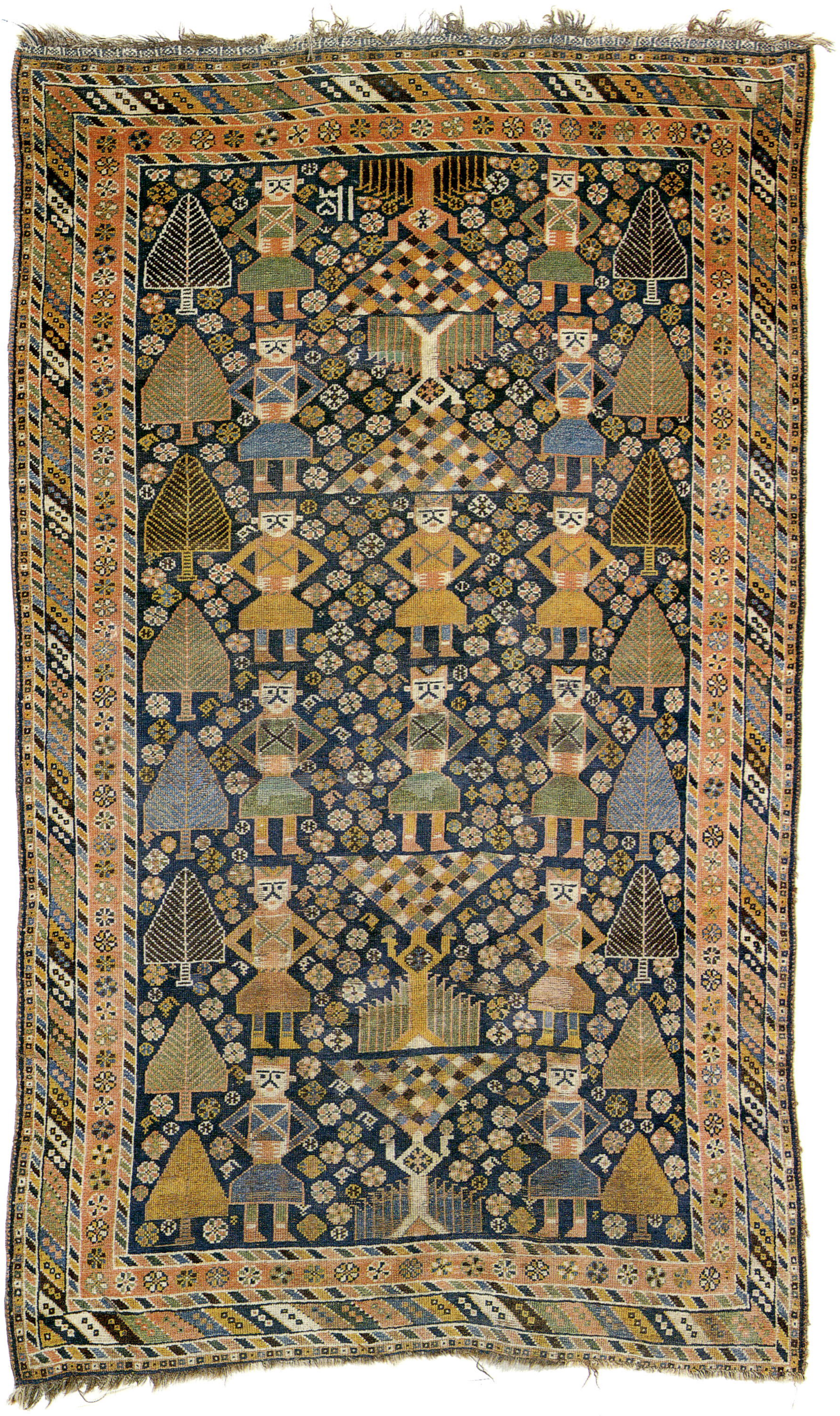

*Kings, Heroes and Lovers*

**63**

**Baluchi Women**
**Baluch of the Zabul area**
**Mid-19th century**

This is one of the oldest rugs of the Zabul region to survive. Even in its somewhat damaged condition it is still a most attractive piece. Some of the strong, happy colours used here, in particular the orange, bright red, bluish-turquoise, and light blue, have not been seen in Baluchi rugs for a long time. Nearly all of the Baluchi rugs of the last century have dark colours among which such contrasting hues as light yellow and green are only occasionally found. In comparison, the oldest of the other rugs of this group appear to be at least a generation younger than this example. The use here of such colours makes one suspect that Baluchi rugs in the past were perhaps characterized by bright, cheerful hues as well.

For rugs depicting tribal people, see p. 50 infra.

*Size:* 5ft 17in x 3ft 0.5in (170 x 92cm)
*Warp:* wool, Z2S, undyed ivory, fairly straight, 1 level
*Weft:* wool, Z2S, loosely plied, undyed ivory to dark brown, 2 shoots, both somewhat undulating
*Pile:* wool, Z2 loosely plied, As1, 0.0625in (2mm)
*Knot count:* 9V x 8H = 72 per sq. in. (36V x 32H = 1152 per sq. dm.)
*Texture:* soft, very thin, very flexible
*Sides:* not original
*Ends:* missing
*Colours* 8, blue-black, blue, light blue, emerald green, red, orange-yellow, brown, ivory

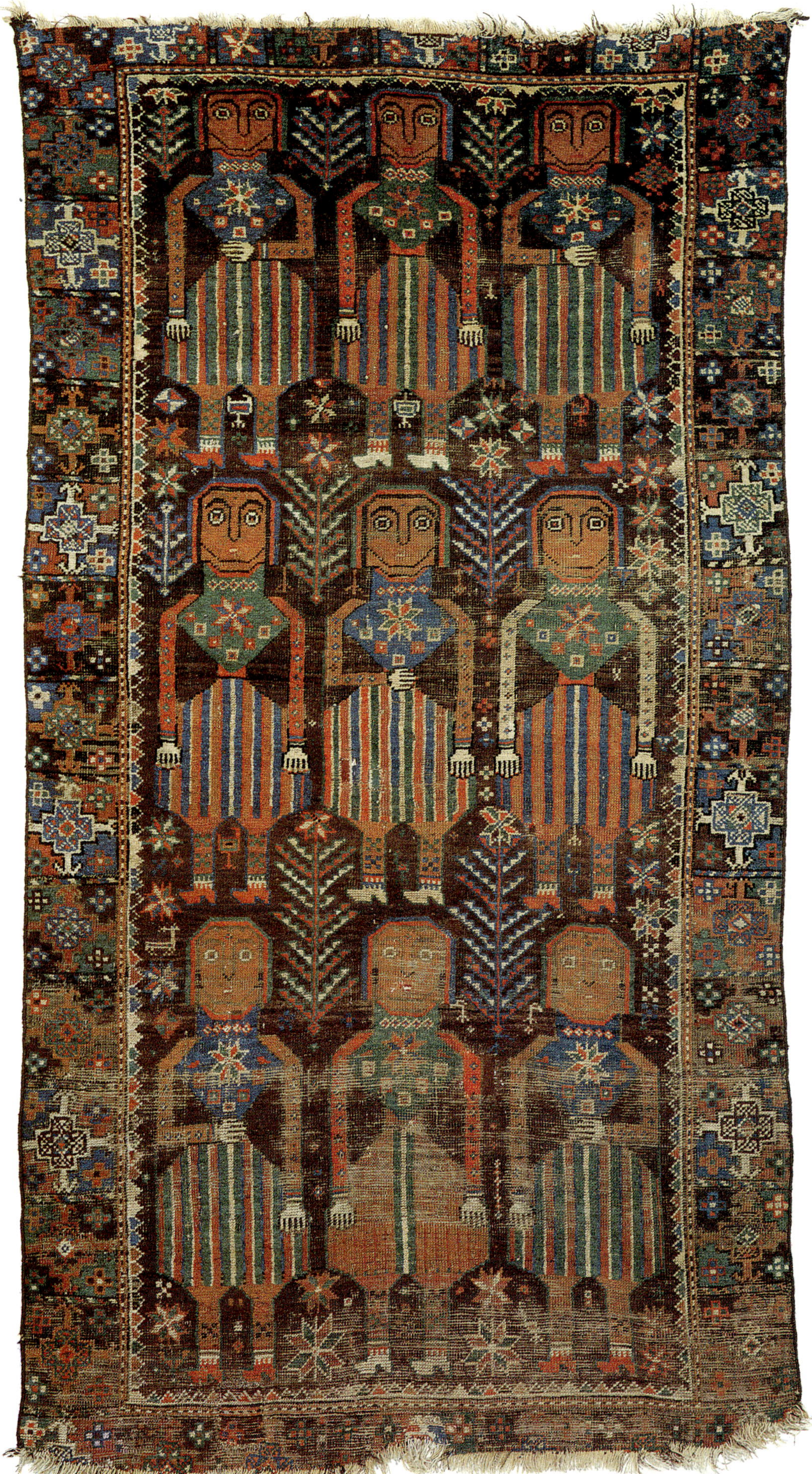

**64**

**Baluchi Men and Women**
**Baluch of the Zabul area**
**Late 19th century**

At first glance the human figures, in three rows, all appear to be very similar. But their facial features are differentiated to show that those figures are not all of the same sex. The men in the centre row have tiny moustaches. Their left hands rest on their waists. The women have a cross-shape mole between their eyebrows, and a curled wisp of hair appears on either side of their faces. Smaller forms of men and women are interspersed among the nine large figures, men between women and women between men. Camels are seen in the cramped space at the top as well as in other parts of the rug. Goats and birds fill in other empty spaces. The man at the left in the centre row draws attention because of his yellow trousers.

For rugs depicting tribal people, see p. 50 infra.

*Size:* 5ft 11in x 3ft 4.5in (180 x 103cm)
*Warp:* wool, Z2S, undyed ivory, straight, 1 level
*Weft:* wool, Z2S, undyed light grey brown, 2 shoots, both undulating
*Pile:* wool, Z2 loosely plied, As1, 0.1875in (4mm)
*Knot count:* 9V x 8H = 72 per sq. in. (36V x 32H 1152 per sq.. dm.)
*Texture:* very soft, thin, very flexible
*Sides:* wool, undyed dark brown, light grey brown, 2 cables, each wrapped around 4 warps
*Ends:* missing
*Colours* 8, dark blue, blue green, dark brown, brown, dark red, dark pink, dark buff, white

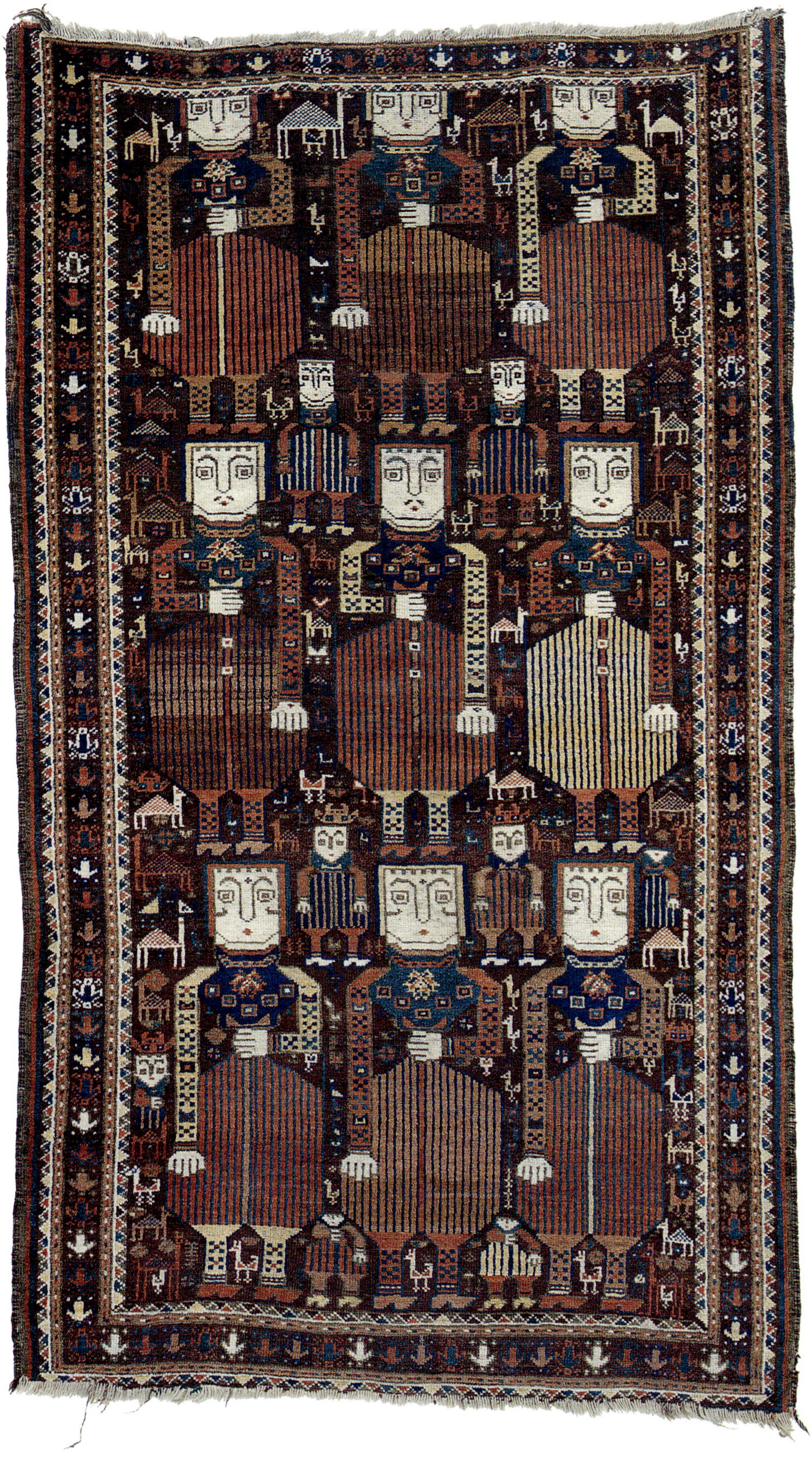

## 65

**Baluchi Men and Women**
**Baluch of the Zabul area**
**Late 19th century**

Despite the fact that the figures here are extremely simple and lack the stripes and decorative touches found in rugs nos. 63 and 64, this rug has a special appeal all its own. The weaver avoided monotony in the main characters by creating a rhythmic effect through her subtle but skilful use of colours. This is another example of outstanding Baluchi weaving in which all elements have been executed with great taste and care. In the border, for instance, the multicoloured stars have been artfully ordered beside each other and seem to exude light. One is reminded of the old Persian saying that 'for each person there is a star.'

For rugs depicting tribal people, see p. 50 infra.

*Size:* 5ft 10.5in x 3ft 10in (179 x 117cm.)
*Warp:* wool, Z2S, undyed ivory, straight, very slightly depressed
*Weft:* wool, Z2S, first 11.75in (30cm) undyed ivory, the rest blue, 2 shoots, both undulating
*Pile:* wool, Z2 loosely plied, As2, 0.25in (3mm)
*Knot count:* 10V x 10H = 100 per sq. in. (40V x 40H = 1600 per sq. dm.)
*Texture:* soft, thin, very flexible
*Sides:* top two-thirds, goat hair, undyed dark brown, 4 cables, each wrapped around 3 warps; lower third, wool, red and blue, chevron wrapping around 12 warps
*Ends:* 1.5625in (4cm) weft-faced plain weave, wool, blue, red, reddish brown, undyed brown, ivory; warp ends tied in bunches
*Colours* 11, dark blue, green blue, dark green, red, orange, light yellow, dark brown, dark purplish brown, brown, light brown, ivory

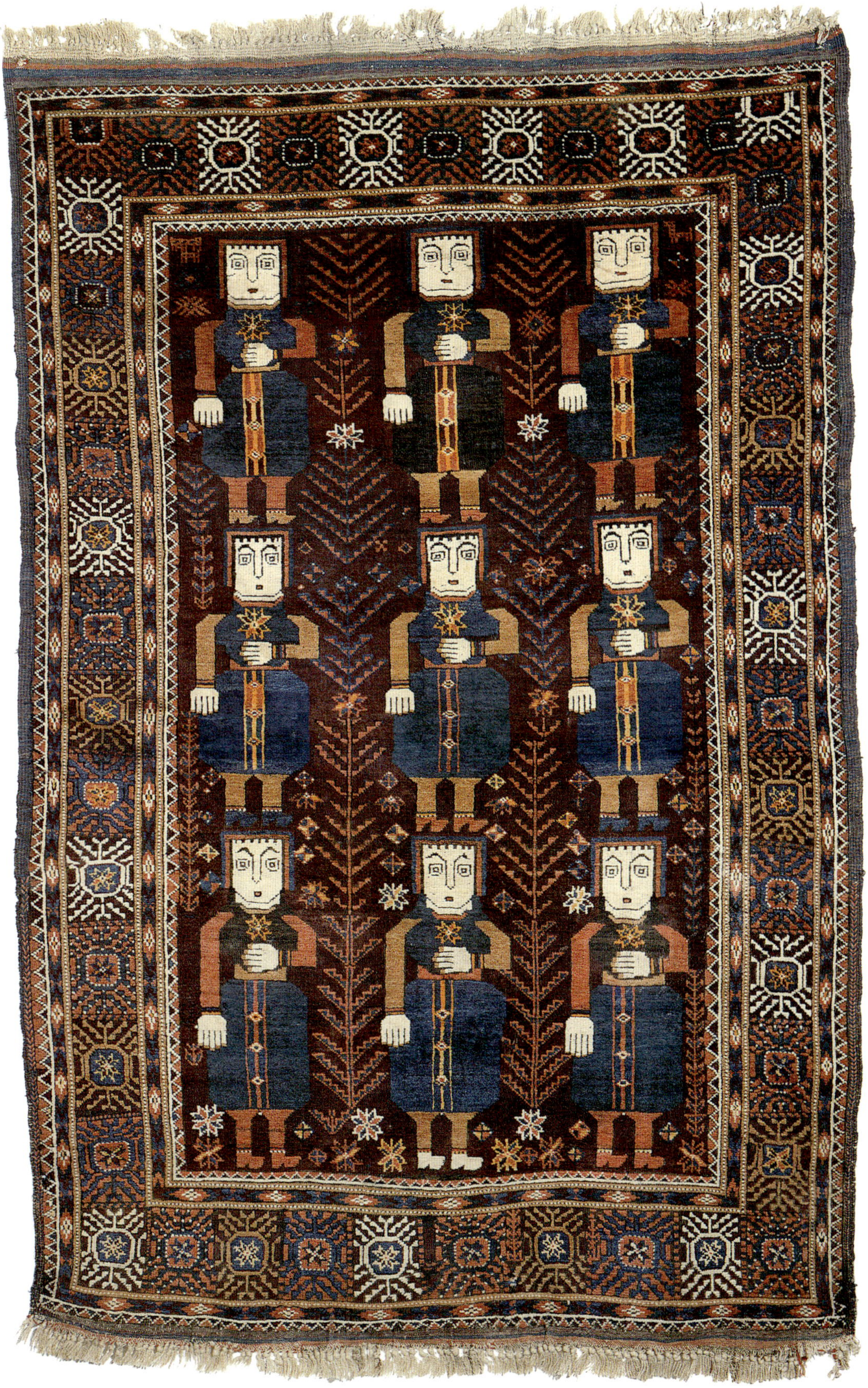

## 66

**A Mounted Khan and His Men**
**Baluch of the Zabul area**
**Late 19th century**

Of all the pictorial rugs of the Zabul area that I have seen, this is the only one that portrays the men of the region in a realistic manner and that succeeds in an exceptional way in capturing their physical appearance. Anyone who has actually seen tall, slender Baluchi men will admire the weaver's achievement here even more.

The desired effect of the design of this rug is apparent in the placement of figures. At the top is a khan mounted on a white horse. The man's face and body are wider than those of the other men. Around him we see flocks of goats and camels. From their numbers we are reminded of the khan's wealth and importance. Next to his horse and in two rows below him are the khan's retainers who stand with exemplary order and respect. Each man's head is covered with a checkered cloth. (Baluchi men normally tie a cloth around their heads or wear one over their heads.) Two small female figures are also seen under the khan's horse. These might be his daughters or wives. The entire composition of the rug clearly seems to be aimed at showing the wealth and power of the khan.

For rugs depicting tribal people, see p. 50 infra.

*Size:* 6ft 9in x 3ft 8in (206 x 112cm)
*Warp:* wool, Z2S, ivory, straight, slightly depressed
*Weft:* wool, Z2S, loosely plied, dark brown, 2 shoots, both undulating
*Pile:* wool, Z2 loosely plied, As3, 0.1875in (4mm)
*Knot count:* 9V x 8H = 72 per sq. in. (36V x 32H = 1152 per sq. dm.)
*Texture:* soft, thin, very flexible
*Sides:* wool, undyed brown, 2 cables, each wrapped around 2 warps (Z6S)
*Ends:* 1.5625in (4cm) weft-faced plain weave, wool, undyed ivory; warp ends knotted in bunches
*Colours* 8, blue-black, orange yellow, very dark brown, reddish brown, light brown, buff, grey, ivory

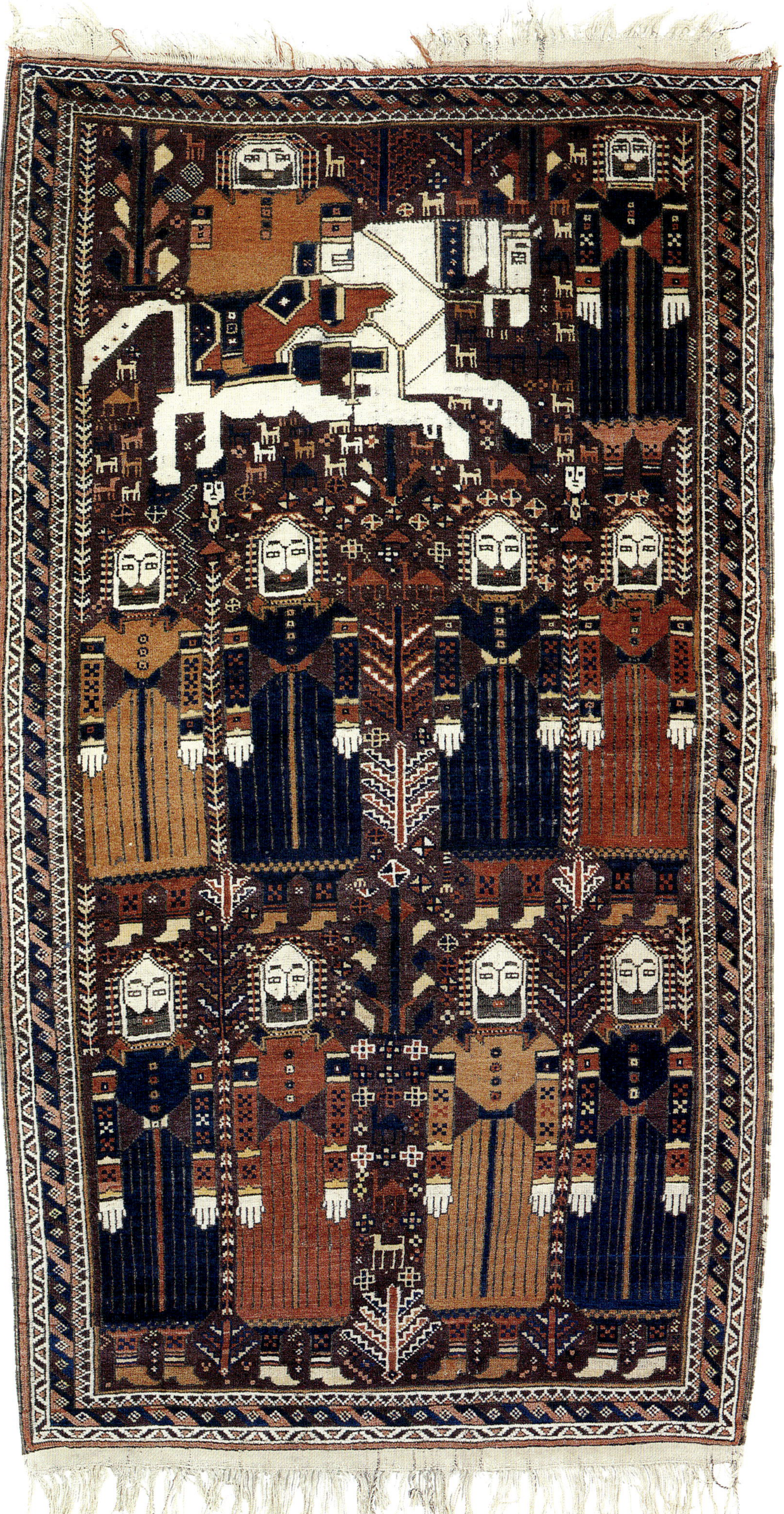

*Kings, Heroes and Lovers*

**67**

**Qashqa'i Men**
**Safi Khani subtribe of the Qashqa'i**
**Late 19th century**

Brightly attired tribal men, placed on either side of a series of medallions, are depicted in this Safi Khani rug. While their faces resemble each other, the colours and designs of their clothing are varied as much as possible. Small figures are crammed into the topmost part of the field with heads even extending into the border. This would be unlikely to happen in a city-made rug and is typical of the kind of freedom and spontaneity of conception and execution employed by tribal weavers.

For rugs depicting tribal people, see p. 50 infra.

*Size:* 8ft 4.75in x 4ft 7.5in (256 x 141cm)
*Warp:* wool (and some goat hair), Z2S, undyed shades of ivory to dark brown, straight, semi-depressed (almost 2 levels)
*Weft:* wool, Z2S, yellow, red, blue, undyed ivory, 2 shoots, both undulating
*Pile:* wool, Z2 loosely plied, Sy2, 0.1875in (5mm)
*Knot count:* 12V x 7H = 84 per sq. in. (48V x 28H = 1344 per sq. dm.)
*Texture:* fairly soft, fairly thick, stiff
*Sides:* wool, yellow and brown, parallel wrapping around 4 warps
*Ends:* missing
*Colours* 8, blue-black, blue, light blue, green, red, orange-yellow, brown, ivory

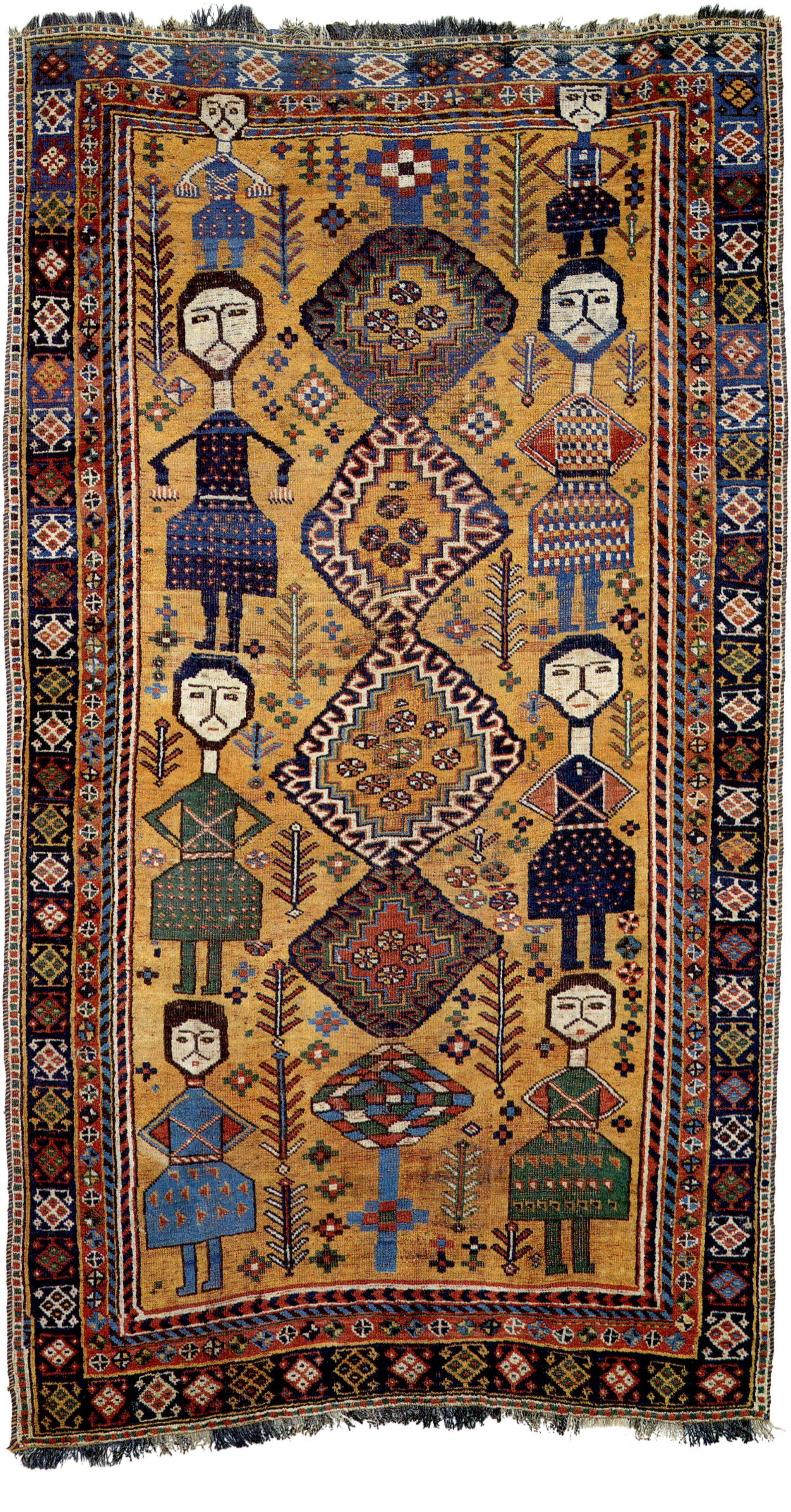

## 68

**Afshar Women**
**Afshar of the Sirjan area**
**Late 19th century**

Even though the subject and the composition of this rug are similar to many other depicting tribal people, the naturalistic appearance of the women and their urban-looking costumes give this rug a different character. Although at first glance their costumes look modern (and Western), a more careful look reveals the traditional style of dress, such as the narrow trousers, and the division of the costumes by two different colours that make them look like two pieces, a blouse and skirt. It is also worth noticing how skilfully the figures of the women have been placed within the *boteh* (paisley) motifs.

For more information about rugs depicting tribal people, see p. 50 infra.

*Size:* 5ft 9.75in x 4ft 1.25in (177 x 125cm)
*Warp:* cotton, Z5S undyed, straight, semi-depressed
*Weft:* cotton, Z3S, undyed, 2 shoots, both undulating
*Pile:* wool, Z2 loosely plied, Sy2, 0.125in (4mm)
*Knot count:* 9V x 9H = 81 per sq. in. (36V x 36H = 1296 per sq. dm.)
*Texture:* soft, somewhat thin, somewhat stiff
*Sides:* wool, all colours of the pile, remains of parallel wrapping around 12 warps
*Ends:* 0.75in (2cm) weft-faced plain weave, undyed
*Colours* 10, black, very dark blue, blue, dark green, light green, dark brown, red, very light pink, ochre, ivory

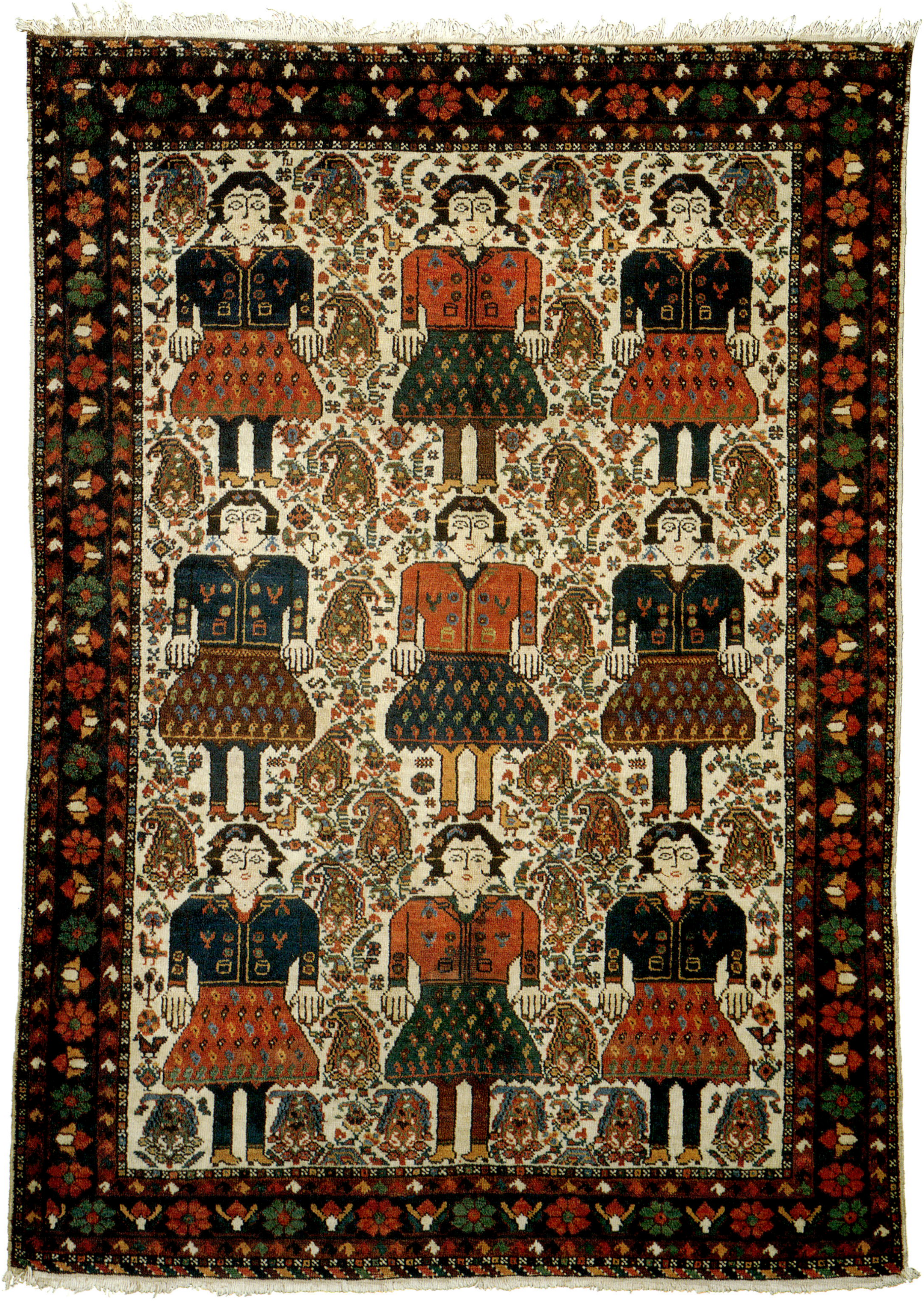

## 69

**Kurdish Women**
**Kurds of the Quchan area**
**Mid-20th century**

The faces of the tribal women in this rug are reminiscent of the art of the Seljuk period in Iran (eleventh to thirteenth centuries). This similarity becomes even more apparent when we look carefully at the connected eyebrows, narrow eyes, and large scale of their faces, which are not shown full face, looking straight out at the viewer, as in other rugs, but rather in three-quarter view as in Seljuk art. The influence of neighbouring tribal groups like the Baluchi and Arab weavers is, however, seen in the arrangement of the elements of the field and in the borders.

For more information about rugs depicting tribal groups, see p. 50 infra.

*Size:* 6ft 10in x 4ft 2.75in (208 x 129cm)
*Warp:* wool, Z2S, undyed ivory to brown, straight, 1 level
*Weft:* wool, Z2S, loosely plied, light brown, 2 shoots, both undulating
*Pile:* wool, Z2, loosely plied, As1, 0.375in (1cm)
*Knot count:* 7V x 7H = 49 per sq. in. (28V x 28H = 784 per sq. dm.)
*Texture:* soft, thick, stiff
*Sides:* wool, undyed dark brown, 4 cables, each wrapped around 4 warps
*Ends:* lower: 0.75in (2cm) weft-faced plain weave, wool, red, light green, undyed dark brown
upper: 2in (5cm) weft-faced plain weave, wool, red, light green, undyed dark brown
*Colours* 7, black, light green, very light green, red, light orange, light purple, ivory

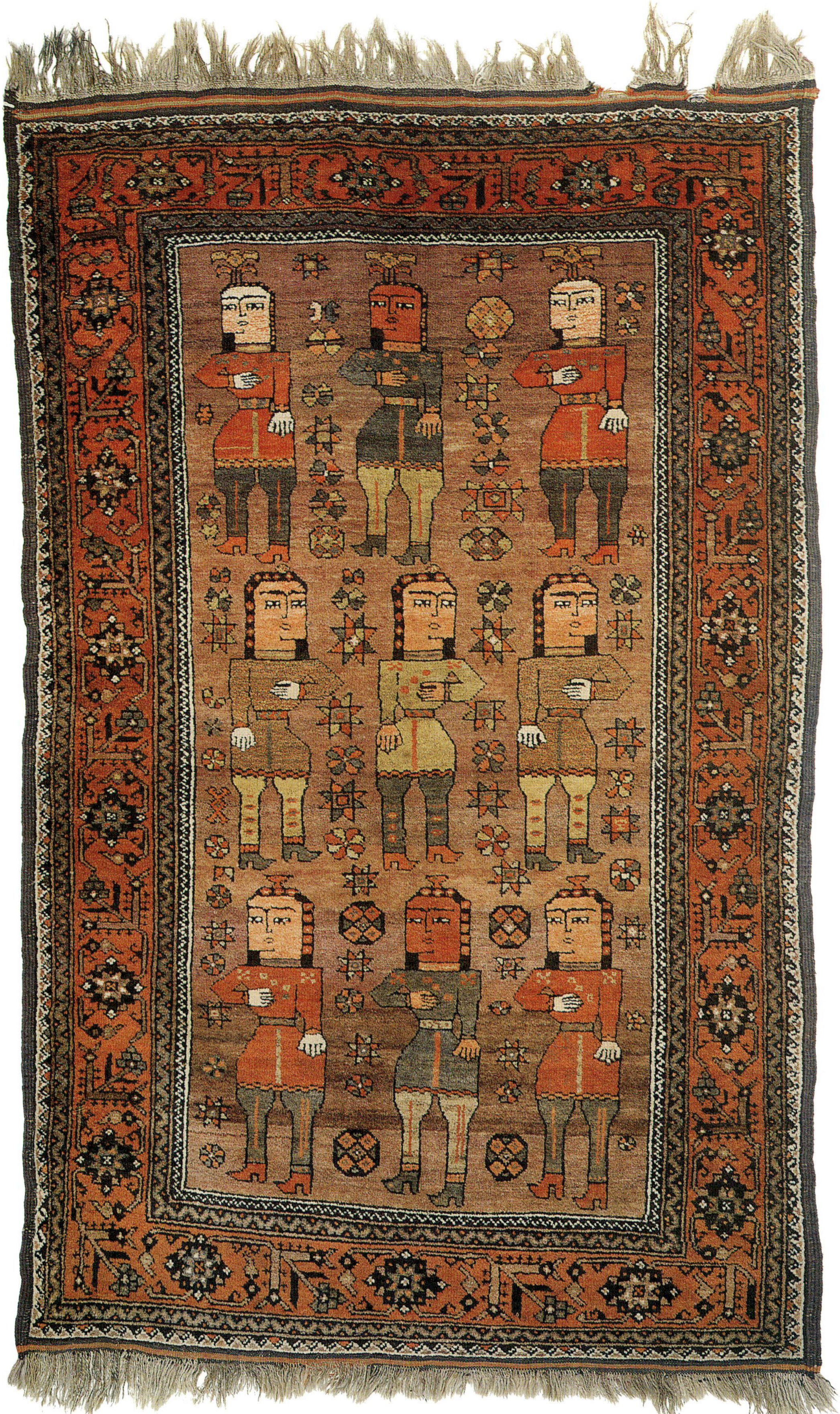

## 70

**Mounted Hunters**
**Qashqa'i**
**Mid-19th century**

Even though constant use has worn down the pile of this rug and left the warps showing, this condition in no way detracts from the vibrancy of colour seen in it. A tribal propensity for filling the field with small, repeating motifs is seen in pleasing fashion here.

This rug reminds one of certain aspects of some of the hunting rugs of the Safavid period, in particular of that in the Poldi Pezzoli Museum in Milan. While the horseback riders wear simple hats typical of the tribes of Fars and lack the soft, miniature-like qualities of Safavid horsemen, the deer in this rug are somewhat similar to those seen in hunting scenes of Persian carpets and miniatures of the sixteenth and seventeenth centuries. It is possible that a silk or cotton textile with small, repetitive pictorial motifs was a source of inspiration for this rug. Other sources the weaver could have drawn on might have been prints based on miniature paintings and painted or printed fabrics such as the *qalamkar* curtains.

For rugs depicting tribal people, see p. 50 infra.

*Size:* 6ft 3.5in x 4ft 10.75in (192 x 149cm)
*Warp:* wool, Z2S, undyed ivory to brown, straight, 1 level
*Weft:* wool, Z2S loosely plied, 2 and 3 shoots (one brownish orange, one buff), all undulating
*Pile:* wool, Z2 loosely plied, Sy1, 0.0625in (2mm)
*Knot count:* 9V x 8H = 72 per sq. in. (36V x 32H = 1152 per sq. dm.)
*Texture:* soft, very thin, extremely flexible
*Sides:* wool, blue, yellow, red, parallel wrapping around 8 warps
*Ends:* lower: missing
upper: 0.75in (2cm) weft-faced plain weave, wool, red, blue
*Colours* 8, blue-black, blue, dark green, dark red, red, yellow, dark brown, ivory

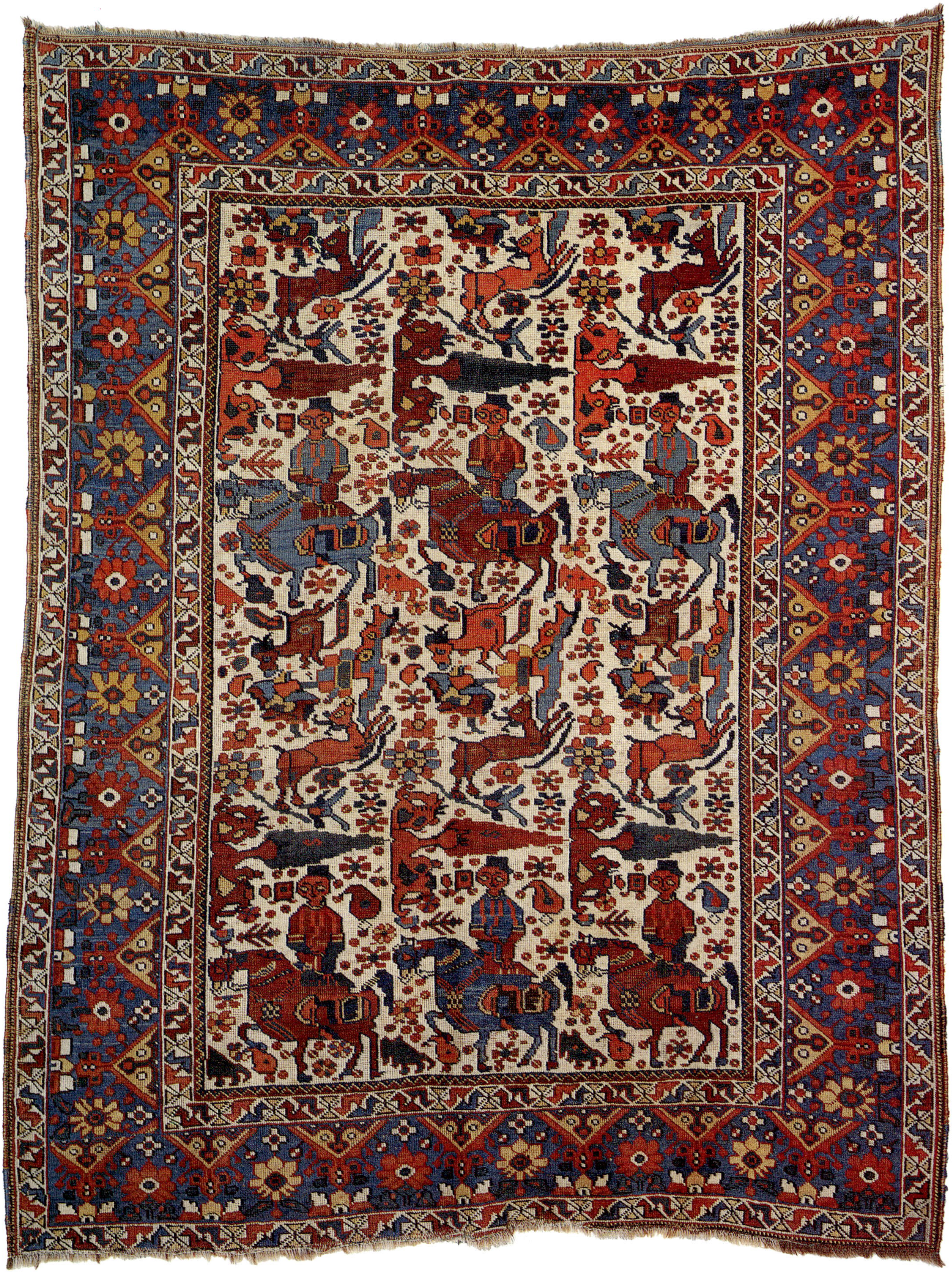

Kings, Heroes and Lovers

**71**

**Horseman and People**
**Hamadan area**
**Early 20th century**

It would appear that this rug has no particular theme, and if any is to be found, it must in some way be related to aspects of life in a village. The portrayal has the delightful simplicity of folk art. Although perhaps no specific story is immediately conveyed to the viewer by the figures in this rug, the weaver is successful in suggesting that there is some relationship between them and that they are symbolic of village life. The dominant figure is a mounted youth. In front of his horse is a man in peasant's clothes; above them stands a person resembling the village mullah; and at the bottom is the bust of a young boy with rosy cheeks. The rest of the field is filled with domesticated animals such as chickens, goats, and horses, and with household objects such as a samovar, sugar bowl, and other types of bowls, as well as with geometric and floral motifs.

For rugs depicting tribal people, see p. 50 infra.

*Size:* 5ft 8in x 4ft 3.25in (173 x 130cm)
*Warp:* cotton, Z4S, undyed, undulating, 1 level
*Weft:* wool, Z2S, brown, 1 shoot, straight
*Pile:* wool, Z2 loosely plied, Sy1, 0.1875in (4mm)
*Knot count:* 7V x 8H = 56 per sq. in. (28V x 32H = 898 per sq. dm.)
*Texture:* fairly soft, fairly thin, very flexible
*Sides:* wool, undyed dark brown, 2 cables, each chevron wrapped around 4 warps
*Ends:* lower: missing
upper: 0.75in (2cm) weft-faced plain weave, undyed cotton, decorated with one row of weft twining in brown and blue wool
*Colours* 11, blue-black, blue, blue green, pink, orange, dark brown, reddish brown, light brown, buff, grey, ivory

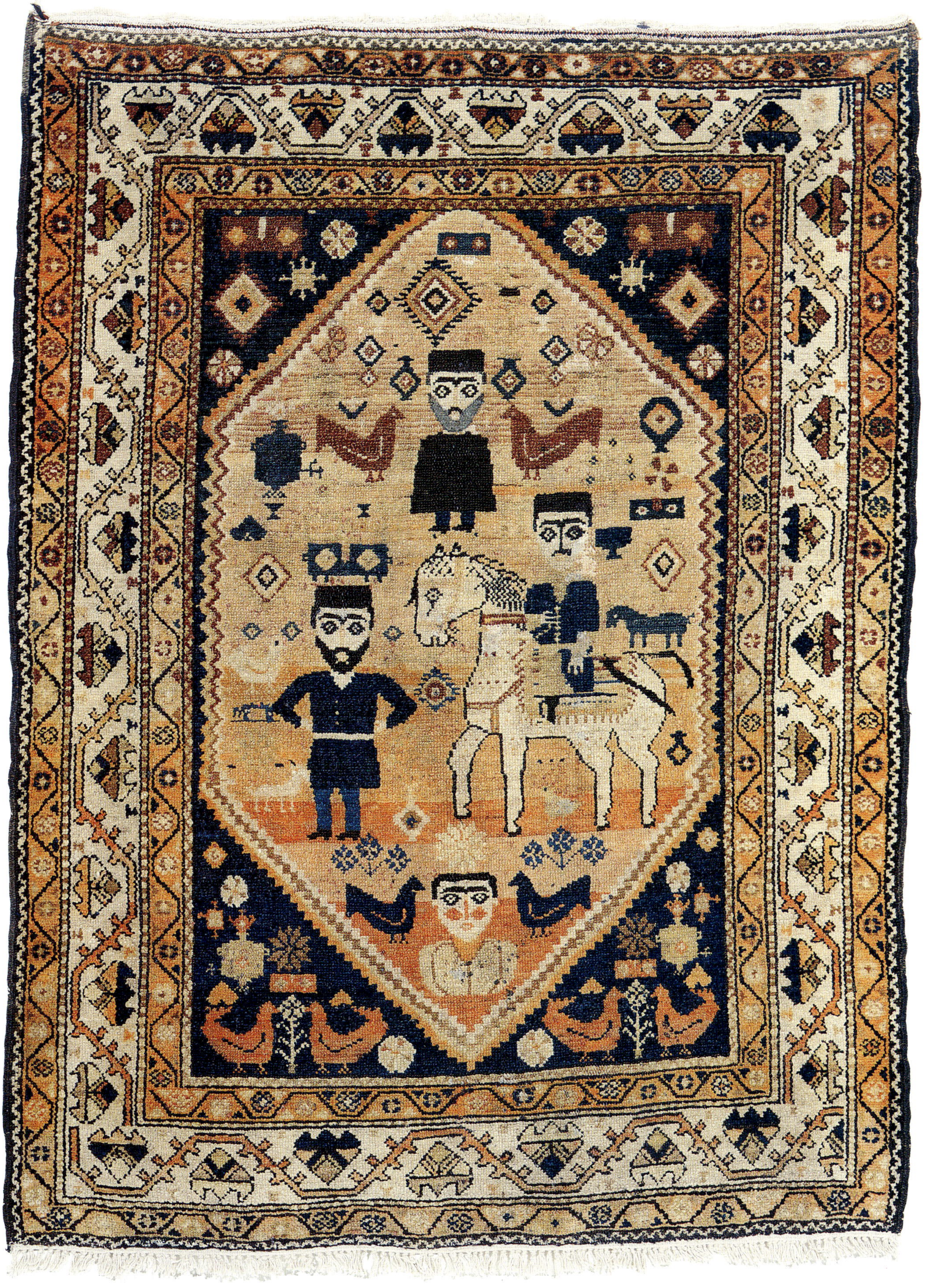

*Kings, Heroes and Lovers*

**72**

**A Khan's Wife and Her Female
   Companion
Afshar of the Sirjan area
Mid-19th century**

This scene perceptively depicts a khan's wife (*bibi*) and her female companion, and clearly indicates the behaviour and personality characteristic of each woman. The former, with her large frame, rests on a chair, the symbol of aristocracy, and holds in her hand a bunch of flowers on which a chicken roosts. At her side stands her thinner companion with hands folded on her breast as a sign of respect. Above and below the khan's wife are two small pools of water in which fish and fowl are swimming. The remaining spaces at the sides are filled with flowers, plants and birds and with ornamentation that is suggestive of the tassels and decorations on the tents of tribal chiefs. In addition to containing a rare picture of one aspect of tribal life in Iran, this rug is representative of the finest Afshar weaving.

For rugs depicting tribal people, see p. 50 infra.

*Size:* 6ft 2in x 4ft 11in (188 x 150cm)
*Warp:* wool, Z2S, undyed ivory, straight, semi-depressed (almost 2 levels)
*Weft:* wool, Z2S, brown, 2 shoots: the first straight, the second undulating; in parts of the upper and lower ends, one shoot of wool and one of cotton (Z2S, blue)
*Pile:* wool, Z2 loosely plied, As4, 0.1875in (5mm)
*Knot count:* 10V x 9H = 90 per sq. in. (40V x 36H = 1440 per sq. dm.)
*Texture:* soft, fairly thin, fairly stiff
*Sides:* wool, red, dark blue, parallel wrapping around 14 warps
*Ends:* 0.75in (2cm) weft-faced plain weave, wool, undyed ivory
*Colours* 10, blue-black, dark blue, light blue, dark green, red, orange, dark brown, brown, buff, ivory

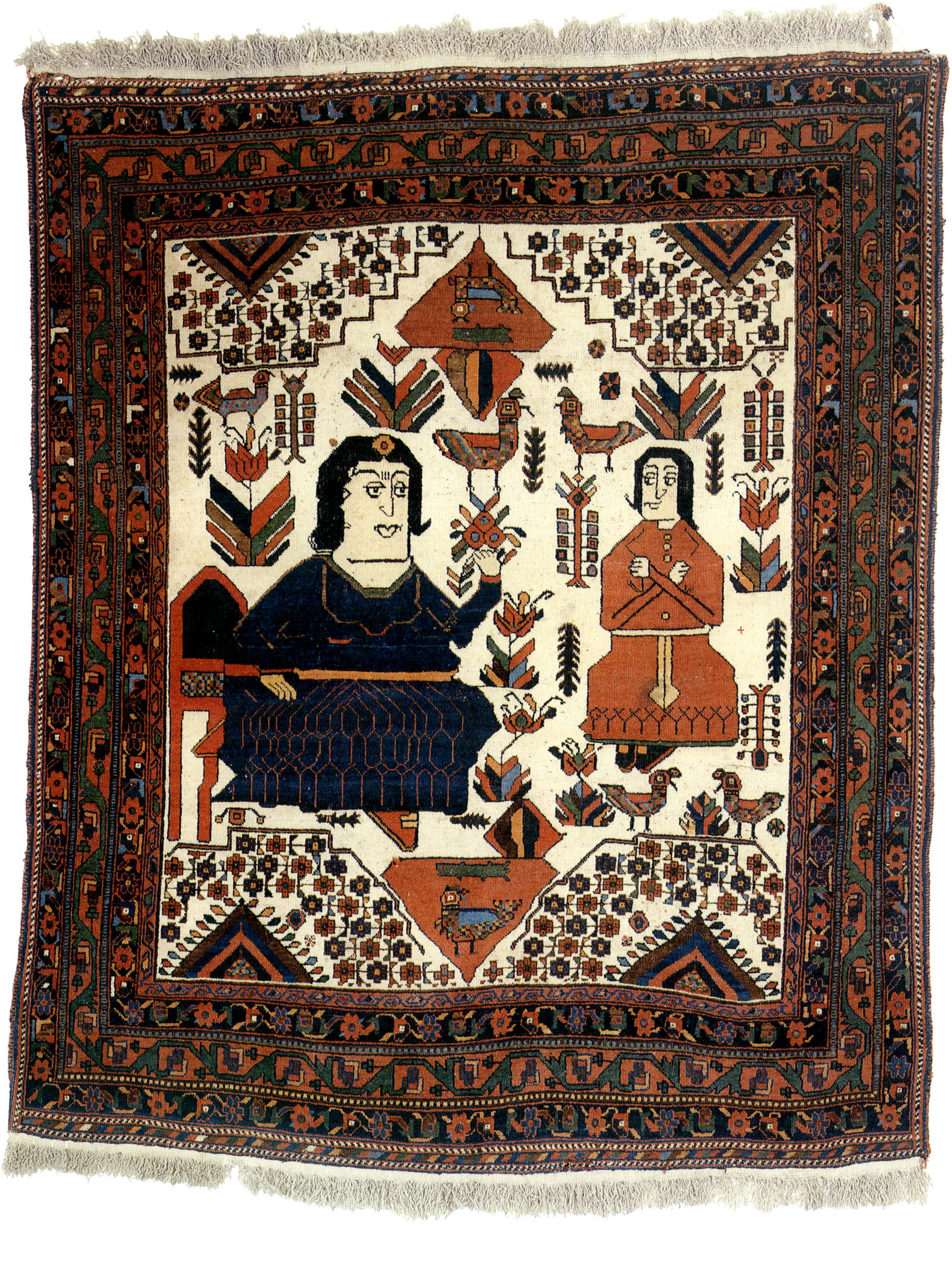

## 73

**Saqi (cup-bearer): A Woman Carrying a Tray of Wine Bottles**
**Firdows area**
**Late 19th century**

Another of the favourite pictorial designs of the Firdows weaver is the cup-bearer, or woman carrying a tray as seen here, a depiction that has been produced in considerable numbers with only minor differences of style. This rug, one of the oldest of the group, suggests that there must be a story hidden behind it. The tray carrier is a theme that appears very commonly in Iranian miniature paintings, especially from Safavid times on, through the Qajar period (see fig. 53). Reminiscent of earlier depictions are the clothes and turban-like headdress of this figure. These features, however, have been somewhat simplified and brought closer to local costume styles. The dark skin characteristic of the people of Firdows is, interestingly enough, shown in the woman's hand and neck.

For rugs depicting tribal people, see p. 50 infra.

*Size:* 5ft 3.5in x 3ft 1.5in (161 x 95cm)
*Warp:* cotton, Z4S, undyed, straight, 1 level
*Weft:* cotton, Z3S, loosely plied, dyed light grey-brown, 2 shoots, both undulating
*Pile:* wool, Z2 loosely plied, As2, 0.31in (8mm)
*Knot count:* 9V x 8H = 72 per sq. in. (36V x 32H = 1152 per sq. dm.) 73 *Texture:* soft, fairly thick, very flexible
*Sides:* wool, pink, parallel wrapping around 6 warps
*Ends:* lower: 0.75in (2cm) weft-faced plain weave, cotton, dyed light grey brown
upper: 0.375in (1cm) weft-faced plain weave, cotton, dyed light grey-brown
*Colours* 12, blue-black, blue, pale blue, olive, red, dark pink, pink, very dark brown, dark brown, pale brown, buff, ivory

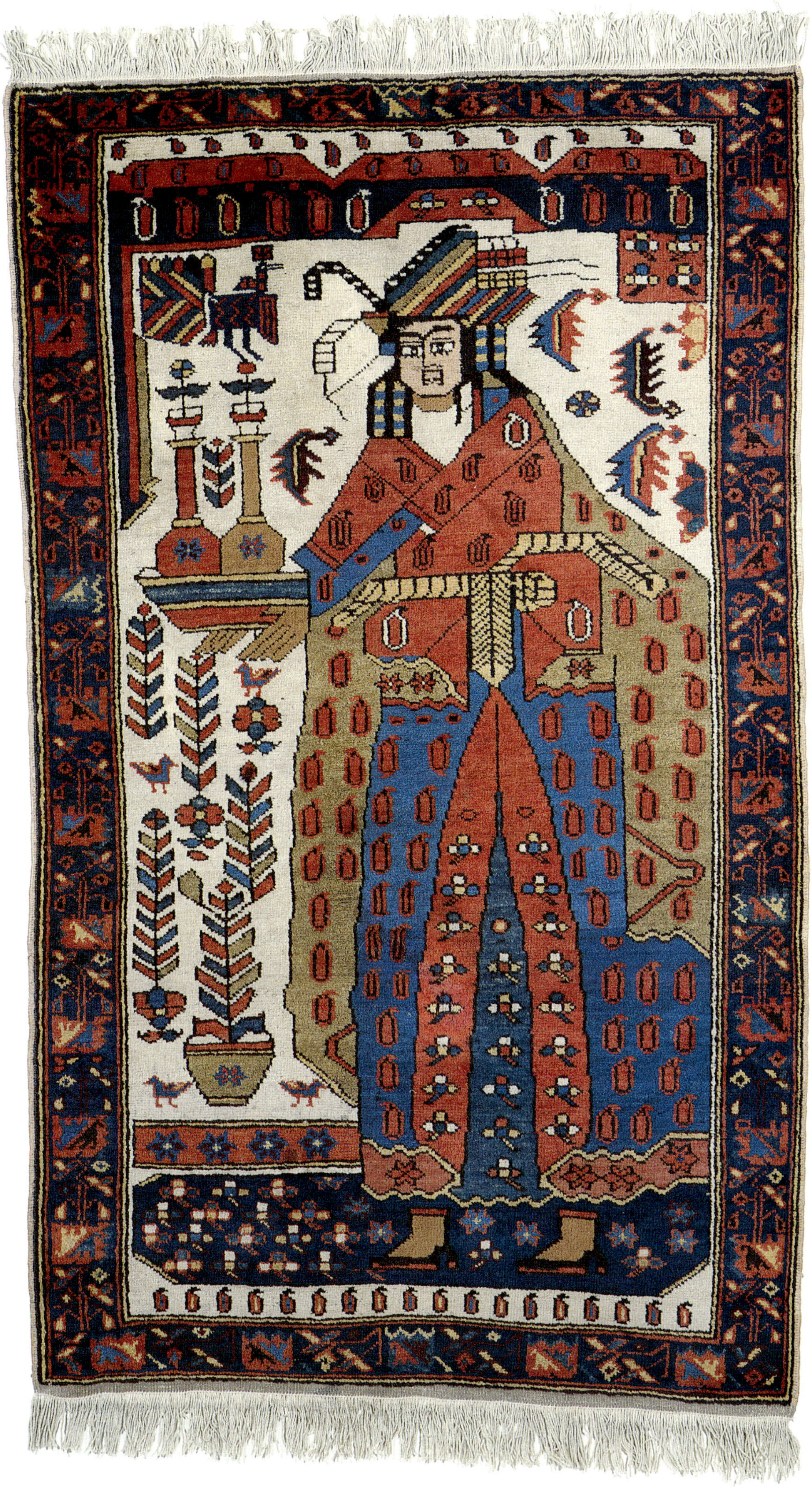

## 74

**Bride and groom**
**Malayir**
**Early 20th century**

This rug depicts a young bride and groom in clothing typical of wedding costume of the area where the rug was woven. The bride is also wearing make-up, as is customary for weddings. The figures are imposingly placed in the midst of an over-all floral pattern, which is very characteristic of Malayir weaving, but which also enhances the festive atmosphere of the scene. The bride and groom appear to be extending their hands toward each other, but in effect are giving flowers to each other, the flowers of the field. This is the only example of this pictorial subject that has come to light, and from every point of view it is most successful.

*Size:* 4ft 7.125in x 3ft 8.125in (140 x 112cm)
*Warp:* cotton, Z3S, undyed, undulating, 1 level
*Weft:* cotton, Z2S, light red, 1 shoot, straight
*Pile:* wool, Z2 loosely plied, Sy1, 0.25in (3mm)
*Knot count:* 11V x 13H = 143 per sq. in. (44V x 53H = 2332 per sq. dm.)
*Texture:* soft, thin, soft
*Sides:* wool, brown, parallel wrapping around 4 warps
*Ends:* missing
*Colours* 10, blue-black, turquoise blue, dark green, light green, dark brown, Sienna red, pink-red, pink, yellow, ivory

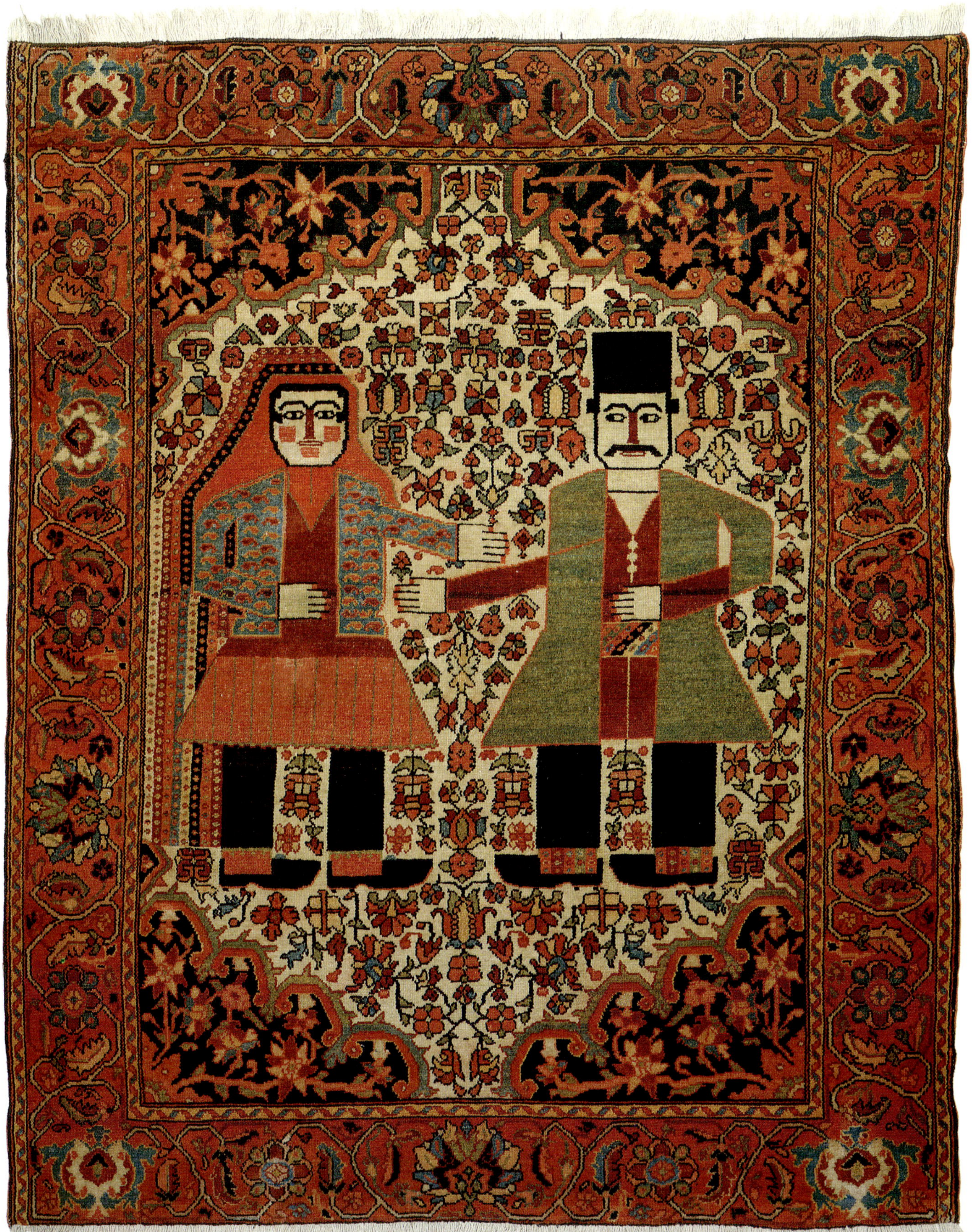

**75**

**Portrait of a Woman**
**Kerman area, probably Ravar**
**Late 19th or early 20th century**

Despite the fact that time has been unkind to this small piece and some of its warps and wefts are now exposed, it still emits a mysterious power, in part conveyed by the woman's eyes. Who is this woman who has so attracted the attention of the Iranian weaver? (See p. 56 infra, and fig. 60, which is clearly the design source of this rug and related examples.) There can be no question about the age of the rug. If it is not a hundred years old, it is not much less, for all of the black wool that is used in her hair and eyebrows is now eroded. A rug of this character was made to hang on the wall, not to be used on the floor, therefore its very worn-out condition suggests that one of its owners didn't respect this rug and seems to have used it as a mere doormat.

*Size:* 2ft 4.5in x 1ft 11in (73 x 58cm)
*Warp:* cotton, Z6S, undyed, straight, 2 levels
*Weft:* cotton, Z3S, undyed, 2 shoots: the first straight, the second undulating
*Pile:* wool, Z2 loosely plied, As3, threadbare
*Knot count:* 16V x 18H = 288 per sq. in. (64V x 72H = 4608 per sq. dm.)
*Texture:* coarse, very thin, fairly flexible
*Sides:* missing
*Ends:* missing
*Colours* 7, blue-black, light blue, dark red, pink, dark brown, brown, ivory

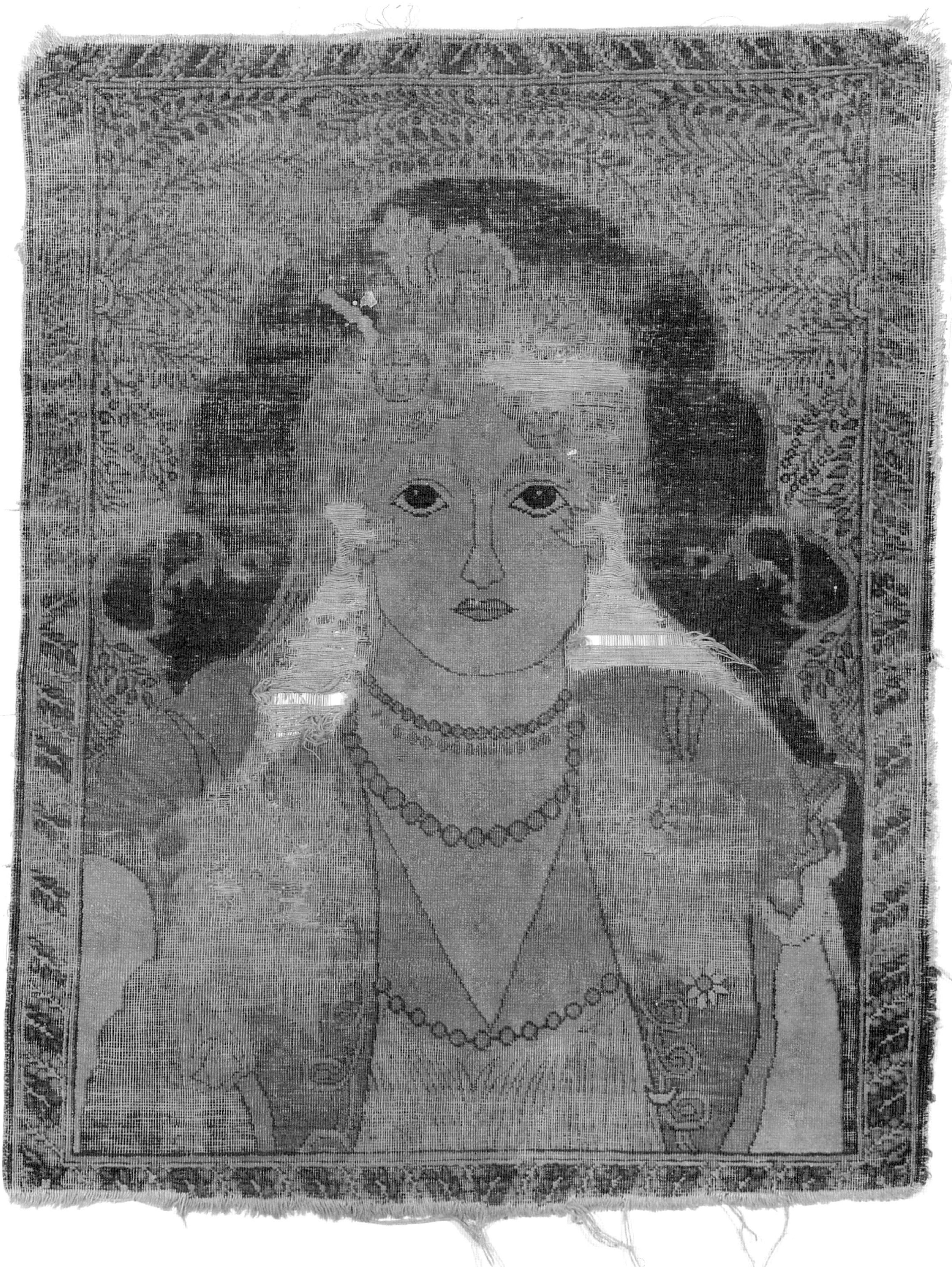

## 76

**Portrait of a Woman**
**Baluch of the Zabul area**
**Late 19th or early 20th century**

The portrait of the woman (see fig. 60 and p. 56 infra) seen in the middle of this Baluchi rug of Zabul appears to have been based on the same image that inspired the small rug no. 75 (from the region of Kerman), despite the fact that these rugs come from different regions. Besides the obvious stylistic similarities, the busts in both are the same size even though the Baluchi piece is several times larger. These two rugs provide a good example of the treatment of a common subject by weavers in different regions. The city weaver of the Kerman area who made rug no. 75, assisted by a cartoon showing the position of each knot, was able to translate accurately and convincingly the soft, curving lines and proportions of the original chromolithograph into a pile rug, while the Baluchi village or nomadic weaver (the Baluch do not use cartoons), copying another rug or a picture rather than a meticulously drawn cartoon, has depicted the same subject in an angular rather than a curvilinear style, with straight, broken lines instead. If we concentrate on the two parallel lines that run along the edge of the woman's vest up along the locks of the woman's hair that frame her face in this rug, we see how simply the face, neck, and collar of the dress are formed by a set of straight lines. Furthermore, many of the flowers on her hair are shown simply as small square and oblong shapes. The small stylized yellow floral motifs that flank the woman's face do not appear in the chromolithograph prototype (fig. 60) but are inspired by the rugs of the Kerman area (such as rug no. 75) that portray this woman, suggesting that this Baluchi rug drew at first hand on a rug from the region of Kerman and at second hand on the chromolithograph as a design source, as seems also to have been the case with rug no. 78, also Baluch work.

*Size:* 5ft 10.5in x 3ft 11.25in (179 x 120cm)
*Warp:* wool, Z2S, undyed light grey-brown, straight, 1 level
*Weft:* wool, Z2S loosely plied, undyed brown, 2 shoots, both undulating
*Pile:* wool, Z2 loosely plied, As1, 0.31in (8mm)
*Knot count:* 10V x 9H = 90 per sq. in. (40V x 36H = 1440 per sq. dm.)
*Texture:* very soft, thick, very flexible
*Sides:* wool, green, red, undyed brown, 2 cables, each wrapped around 3 warps
*Ends:* remains of 0.75in (2cm) weft-faced plain weave, wool, undyed ivory, light blue, warp ends knotted in bunches
*Colours* 10, blue-black, light blue, dark green, very light green, red, pink, pale pink, orange, brown, ivory

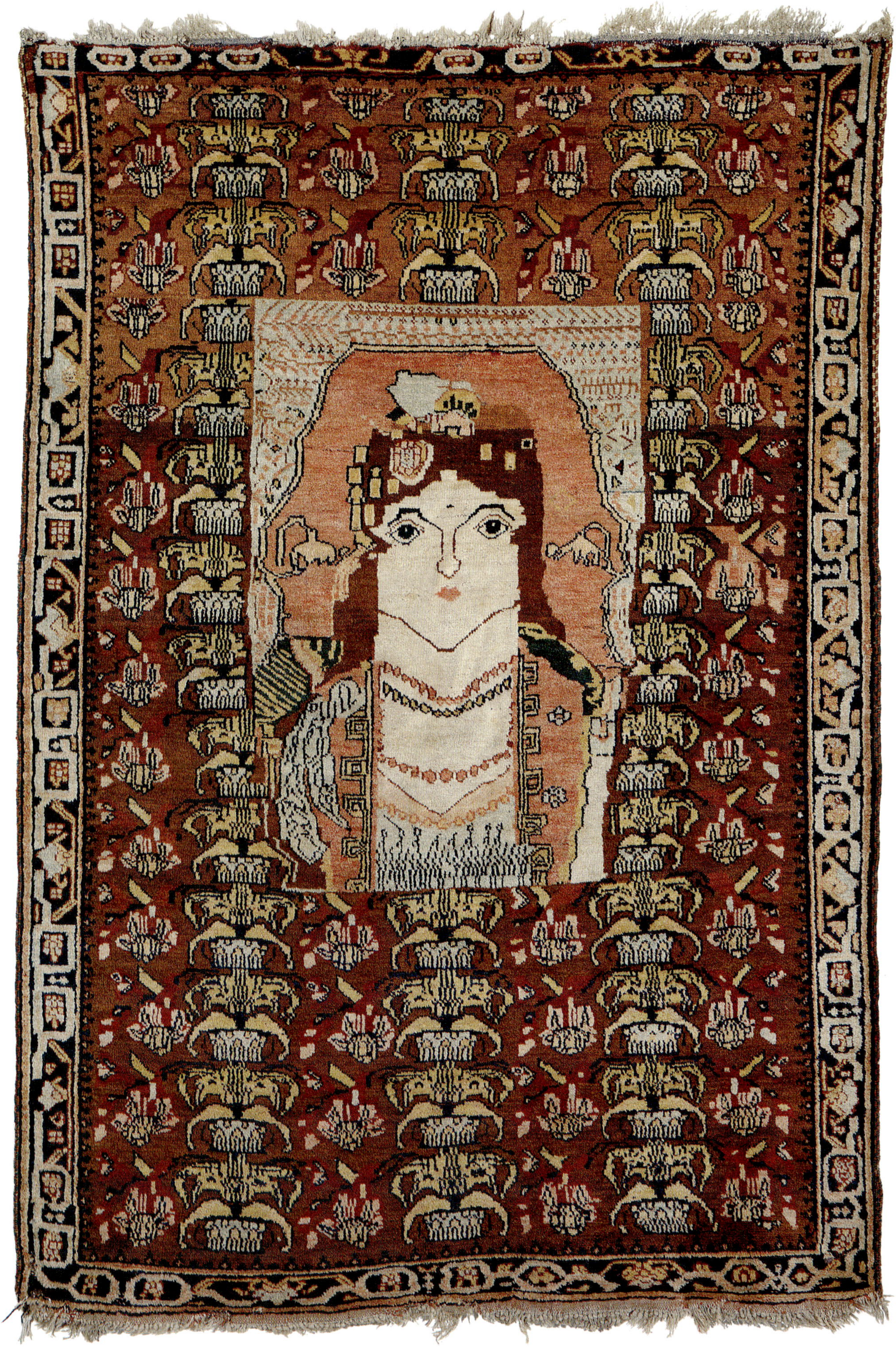

*Kings, Heroes and Lovers*

**77**

**Portrait of a Woman**
**Khamsah Confederation, Arab tribe**
**Inscription: [illegible words in Arabic and Persian]**
**Dated: *1323 (1905 AD)***

In this example of the anonymous beautiful woman (see fig. 60 and p. 56 infra) she is placed skilfully and imaginatively in a completely different framework by a weaver of the Khamsah Confederation. On the one hand, an almost complete medallion in the style of traditional carpets with purely abstract designs is created in the centre of the rug, with the busts (shown as if reflected in water or as on playing cards) enjoying an important role in the central area. On the other hand, the reflection of the image creates different views in this rather large rug. In the centre at the point where the busts join is a blue ground with an inscription in Arabic and Persian that is not legible. Even if the inspiration for this pattern came from playing cards, the weaver has produced something most creative.

*Size:* 6ft 10.5in x 5ft 6in (210 x 168cm)
*Warp:* cotton, Z2S, undyed, nearly straight, semi-depressed
*Weft:* cotton, Z2S, pale pink, 2 shoots, both slightly undulating
*Pile:* wool, Z2 loosely plied, As3, 1.5625in (4mm)
*Knot count:* 9V x 9H = 81 per. sq. in. (36V x 36H = 1296 per sq. dm.)
*Texture:* soft, thin, very flexible
*Sides:* wool, dark red, dark green, chevron wrapping around 8 warps
*Ends:* missing
*Colours* 15, blue-black, medium blue, light blue, dark green, light green, dark red, red, dark pink, pink, orange, lemon yellow, black brown, brown, light brown, ivory

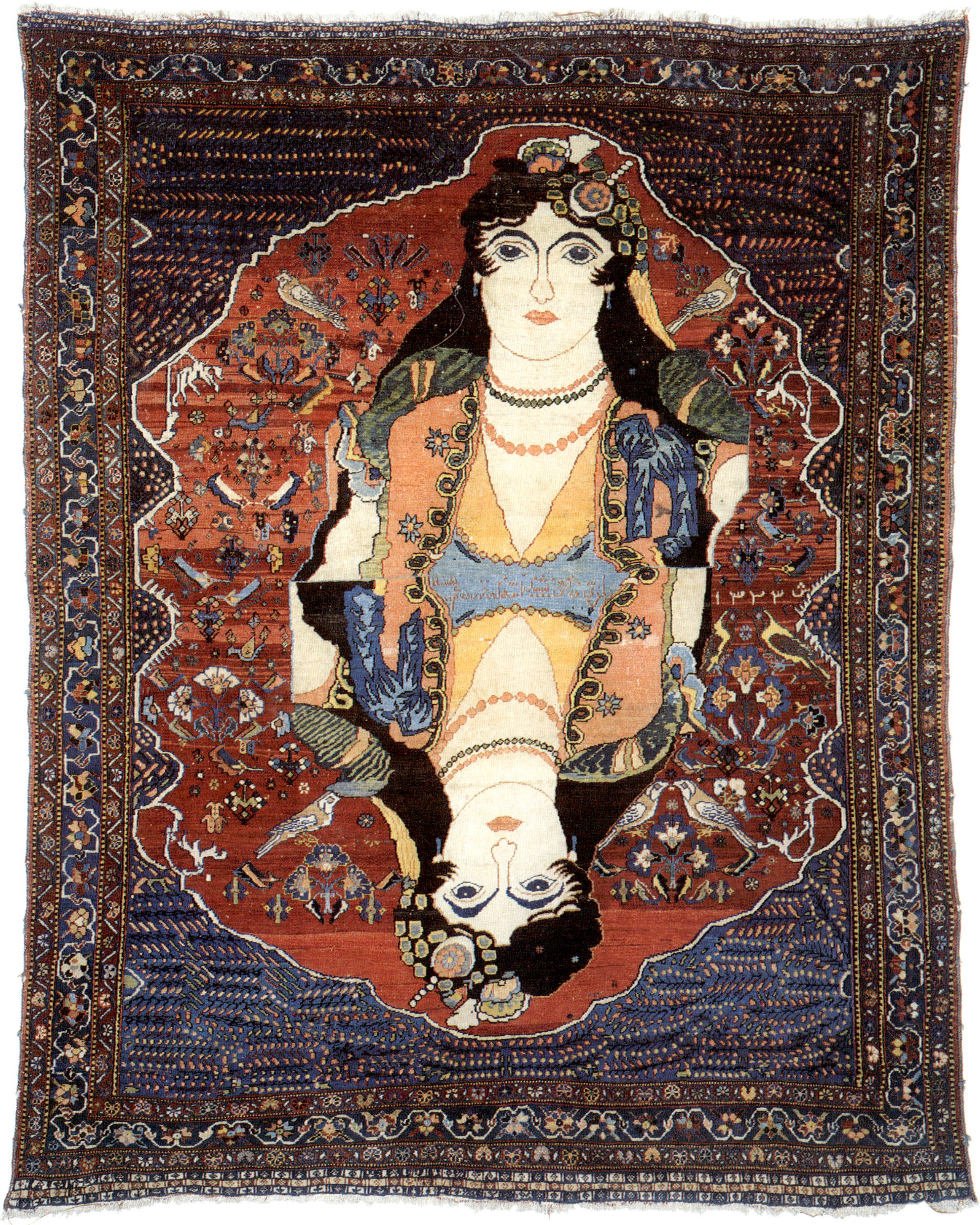

Kings, Heroes and Lovers

**78**

**Portrait of a Woman
Baluch of the province of Khurasan
Mid-20th century**

Here is another interpretation of the bust of the beautiful woman (see fig. 60 and p. 56 infra) seen in rugs nos. 75-77. Her large, black eyes set of by her white skin more than anything else attract the viewer's attention and dominate the other colours designs.

This is very probably the work of a Baluchi weaver of Khurasan in eastern Iran as opposed to a Baluchi weaver of Zabul (who wove rug no. 76). To a large extent it is a successful rendition of the curves and consequently of the natural proportions of the original, which would indicate the influence of city weaving. This rug shows that the depiction of this idealized woman continued to interest rug weavers until very recently.

*Size:* 3ft 5in x 2ft 4.75in (104 x 73cm)
*Warp:* wool, Z2S, undyed ivory, straight, semi-depressed
*Weft:* wool, Z2S loosely plied, dark blue, 2 shoots: the first straight, the second undulating
*Pile:* wool, Z2 loosely plied, Sy3, 0.25in (6mm)
*Knot count:* 11V x 9H = 99 per sq. in. (44V x 36H = 1584 per sq. dm.)
*Texture:* soft, fairly thick, very flexible
*Sides:* wool, dark red, 2 cables, each wrapped around 3 warps
*Ends:* 1.5625in (4cm) weft-faced plain weave, wool, first 0.75in (2cm) decorated with 3 rows of countered weft-twining in red, blue, pink, green, and black; the ends of every 3 warps knotted together
*Colours* 11, blue-black, turquoise blue, dark green, green, purplish red, pink, brownish orange, mustard yellow, brown, olive brown, ivory

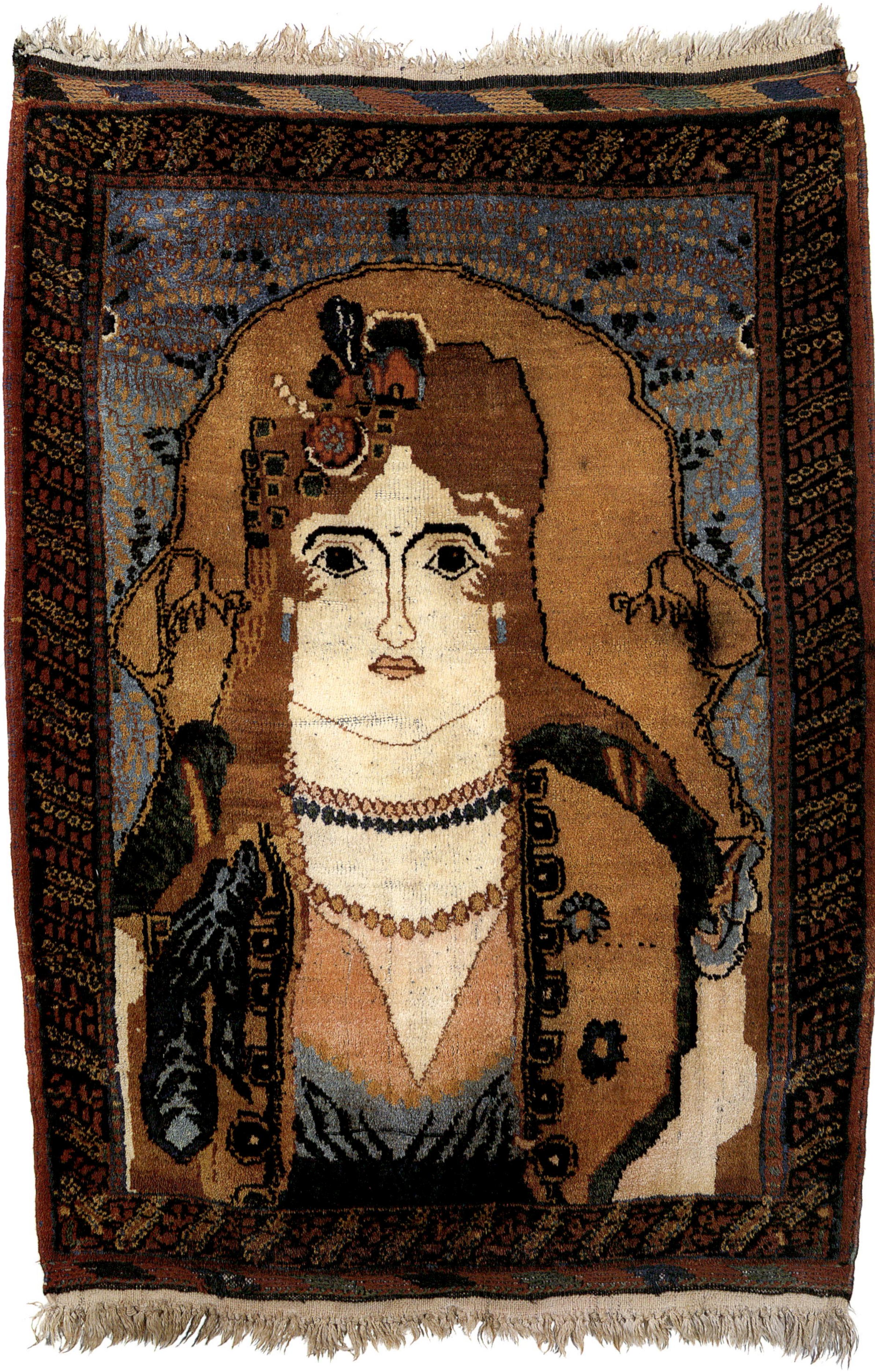

**79**

**Standing Woman and Dog**
Bakhtiyari, village of Shamsabad
Inscription: ***Ordered by His Excellency, Amir Mujahid, woven by Bakhtiyari [in the] year 1324 (1906 AD)***

This is one of several rugs with pictures of women commissioned by Yusuf Khan Amir Mujahid Bakhtiyari (see nos. 80 and 81). On p. 56 infra information is given about the source of this type of picture (this one, discussed on p. 57, may have been based on a European postcard) and the extent to which the pictures of beautiful European women were enjoyed by the people and artists of Iran in the nineteenth and early twentieth centuries. The light brown hair, clothes, manner in which this woman stands with a basket of flowers in her hand, and dog in front of her, all recall photographs of European women commonly seen in Iran at the end of the last century and the beginning of the present one. However, the Iranian rug weaver has imparted a special life and quality to her version of the photographic image. The facial features have been simplified and idealized, and convey a certain air of nobility as well as innocence and purity. The woman's alluring eyes, which are fixed on an undetermined point in the distance, instil silence and respect in the viewer. The two parrots on either side of her head and the two trees that form an arch over her seem to protect her.

*Size:* 6ft 4in x 5ft 2.25in (193 x 158cm)
*Warp:* cotton, Z3S, undyed, straight, 2 levels
*Weft:* cotton, Z5S, undyed, 2 shoots: the first straight, the second undulating
*Pile:* wool, Z2 loosely plied, Sy3, 0.25in (3mm)
*Knot count:* 12V x 12H = 144 per sq. in. (48V x 48H = 2304 per sq. dm.)
*Texture:* soft, thin, fairly stiff
*Sides:* wool, red, parallel wrapping around 6 warps
*Ends:* lower: 0.75in (2cm) weft-faced plain weave, undyed cotton
upper: 1.1875in (3cm) weft-faced plain weave, undyed cotton
*Colours* 9, blue-black, dark green, light green, very light green, pink, yellow, dark brown, light brown, ivory

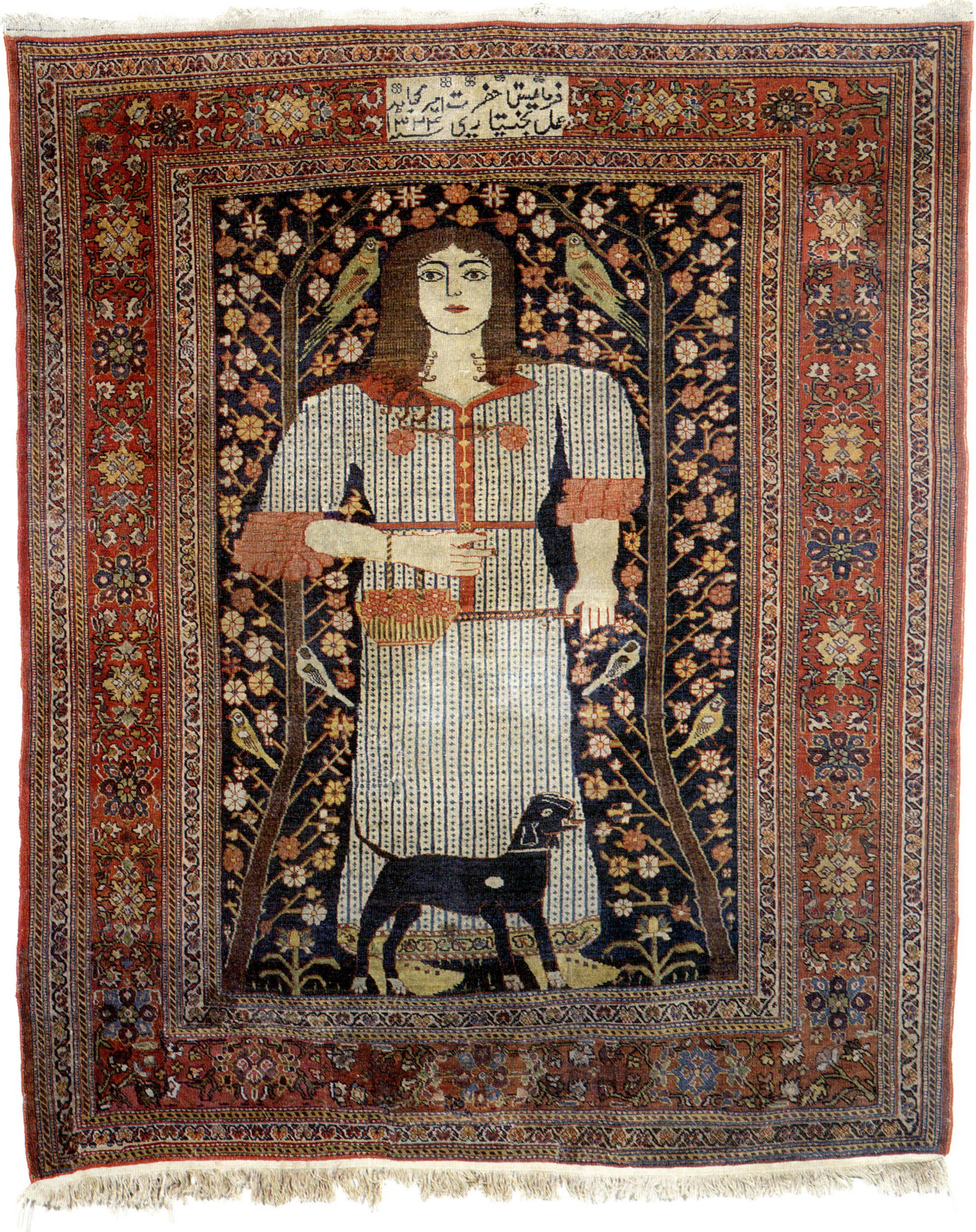
فرمایش حضرت امیر مجاهد
عمل بختیاری ۱۳۲۴

## Kings, Heroes and Lovers

**80**

**Standing Woman**
**Bakhtiyari, village of Shamsabad**
**Inscription:** *Ordered by His Excellency Amir Mujahid, woven by Bakhtiyari [in the] year 1309 (1891 AD)*

This is another example of the woman who was the object of Yusuf Amir Mujahid Bakhtiyari's interest. An indication of the tribal identity of the weaver of other rugs depicting this woman also appears at the top of this one. According to its date woven into this rug this must be the oldest of the three rugs depicting this woman (nos. 79, 80, 81). The same prototype seems to have been used for the woman portrayed here and the central figure in rug no. 81 (see p. 56 infra, especially p. 57). The fact that the rug illustrated here is executed in a limited range of colours (mainly blue-black and ivory), might suggest that it was based on a black and white photograph. The dominance of only two colours, however, is not sufficient reason to think that was the case, for even if it had been, the weaver could have added colour in at least the border in the woven version of the picture; instead she apparently consciously chose to use two predominant, contrasting tones. The dark blue clothing of the woman appears like velvet against the white field and is reminiscent of a style current among aristocratic women at the beginning of the century in Iran.

*Size:* 6ft 8.25in x 5ft 11in (204 x 155cm)
*Warp:* cotton, 3(Z2S)S, undyed, straight, semi-depressed
*Weft:* cotton, Z3S, undyed, 2 shoots: the first straight, the second undulating
*Pile:* wool, Z2 loosely plied, Sy2, 0.0625in (2mm)
*Knot count:* 12V x 11H = 132 per sq. in. (48V x 44H = 2112 per sq. dm.)
*Texture:* soft, thin, flexible
*Sides:* wool, undyed dark brown, parallel wrapping around 9 warps
*Ends:* 0.75in (2cm) weft-faced plain weave, undyed cotton
*Colours* 7, blue-black, very light green, red, dark brown, light brown, grey, ivory

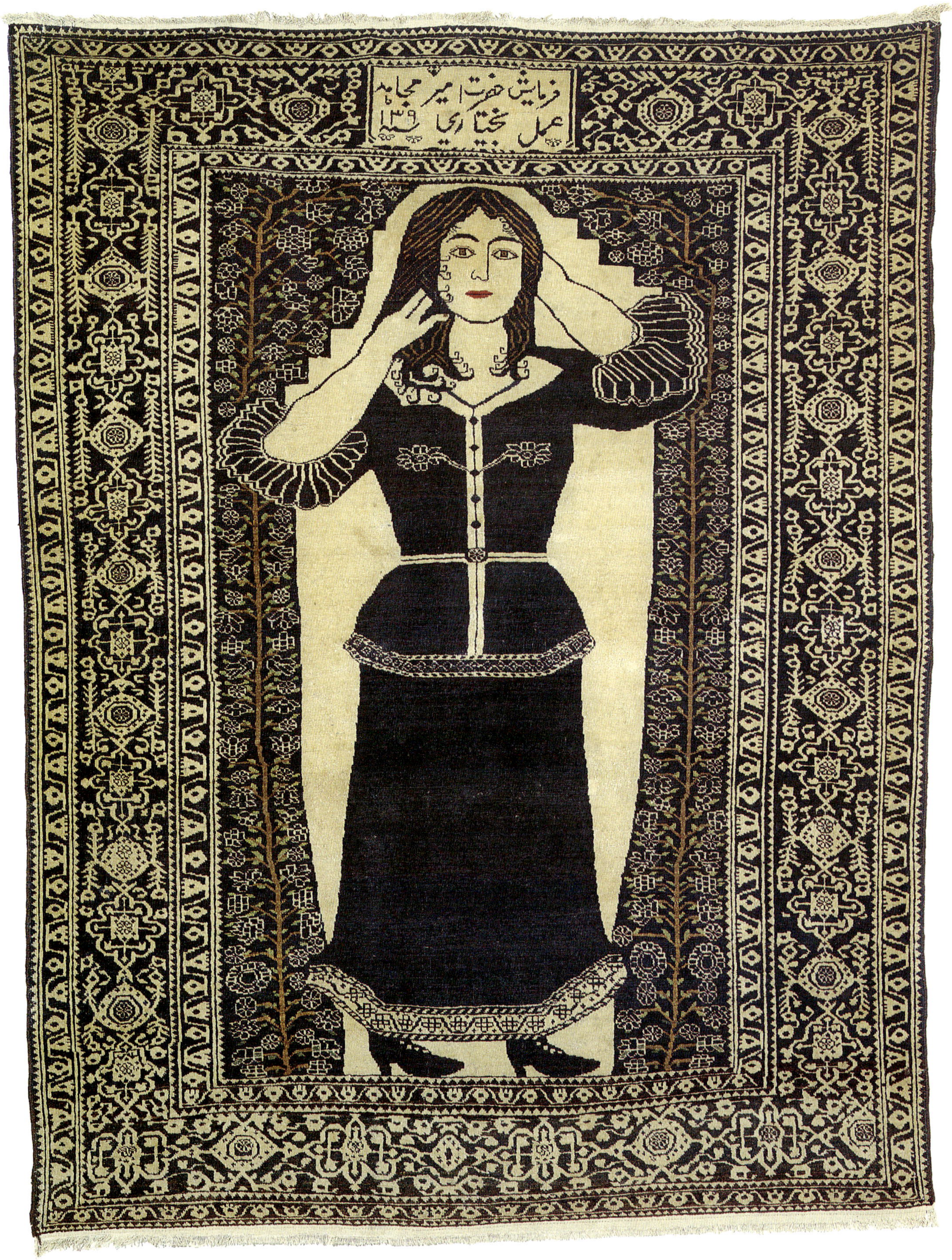
فرمایش حضرت امیر مجاهد
عمل بختیاری سنه ۱۳۹

**81**

**Three Women**
**Bakhtiyari, village of Shamsabad**
**Inscription:** ***Ordered by His Excellency Amir Mujahid, woven by Bakhtiyari [in the] year 1329 (1911 AD)***

Yusuf Khan Amir Mujahid Bakhtiyari's special interest in the central woman portrayed here led him to order several rugs depicting her. Rugs nos. 79 and 80 show two different versions of the portrait of this European woman (see p. 56 infra, especially p. 57). In this example the weaver combined aspects of rugs nos. 79 and 80. The woman of rug no. 80, with the same pose and clothes, has been placed between the two other women in this example, and the dog in rug no. 79 has been placed in front of her here. The two other women, whose clothes and pose (the one on the right reversed for symmetry) are very similar to those of the woman shown in rug no. 79. The woman on the right also carries a basket of flowers as does the woman in rug no. 79. The other woman in this rug is holding a tar, an Iranian stringed instrument. Each woman is holding a flower in her other hand. In this rug the weaver has emphasized the Iranian costumes of the women on either side of the central figure by decorating their jackets with large *boteh* (paisley) motifs, a great favourite with Iranians. The weaver's reason for increasing the number of women is very probably the large size of this rug. A rug of these large dimensions is most exceptional among pictorial rugs, which are normally of a convenient size to hang on a wall. This rug, however, was ordered by a Bakhtiyari chief named Yusuf Khan Amir Mujahid for the floor of the reception room in his own residence in Shamsabad (see p. 57) and it was undoubtedly intended to complement rugs nos. 79 and 80, which were hung on the wall in the same room. Here, as in rug no. 79, the flowering trees form an arch over the women, and birds and small animals perch symmetrically on their branches.

*Size:* 11ft 10.5in x 9ft 7.75in (362 x 294cm)
*Warp:* cotton, Z3S, undyed, straight, 2 levels
*Weft:* cotton, Z3S, undyed, 2 shoots: the first straight, the second undulating
*Pile:* wool, Z2 loosely plied, Sy3, 0.0625in (2mm)
*Knot count:* 12V x 16H = 192 per sq. in. (48V x 64H = 3072 per sq. dm.)
*Texture:* soft, thin, fairly stiff
*Sides:* wool, red, parallel wrapping around 6 warps
*Ends:* 1.1875in (3cm) weft-faced plain weave, undyed cotton, decorated with 1 row of weft twining in red and yellow wool
*Colours* 12, blue-black, blue, light blue, green, light green, red, pink, yellow, mustard, brown, light brown, ivory

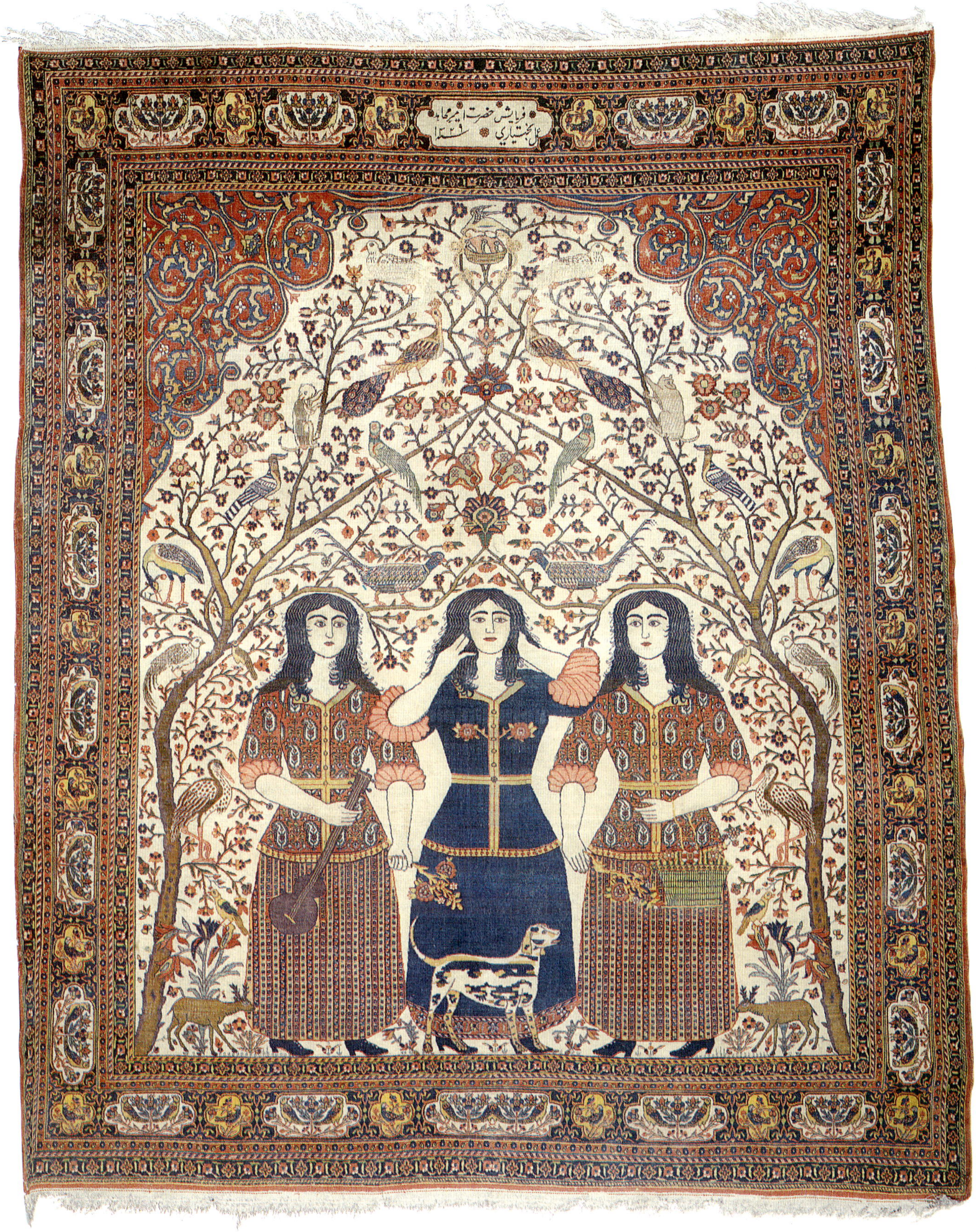

**82**

**Lion (Tiger?)**
**(Although the animal depicted in this rug resembles a tiger, the tribal people still call it a lion)**
**Qashqa'i**
**Inscription:** *Ordered by Nasrullah Khan [in the] year [1]336 (1918 AD)*

This rug is the mate to a rug showing the same animal (which has both stripes and spots) walking to the left (in symmetrical mirror image to this one) published in colour in my exhibition catalogue *Lion Rugs from Fars* (Tehran, 1978), no. 37, pp. 102-103; and in black and white in my catalogue *Lion Rugs from Fars* (Washington, DC, 1974), no. 1, p. 30 (see also p. 18). There are minor differences between these two rugs (the lion in the other example is shown with his mouth open), but both were commissioned by the same person and were almost certainly made by the same weaver, and they both have the same date woven into them. Actually, two dates, 1115 (1703 AD) and 1336 (1918 AD), were woven into the other rug, the former slightly paler and the latter as part of the inscription. According to information gathered during research conducted in the Marv Dasht area east of Shiraz, these two rugs were woven in that area. A Qashqa'i khan named Nasrullah Khan is known to have lived there three generations ago, and to have died in the late nineteenth century. We believe that this was the Nasrullah Khan referred to in the inscription in these two rugs as the person who ordered them. If this is correct, the rug must be nearly one hundred years old. The high quality of the rug from the point of view of material and colour is a further indication that this rug could be nearly a hundred years old. Moreover, unlike many more recent lion rugs, this one is very finely woven and is very thin. The lion of the rug has a special dignity. Being placed on a blue ground that is devoid of other ornamental touches adds to its magnificence and power.

For rugs depicting animals, particularly lions, see p. 58 infra.

*Size:* 7ft 2.5in x 4ft 11in (220 x 150cm)
*Warp:* wool, Z2S, undyed ivory, straight, 1 level
*Weft:* cotton, Z6S, undyed and dyed buff; 2 shoots: both undulating
*Pile:* wool, Z2 loosely plied, As1, 0.25in (3mm)
*Knot count:* 12V x 11H = 132 per sq. in. (48V x 44H = 2112 per sq. dm.)
*Texture:* velvety, very thin, flexible
*Sides:* wool, all colours used for the pile, parallel wrapping around 4 warps in 3- to 4-inch vertical sections of each colour
*Ends:* missing
*Colours* 11, blue-black, dark blue, blue, greenish blue, turquoise green, reddish purple, orange, aubergine, brown, light brown, ivory

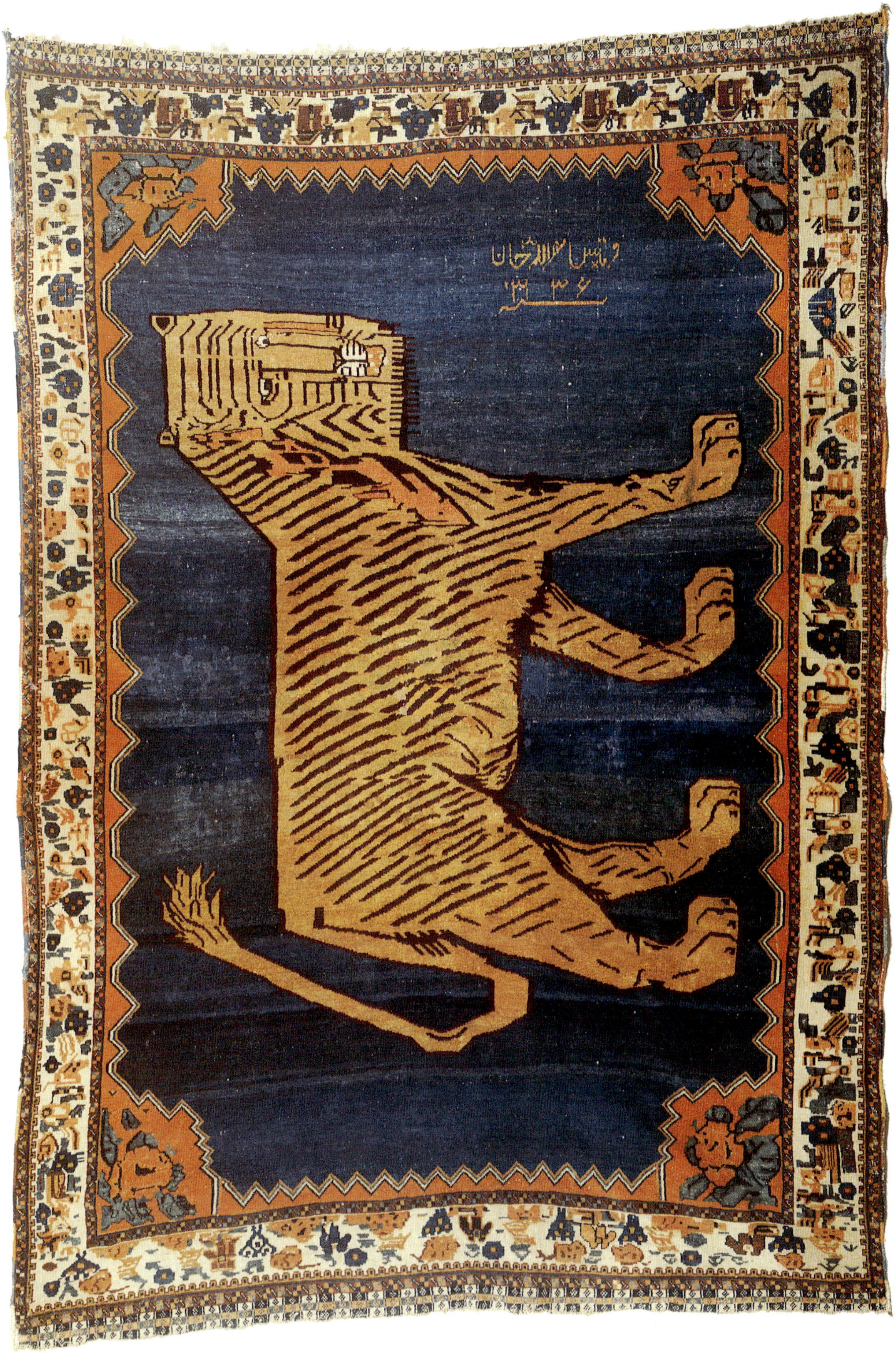

## 83

**Lion**
**Lori, Boyer Ahmad**
**Mid-19th century**

The animal depicted here by a Boyer Ahmad Lor more closely resembles a tiger than a lion, but this type of image is called 'lion rug' by the tribal people of the province of Fars. The lion must have an interesting story behind it for it has attracted the attention of many tribal weavers in Iran (see p. 58 infra). I have seen examples of those woven by the Qashqa'i as well as another example of a rug depicting a lion that is Shahsavan work (no. 84).

In my exhibition catalogue, *Lion Rugs from Fars* (Washington, DC, 1974; no. 18 on p. 45, see also p. 23) a Qashqa'i rug very similar to this Lori rug is illustrated. The following anecdote is in circulation among the Qashqa'i in Fars province about the lion depicted in rug no. 18 in that catalogue: there was an old lioness whose teeth had fallen out (making her harmless) and who became the mascot of the children of a tribe.

This lion rug must be considered one of the very best examples of Lori weaving. In spite of its age it has remained in excellent condition. It is the type of rug known in Iran as a *gabbeh* (see p. 67).

*Size:* 6ft 3.5in x 5ft 0.5in (192 x 153cm)
*Warp:* wool, Z2S, undyed ivory to brown, straight, semidepressed depressed
*Weft:* wool, Z2S, dark red, 4in (10cm) at the top undyed ivory, 3 to 5 shoots: the first, third and fifth straight, the second and fourth undulating
*Pile:* wool, Z2 loosely piled, Sy3, 0.25in (6mm)
   *Knot count:* 7V x 8H = 56 per sq. in. (28V x 32H = 896 per sq. dm.)
*Texture:* very soft, fairly thick, flexible
*Sides:* wool, red, green, chevron wrapping around 4 warps
*Ends:* lower: missing
   upper: 2 inches (5cm) weft-faced plain weave, wool, blue, dark brown, undyed ivory; half turned under and sewn down
*Colours:* 10, blue-black, blue, sky blue, light green, very light green, dark brown, dark buff, red, yellow, white

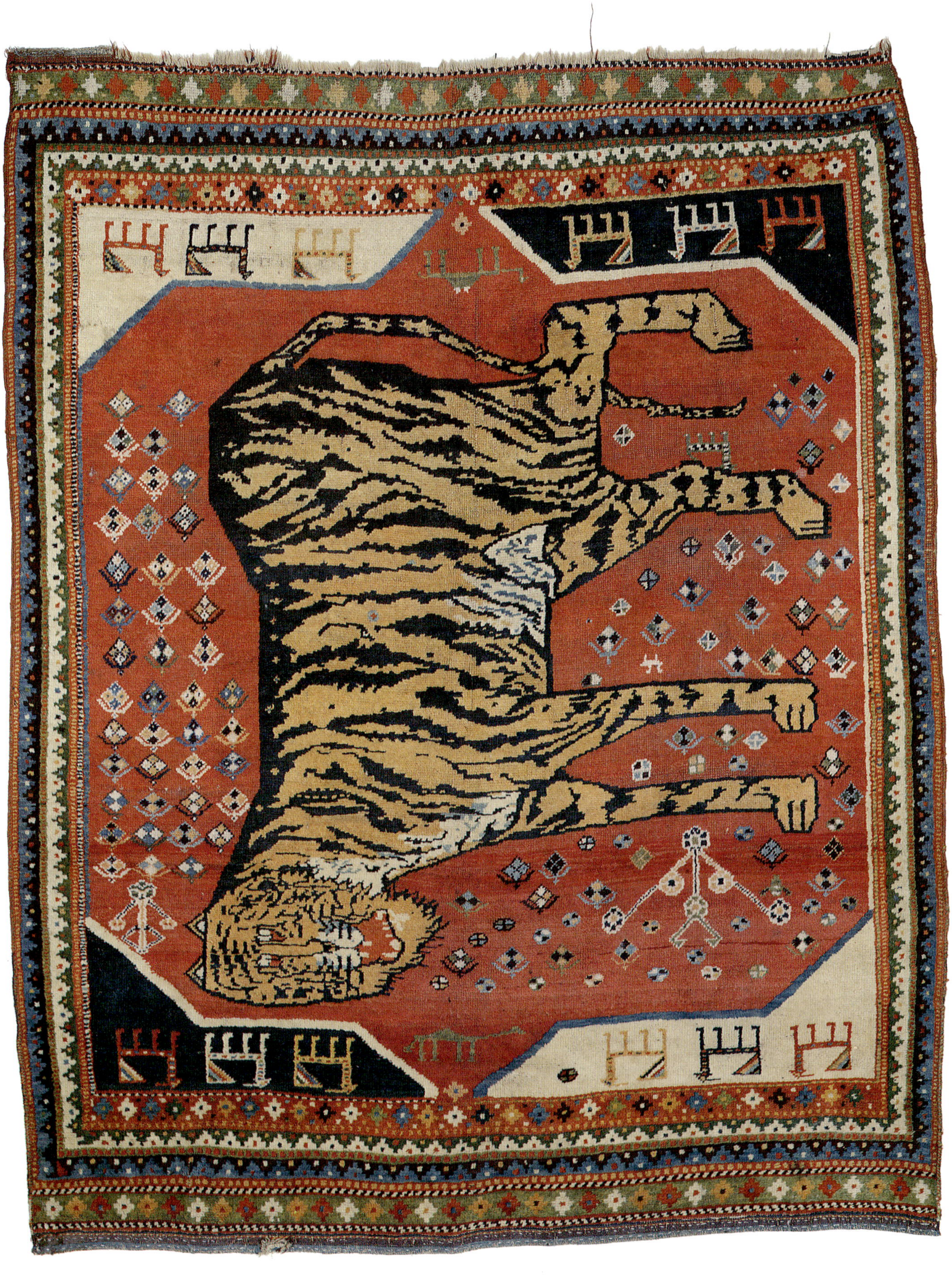

*Kings, Heroes and Lovers*

**84**

**Two Lions**
**Shahsavan of the Khamsah area of Hamadan Province**
**Late 19th century**

The importance of the lion motif among the people of Iran and the antiquity of its use by tribal weavers, especially the Qashqa'i, are discussed on p. 58 infra. This lion rug, however, was woven long ago by the nomads in the Khamsah area of the province of Hamadan. Although the Shahsavan of that area did very little pile weaving in the past, this rug can still be attributed to them mainly because of the weave and the colours, which are similar to some of the pile rugs made by the Shahsavan of the Khamsah area. While this is the only example from that area in this book, a hypothesis about the likelihood of earlier Shahsavan rugs depicting lions is supported by the fact that there are numerous stone statues of lions carved in the round used as grave markers not only in Fars and Bakhtiyari provinces but also in Azerbayjan and Zanjan, neighbouring provinces of the tribes and nomads of the Khamsah area of Hamadan.

There may perhaps be some relationship between this rug and no. 83, with this difference, however, that the two lions of this example were woven in a more linear and chunky fashion. The stripes on the skin of the lions are so stylized that most of them resemble regular geometric forms. The lion on the right has turned its head to one side, while the one on the left, with eyes one above the other, has taken on a strange appearance.

Different shades of red, reflecting an irregular rate of fading with the passing of time, contribute added depth to the space surrounding the lions.

*Size:* 12ft 11.5in x 5ft 3in (395 x 160cm)
*Warp:* cotton, Z10S, undyed, straight, 1 level
*Weft:* wool, Z2S loosely plied, undyed light brown, 2 shoots, both undulating
*Pile:* wool, Z2 loosely plied, Sy1, 0.25in (3mm)
*Knot count:* 7V x 6H = 42 per sq. in. (28V x 24H = 672 per sq. dm.)
*Texture:* soft, fairly thin, very flexible
*Sides:* wool, undyed brown, parallel wrapping around 4 warps
*Ends:* lower: 1.1875in (3cm) weft-faced plain weave, wool, undyed brown
upper: missing
*Colours* 10, dark blue, blue, green, red, pink, orange, yellow, dark brown, light brown, ivory

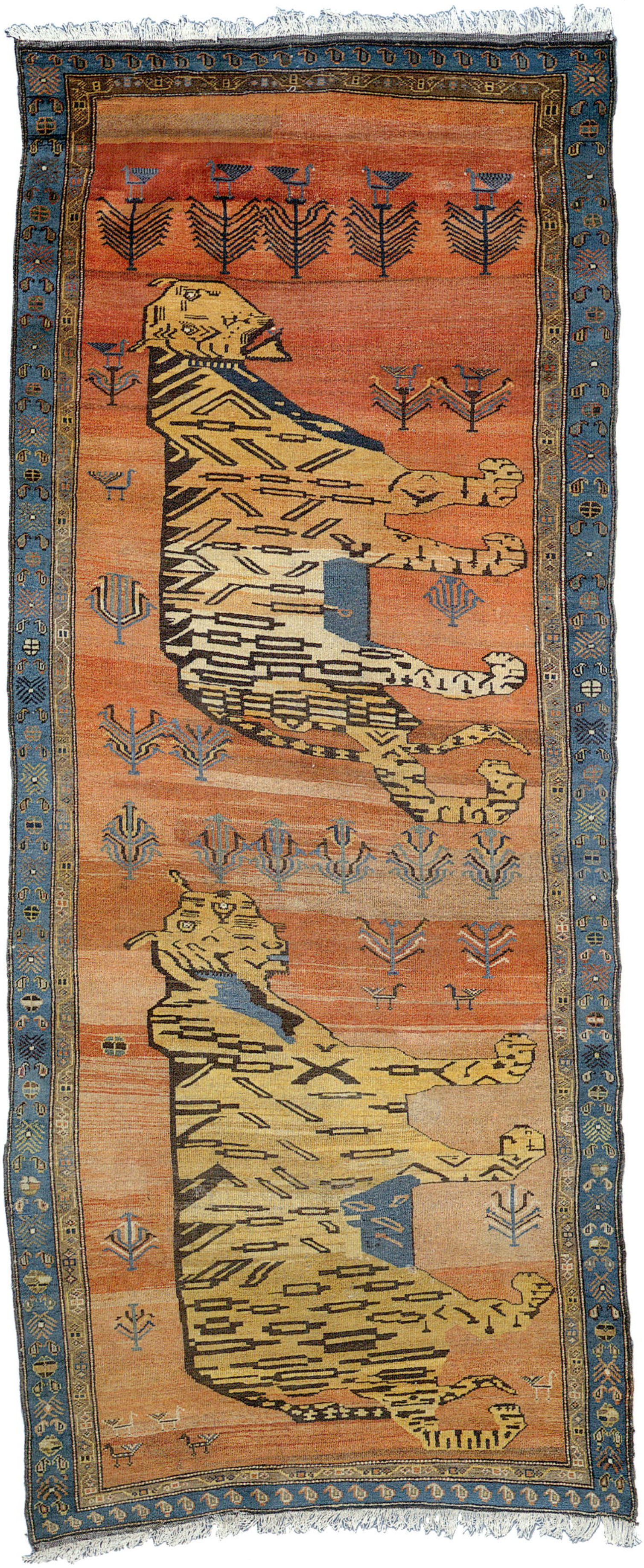

## Kings, Heroes and Lovers

**85**

**Lion**
**Qashqa'i**
**Mid-19th century**

Many of the characteristics of this lion remind one of the stone lions found in tribal graveyards in the Fars and Bakhtiyari provinces. The chunky style, the open mouth, the way in which the tail is brought back over the body, and the collar around the lion's neck, all are characteristics of the stone lions of the above-mentioned regions (see fig. 54). In spite of the attempt made to depict the ferocity of this lion (baring his fangs), the collar around its neck indicates the friendship and closeness which usually exist between a domesticated animal and its master. This collar is seen around the necks of most stone lions as well and is a sign of the affection Iranians feel toward this animal (see p. 58 infra).

The small, stylized figures of men, women, birds, and animals above and below the lion, as well as the sketchy suggestion of stripes and spots on the lion's body, add to the charm of this rug. This is an example of a type of rug known in Iran as a *gabbeh* (see p. 67).

*Size:* 6ft 11in x 3ft 7.75in (211 x 111cm)
*Warp:* wool, Z2S, undyed, ivory, straight, 1 level
*Weft:* wool, Z2S loosely plied, undyed reddish brown, 4 shoots: all undulating
*Pile:* wool, Z2 loosely plied, As1, 0.0625in (2mm)
*Knot count:* 6V x 6H = 36 per sq. in. (24V x 24H = 576 per sq. dm.)
*Texture:* fairly soft, fairly thin, very flexible
*Sides:* wool, red and yellow, remains of chevron wrapping around 6 warps
*Ends:* 2in (5cm) weft-faced plain weave, wool, red and undyed ivory; half turned under and sewn down; decorated with 2 rows of weft twining in yellow and red wool
*Colours* 6, blue-black, purple red, greenish-yellow, dark brown, light brown, ivory

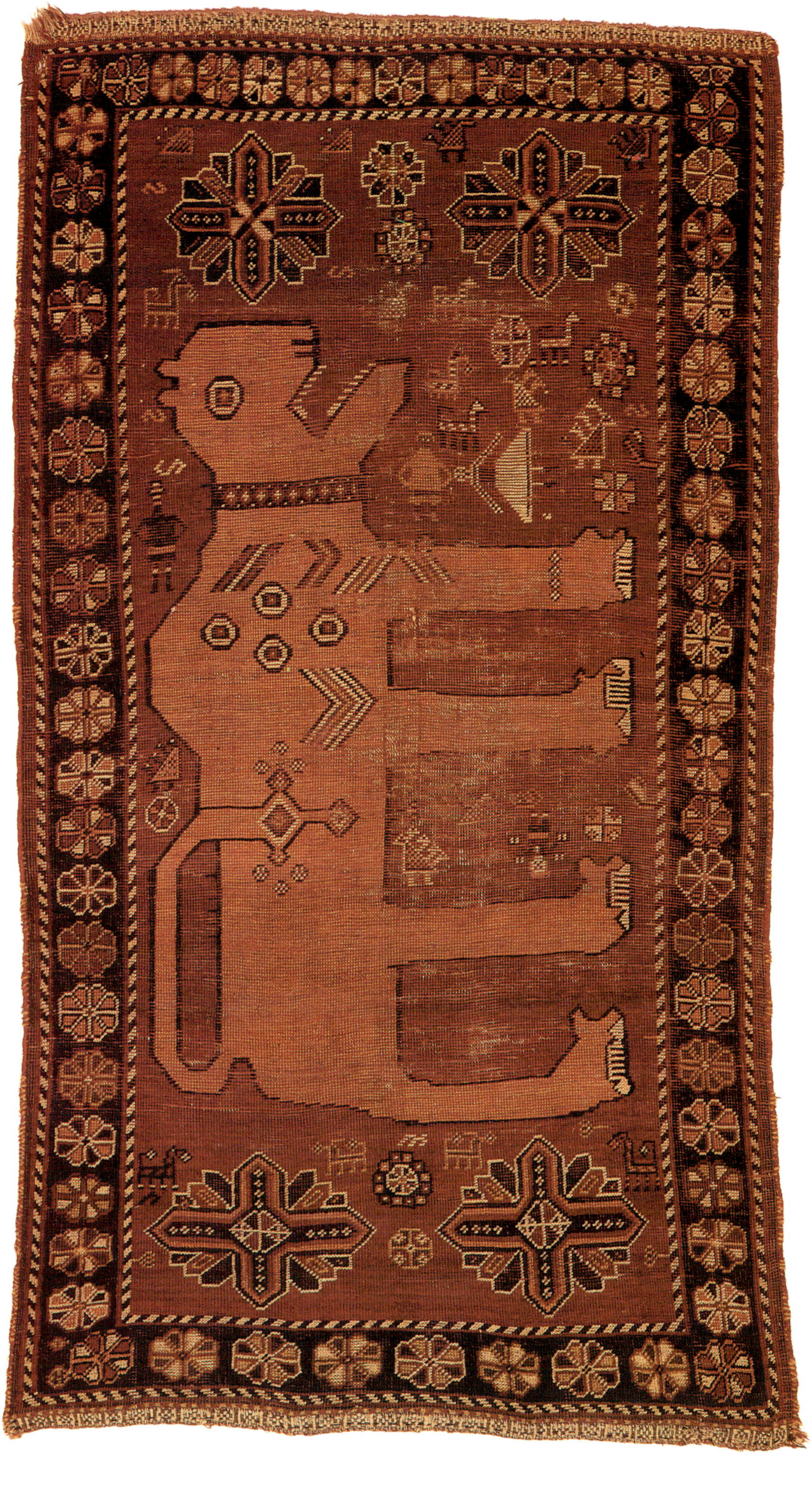

**86**

**Lion and Sun**
**Bijar area**
**Inscription:** *[in the]* **year 1339 (1920 AD)**

Although the Lion and Sun officially became the symbol of the Iranian state in 1836 AD during the reign of Muhammad Shah, this motif has been used by Iranians on coins, emblems, standards, and other objects over the last six hundred years (for discussion of this motif, see pp. 58, 60 and figs. 63a, 63b). During the last two centuries, this motif has also attracted the attention of rug weavers, but most of them have woven it in small size and on the same scale as other small designs in a rug, as for example in nos. 5, 6, and 7. It is far less common to see the lion and sun used as a large medallion and as the major design element.

In this rug the weaver filled the empty spaces with flowers and birds. One of these birds perches on the sun behind the lion; another alights on a flower below the lion. (For rugs depicting animals, particularly lions, see xref p. 58 infra.)

*Size:* 3ft 10in x 3ft 3.75in (117 x 101cm)
*Warp:* wool, Z2S, undyed, ivory, straight, 2 levels
*Weft:* wool, Z2S, 2 shoots: the first undyed ivory, straight; the second, light red, undulating
*Pile:* wool, Z2 loosely plied, Sy2, 0.5in (6mm)
*Knot count:* 7V x 9H = 63 per sq. in. (28V x 36H = 1008 per sq. dm.)
*Texture:* fairly soft, fairly thin, fairly stiff
*Sides:* not original
*Ends:* missing
*Colours* 7, dark blue, light green, maroon, dark pink, dark brown, yellow, ivory

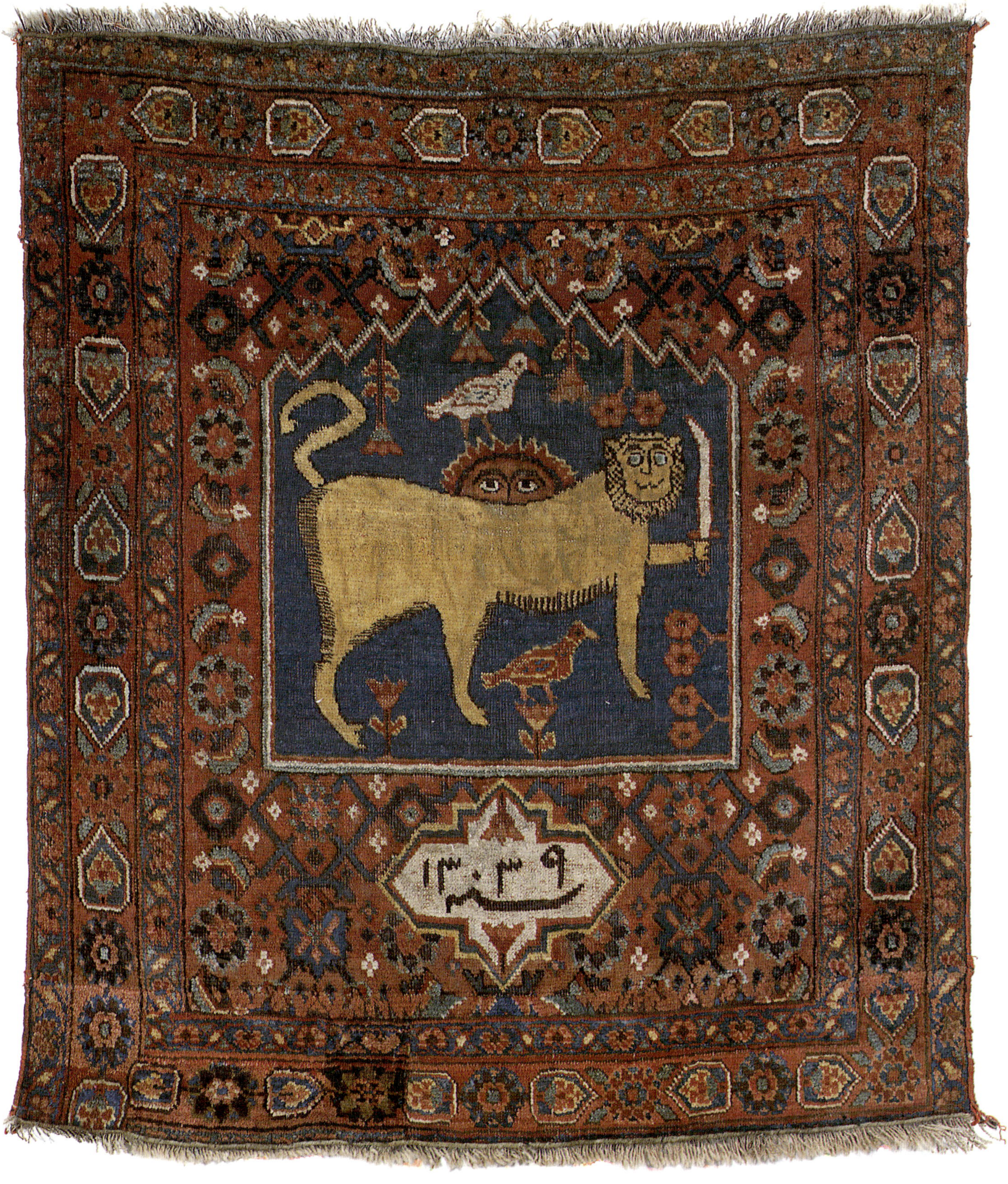
١٣٠٣٩

**87**

**Lion
Afshar of the region of Kerman
Mid-19th century**

The Afshars who live in southeastern Iran (between Shiraz and Kerman) share certain designs with the Qashqa'i. Although until now only a few examples of Afshar lion rugs have come to hand, the age and power of these suggest a long history of lion-rug weaving in that tribe. It is believed that this rug is over one hundred years old, but the large scale and natural proportions of this lion have a fortuitous similarity to those of Qashqa'i rugs whose lions are believed to be based upon English and Indian blankets depicting a lion, which were used during the first World War. Iranians were, however, aware of the naturalistic proportions of the lion before the importation of the blankets. (For a discussion of rugs depicting animals, particularly lions, see p. 58 infra.)

*Size:* 5ft 8in x 4ft 2in (173 x 126cm)
*Warp:* wool, Z2S, undyed ivory; cotton, Z3S and Z2S, undyed white mixed with undyed brown wool, Z1, and undyed brown goat hair; straight, semi-depressed
*Weft:* cotton, Z3S, undyed, white, 2 shoots: the first straight, the second undulating
*Pile:* wool, Z2, loosely plied, Sy3, 0.25in (3mm)
*Knot count:* 3.5 v x 5H = 17.5 per sq. in. (14V x 20H = 280 per sq. dm.)
*Texture:* soft, rather thin, flexible
*Sides:* not original
*Ends:* missing
*Colours* 8, blue-black, dark blue, green, light green, red, pink, brown, ivory

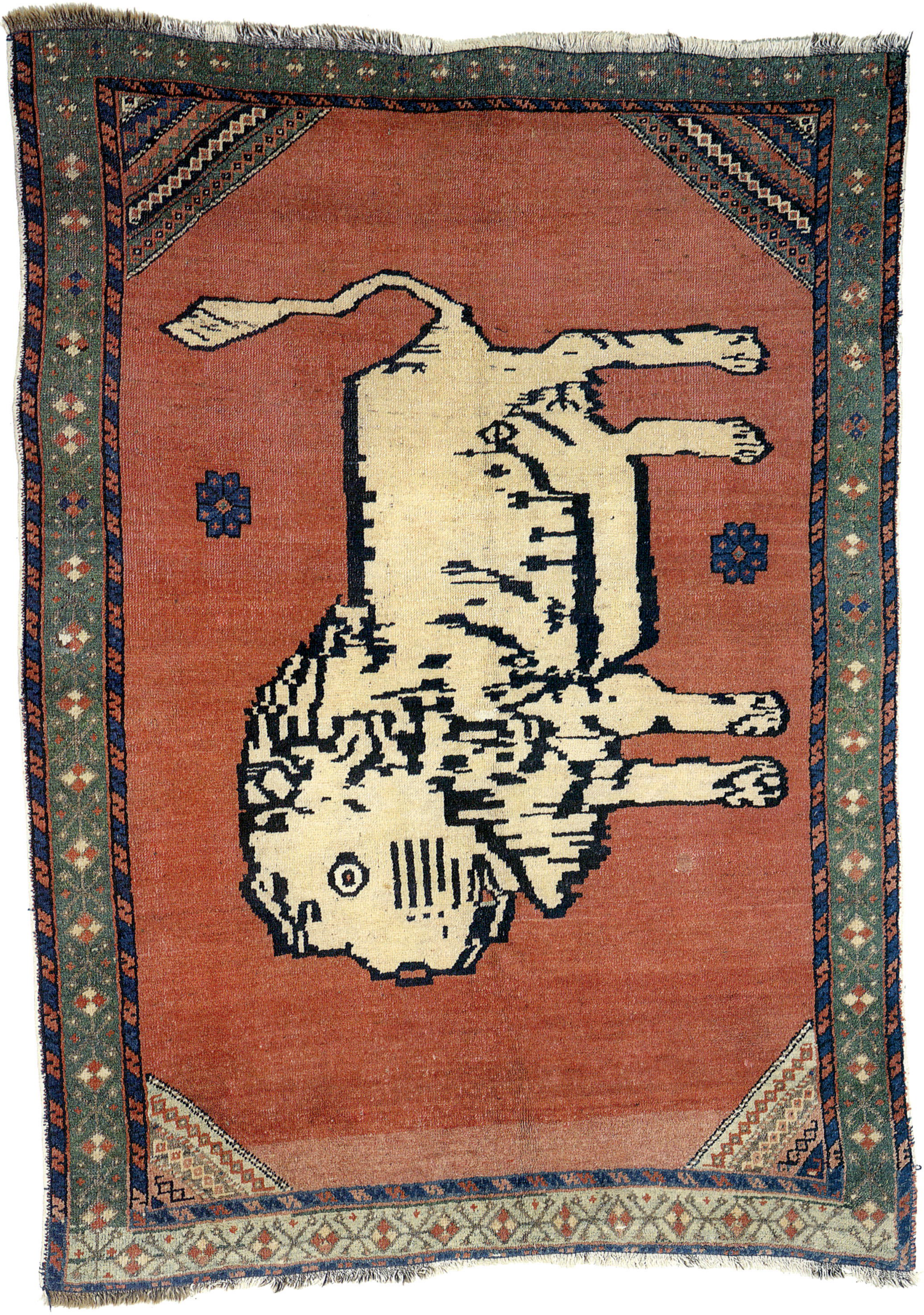

*Kings, Heroes and Lovers*

**88**

**Lion**
**Doqozlou clan of the Shish Boluki subtribe of the Qashqa'i**
**Early 20th century**

This lion is another example of the simplified depictions in the weavings of the Qashqa'i tribes. The background here is unadorned except for the variations in shades of red and occasional lines of very dark blue, which in some places create a honeycomb pattern. In recent years a large number of similar lions have been woven in rugs in a variety of forms against spotted backgrounds locally referred to as *namak va filfil* (salt and pepper).

For rugs depicting animals, and lions in particular, see p. 58 infra.

*Size:* 5ft 8in x 3ft 1in (170 x 94cm)
*Warp:* cotton, Z4S, undyed, white, straight, 1 level
*Weft:* wool, Z2S loosely plied, undyed dark brown and dyed black, 2 to 3 shoots, all undulating; and cotton, Z2S, undyed white, 4 to 5 shoots, all undulating
*Pile:* wool, Z2 loosely plied, Sy1, 0.1875in (4mm)
*Knot count:* 3V x 3.5 H = 10.5 per sq. in. (12V x 14H = 168 per sq. dm.)
*Texture:* soft, rather thick, fairly stiff
*Sides:* wool, brown and red, parallel wrapping around 6 warps
*Ends:* lower: undyed black goat hair
upper: 1.1875in (3cm) weft-faced plain weave, purple wool, turned under and sewn down
*Colours* 12, brown, grey, blue-black, turquoise, dark green, olive, dark red, red, orange, yellow, brown, ivory

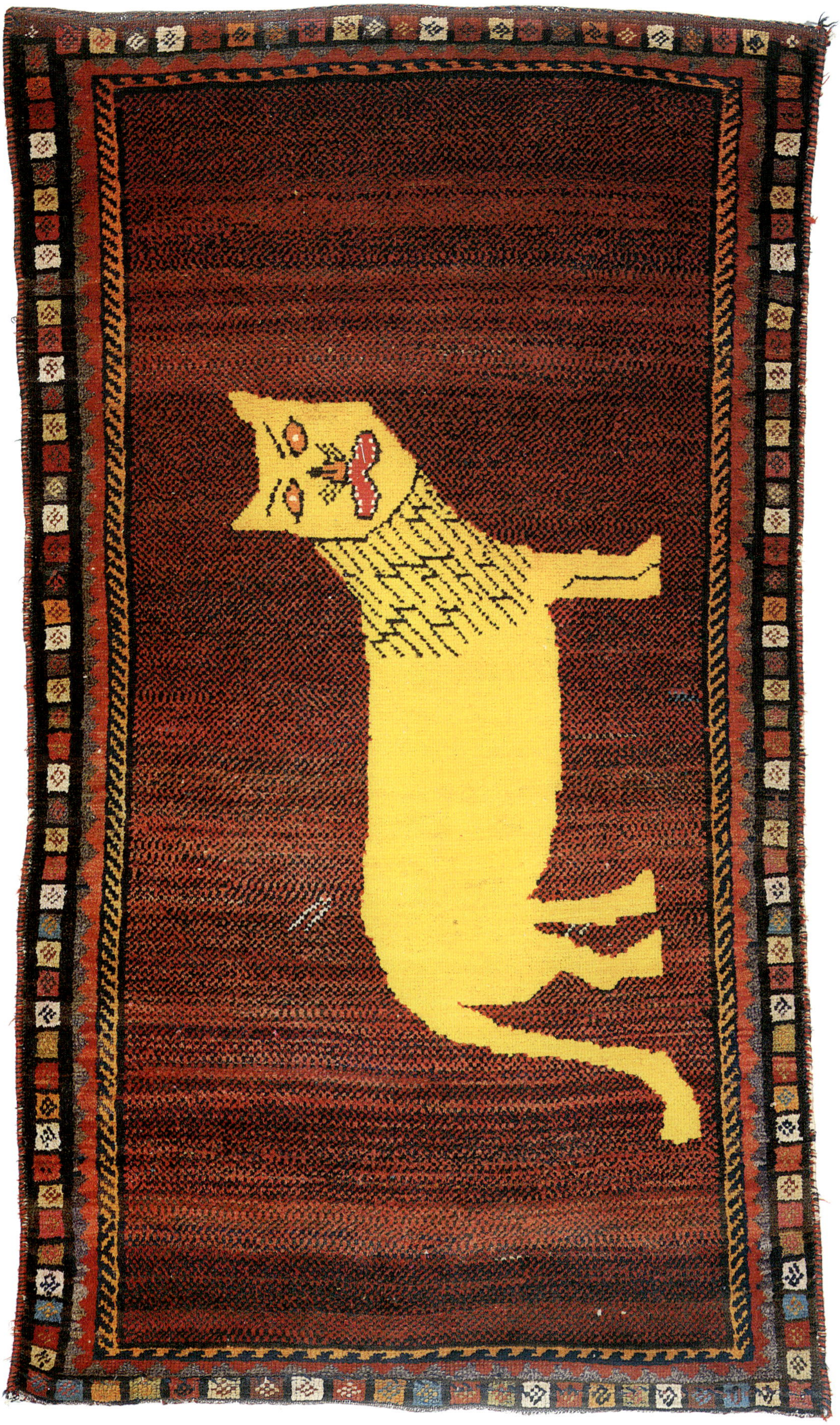

*Kings, Heroes and Lovers*

**89**

**Lion**
**Shirvan region of the Caucasus**
**Late 19th century**

We have seen that the lion motif was popular with nomadic and village rug weavers in Iran, particularly in Fars Province, and also in the northwest. Although this rug is the first depicting a lion woven in the Shirvan area of the Caucasus that I have seen, I feel certain that it is not the only one that was woven in the Caucasus (where Persian cultural influence was felt well into the present century), for the lion figure seems to have caused the weaver little difficulty, which would seem to indicate the lion was not an unfamiliar motif for weavers in the Caucasus.

For rugs depicting animals, and lions in particular, see p. 58 infra.

*Size:* 4ft 10in x 3ft 6in (148 x 106cm)
*Warp:* wool, Z4S, undyed ivory, straight, 1 level
*Weft:* wool, Z2S, undyed dark brown except for 7.875in at the top which are undyed ivory, 2 shoots, both undulating
*Pile:* wool, Z2 loosely plied, Sy1, 0.1875in (4mm)
*Knot count:* 10V x 8H = 80 per sq. in. (40V x 32H = 1280 per sq. dm.)
*Texture:* soft, fairly thin, flexible
*Sides:* wool, dark blue, 2 cables, each wrapped around 3 warps
*Ends:* 0.75in (2cm) countered weft-twining (*sumak* brocading) wool, dark blue, undyed ivory
*Colours* 14, blue-black, blue, light blue, dark green, light green, dark red, flame red, orange, orange-yellow, lemon yellow, black brown, brown, dark brown, ivory

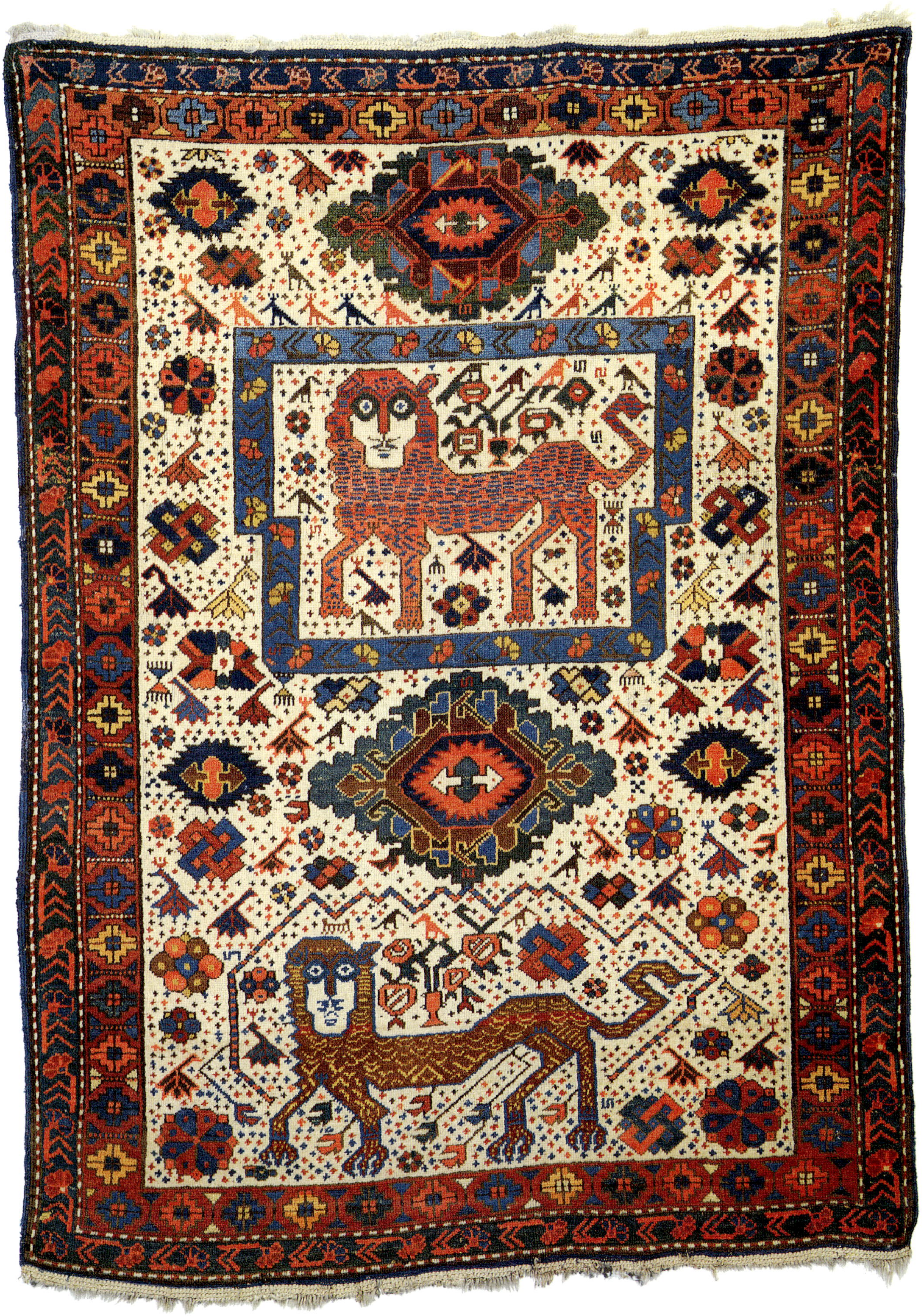

*Kings, Heroes and Lovers*

**90**

**Camels**
**Kashkuli subtribe of the Qashqa'i**
**Mid-20th century**

While the camel has long played a significant role in the lives of the tribes of Iran it has seldom constituted the principal subject of a rug. This does not mean to say, however, that camels do not appear in tribal rugs. Quite often they are found in borders and form part of field designs, but usually in very small dimensions. The rug here is exceptional because the camels here are large and constitute the main focus in the centre, in a square medallion. As we have already seen, this arrangement is frequently encountered in the case of lion rugs. Of note is the choice of light blue for the baby camel. The weaver was apparently eager to set it off from the other two.

For rugs depicting animals, see p. 58 infra.

*Size:* 7ft 6.5in x 4ft 5in (230 x 135cm)
*Warp:* wool, Z2S, undyed ivory, brown, slightly undulating semi-depressed
*Weft:* wool, Z1, brownish red, 3 to 5 shoots: the first, third, and fifth straight; the second and fourth undulating
*Pile:* wool, Z2 loosely plied, Sy3, 0.1875in (4mm)
*Knot count:* 6V x 6H = 36 per sq. in. (24V x 24H = 576 per sq. dm.)
*Texture:* very soft, thick, very flexible
*Sides:* wool, red and blue, parallel and chevron wrapping around 5 warps
*Ends:* lower: missing
upper: 0.75in (2cm) weft-faced plain weave, wool, blue, reddish brown
*Colours* 11, blue-black, blue, light blue, dark green, green, purplish red, red, orange yellow, dark brown, light brown, ivory

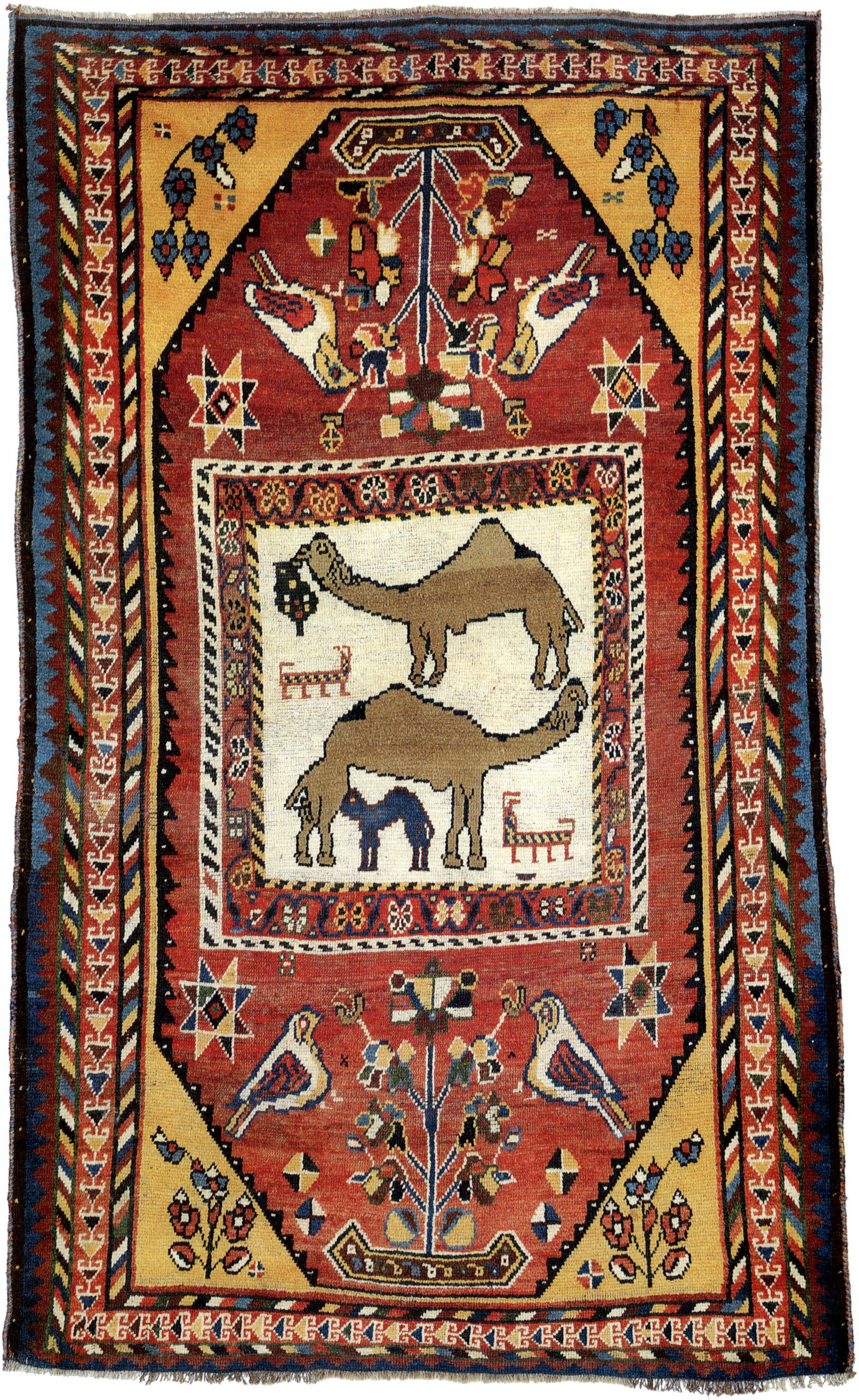

## 91

**Groom, Mare, and Foal**
**Dargazin area**
**Dated:** *1328 (1910 AD)*

The scene of a groom, mare, and foal has been positioned neatly in a central medallion which in turn conforms to the shapes of the figures contained. A black field for the medallion provides a very effective foil, setting the scene off to best advantage. The placement of an open umbrella between the mare and groom has caused a slight, but not awkward, distortion of the man's right shoulder and arm. Designs on the horse-cover in the centre of the rug help to tie together harmoniously the central section and the surrounding border.

*Size:* 6ft 5in x 4ft 5in (196 x 135cm)
*Warp:* cotton, Z5S, undyed, undulating, 1 level
*Weft:* cotton, Z16S, undyed, 1 shoot, nearly straight
*Pile:* wool, Z2 loosely plied, Sy1, 0.0625in (2mm)
*Knot count:* 10V x 9H = 90 per sq. in. (40V x 36H = 1440 per sq. dm.)
*Texture:* fairly soft, thin, very flexible
*Sides:* wool, undyed brown, parallel wrapping around 3 warps
*Ends:* lower: missing
upper: 0.75in (2cm) weft-faced plain weave, undyed cotton
*Colours* 10, black, blue-black, blue, brownish olive, red, purplish pink, lemon yellow, brown, light brown, white

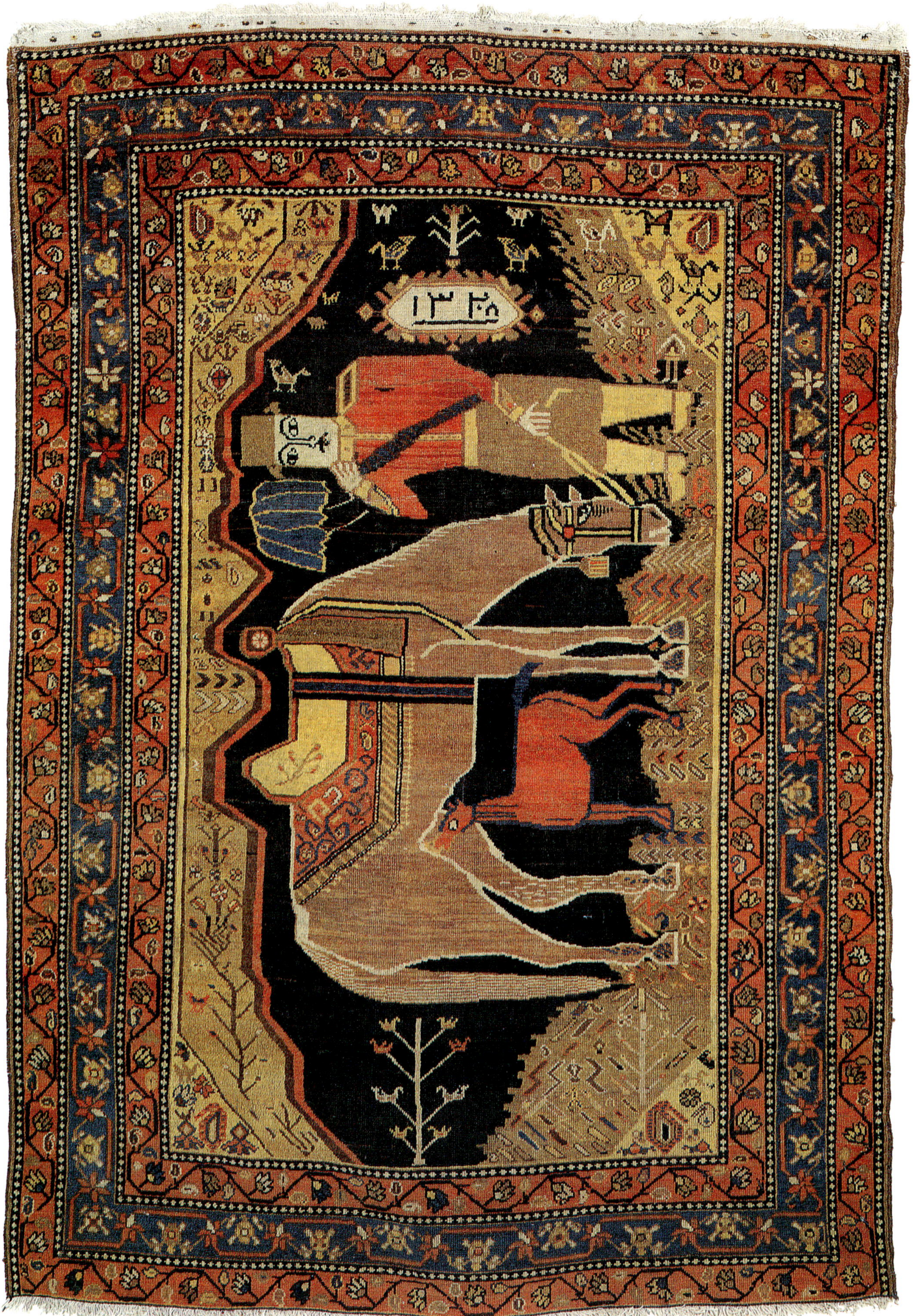

*Kings, Heroes and Lovers*

**92**

**Horse and Groom**
**Dargazin area**
**Late 19th century**

In spite of all the similarities between this rug and no. 91, this is an individual creation. The slightly different treatments of similar subject matter are in fact complementary. While the other depicted a light-coloured mare and foal on a dark background, this shows a single, dark horse on a light background. There is no way of knowing if these were woven as a pair, but one can imagine that this rug depicts the mate of the mare in the other. The groom, with an open umbrella or parasol, is also present in this rug, but oriented at a right angle to the standing horse. The smaller figures in the background help to complete the story of the rug, which is probably connected with the hunting activities of the horse's owner. We find the groom sitting and waiting on a stone bench next to a tent, while two gazelles, which have probably been taken in a hunt, are seen in front of it.

*Size:* 6ft 2.5in x 4ft 2.75in (189 x 129cm)
*Warp:* cotton, Z3S, undyed, undulating,1 level
*Weft:* cotton, Z3S, undyed, 1 shoot, straight
*Pile:* wool, Z2 loosely plied, Sy1, 0.0625in (2mm)
*Knot count:* 9V x 9H = 81 per sq. in. (36H x 36V = 1296 per sq. dm.)
*Texture:* fairly soft, thin, very flexible
*Sides:* wool, pale brown, parallel wrapping around 4 warps
*Ends:* not original
*Colours* 12, black, blue-black, blue, light blue, very light green, red, pink, orange, yellow, light brown, olive brown, ivory

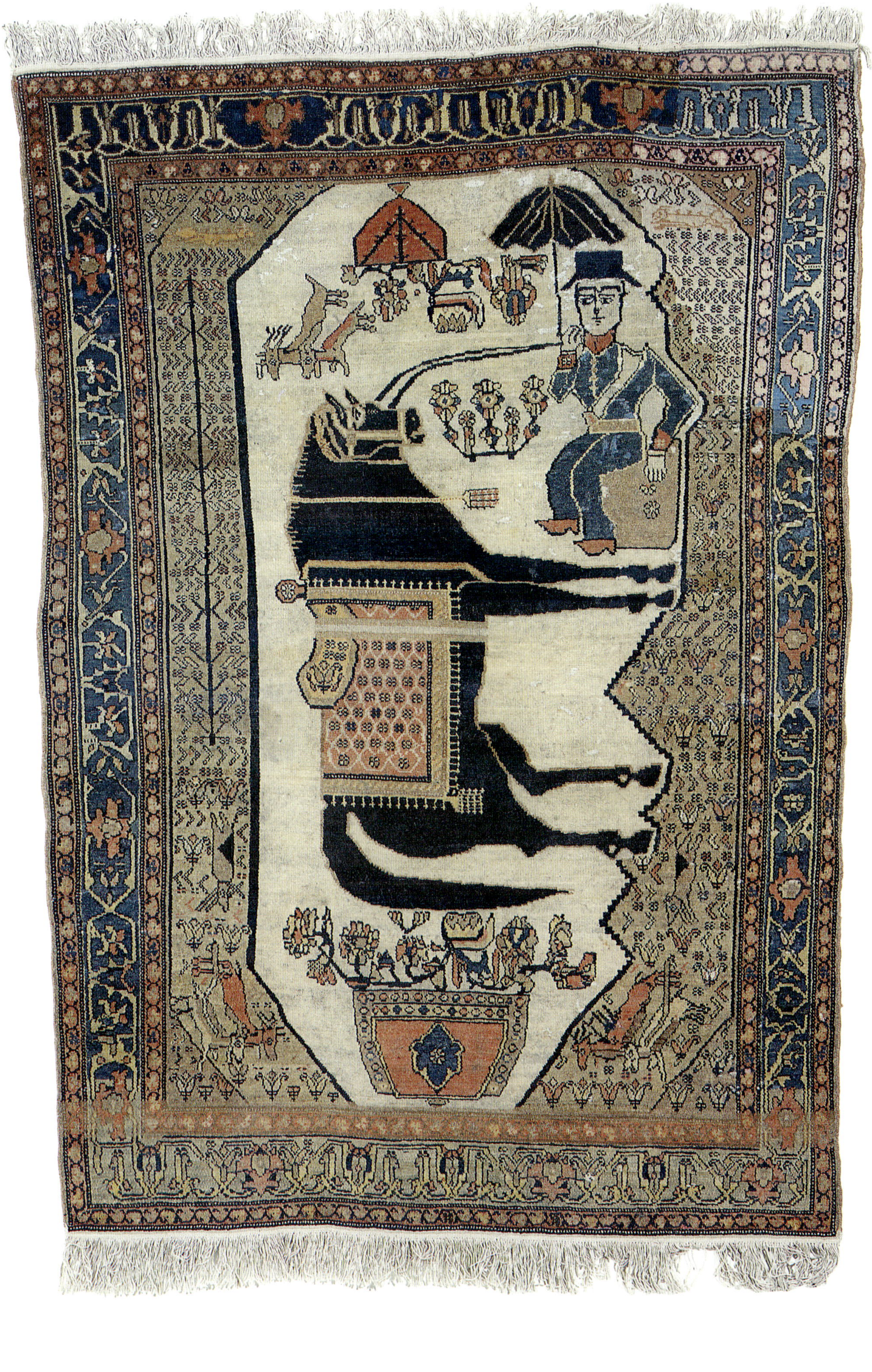

*Kings, Heroes and Lovers*

**93**

**Hunter on Horseback, and Roosters
Shirvan region of the Caucasus
Late 19th-century**

This rug features a hunting scene. Depicted in the middle of the rug are a horse and a mounted hunter, who is pointing out a bird resembling a pheasant to the falcon that perches on his other arm. The prey rests in a tree at the foot of which the hunter's dog barks and tries to climb up. The pose and appearance of the hunter (with the bird on his wrist) and his horse are reminiscent of sixteenth- and seventeenth-century scenes in Persian miniature paintings depicting princes out hunting. This scene fills the central panel of the rug. In the four corners are squares each containing the picture of a rooster. These roosters seem to have no direct connection with the principal theme of the rug and are used mainly to fill the four corners and preserve the traditional medallion-and-cornerpiece layout (see p. 12).

*Size:* 6ft 6in x 4ft 1.5in (198 x 126cm)
*Warp:* wool, Z3S, undyed ivory, undyed dark brown (some warps plied with both), straight, 1 level
*Weft:* cotton, Z3S, undyed, 2 shoots, both undulating
*Pile:* wool, Z2 loosely plied, Sy1, 0.1875in (4mm)
*Knot count:* 13V x 9H = 117 per sq. in. (52V x 36H = 1872 per sq. dm.)
*Texture:* fairly soft, thin, fairly flexible
*Sides:* cotton, selvage formed with wefts of the rug in 2 cords, each wrapped around 2 warps
*Ends:* 0.625in (1.5cm) weft-faced plain weave, wool, undyed brown and ivory; warp ends knotted in groups of 4 to form a compact net with 2 rows of knots
*Colours* 11, black, purplish-grey, light grey, green, light green, red, orange, yellow, dark brown, brown, ivory

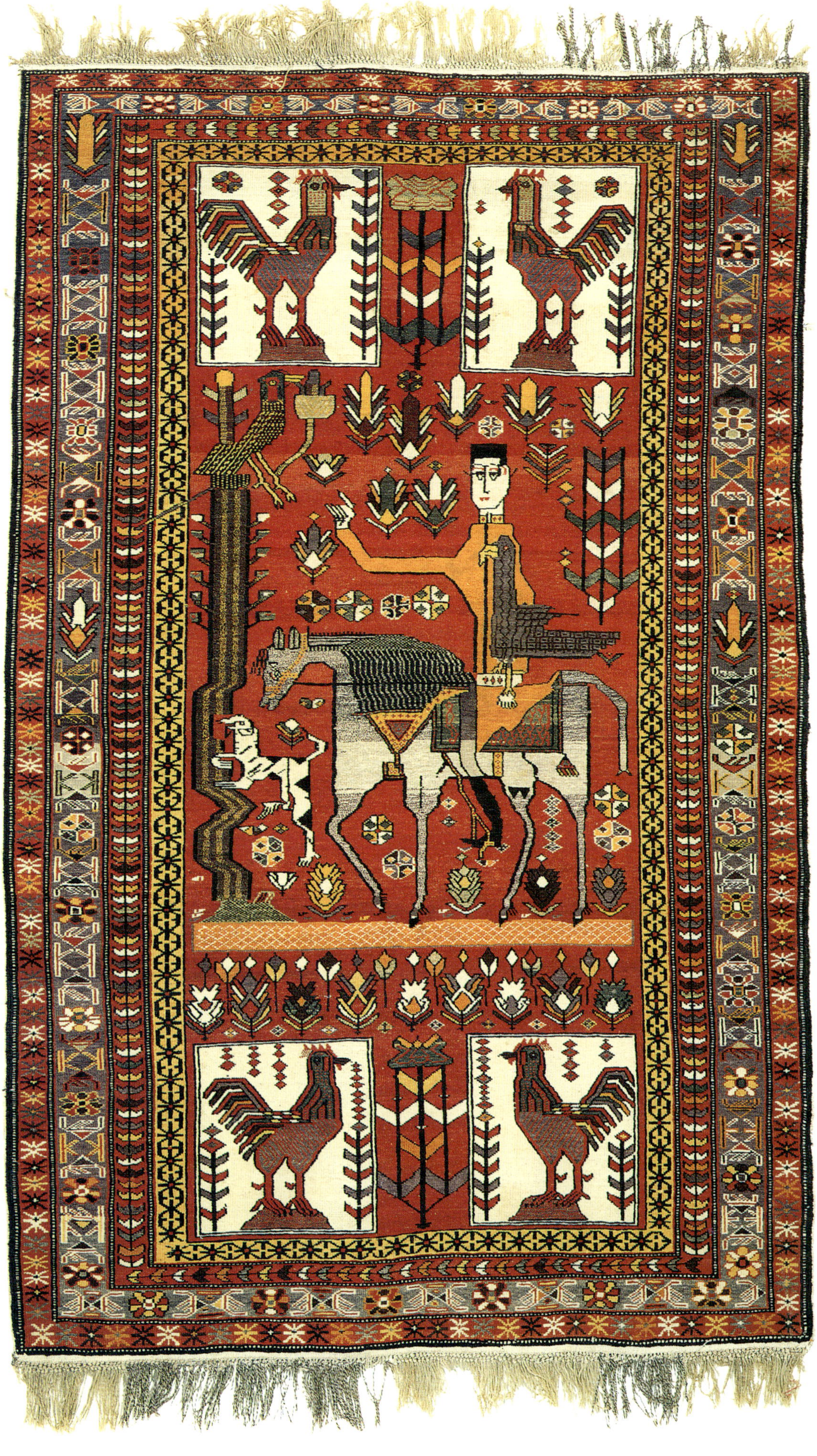

**94**

**Animals**
**Tabriz**
**Early 20th century**

In most pictorial rugs that include a collection of animals there is also a theme or story, such as the court of Solomon, the story of Majnun, or a hunting scene. In this rug there are a number of different animals, but they convey no theme or story. Such a scene, very rare and exceptional in rugs, is known among the traditional painters and craftsmen of Iran as *jangal-i mawla* ('forest of the master'; see p. 59). The border contains a procession of animals, which lends a note of order to the confusion of animals, birds, and serpents in the field, which include a delightfully wide range of naturalistically rendered breeds as well as a lion attacking a gazelle or deer, a traditional symbolic motif in classical Iranian art.

*Size:* 6ft 4in x 4ft 2.75in (193 x 129cm)
*Warp:* cotton, Z4S, undyed, straight, semi-depressed
*Weft:* cotton, undyed, 2 shoots: the first straight, Z6S; the second undulating, Z4S
*Pile:* wool, Z2 loosely plied, Sy2, 0.1875in (5mm)
*Knot count:* 12V x 10H = 120 per sq. in. (48V x 40H = 1920 per sq. dm.)
*Texture:* fairly soft, relatively thick, stiff
*Sides:* wool, undyed light brown, remains of parallel wrapping 4 warps
*Ends:* missing
*Colours* 10, dark blue, light blue, very light green, red, pink, very dark brown, dark brown, light brown, tan, ivory

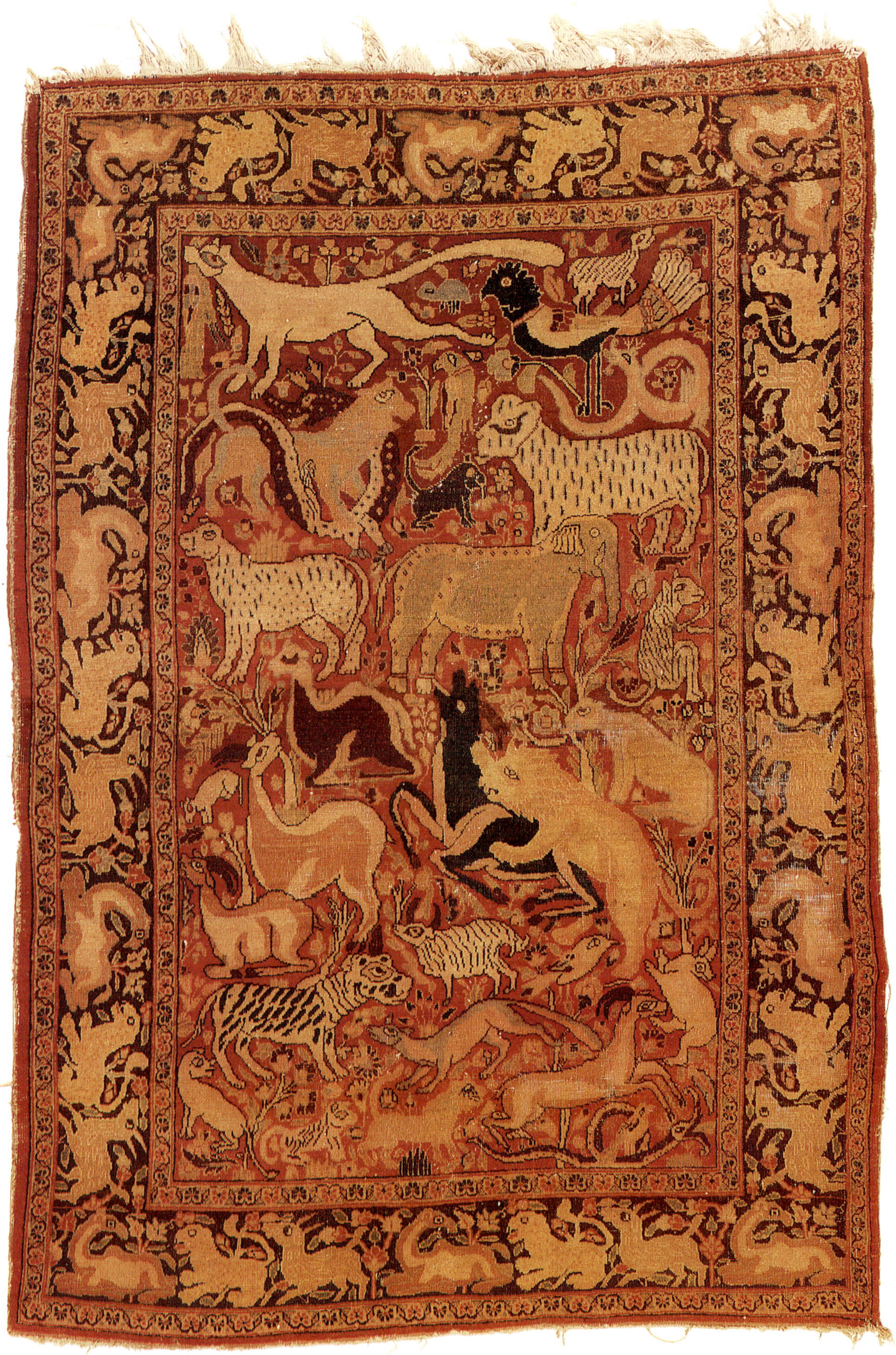

## 95

**Animals**
**Bijar**
**Dated: *1349 (1930 AD)***

The subject and composition of this rug are very much like the previous one, no. 94. This one, however, was made in Bijar and has much livelier colours. The animals are not placed in any particular order; domestic animals mingle with wild beasts in a Persian peaceable kingdom. Some are in realistic colours, while others reflect the imagination of the weaver—and a convention of Persian miniature painting, as in a pink lion, a blue sheep, or a green deer. The animals are less crowded in this rug, as compared with the previous one, and features of the landscape are indicated, such as hills, brooks, goat paths, leafy plants, and a palm tree. A pleasing sense of order is unobtrusively effected by placing more of the larger animals in the lower part of the rug and by placing a seated camel in each of the lower corners. In contrast to the previous rug, the dark blue border here features graceful birds and naturalistic flowering plants, which complement the animals of the rich red field.

*Size:* 9ft 11.875in x 5ft 5in (273 x 165cm)
*Warp:* cotton, Z7S, undyed, straight, depressed
*Weft:* cotton, undyed, 2 shoots: the first straight, Z5S; the second undulating, Z3S
*Pile:* wool, Z2 loosely plied, Sy2, 0.1875in (4mm)
*Knot count:* 10V x 13H = 130 per sq. in. (40V x 53H = 2120 per sq. dm.)
*Texture:* fairly soft, relatively thick, stiff
*Sides:* wool, dark blue, parallel wrapping around 4 warps
*Ends:* 0.75in (2cm) balanced plain weave, undyed cotton
*Colours* 12, blue-black, light blue, olive green, green, light green, dark brown, light brown, orange, deep red, pink, ivory, white

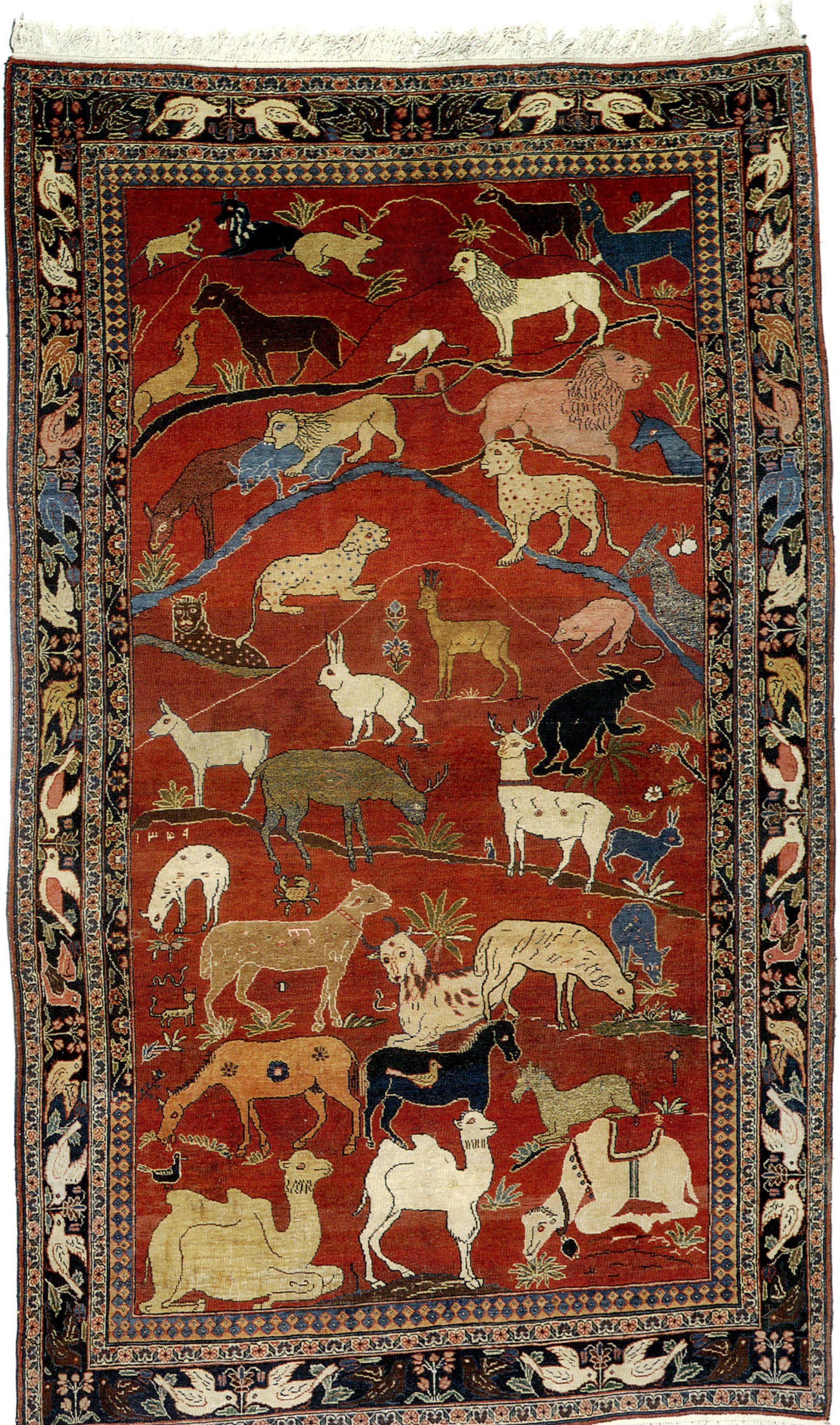

## 96

**Tiger, Man, Sheep, and Dragon**
**East Turkestan, possibly Khotan**
**Dated:** *1210 (1795 AD)*

As explained on p. 60, I have not succeeded in identifying the exact subject of this rug. Its provenance seemed equally difficult to determine, but I have suggested a solution to that enigma.

The man's posture and movement lead one to think that he is perhaps victorious over the dragon and tiger (leopard?) and is protecting the pregnant black sheep, or that the sheep is a symbol of his wealth and the dragon and tiger are symbols of his power.

In any case, all aspects of this rug, from the material (silk) to the unusual border depicting snakes, as well as the elusive theme of the four central panels, all make it exceptional and unique in my experience.

*Size:* 5ft 5.5in x 13ft 4.25in (166 x 408cm)
*Warp:* silk, Z2S, blue to light blue, straight, semi-depressed
*Weft:* silk, Z?S, 2 shades of blue, 3 shoots (occasionally 2): the first and third straight, the second undulating
*Pile:* silk, Z?S, As3, 0.25in (3mm)
*Knot count:* 7V x 10H = 70 per sq. in. (28V x 40H = 1120 per sq. dm.)
*Texture:* thin, flexible
*Sides:* wool, purplish red, parallel wrapping around 4 warps
*Ends:* lower: 1.1875in (3cm) balanced plain weave, silk, light blue; warp ends are left as uncut twisted loops
upper: same except the warp ends are cut, a few are still tied in groups
*Colours* 8, blue, light blue, light green, purple red, pink, yellow, dark brown, ivory

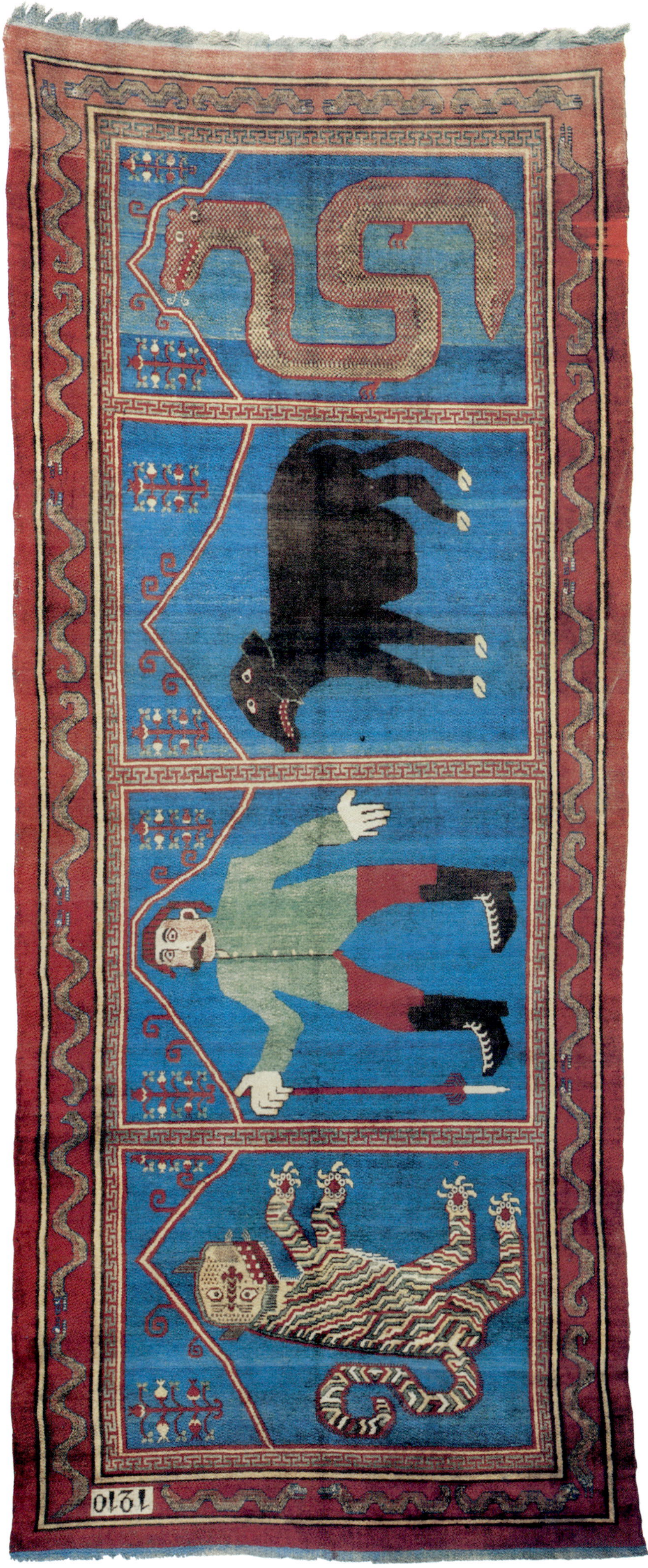

# NOTES

1 The major theoretical distinction between the two major sects of Islam—Sunnism and Shi'ism—is the issue of who was the rightful successor to the prophet Muhammad The Shi'ites proclaim that the rightful successors were Muhammad's immediate descendants, the imams, beginning with 'Ali ibn Abi Talib, his cousin and son-in-law. The Sunnis traditionally maintain that Muhammad's successors are to be elected.
2 Samuel R. Peterson, 'The Ta'ziyeh and Related Arts', in *Ta'ziyeh: Ritual and Drama in Iran*, ed. Peter J. Chelkowski (New York, 1979), pp. 74-84. I am particularly grateful to Mr Peterson for bringing these new insights to my attention, especially those about the influence of *Ta'ziyeh* ceremonies.
3 Aboumansour Abd al-Malik ibn Muhammad ibn Isma'il al-Thaalibi, *Histoire des rois de Perse*, ed. and transl. H. Zotenberg, Paris, 1900, p. 9.
4 Sa'di, *The Bustan of Sa'di*, transl. G.M. Wickens (Toronto, 1974), verses 398-406, pp. 25-26.
5 Jenny Housego, 'The Nineteenth-century Persian Carpet Boom,' *Oriental Art*, vol. 19, no. 2, summer, 1973, pp. 169-171.
6 Comte Julian de Rochechouart, *Souvenirs d'un voyage en Perse*, Paris, 1867, p. 261.
7 Pierre Amédée Eilien Probe Jaubert, *Voyage en Arménie et en Perse, fait dans les années 1805 et 1806*, Paris, 1821, pp. 236-237.
8 George Widengren, *Mani and Manichaeism*, transl. Charles Kessler, London, rev. ed. 1965, illus. between pp. 72 and 73.
9 Jes P. Asmussen, selected and partly transl., *Manichaean Literature*, New York, 1975, p. 21.
10 B. W. Robinson, 'The Tehran Nizami of 1848 and Other Qajar Lithographed Books', in *Islam in the Balkans/Persian Art and Culture of the 18th and 19th Centuries*, ed. Jennifer M. Scarce, Edinburgh, 1979, pp. 61-65.
11 Abdolhosein Ehsani, *Majmu'ah-yi Qalamkar-i Iran* (A Collection of Iranian Qalamkar), Tehran, 1971; and Annette and Hermann Landolt-Tuller, *Qalamkar-Druck in Isfahan*, Basel, 1977.
12 Yahya Zoka, *Tarikh-i 'Aksi va 'Akkasan-i Pishgam dar Iran* (A History of Avant-garde Photography and Photographers in Iran), Tehran, 1990.
13 Mehdi Bamdad, *Sharh-i hal-i rijal-i Iran dar qarn 12, 13, 14 hijri* (Biography of the Dignitaries of Iran in the 18th, 19th, and 20th Centuries), Tehran, 1969, vol. 1, p. 513.
14 A. Cecil Edwards, *The Persian Carpet* (London, 1953), p. 218, no. 203.
15 'Ali ibn Husayn Mas'udi, *Al-Tanbih wa-'l-ashraf* (Warnings and Remarks), Cairo, 1938, p. 92.
16 'Aruzi Samarqandi, *Chahar maqalah* (Four Discourses), Berlin, 1927; rev. ed. by Muhammad Mo'in, Tehran, 1985, p. 120.
17 Yahya Zoka, 'Muhammad Zaman, nakhustin nigargar-i Irani kih bi Urupa firistadah shud' (Muhammad Zaman, The First Iranian Painter Sent to Europe), in Yahya Zoka, *Nagahi bi nigargari-yi Iran dar sadaha-yi davazdahum va sizdahum* (A Look at Iranian Painting in the 12th and 13th Centuries [18th and 19th Centuries AD]), Tehran, 1974, p. 40.
18 *Ibid.*, p. 41.
19 Richard N. Frye, *The Heritage of Persia* (Cleveland, 1963), p. 35.
20 Muhammad Javad Mashkoor, *Iran dar 'ahd-i bastan, dar tarikh-i aqwam va padishahan pish az Islam* (Iran in Ancient Times, The History of Tribes and Kings before the Islamic Era), Tehran, 1968, p. 75.
21 Hakim 'Abu 'l-Qasim Firdawsi, *Shahnamah Firdawsi* Tehran 1971, p. 15.

22 Arthur Christensen, *Les Types du premier homme et du premier roi* Leiden, 1934, p. 140.
23 Mary Boyce, *A History of Zoroastrianism*, Leiden, 1975, vol. 1, p. 3.
24 Roman Ghirshman, *Iran, From the Earliest Times to the Islamic Conquest*, Baltimore, 1961, p. 61.
25 Frye, *op. cit.*, pp. 2-3.
26 Boyce, *op. cit.*, pp. 144-145, 274-275.
27 Christensen, *Les Types*, p. 18.
28 Zayn al-Abedin Shirvani, *Bustan-i siyahah*, (Garden of Travels), Tehran, 1897, p. 129.
29 *Majma' al-tavrikh va al-qasas* (Summary of the Histories and Stories), quoted in Yahya Zoka, 'Shahnamah va bastan shinasi, nawruz dar Shahnamah va rabitah-yi an ba Takht-i Jamshid', (Shahnamah and Archaeology, Nawruz in the *Shahnamah* and Its Relationship with Persepolis), *Hunar va Mardum* (Art and People), no. 186 (March-April, 1978), pp. 2-15. 73 30 Yahya Zoka, 'Takhtha-yi Saltanat-i Iran' (Iranian Royal Thrones), *Hunar va Mardum* (Art and People), no. 60, September/October, 1968, pp. 47-59.
31 For more information about the jewels in this throne see V. B. Meen and A. D. Tushingham, *Crown Jewels of Iran*, Toronto, 1968, pp. 54-55.
32 I Kings 10: 18-21.
33 Firdawsi, *Shahnamah*, p. 330.
34 Mashkoor, *op. cit.*, p. 111.
35 Brian M. Fagan, *Return to Babylon: Travellers, Archaeologists, and Monuments in Mesopotamia*, Boston, 1979, pp. 71-82.
36 John Malcolm, *The History of Persia*, London, 1815, *passim*.
37 Erich F. Schmidt, *Persepolis*, Chicago, 1970, vol. 1, *passim*; and Roman Ghirshman, *Perse*, Paris, 1963, pp. 147-222.
38 Habibollah Payman, *Il-i Qashqa'i* (Qashqa'i Tribes), Tehran, 1969, p. 76.
39 Gholam 'Ali Homayun, *Asnad-i musavvar-i Urupa'iyan az Iran* (European Illustrated Documents of Iran), Tehran, 1970, vol. 1, p. 74.
40 Homayun, *op. cit.*, p. 167.
41 Eugène Flandin and Pascal Coste, *Voyages en Perse moderne, les années 1840 et 1842*, Paris, 1843, 1854, vol. 3, fig. 154.
42 Homayun, *op. cit.*, p. 167.
43 Siawosch Azadi, *Persische Teppiche*, Hamburg, 1971, p. 197, no. 91.
44 Another example, on a dark blue ground and dated 1310 (1892 AD) and inscribed at the top in reversed lettering *Abdullah Qashqa'i Arayish-i Jamshid*, is published in *Hali*, vol. 1, no. 4, winter, 1978, p. 26.
45 Sayyid Muhammad Taqi Mostafavi and 'Ali Sami, *Takht-i Jamshid* (Persepolis), Shiraz, 1969, pp. 32-33.
46 Percy Molesworth Sykes, *A History of Persia*, London, 1915, vol. 1, pp. 195-213. For Darius I's ancestry, see also A. T. Olmstead, *History of the Persian Empire*, Chicago, 1959, pp. 214-215.
47 Mashkoor, *op. cit.*, p. 55.
48 Edwards, *op. cit.*, p. 140.
49 Fursat al-Dawlah-yi Shirazi, *Athar-i 'Ajam* (Works of the Iranians), Bombay, 1896, p. 291.
50 Charles Félix Marie Texier, *Description de l'Arménie, la Perse, et la Mesopotamie*, Paris, 1842, 1852, vol. 2, pp. xvii, 207-208, pls. 149, 150. See also Arthur Upham Pope, *A Survey of Persian Art*, Tokyo, 1967, vol. 7, p. 161, illus. B and C.
51 Texier, *op. cit.*, vol. 2, pp. xvii, 207.

52 Sykes, *op. cit.*, pp. 399-409.
53 For Shapur I's contribution to Iranian arts see Georgina Herrman, *The Iranian Revival* (Oxford, 1977), pp. 91-99.
54 On the Bishapur excavations see Roman Ghirshman, *Bichapour*, vol. 1 (Paris, 1971) and vol. 2 (Paris, 1956).
55 Cited in Zoka, 'Muhammad Zaman', p. 57.
56 Malcolm, *op. cit., passim*. Portrait of Shah 'Abbas facing p. 525 of vol. 1.
57 Sykes, *op. cit.*, vol. 2, p. 172.
58 Sykes, *op. cit.*, vol. 2, pp. 247-274.
59 Ahmad Kasravi, preface to Mirza Mehdi Astarabadi, Naghavi Pakbaz, Muhammadi Malayeri, and Laurence Lockhart, *Nadir Shah* (Tehran, 1966), pp. 5-9.
60 Sykes, *op. cit.*, vol. 2, pp. 289-322.
61 Robert Ker Porter, *Travels in Georgia, Persia, Armenia, Ancient Babylonia*, vol. 1 (London, 1821), pp. 327-328.
62 Sykes, *op. cit.*, vol. 2, pp. 323-338.
63 Sykes, *op. cit.*, vol. 2, pp. 339-405.
64 Sykes, *op. cit.*, vol. 2, pp. 406-420.
65 Sykes, *op. cit.*, vol. 2, pp. 421-540.
66 Sykes, *op. cit.*, vol. 2, pp. 541-561.
67 Firdowsi, *The Epic of the Kings: Shah-Nama, the national epic of Persia*, transl. Reuben Levy (London, 1967), pp. 47-80.
68 Nasrollah Falsafi, 'Tarikh-i qahvah khanah dar Iran' (The History of the Coffee House in Iran), *Sukhan* (Word), no. 4, March/April 1955, Tehran, pp. 258-268.
69 Khusraw Khosravi, 'Mutali'-i darbarah-yi qahvah khanah-ha' (A Study Concerning Coffee Houses), *Kavush* (Research), no. 9, January/February 1962, Tehran, pp. 84-92.
70 Firdawsi, *The Epic*, pp. 64-80.
71 Firdawsi, *The Epic*, pp. 146-151.
72 Very readable versions of three of the stories are available in Peter J. Chelkowski, *Mirror of the Invisible World, Tales from the Khamsah of Nizami* (New York, 1975).
73 Arthur Christensen, *L'Iran sous les Sassanides* (Copenhagen, 1936), pp. 460-461.
74 *Ibid.*
75 *Ibid.*
76 *Ibid.*, p. 456.
77 Muhammad Dabir Siyaghi, ed., *Safarnamah-i Hakim Nasir-i Khusraw Qubadiyani Marvazi* (Travel Account of Nasir Khusraw Qubadiyani), (Tehran, 1977), p. 170; 'Ala al-Din Demirchi, 'Jughrafi-yi tarikhi-yi Firdaws' (The Historical *Geography of Ferdows*), *Hunar va Mardum* (Art and People), no. 106, July/August 1971, p. 42.
78 Khusraw II (Khusraw Parviz, 'the Victorious', 591-628 AD, the last great ruler of the Sasanian dynasty, whose capital was at Ctesiphon, the Islamic name for which is Mada'in); Chelkowski, *op. cit.*, pp. 21-48.
79 Chelkowski, *op. cit.*, pp. 49-68.
80 'Darwish,' by D. B. MacDonald, in *Encyclopedia of Islam*, Leiden, 1913, vol. 1, pp. 949-951.
81 Cf. 'Tassawuf,' by Louis Massignon, in *Encyclopedia of Islam*, Leiden, 1924, vol. 4, pp. 681-685.
82 Abdol Hossein Zarrinkub, *Arzish-i miras-i Sufiyah* (The Value of the Sufi Heritage), Tehran, 1978, pp. 31-32; Laleh Bakhtiar, *Sufi Expressions of the Mystic Quest*, London, 1976; and Seyyed Hossein Nasr, *Sufi Essays*, London, 1972, *passim*.
83 *Ibid.*
84 *Ibid.*
85 *Ibid.*
86 *Ibid.*
87 *Ibid.*
88 Na'ib Sadr Shirazi Muhammad Masun, *Tara'iq al-haqa'iq* (The Ways of the Truths), Tehran, 1898-1901, vol. 3, pp. 91-97.
89 *Ibid.*
90 Samuel R. Peterson, 'Painted Tiles at the Takiyah Mu'avin ul-Mulk, Kirmanshah,' in *Akten des VII Internationalen Kongresses für Iranische Kunst und Archaeologie*, München, 7-10 September, 1976 (Berlin, 1979), pp. 618-628.
91 Bakhtiar, *op. cit.*, p. 38.
92 Marilyn Ereshefsky, 'Animal Skin Prayer Rugs', in Jere L. Bacharach and Irene A. Bierman, *The Warp and Weft of Islam* (Seattle, 1978), pp. 47-52.
93 Kurt Erdman, *Oriental Carpets* (Tübingen, Germany, 1955; rep. Fishguard, Wales, 1976), no. 151.
94 Arthur Upham Pope, *A Survey of Persian Art* (London, 1938-1939; rep. Tokyo, 1964-1965), vol. 2, Pl. 275; and Joseph V. McMullan, *Islamic Carpets* (New York, 1965), Pls. 30, 32.
95 McMullan, *op. cit.*, pls. 30, 32.
96 Zayn al-'Abidin Shirvani, *op. cit.*, pp. 354-355.
97 *Ibid.*, pp. 355-359.
98 In addition to those in Julfa and the central regions of Iran, a large number of Armenians lived in Azarbayjan and in the villages around Tabriz.
99 Sa'di, *op. cit.*, p. 3.
100 I am indebted to Sarah B. Sherrill; K. Abraham Chorekchan, professor of Middle Eastern Art and Literature, University of Pennsylvania; and Malcolm Topalian for the interpretation of this carpet and the resumé of the relevant details from the Armenian national epic of David of Sassoun.
101 Tofik Firuzan, 'Darbarah-yi tarkib va saziman-i Ilat va 'asha'ir-i Iran' (Concerning the Social Structure of the Tribes of Iran), *Ilat va 'Asha'ir*, Tehran, 1983; and Morteza Ravandi, *Tarikh-i ijtima'i-yi Iran* (The Social History of Iran), Tehran, 1972, vol. 3, p. 283.
102 'Ali Akbar Dihkhuda, *Lughat-namah* (Encyclopedic Dictionary), (Tehran, 1971), no. 172, p. 432.
103 See Jean Pierre Digard, *Techniques des nomades baxtiyari d'Iran* (Cambridge, England, 1981).
104 Lisan al-Saltanah Sipihr, *Tarikh-i Bakhtiyari* (The History of the Bakhtiyari), Tehran, 1910, rep. 1977, pp. 6, 141, 385.
105 Mashkoor, *op. cit.*, p. 290.
106 'Balocistan,' by Longworth Dames, in *Encyclopedia of Islam*, Leiden, 1913, vol. 1, pp. 625-640.
107 See Pierre Oberling, *The Qashqa'i Nomads of Fars* (The Hague), 1974); Lois Beck, *The Qashga'i People of Southern Iran* (Los Angeles, 1981).
108 Ahmad Kasravi, 'Afsharha-yi Khuzistan' (Afshars of Khuzistan), *Karvand-i Kasravi, majmu'ah-yi 78 maqalah va guftar az Ahmad Kasravi bi kushish Yahya Zoka* (Works of A. Kasravi, a Collection of 78 Articles and Topics by Ahmad Kasravi Edited by Yahya Zoka), Tehran, 1974, pp. 43-52.
109 Rug no. 68 is illustrated on p. 29 of my article 'The Afshar, Part 1: A Tribal History,' *Hali*, Issue 37, January/February 1988, pp. 22-29. The article gives further history of the Afshars in various parts of Iran.
110 Edwards, *op. cit.*, p. 212.
111 See Richard Tapper, *Pasture and Politics, Economics, Conflict and Ritual Among Shahsevan Nomads of Northwestern Iran* (London, 1979); Parviz Tanavoli, *Shahsavan* (Fribourg, Switzerland and New York, 1985).
112 'Abd al-Husayn Zarinkub, *Tarikh-i Iran ba'd az Islam* (History of Iran in the Islamic Era), Tehran, 1978, p. 432.
113 See Fredrik Barth, *Nomads of South Persia, the Basseri Tribe of the Khamsah Confederacy* (Oslo, 1965).
114 Ruhollah Khaleqi, *Sarguzasht-i musiqi-yi Iran* (The Story of Music in Iran), Tehran, 1955, vol. 2, p. 234.
115 I am grateful to Sarah B. Sherrill for this suggestion.
116 'Dreams, reveries, and sweet seductions were all used to lure the would-be purchaser. If the scantily clad pin-up and femme-fatale on the pack were insufficient, then the smoker was offered access to the exotic mysteries of the Middle East, harems, pyramids, and palm trees. Many designers relished the opportunity to introduce richness and colour, often with bizarre results.' (Chris Mullen, *Cigarette Pack Art*, New York, 1979, p. 75).
117 *The TMA Directory of Cigarette Brand Names 1913-1977*, published in 1978 by the Tobacco Merchants Association of the United States, p. 30.
118 Illustrated in Mullen, *op. cit.*, p. 77. 'Part of the smoker's dream was the seductive and beautiful woman . . . the dream of the white slave in the harem is widely used, particularly to emphasize the Turkish or Egyptian type of cigarette. She features in the harem pack (UK, about 1935) and at her proudest in Major Drapkin's Crayol (UK, about 1900) . . . The Crayol pack [featured] a sleek handmaiden in a visibly Middle Eastern landscape . . . The popularity of Turkish and Egyptian cigarettes earlier in the century assured a maximum of Middle Eastern themes.' (*Ibid*).
119 I would like to thank Holly Chase for bringing this information regarding Tunisia to my attention.
120 Rugs. nos. 79 and 81 are illustrated as Figs. 3 and 20 in Ian Bennett's article 'Carpets of the Khans, Part 1,' *Hali*, Issue 43, February 1989, pp. 40-51.

## Kings, Heroes and Lovers

121  A photograph taken about 1908 of Yusuf Khan Amir Mujahid and a photograph of the interior of his house in Shahr-i Kord appear as figs. 6 and 2 respectively in Bennett, *op. cit.*

122  Parviz Tanavoli, *Lion Rugs of Fars*, Washington, DC, 1974, and Tehran, 1978. These two earlier exhibition catalogues are superseded by an expanded treatment of this subject in the exhibition catalogue *Lion Rugs: the Lion in the Art and Culture of Iran*, Basel, 1985.

123  In Persian the word *murgh* is used for both bird and hen, and in using the general term bird here we include different kinds of fowl; some species, such as the hoopoe, falcon, and peacock were more favoured than others by crafts people.

124  Yahya Zoka, 'Religious Symbolism in Achaemenid Art,' in Arthur Upham Pope, *A Survey of Persian Art*, vol. 15, ed. Jay Gluck (Tokyo, 1974), p. 3462.

125  *Ibid.*; and Jacques Duchesne-Guillemin, *Symbols and Values in Zoroastrianism* (New York, 1966), pp. 39-42, 65-76, 130-132.

126  Parviz Tanavoli, *Lion Rugs: the Lion in the Art and Culture of Iran*, pp. 36-39.

127  Yahya Zoka, *Tarikhchah-yi taghyirat va tahavulat-i darafsh va 'alamat-i dawlat-i Iran az aghaz-i sadah-yi sizdahum-i hijri-yi qamari ta imruz* (A Short History of the Changes and Transformations of the Flag and Emblem of the Government of Iran, from the Beginning of the 13th Century AH. [19th Century AD] to the Present), Tehran, 1965, p. 14.

128  Tanavoli, *Lion Rugs: the Lion in the Art and Culture of Iran*.

129  *Ibid*.

130  Rug no. 96 is illustrated and discussed further in my article '"Samarkand" Pictorial Saf,' *Hali*, Issue 40, July/August 1988, pp. 14-15.

131  Hans Bidder, *Carpets from Eastern Turkestan* (New York, 1964), p. 45.

133  Bidder, *op. cit.*, p. 49-53.

# BIBLIOGRAPHY

Arberry, A.J., ed., *The Legacy of Persia*, Oxford, 1953
Asmussen, Jes P., selected and partly transl., *Manichaean Literature*, no. 22 in Persian Heritage Series, Ehsan Yar-Shater, gen. ed., New York, 1975.
Astarabadi, Mirza Mehdi, Naghavi Pakbaz, Muhammadi Malayeri, and Laurence Lockhart, *Nadir Shah*, Tehran, 1966.
Azadi, Siawosch, *Persische Teppiche*, Hamburg, 1971.

Bakhtiar, Laleh, *Sufi Expression of the Mystic Quest*, London, 1976.
Bamdad, Mehdi, *Sharh-i hal-i rijal-i Iran dar qarn 12, 13, 14 hijri* (Biography of the Dignitaries of Iran in the 18th, 19th, and 20th Centuries), Tehran, 1969.
Barth, Fredrik, *Nomads of South Persia, The Basseri Tribe of the Khamsah Confederacy*, Oslo, 1965.
Beck, Lois, *The Qashga'i People of Southern Iran*, Los Angeles, 1981.
Bennett, Ian, 'Carpets of the Khans, Part I,' *Hali*, Issue 43, February 1989, pp. 40-51.
Bidder, Hans, *Carpets from Eastern Turkestan*, New York, 1964.
Biggs, Robert D., ed., *Discoveries from Kurdish Looms*, Evanston, Illinois, 1983.
Bosworth, Clifford Edmund, *The Islamic Dynasties*, Edinburgh, 1967.
Boyce, Mary, *A History of Zoroastrianism*, Leiden, 1975.
Browne, Edward G., *A Literary History of Persia*, 4 vols., Cambridge, England, 1969.

Chardin, John, *The Travels of Sir John Chardin into Persia and the East-Indies*, London, 1686.
——, *Travels in Persia*, London, 1927.
Chelkowski, Peter J., *Mirror of the Invisible World: Tales from the Khamsah of Nizami*, New York, 1975.
——, ed., *Ta'ziyeh: Ritual and Drama in Iran*, New York, 1979.
Christensen, Arthur, *L'Iran sous les Sassanides*, Copenhagen, 1936.
——, *Les Types du premier homme et du premier roi*, Leiden, 1934.
Clavijo, Ruy Gonzalez, *Clavijo, Embassy to Tamerlane, 1403-1406*, transl. Guy Le Strange, New York, 1928.

Demirchi, 'Ala al-Din Azari, 'Jughrafiya-yi tarikhi-yi Firdaws' ('The Historical Geography of Firdows'), *Hunar va Mardum* (Art and People), no. 106, July-August, 1971, Tehran.
Digard, Jean Pierre, *Techniques des nomades baxtiyari d'Iran*, Cambridge, England, 1981.
Duchesne-Guillemin, Jacques, *Symbols and Values in Zoroastrianism*, New York, 1966.

Eagleton, William, *An Introduction to Kurdish Rugs and Other Weavings*, New York and London, 1988.
Edwards, A. Cecil, *The Persian Carpets*, London, 1953.
Ehsani, Abdolhosein, *Majmu'ah-yi Qalamkar-i Iran* ('A Collection of Iranian *Qalamkar*'), Tehran, 1971.
Emery, Irene, *The Primary Structures of Fabrics*, Washington DC, 1966.
*Encyclopedia of Islam, A Dictionary of the Geography, Ethnography and Biography of the Muhammadan Peoples*, Leiden, various dates.
Erdmann, Kurt, *Oriental Carpets*, Tübingen, Germany, 1955; rep. Fishguard, Wales, 1976.
Ereshefsky, Marilyn, 'Animal Skin Prayer Rugs,' in *The Warp and Weft of Islam*, ed. Jere L. Bacharach and Irene A. Bierman, Seattle, 1978.

Fagan, Brian M., *Return to Babylonia: Travellers, Archaeologists, and Monuments in Mesopotamia*, Boston, 1979.
Falk, S. J., *Qajar Painting, Persian Oil Painting of the 18th and 19th Centuries*, London, 1972.
Falsafi, Nasrollah, 'Tarikh-i qahva khaneh dar Iran' ('The History of the Coffee House in Iran'), *Sukhan* (Word), no. 4, March-April, 1955, Tehran, pp. 258-268.
Farid al-Din 'Attar, *The Conference of the Birds* (Mantiq ut-Tair), Boulder, Colorado, 1971.
Farid al-Din 'Attar, *The Conference of the Birds*, transl. with an intro. by Afkham Darbandi and Dick Davis, London, 1984.
Firdowsi, Hakim Abolghasem, *The Epic of the Kings: Shah-Nama, the national epic of Persia*, transl. Reuben Levy, London 1967.
—— *Shahnamah-yi Firdawsi*, Tehran, 1971.
Firuzan, Tofig, 'Darbarah-yi Tarkib va Saziman-i Ilat va 'Asha'ir-i Iran' ('Concerning the Social Structure of the Tribes of Iran'), *Ilat va 'Asha'ir*, Tehran, 1983.
Flandin, Eugène, and Pascal Coste, *Voyages en Perse moderne, les années 1840 et 1842*, Paris, 1843, 1854.
Frye, Richard N., *The Heritage of Persia*, Cleveland, 1963.

Garthwaite, Gene, *Khans and Shahs*, Cambridge, 1983.
Ghirshman, Roman, *Bichapour*, 2 vols., Paris 1956, 1971.
——, *Iran, From the Earliest Times to the Islamic Conquest* (Paris, 1951), rep. Baltimore, 1961.
——, *Iran, Parthians and Sassanians*, London, 1962.
——, *Perse*, Paris, 1963.
——, *Persia, From the Origins to Alexander the Great*, London, 1964.
Gluck, Jay, and Sumi Hiramoto Gluck, eds., *A Survey of Persian Handicraft*, Tehran, 1977.

Herrmann, Georgina, *The Iranian Revival*, Oxford, 1977.
Homayun, Gholam 'Ali, *Asnad-i musavvar-i Urupa'iyan az Iran* ('European Illustrated Documents of Iran'), Tehran, 1970.
Housego, Jenny, 'The Nineteenth-century Persian Carpet Boom,' *Oriental Art*, vol. 19, no. 2 (Summer 1973).
——, *Tribal Rugs*, London, 1978.
Hubel, Reinhard G., *The Book of Carpets*, New York, 1964.

Jalal al-Din Mirza, *Namah-yi Khusravan* ('Book of Kings'), Tehran, 1868, and Vienna, 1880.
Jaubert, Pierre Amédée Emilien Probe, *Voyage en Arménie et en Perse, fait dans les années 1805 et 1806* (Paris, 1821).
Jazayiri, Mawlana Muhammad, *Qissas al-Anbiya'* ('Stories of the Prophets'), Tehran, n.d.

Kasravi, Ahmad, 'Afsharha-yi Khuzistan' (Afshars of Khuzistan), in *Karvand-i Kasravi, majmu'ah-yi 78 maqaleh va guftar az Ahmad Kasravi bi kushish Yahya Zoka* ('Works of Ahmad Kasravi, a Collection of 78 Articles and Topics by Ahmad Kasravi Edited by Yahya Zoka'), ed. Yahya Zoka, Tehran, 1974.
Khaleqi, Ruhollah, *Sarguzasht-i musiqi-yi Iran* ('The Story of Music in Iran'), Tehran, 1955.
Khosravi, Khusraw, 'Mutali' darbarah-yi qahvah khanah-ha' (A Study Concerning Coffee Houses), *Kavush* ('Research'), no. 9, January-February 1962, pp. 84-92.

Landolt-Tüller, Annette and Hermann, *Qalamkar-Druck in Isfahan*, Basel, 1977.
Lewis, Bernard, ed., *World of Islam*, London, 1976.

Malcolm, John, *The History of Persia*, 2 vols., London, 1815.
Martin, D.W., 'The Gabbehs of Fars, An Abstract Tribal Art,' *Hali*, vol. 5, no. 4, 1983, pp. 462-473.
Mashkoor, Muhammad Javad, *Iran dar 'ahd-i bastan, dar tarikh-i aqwam va padishahan pish az Islam* ('Iran in Ancient Times, The History of Tribes and Kings Before the Islamic Era'), Tehran, 1968.
Mas'udi, 'Ali ibn Husayn, *Al-Tanbih wa-'l-ashraf* ('Warnings and Remarks'), Cairo, 1938.
McMullen, Joseph V., *Islamic carpets*, New York, 1965.
Meen, V. B., and A. D. Tushingham, *Crown Jewels of Iran*, Toronto, 1968.
Mostafavi, Sayyid Muhammad Taqi, and 'Ali Sami, *Takht-i Jamshid* ('Persepolis'), Shiraz, 1969.
Mullen, Chris, *Cigarette Pack Art*, New York, 1979.

Na'ib Sadr Shirazi Muhammad Masum, *Tara'iq al-Haqa'iq* ('The Ways of Truths'), Tehran, 1898-1901.
Nasr, Seyyed Hossein, *Sufi Essays*, London, 1972.

Oberling, Pierre, *The Qashqa'i Nomads of Fars*, The Hague, 1974.
Olmstead, A. T., *History of the Persian Empire*, Chicago, 1959.

Payman, Habibollah, *Il-i Qashqa'i* ('The Qashqa'i Tribe'), Tehran, 1969.
Peterson, Samuel R., 'Chairs and Change in Qajar Times,' in *Modern Iran, The Dialectics of Continuity and Change*, eds. Michael E. Bonine and Nikki R. Keddie, Albany, 1981, pp. 383-446.
——, 'Painted Tiles at the Takieh Mu'avin ul-Mulk, Kirmanshah,' in *Akten des VII Internationalen Kongresses für Iranische Kunst and Archaeologie*, München, 7-10 September, 1976, Berlin, 1979, pp. 618-628.
——, 'Shi'ism and Late Iranian Arts,' UMI 8127951, Ann Arbor, Michigan: University Microfilms International, 1981.
——, 'The Ta'ziyeh and Related Arts,' in *Ta'ziyeh: Ritual and Drama in Iran*, ed. Peter J. Chelkowski, New York, 1979.
Pope, Arthur Upham, ed., *A Survey of Persian Art*, London, 1938-1939, rep. Tokyo, 1964-1965.
Porter, Robert Ker, *Travels in Georgia, Persia, Armenia, Ancient Babylonia*, 2 vols., London, 1821, 1822.

Qarahnejad, Hasan, 'Qalamkar Cloth,' *Hunar va Mardum* ('Art and People',) no. 183, 1978.

Ravandi, Morteza, *Tarikh-i ijtima'i-yi Iran* ('The Social History of Iran'), Tehran, 1972.
Robinson, B. W., 'The Court Painters of Fath 'Ali Shah,' *Eretz-Israel*, 1964.
——, *A Descriptive Catalogue of the Persian Paintings in Bodleian Library*, Oxford, 1958.
——, 'The Tehran Nizami of 1848 and Other Qajar Lithographed Books,' in *Islam in the Balkans/Persian Art and Culture of the 18th and 19th Centuries*, ed. Jennifer M. Scarce, Edinburgh, 1979, pp. 61-65. 73 de Rochechouart, Comte Julien, *Souvenirs d'un voyage in Perse*, Paris, 1867.

Sa'di, *The Bustan of Sa'di*, transl G.M. Wickens, Toronto, 1974.
Samarqandi, 'Aruzi, *Chahar Maqalah* ('Four Discourses'), Berlin, 1927; rev. ed. by Muhammad Mo'in, Tehran, 1985.
Scarce, Jennifer M. ed., *Islam in the Balkans/Persian Art and Culture of the 18th and 19th Centuries*, Edinburgh, 1979.
Schmidt, Erich F., *Persepolis*, Chicago, 1970.
Shirazi, Fursat al-Dawlah, *Athar-i 'Ajam* ('Works of the Iranians'), Bombay, 1896.
Shirvani, Zayn al-'Abidin, *Bustan-i Siyahah* ('Garden of Travels'), Tehran, 1897.

Sipihr, Lisan al-Saltanah, *Tarikh-i Bakhtiyari* ('The History of the Bakhtiari'), Tehran, 1910, rep. 1977.
Siyaghi, Muhammad Dabir, ed., *Safarnamah Hakim Nasir-i Khusraw Qubadiyani Marvazi* ('Travelogue of Hakim Nasir-i Khusraw Qubadiyani Marvazi'), Tehran, 1977.
Stanzer, Wilfried, *Kordi*, Vienna, 1988.
Sykes, Percy Molesworth, *A History of Persia*, 2 vols., London, 1915.

Tanavoli, Parviz, 'The Afshar, Part 1: A Tribal History', *Hali*, Issue 37, January/February 1988, pp. 22-29.
——, 'Gabbeh', *Hali*, vol. 5, no. 4, 1983, pp. 474-476.
——, *Lion Rugs from Fars*, Washington, D.C., 1974.
——, *Lion Rugs from Fars*, Tehran, 1978.
——, *Lion Rugs: The Lion in the Art and Culture of Iran*, Basel, 1985.
——, '"Samarkand" Pictorial Saf', *Hali*, Issue 40, July/August 1988, 14-15.
——, *Shahsavan*, Fribourg, Switzerland, and New York, 1985.
Tapper, Richard, *Pasture and Politics, Economics, Conflict and Ritual Among Shahsevan Nomads of Northwestern Iran*, London, 1979.
Tavernier, Jean Baptiste, *Les six voyages de Jean Baptiste Tavernier, en Turquie, en Perse, et Aux Indes*, Paris, 1679.
Texier, Charles Felix Marie, *Description de l'Armenie, la Perse, et la Mesopotamie*, 2 vols., Paris, 1842, 1852.
Al-Thaalibi, Aboumansour Abd al-Malik ibn Muhammad ibn Isma'il, *Histoire des rois de Perse*, ed and transl. H. Zotenberg, Paris, 1900.
Tolegian, Aram, transl., *David of Sassoun, Armenian folk Epic*, New Haven, 1961.

Widengren, George, *Mani and Manichaeism*, transl. Charles Kessler, London, rev. ed. 1965.
Wulff, Hans E., *The Traditional Crafts of Persia*, Cambridge, Massachusetts, 1966.

Zakaria ibn Muhammad ibn Mahmud, *'Aja'ib al-Makhluqat* ('The Wonders of Creation'), Tehran, 1866.
Zarrinkoob, Abdol Hossein, *Arzish-i miras-i Sufiyah* ('The Value of the Sufi Heritage'), Tehran, 1978.
——, *Tarikh-i Iran ba'd az Islam* ('History of Iran in the Islamic Era'), Tehran, 1965.
Zoka, Yahya, *Nigahi bih nigargari-yi Iran dar sadaha-yi davazdahum va sizdahum* ('A Look at Iranian Painting in the 12th and 13th Centuries [18th and 19th Centuries AD]'), Tehran, 1974.
—— 'Partuvi nawvin bar din-i Hakhamanishian', ('New Light on the Religion of the Achaemenians'), *Hunar va mardum*, nos. 124, 125 (February/March, 1973).
——, 'Religious Symbolism in Achaemenid Art', in Arthur Upham Pope, *A Survey of Persian Art*, vol. 15, ed. Jay Gluck (Tokyo, 1974), pp. 3458-3465.
——, 'Shahnamah va bastan shinasi, nawruz dar Shahnamah va rabitah-yi an ba Takht-i Jamshid' ('*Shahnamah* and Archaeology, Nawruz in the *Shahnamah* and Its Relationship with Persepolis'), *Hunar va mardum*, no. 186 (March/April, 1978), pp. 2-15.
——, 'Takhtha-yi saltanat-i Iran' ('Iran's Royal Thrones') *Hunar va mardum*, no. 60 (September/October, 1968).
——, *Tarikhchahah-yi taghyirat va tahavulat-i darafsh va 'alamat-i dawlat-i Iran az aghaz-i sadah-yi sizdahum hijri-yi qamari ta imruz* ('A Short History of the Changes and Transformations of the Flag and Emblem of the Government of Iran, from the Beginning of the 13th Century AH. [19th Century AD] to the Present'), Tehran, 1965.
——, *Tarikh-i 'Aksha va 'Akkasan-i Pishgam dar Iran* ('A History of Avant-garde Photography and Photographers in Iran'), Tehran, 1989.

# INDEX

Abadeh 53, 174
Abazar Ghaffari 39
'Abbas Mirza 10
'Abdullah Qashqa'i 20
Abrahan 39 infra, 204
Abu 'Ali Sina 13
Abu Nasr 'Iraqi 13
Abulqasem-Qa'im Maqam 26
Achaemenids 21
Afghan invasions 8
Afghanistan 34
Afghans 25
Afrasiyab 30, 31, 32
Afshars 19, 25, 28, 47, 51, 53 infra, 218, 238, 246, 274
Agha Muhammad 51
Ahmad Shah 27 infra, 28, 162, 166, 168, 170, 172, 224, 226
Ahmad shrine 59
Ahriman 8, 16
Ahura Mazda 21, 128
Akvan 32 infra, 182
Alexander the Great 19, 52
'Ali 39, 58
'Ali-Allahis 192
'Ali Shah 26 infra
Alvand 18
Animals 290, 292
Anushirvan 35
Arab tribes 54 infra
Arab tribes of Khamsah Confederation 54 infra
Arabesques 9
Arabia 7, 21, 37
Arabs 9, 196, 222
Arak 21, 22 passim, 23, 33, 48, 132, 194
Archers 186
Ardabil 54
Arisaq Osep 49
Armenia 21, 35, 36
Armenians 59, 218
Artists 25
'Aruzi Samarqandi 13
Aryans 15
Ashaqibash Turkomans 51
Ashtiyan 22
Asia Minor 53
Assad 37
*Athar-i 'Ajam* 14, 23
Atossa 21
Atrak 52
*Avesta* 15
Axe (*tabarzin*) 44, 210, 212
Azod al-Mulk 28
Azarbayjan 48, 53, 59, 270
Azhar Imamzadeh 19

Babylonia 21
Baharlu 54
Bahman 15
Bakhtiyari Lors 53

Bakhtiyaris 51 infra, 57, 59, 61, 260, 262, 264, 272
Baku 26
Baluch of Khurasan 126, 258
Baluchis 28, 34, 51, 52 infra, 57, 61, 190
Baluchis, Zabul area 206, 208, 228, 230, 232, 234, 254
Baluchistan 52
Bandar 'Abbas 55
Bani Amir 37
Barbad 34, 35, 37
Baseri 54 passim
Beggar's bowl (*kashkul*) 44, 210, 212
Belkis, Queen of Sheba 56
Bible 18, 39
Bijar 48, 54, 58, 154, 272, 292
Birjand 158
Bishapur 23
Bisotun 36
Boar 186
Bojnurd 52
Bokhara 27
Bolshevik Revolution 28
Bombay 10
Boteh 10, 58, 218, 238, 264
*Boteh jegheh* 24
Bowl of Jam 16
Boyer Ahmadi Lors 28, 51, 52 infra
Bride 250
British 26, 27, 28
*Bundahishn* 16
*Bustan* of Sa'di 48
*Bustan al-Siyahah* 16
Byzantines 36, 48

Cairo 57
Calcutta 10
Camels 34, 206, 282
Caps, dervish 44
Caspian Sea 54
Cats 58
Caucasus 28, 48
Celebrations 9
Central Asia 10
Chahar Mahal-i Bakhtiyari 51, 52, 148
*Chahar Maqalah* 13
Chair 150
Chardin, J 20
China 32
Chocolate boxes 8
Chowgan pass 23
Christians 46
Chromolithographs 57
Cigarette packages 57
Cilicia 21
Coco de mer 45
Colours 67 infra
Constantinople 36
Coste, P 20
Crown Jewels 17
Cudgel (*mantasha*) 44

Curtains 25
Cyrus the Great 21 passim
Daghestan 26
Dar al-Funun 11
Dargazin 19, 110, 284, 286
Darius I 16, 17, 19 infra
Darjazin 62
*Dastur* 11
Dates 62
David M Arka 49
David of Sassoun 48 infra, 220
Deer 58
Demons 31
Dervishes 42 infra, 214, 216, 224
Dih Bid 55
Direction of spin 63 infra
Djinns 17
Dogs 260
Doqozlou of Shish Boluki 278
Dorokhsh 27, 158
Dutch East India Company 14, 20
Dyestuffs 62 infra

Ecbatana 19
Edwards, A C 11
Egypt 21, 49
Elam 21
End finishes 65 infra
English East India Company 20
English/Indian blankets 274
Epics 9
Erivan 26
European diplomats 106
European exotica 11
European paintings 26
European postcards 8
European prints 8
European travellers 14
European women 56

Farhad 30, 33, 35 infra
Farid al-Din 'Attar 45, 218
Farrashabad 53
Fars 28, 51, 53, 59
Fath 'Ali Shah 8, 10, 14, 17, 18, 24, 25 infra, 152, 154
Fatimids 49
Fayz 'Ali Shah 43
Ferahan 22 passim, 62, 144, 146
Figural representation 8
Firdawsi 13, 18, 21, 178
Firdows 34, 184, 186, 222, 248,
Flandin, E 20
French East India Company 20
Fursat al-Dawlah 14, 23
*Gabbehs* 67 infra, 172, 272
Gabriel 40 infra, 206
Galileo 15
Galleh-Dar 53
Ganjeh 33
Gayomard (Kiyumars) 16

Germany 57
Golestan, treaty 26
Golgun 36, 37
Greece 21
Grooms 58, 250
Grotefend, G F 19
Gulistan Palace 17

Habibullah 134
Haji Khanomi 45
Hajir 31
Hajji Mullah Hassan 152
Hamadan 15, 18, 28, 34, 53, 54, 61, 106, 108, 112, 114, 116, 118, 124, 162, 170, 198, 200, 218, 244
Harun-i Velayat shrine 59
Hasan 39
Hasan Khan 11
Hashtrud 54
Hat (*taqieh*) 44
*Herati* 21
Herodotus 19, 21
Hindus 45
Hirmand 53
Hisham b. 'Abd al-Malik 13
Historical figures 7
Hormuzd 35
Horn 210
Horses 58, 284, 286
Hunters 242, 288
Hunting 186
Husayn 39
Hushang Shah 13, 15 infra, 18 passim, 104, 106, 108, 110, 112, 114, 116, 118, 120, 122, 124, 126

Iblis 39
Ibn Salam 37
Ibrahim b. Shah Rukh Shah 20
Idolatry 7
Illustrated books 9 infra
Inanlu 54
India 25
Isaac 39
Isfahan 9, 11, 14, 17, 24, 36, 51, 53, 54, 150
Ishmael 39 infra, 204
Istakhr 13, 16

Jalal al-Din Mirza 14, 23, 134
Jamshid 16
Jan(-i) Khan Qashqa'i 19, 20, 53
*Jangal-i mawla* 59
Jaubert, P Amédée 9
Jozan 130

Kahak 19, 198
Kandahar 21, 52
Karabagh 26, 28, 47, 48 passim, 180, 220
Karekin Vartabed Servantziants 48
Karim Khan 51
Kashan 9, 11, 25, 34, 152, 210
Kashkuli of Qashqa'i 62, 282
Kashmir 45
Kavus 31
Kay Khusraw 32
Kemal al-Mulk 26
Keri Toros 49
Kerman 9, 11, 14, 24, 53, 54, 56, 57, 156, 208, 252, 254, 274
Kermanshah 35, 36, 154, 176
Khalaj 53
Khamsah Confederation 53, 54 infra, 57, 256
Khamsah of Hamadan 270
*Khamsah* of Nizami 19, 30, 33 infra, 35 infra

Khan, Richard 11
*Khanaqah* 43, 45, 210
*Khans* (courtiers) 27
*Khans* (tribal leaders) 11
Khiva 27
Khotan 59 passim, 60
*Khuda'i-namah* 13
Khurasan 10, 34, 52, 54, 57
Khusraw and Shirin 9, 30, 33, 184, 186, 188, 190, 192, 194, 196
Khusraw (Parviz) 33, 35 infra, 202
Khuzistan 51, 53
Kiyumars 15
Knot density 65 infra
Knots 64 infa
Koh Kiluyeh 52, 53
Kourkik Jelalin 49
Kurds 51, 240
Kurds of Khurasan 52 infra

*Lachak* 12
*Lachak turanj* 21
Landes, A D des 20
Lar 55
Layla 33
Layla and Majnun 9, 30, 34, 37 infra, 198, 200
Lebanon 21
Leo 58
Leopard 45
Leopard skin 214, 216
Lilihan 33, 48, 194
Lions 58 infra, 266, 268, 270, 272, 274, 278, 280
Lisan al-Saltanah Sipihr 51
Lithographs 11, 16, 25, 26
Lor-i Buzurg 51
Lor-i Kuchik 51
Lorestan 51
Lori-Boyer Ahmad 226, 268
Lors 51 infra
Lutf 'Ali Khan Zand 44

Ma'sum 'Ali Shah Dakani 43
Mada'in 35
Madder 62
Mahan 43
Mahin Banu 35
Majnun 290
Makran 53
Malayer 19, 22, 28, 61, 120, 122, 124, 130, 160, 168, 250
Malcolm, Sir John 19, 24
*Mantiq al-Tayir* 45
Marble Throne (*Takht-i Marmar*) 18
Mary and Jesus (Madonna and Child) 39, 40 infra, 208
Maryam Banu 36
Mas'udi 13
Mashig 16
Mashiyanig 16
Mazandaran 18, 53
Mecca 39, 45
Mehregan 19
Mehrgerd 53
Mher 49
Middle Persian 15
Miniatures 7
Mir Latif Khan Shohrati 148
Mirza Mutallib 14
Mithraism 58
Moghan 25, 54
Mohtasham 152
Mongols 7, 48
Mordants 62
*Morgh u mahi* 21

Mosul 44
Mt Dena 52
Mt Rahmat 19
Muhammad, the Prophet 39
Muhammad 'Ali Mirza Dawlatshah 154
Muhammad 'Ali Shah 22, 27 infra, 166
Muhammad Jazayiri 39, 204
Muhammad Juki 182
Muhammad Shah 26 infra, 156, 272
Muhammad Taqi Khan 176
Muhammad Zaman 24
Mushtaq 'Ali Shah 44, 210
Muzaffar al-Din Shah 27
Mythical figures 7

Nadir Shah 8, 17, 24, 51, 52, 150
Nadir Throne (*Takht-i Nadiri*) 17
Nafar 54
Nahavand 19, 34, 188, 212
*Namah-yi Khusravan* 14, 23
*Namak va filfil* 278
Napoleon 9
*Naqsh-i ghalat* 12
Nasir al-Din Shah 11, 26 infra, 128, 156, 158, 160, 162, 164
Nasir Khusraw 34
Naw Ruz 15, 16, 19, 25
Nazem 45
Neyriz 55
Ni'matollah Vali 43
Ni'matullahi order 43
Nikisa 37
Nishapur 45
Nomadic areas 7
Nomads 50
Nowfal 37
Nur 'Ali Shah 43 passim, 210, 212

Oil paintings 7
Old Testament 17
Ormazd 16
Ottomans 7, 24, 25
Owls 58

Paintings 8, 26, 196
Paintings on glass (*shamayel*) 39
*Pardeh* 9
Parthians 48
Patrons 7
Peacock Throne (*Takht-i Tavus*) 17 infra, 25
Persepolis 16, 19, 52, 104, 128
Persian-speaking tribes 51 infra
Photographs 7, 9, 10 infra, 20, 27, 28 passim, 39
Pile height 65 infra
Pishdadis 15
Ply 63 infra
Populations 50
Porter, R Ker 25, 26
Pouch (*chantah*) 44, 212
Prints 7
*Pust-i palang* 44 passim
Pythagoras 15

*Qab-i ayinah* 170
Qajars 7, 11, 50, 51, 122, 14, 154
*Qalamkar* 9, 10 infra, 14, 16, 18, 28, 158, 170, 194, 196
*Qalichaha-yi surati* 7
Qambar 39, 43
Qashqa'is 20, 45, 50, 52, 53 infra, 62, 124, 128, 196, 224, 236, 242, 266, 268, 270, 272, 278
Qavam al-Saltanah 176
Qays 37

# Index

Qazvin 54, 164
Qizilbash 24, 47, 48, 54
Quchan 52, 240
Queen Victoria 15
Qum 54 passim
Qur'an 17

Rakhsh 31, 32, 182
Ravar 252
Rawlinson, H C 19
Reza Khan, Iqbal al-Saltanah 11
Reza Shah 28 infra, 56, 174
Rhubarb 16
Rochechouart, J de 9
Romans 48
Roosters 288
Rudehen 34, 192
Russians 26, 27, 28, 59
Rustam 30 infra, 178, 180, 182

Sa'di 8
Sadeh festival 15
Sadhus 45
Safavids 7, 8, 13, 31, 51, 136
Safi Khani, Qashqa'i 172, 236
Sakae 21
Samangan 31
Samarkand 27, 59, 60
Saqi 248
Saragati 21
Sarah 39
Saruq 15, 21, 22 passim, 61, 130, 132, 134, 136, 138, 140, 142, 178, 214, 216
Sasanians 10, 13, 15, 21, 134
Saveh 19, 54, 202
Sayyid Zia al-Din 176
Scythians 15
Seljuks 19, 48, 53, 60, 240
Shabdiz 34, 35
Shah 'Abbas 14, 24 infra, 31, 48, 52, 54, 136, 148
Shah Safi 14
Shah Tahmasp 14, 54
Shah Tahmasp II 25
*Shahnamah* 13, 15 passim, 16, 21, 30 passim, 33, 178, 182
*Shahr-i farang* 11
Shahr-i Kurd 57
Shahreza 53, 196
Shahsavan 19, 24, 47, 51, 54 infra, 218, 270
Shamsabad 57, 260
Shapur 15, 14, 21 infra, 130, 132, 134, 136, 138, 140, 142, 144, 146, 178
*Shaykh* 42 infra
Shaykh San'an 42, 45, 218
Shekar 36
Shi'ism 7, 8
Shi'ites 47, 52, 58
Shir-i Khuda 58
Shiraz 20, 23, 54
Shirin 35 infra
Shirin and Farhad 34, 198
Shirin and Farhad/Majnun 202
Shiruyeh 37
Shirvan 47, 48, 52, 280, 288
Shish Boluki 62
Shubayr 39
Siberia 15
Side finishes 66 infra
Sind 21
Sistan 30, 52
Siyamak 15
Siyar al-Muluk (al-Fars) 13
Sizes 63 infra
Solomon 16, 17, 18, 20, 290
Storytellers 31

Stuys, Jan J 20
Sufi poetry 44
Sufis 42 infra
Suhrab 31 infra, 180
Sultaniyah 17
Sun 58, 272
Sunnis 52
Sunnism 7
Syria 21, 53

*Ta'ziya* 8
Tabas 34
Tabriz 9, 10, 11, 24, 26, 54, 208, 290
Tafresh 22 passim
Tahirids 51
Tahminah 31
Tahmuras 8
Takht-i Jamshid 20
Takht-i Sulayman 20
Taleqan 164
Tantrism 45
*Taqcheh* 11
Taqdis 33, 35
Tartars 48
Tavernier, J-B 20
Teahouses 11, 31
Tehran 8, 10, 52, 164
Tents 54
Texier, C F M 23
Texture 65
Tha'labi 8, 33
Throne of Solomon (*Takht-i Sulaymani*), see Marble Throne (*Takht-i Marmar*)
Throne of the Sun 17
Tiger 45, 266
Timur (Tamerlane) 20, 43
Timurids 43, 60
Toilet articles 8
Toor Gaitzagin 49
Torkmanchay 26
Tribal rugs 8
Trousers 56
Trumpet 210
Tukomanchay 48
Tun 34
Tunisia 57
Turan 12, 31 passim
Turfan 10
Turkestan 60
Turkish-speaking tribes 53 infra
Turkomans 47
Turks 7, 31
Tzenov Ohan 49

Uffizi 14
United States 11
Urban centres 11
Uzbeks 24, 52

*Vagirah* 11
Van 48
Varamin 54
Veil 56
Verti Osepiantz 49
Vienna 23
Village rugs 8
Villages 7

Warps 63 infra
Weaving terminology 61
Wefts 63 infra
White Demon 178
White Fortress 31
Women 228, 238, 240, 248, 252, 254, 256, 258, 260, 262, 264

Workshops 7
World War I 28

Xenophon 19
Xeres I 16, 19 infra, 21 passim, 128

Yarkand 60
Yasuj 52
Yusuf Khan Amir Mujahid 57, 260, 262, 264

Zabul 52, 53, 190, 258
Zabulistan 31, 32
Zahhak 16
Zal 30
Zands 8, 51
Zanjan 19, 54, 106, 166, 270
Zarand 19, 112
Zhandah Razm 31
Zoroastrians 15, 128
*Zurkhanah* 30
Zayn al-'Abidin Shirvani 47